# ISRAEL AND PALESTINE

# ISRAEL AND PALESTINE

## Reappraisals, Revisions, Refutations

### Avi Shlaim

**VERSO**

London • New York

# 4218/1120

Earlier versions of the chapters included in this volume
have appeared in the following publications:
Chapter #1, in Wm. Roger Louis, ed., *Yet More Adventures with Britannia* (London: I.
B. Tauris, 2005); #2, in Mary Coll, ed., *Faithful Companions: Collected Essays Celebrating
the 25th Anniversary of the Kate O'Brien Weekend* (Limerick: Mellick Press, 2009); #3,
#5, #8, #15 *Journal of Palestine Studies*; #4, #6, #7, #9, #10, #12, #13, #18, #20, *London
Review of Books*; #11, #29, *Guardian*; #14, in Jane Davis, ed., *Politics and International
Relations in the Middle East* (Aldershot: Edward Elgar, 1995); #16, in Louise Fawcett
ed., *International Relations of the Middle East* (Oxford: Oxford University Press, 2005);
#17, #26, *New York Review of Books*; #19, *Israel Studies*; #21, *The Nation*; #22, in Ken
Booth and Tim Dunne eds., *Worlds in Collision: Terror and the Future of World Order*
(London: Palgrave, 2002); #23, *Logos*; #25, *Islamica*; #27, in Adel Iskandar and Hakem
Rustom, eds., *Emancipation and Representation: On the Intellectual Meditations of Edward
Said* (Berkeley: University of California Press, forthcoming); #30, *Jewish Chronicle*

First published by Verso 2009
© Avi Shlaim 2009
All rights reserved

1 3 5 7 9 10 8 6 4 2

**Verso**
UK: 6 Meard Street, London W1F 0EG
US: 20 Jay Street, Suite 1010, Brooklyn, NY 11201
www.versobooks.com

Verso is the imprint of New Left Books

ISBN-13: 978-1-84467-366-7

**British Library Cataloguing in Publication Data**
A catalogue record for this book is available from the British Library

**Library of Congress Cataloging-in-Publication Data**
A catalog record for this book is available from the Library of Congress

Typeset by Hewer Text UK Ltd, Edinburgh
Printed in the US by Maple Vail

To Tamar

# Contents

# Introduction

The Israeli–Palestinian conflict is one of the most bitter, protracted, violent and seemingly intractable conflicts of modern times. This book brings together my writings on the Palestine question over the last quarter of a century. With the exception of the chapter on the Balfour Declaration of 1917, the time span of this volume begins with the Palestine War of 1948 and ends with the savage war launched by Israel on Gaza in December 2008. Between these melancholy dates fall nearly all the events discussed in the following pages.

The chapters in this book, although they were written at different times, have one thing in common: they are a testimony to an alternative view, to a more critical way of looking at the past. They are also grounded in the belief that the past is our best guide for understanding the present and for predicting the future. Only by coming to grips with the tangled and tortured history of this conflict can we make sense of it. Alongside the political conflict between Israelis and Palestinians runs a parallel conflict between two distinct national narratives. Only by taking full account of these two narratives can we form a true picture of the character and dynamics of this tragic conflict, and of the prospects for its resolution.

I belong to a small group of scholars who are sometimes labelled the 'revisionist Israeli historians' and sometimes the 'new historians'. The original group included Benny Morris of the Ben-Gurion University of the Negev and Ilan Pappé of Haifa University. We were called the 'new historians' because we challenged the standard Zionist version of the causes and course of the Arab–Israeli conflict. More specifically, we challenged the many myths that have come to surround the birth of Israel and the first Arab–Israeli war of 1948. Benny Morris, who coined the term 'the new historiography', radically changed his views on the nature of this conflict following the outbreak of the second intifada in 2000 and the Palestinian resort to violence and suicide attacks. He began to lay virtually all the blame for the failure to reach a political settlement at the door of the Palestinians. Ilan Pappé and I, on the other hand, held on to our belief that Israel bears the primary responsibility for both the persistence and the escalation of the conflict.

Many different issues are explored in the chapters that follow, which are arranged in only a rough chronological order. As such, it might help the reader to know at the beginning of the journey that much of what follows turns on three main watersheds: the creation of Israel in May 1948; the Six-Day War of June 1967; and the Oslo Accord signed on 13 September 1993. Each of these episodes is the subject of heated debate among scholars, and among the protagonists on both sides.

The first debate is about 1948. I believe that the creation of the State of Israel involved a terrible injustice to the Palestinians. But I fully accept the legitimacy of the State of Israel within its pre-1967 borders. My critics claim that these two statements are contradictory, that a state based on injustice cannot be legitimate. My reply is as follows. As a result of the creation of Israel, the Palestinians suffered dispossession and dispersal. Over 700,000 Palestinians, roughly half of the indigenous Arab population, became refugees. The name Palestine was wiped off the map. This outcome of the war constituted not merely an injustice but a profound national trauma, a catastrophe or al-Nakba, as it is called in Arabic.

But the Jews also suffered an injustice, perhaps the greatest injustice of the twentieth century – the Holocaust. The Jews are a people and, like any other people, they have a natural right to national self-determination. In the aftermath of the Second World War, the moral case for a Jewish state became unassailable. In the circumstances of 1948, after the hideous suffering inflicted on the Jews of Europe by Nazi Germany, it was an inescapable fact that something on a titanic scale had to be done for them and there was nothing titanic enough except Palestine. This was the background to the UN resolution of 29 November 1947 for the partition of Palestine into two states, one Jewish and one Arab.

The UN resolution provided an international charter of legitimacy for the Jewish state. True, the Arabs were not responsible for the barbaric treatment of the Jews in the heartland of Christian Europe. Most Arabs consequently felt that the gift of part of Palestine to the Jews was illegal. However, a resolution passed by the UN General Assembly by a large majority cannot be illegal. It may be unjust but not illegal. Injustice and illegality are not the same thing. What is legal is not necessarily just. Moreover, in 1949 Israel concluded armistice agreements with all its Arab neighbours: Lebanon, Syria, Jordan and Egypt. These are the only internationally recognised borders that Israel has ever had. And these are the only borders that I regard as legitimate.

The second great watershed in the modern history of the Middle East was June 1967. In the course of its spectacular victory in the Six-Day War, Israel captured the Golan Heights from Syria, the West Bank from Jordan, and the Sinai Peninsula from Egypt. On 22 November 1967, the UN Security Council passed resolution 242. The preamble emphasised the inadmissibility of the acquisition of territory by war, and the resolution itself called on Israel to give up the territories it had captured in return for peace with its neighbours. For the first time in its history Israel had something concrete to offer the Arabs in return for recognition and peace. But Israel preferred land to peace. Within a matter of months after the guns fell silent, Israel began to build civilian settlements in the occupied territories in blatant contravention of the Fourth Geneva Convention. Israel became a colonial power. For my part, as I have said, I still accept the legitimacy of the State of Israel within its pre-1967 borders. But

I reject, and reject utterly, completely and uncompromisingly, the Zionist colonial project beyond these borders.

The third great watershed was the Oslo Accord, signed on 13 September 1993 on the White House lawn and clinched with the historic handshake between Yasser Arafat and Yitzhak Rabin. The Oslo Accord was the first ever agreement between the two principal parties to the Arab–Israeli conflict: Israelis and Palestinians. The brave words 'a Palestinian state' did not appear in the text of the Oslo Accord. The signature did, however, signify three things: the PLO's recognition of the State of Israel and its right to exist; Israel's recognition of the PLO as representative of the Palestinian people; and the two sides' agreement to resolve all their outstanding differences by peaceful means.

Soon after the Oslo Accord was signed, I had a debate with the late Edward Said, who was an old and dear friend, in the 21 October 1993 issue of the *London Review of Books*. My article is not reprinted in this volume because, frankly, it did not stand the test of time. Edward made the case against the Oslo Accord; I made the case for. Edward's article was called 'A Palestinian Versailles'. His argument was that the Oslo Accord was an instrument of Palestinian surrender that compromised fundamental Palestinian national rights. It did not involve the promise, let alone the guarantee, of an independent Palestinian state at the end of the transition period. Edward regarded Oslo as an agreement between a very strong party and a very weak party, which was bound to reflect the balance of power between these two parties.

I conceded at the outset all the shortcomings and omissions of the Oslo Accord, but regarded it as an important step in the right direction. For all its limitations, it seemed to me like a major breakthrough in the 100-year history of this deep, existential conflict. I believed that it would set in motion an irreversible – a gradual and controlled, but still irreversible – process of Israeli withdrawal from nearly all of the occupied territories, and that an independent Palestinian state would emerge by the end of the transition period.

In the years since 1993, I have often asked myself: who was right and who was wrong? Who had the correct analysis? When things were going well, when progress was being made, when Oslo II was signed, for example, I thought that I was right and that Edward Said was wrong. When the political process stalled with the inevitable return to violence, I thought that Edward Said was right and I was wrong. From today's vantage point, 16 years on, it is indisputable that I was wrong and Edward Said was right in his analysis of the nature and limitations of the Oslo Accord. This volume includes a number of essays on Rabin's successors and on the part they played in destroying the foundations he had built for what Yasser Arafat often called 'the peace of the brave'. My view, in a nutshell, is that Yitzhak Rabin was the only prime minister in Israel's history who had the courage, honesty and determination to move forward with the Palestinians towards a resolution of the conflict.

Among the wreckers of the Oslo Accords a special place is reserved for Ariel Sharon, the Likud leader and Israel's prime minister from 2001 to 2006. George W. Bush famously described Sharon as a man of peace and, by his lights, Sharon probably was. But by any reasonable standard, Sharon was a man of war. He was the champion of violent solutions, the unilateralist *par excellence*, a Jewish Rambo. Sharon personified the most brutal, colonial, reactionary and racist trends in Zionism. In dealing with the local Arabs, the Zionist movement always relied heavily on military force and on creating 'facts on the ground' in the shape of Jewish settlements on disputed territory. Jewish settlements pre-empted the negotiations that were supposed to determine the fate of the territory. Sharon's government refused to resume the negotiations on the final status of the occupied territories, as stipulated in the Oslo Accord. Instead it acted ruthlessly in expanding Jewish settlements, demolishing Palestinian houses, constructing a 'security barrier' through the West Bank, undermining the Palestinian Authority, and breaking up the West Bank into a collection of enclaves with no territorial contiguity. In a word, the overarching aim of the government was politicide: to deny the Palestinians any independent political existence in Palestine.

Under Ehud Olmert, Sharon's deputy and successor, this policy of shunning diplomacy and relying exclusively on military power reached its climax with the assault on Gaza that started on 27 December 2008. Official Israeli propaganda depicted 'Operation Cast Lead' as an act of self-defence intended to stop Hamas rocket attacks on civilians in southern Israel. But the real aim of the attack was to drive Hamas (which had won a fair and free election in January 2006) out of power, to terrorise the people of Gaza into submission, to crush all forms of resistance to Israeli occupation, and to suppress the Palestinian struggle for independence and statehood. It was a naked attempt by Israel to impose its own terms on the Palestinians without the slightest regard for their democratic procedures, their rights, or their legitimate aspirations. One of the most deplorable aspects of this war was the indiscriminate bombing by the Israeli army (or Israel Defence Force, as it calls itself); the unbridled brutality towards civilians; and the attacks on UN schools and food depots. The International Criminal Court is urgently considering whether the Palestinian Authority is 'enough like a state' for it to bring a case alleging that Israeli troops committed war crimes in the recent conflict. Even without war crime trials, the vicious assault on the people of Gaza has irreversibly shattered any claim that Israel might once have had to hold the moral high ground.

The death and destruction inflicted by Israel on the innocent civilians of Gaza raises a question: how does a people that has been the victim of such indescribable callousness come to be the cruel tormentor of another people? I confess that I find this subject rather painful and I do not have a satisfactory answer to the question. Salo Baron, the American Jewish historian, spoke of the lachrymose version of Jewish history – history as a never-ending chain of Jewish suffering, culminating in the Holocaust. The Jews do indeed have a fair claim to be among the most persecuted, if not the most persecuted people in history. But the history of Israel is different. Since 1948 the Israelis have had the whip hand, and their victory in June 1967 has turned them into violent oppressors. Edward Said had a different perspective to that of the majority of Palestinians on the relationship between Israelis and Palestinians, describing the latter as the victims of victims. From his perspective both peoples were 'communities of suffering'. It is precisely because the Jews suffered so much at the hands of the Nazis, according to Said, that they became obsessed with security and ended up as oppressors. This perspective helps to explain the psychology behind Israel's violence and inhumanity towards the Palestinians, but it does not justify them.

Is there a peaceful, non-violent solution to this century-old conflict? It seems to me that the only fair and reasonable solution is the partition of Palestine, in other words, a two-state solution. By signing the Oslo Accord the Palestinians abandoned the armed struggle and opted for a two-state solution. They gave up their claim to 78 per cent of mandatory Palestine in the expectation that they would get an independent state on the remaining 22 per cent, consisting of the West Bank and the Gaza Strip. But over the last decade Israel has moved steadily to the Right and as a result its terms for a settlement have hardened. The Likud does not accept the case for an independent Palestinian state. Parties further to the Right advocate overtly racist policies like the mass expulsion of Palestinians. Nor is the attitude of successive Israeli governments towards the Palestinians conducive to reconciliation. Reconciliation cannot be imposed by the strong on the weak. Genuine reconciliation can only grow out of mutual respect and equality.

Despite the serious deterioration in the relations between Israelis and Palestinians in the last decade, I refuse to give up hope. At present Israelis and Palestinians are locked into a horrific dance of death. But in the longer term Israelis may come to realise the error of their ways. They may eventually grasp that there is no military solution to what is essentially a political problem. One day they may stop deluding themselves that their country's security can be guaranteed by the unilateral exercise of extreme force. For my part, I draw comfort from the historical knowledge that nations, like individuals, can act rationally – after they have exhausted all the other alternatives.

*Avi Shlaim*
*Oxford, April 2009*

# *Chronology*

| | |
|---|---|
| 29 Nov. 1947 | UN resolution for the partition of Palestine |
| 15 May 1948 | Proclamation of the State of Israel |
| 15 May 1948– | |
| 7 Jan. 1949 | First Arab–Israeli War |
| 4 Apr. 1950 | Jordan annexes West Bank, including East Jerusalem |
| 29 Oct– | |
| 7 Nov. 1956 | The Suez War |
| 29 May 1964 | Creation of the Palestine Liberation Organisation (PLO) |
| 23 Feb. 1966 | Left-wing coup in Syria followed by increased PLO activity against Israel |
| 5–10 June 1967 | The Six-Day War |
| 27 June 1967 | Israel annexes East Jerusalem |
| 26 July 1967 | Allon Plan presented to Cabinet |
| 1 Sept. 1967 | Arab League summit at Khartoum |
| 22 Nov. 1967 | UN Security Council passes resolution 242 |
| 21 Mar. 1968 | Battle of al-Karameh |
| Mar. 1969– | |
| Aug. 1970 | The Israeli–Egyptian War of Attrition |

| | |
|---|---|
| Sept. 1970 | 'Black September': Jordan crushes Palestinian *fedayeen* |
| 6–26 Oct. 1973 | The Yom Kippur War [the October War] |
| 22 Oct. 1973 | UN Security Council resolution 338 calls for direct negotiations |
| 26–29 Oct. 1974 | Arab League summit at Rabat recognises the PLO as 'the sole legitimate representative of the Palestinian people' |
| 17 May 1977 | Rise to power in Israel of right-wing Likud Party |
| 19–21 Nov. 1977 | Sadat's visit to Jerusalem |
| 17 Sept. 1978 | Israel and Egypt sign the Camp David Accords |
| 26 Mar. 1979 | Israel–Egypt peace treaty is signed at the White House |
| 6 June 1982 | Israeli invasion of Lebanon |
| 21 Aug. 1982 | PLO fighters are evacuated from Beirut |
| 16 Sept. 1982 | The massacre of Sabra and Shatila |
| 10 June 1985 | Israel withdraws from Lebanon, but forms 'security zone' in the south |
| 1 Oct. 1985 | Israel bombs PLO headquarters in Tunis |
| 9 Dec. 1987 | Outbreak of the first intifada |
| 31 July 1988 | King Hussein announces Jordan's disengagement from the West Bank |
| 15 Nov. 1988 | Palestine National Council in Algiers conditionally accepts UN resolutions 181, 242, and 338 |
| 14 Dec. 1988 | Yasser Arafat accepts US terms for talks with the PLO |
| 20 June 1990 | US suspends dialogue with the PLO |
| 2 Aug. 1990 | Iraq invades Kuwait |
| 16 Jan.– 28 Feb. 1991 | The First Gulf War |
| 30 Oct. 1991 | Middle East peace conference convenes in Madrid |
| 10 Dec. 1991 | Bilateral Arab–Israeli peace talks begin in Washington |

| | |
|---|---|
| 16 Dec. 1992 | Israeli deportation of 415 Hamas activists |
| 19 Jan. 1993 | Knesset repeals ban on contacts with the PLO |
| 25 July 1993 | Israel launches Operation Accountability in south Lebanon |
| 10 Sept. 1993 | Israel and PLO exchange letters formally recognising each other |
| 13 Sept. 1993 | Israel–PLO Declaration of Principles on Palestinian Self-Government is signed in the White House |
| 25 Feb. 1994 | Massacre of Palestinians at Tomb of the Patriarchs in Hebron |
| 4 May 1994 | Israel and PLO reach agreement in Cairo on the application of the Declaration of Principles |
| 26 Oct. 1994 | Israel and Jordan sign a peace treaty |
| 2 Feb. 1995 | First summit between leaders of Egypt, Jordan, PLO and Israel |
| 28 Sept. 1995 | Israeli–Palestinian Interim Agreement on the West Bank and the Gaza Strip (Oslo II) is signed |
| 4 Nov. 1995 | Yitzhak Rabin is assassinated and Shimon Peres succeeds him |
| 5 Jan. 1996 | Hamas master bomb-maker Yahya Ayyash ('the engineer') is assassinated by Israel |
| 21 Jan. 1996 | First Palestinian elections |
| 25 Feb. 1996 | A Hamas suicide bomber blows up a bus in Jerusalem |
| 2–4 Mar. 1996 | Four Hamas suicide bombs kill 59 Israelis |
| 13 Mar. 1996 | Anti-terrorist summit of 27 states is held in Sharm el-Sheikh |
| 11 Apr. 1996 | Israel launches Operation Grapes of Wrath in south Lebanon |
| 24 Apr. 1996 | The Palestinian National Council amends the Palestinian National Charter |
| 25 Sept. 1996 | Clashes following opening of tunnel in the Old City of Jerusalem |
| 15 Jan. 1997 | The Hebron Protocol is signed |

| 18 Mar. 1997 | Construction begins of Jewish housing at Har Homa in East Jerusalem |
| 23 Oct. 1998 | Binyamin Netanyahu and Yasser Arafat sign the Wye River Memorandum |
| 4 Sept. 1999 | Ehud Barak and Yasser Arafat sign the Sharm el-Sheikh Memorandum |
| 24 May 2000 | IDF withdraws unilaterally from South Lebanon |
| 11–25 July 2000 | The Camp David summit |
| 28 Sept. 2000 | Ariel Sharon visits Temple Mount. Outbreak of the al-Aqsa intifada |
| 23 Dec. 2000 | President Clinton presents his 'parameters' |
| 21–28 Jan. 2001 | Israeli–Palestinian negotiations at Taba in Egypt |
| 27 Mar. 2002 | Suicide bomber kills 29 and wounds close to 150 in Park Hotel, Netanya |
| 28 Mar. 2002 | Arab League summit in Beirut approves Saudi peace plan |
| 29 Mar. 2002 | Israel launches Operation Defensive Shield in the West Bank |
| 24 June 2002 | President Bush calls for 'provisional' Palestinian state under new leadership |
| 20 Mar. 2003 | United States and Britain invade Iraq |
| 30 April 2003 | The Quartet issues the road map. Mahmoud Abbas appointed Palestinian prime minister |
| 2 June 2003 | Summit meeting in Aqaba to launch the road map |
| 6 Sept. 2003 | Mahmoud Abbas resigns as prime minister |
| 11 Sept. 2003 | Israeli Cabinet decides in principle to 'remove' Arafat |
| 1 Dec. 2003 | Unofficial 'peace agreement' is signed in Geneva |
| 22 Mar. 2004 | Israel assassinates Hamas leader Sheikh Yassin |
| 11 Nov. 2004 | Yasser Arafat dies and Mahmoud Abbas succeeds |
| 18 Dec. 2004 | Ariel Sharon announces unilateral withdrawal from Gaza |
| 9 Jan. 2005 | Mahmoud Abbas is democratically elected as president |

| August 2005 | Israel withdraws unilaterally from the Gaza Strip |
|---|---|
| 25 Jan 2006 | Hamas victory in Palestinian legislative elections |
| March 2006 | Over 40 Qassam rockets fall on Sderot. IDF responds with shelling of launching sites and IAF raids |
| 27 June 2006 | Palestinian Prisoners' Document |
| 28 June 2006 | Israel launches operation Summer Rains in the Gaza Strip to recover kidnapped soldier Gilad Shalit and stop Qassam rocket fire |
| 12 July– 14 Aug. 2006 | Second Lebanon War |
| 26 Nov. 2006 | Israelis and Palestinians announce Gaza truce |
| 8 Feb. 2007 | Palestinian Unity Agreement in Mecca |
| 19 Feb. 2007 | Trilateral Israeli–Palestinian–American summit in Jerusalem |
| 15 June 2007 | Hamas forces drive Fatah out of the Gaza strip. President Abbas dissolves the unity government |
| 25 June 2007 | Sharm el-Sheikh Summit II |
| 27 Nov. 2007 | Annapolis Summit |
| 19 June 2008 | Egyptian-brokered Israel–Hamas truce in Gaza |
| 4 Nov. 2008 | Israel violates the truce |
| 9 Nov. 2008 | Quartet meeting at Sharm el-Sheikh reaffirms support for the Annapolis peace process |
| 27 Dec. 2008– 18 Jan. 2009 | Israel's Operation Cast Lead in the Gaza Strip |

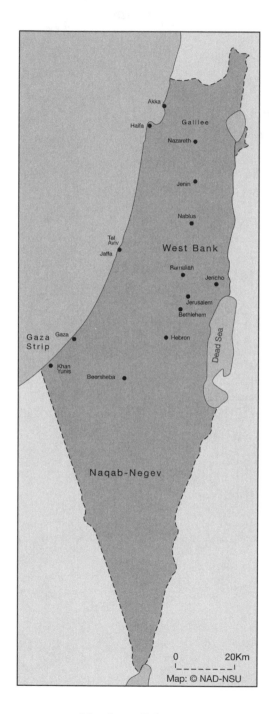

| | 1947 UN Partition Plan lines |
| | Proposed Jewish State |
| | Proposed Arab State |

Mandatory Palestine

The 1947 UN Partition Plan

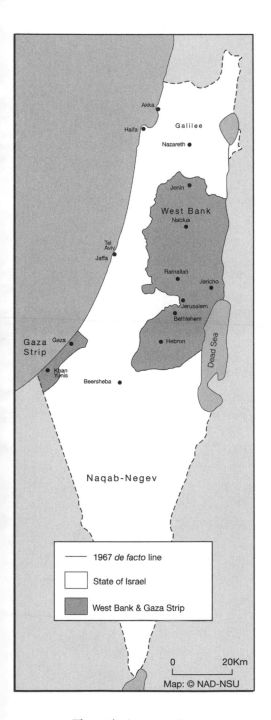

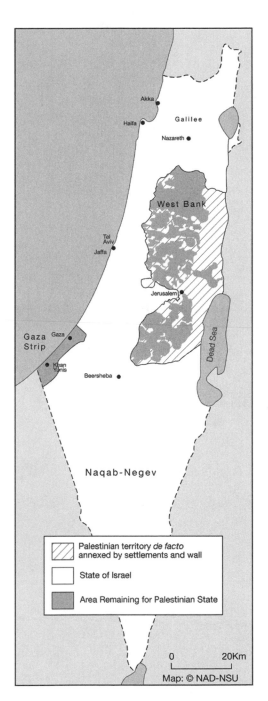

The 1949 Armistice Lines

Israeli Settlements on the West Bank

# PART I

## 1948 and After

# ONE

# *The Balfour Declaration and its Consequences*

Occasionally there are topics that have been written about at such length that it helps to clear the air, or to establish a vantage point from which to consider the subject anew. My aim therefore is to take a fresh look at the Balfour Declaration in the light of recent scholarship. I propose to focus on the Declaration itself, on the motives behind it, the way it was implemented, the conflicts to which it gave rise, and on its consequences for Britain's position as the paramount Western power in the Middle East. I begin with a note on background.

British imperialism in the Middle East during the First World War was – to use a British understatement – intricate. In 1915 Britain promised Hussein, the Sharif of Mecca, that it would support an independent Arab kingdom under his rule in return for his mounting an Arab revolt against the Ottoman Empire, Germany's ally in the war. The promise was contained in a letter dated 24 October 1915 from Sir Henry McMahon, the British High Commissioner in Egypt, to the Sharif of Mecca in what later became known as the McMahon–Hussein correspondence. The Sharif of Mecca assumed that the promise included Palestine. In 1916 Britain reached a secret agreement with France to divide the Middle East into spheres of influence in the event of an Allied victory. Under the terms of the Sykes–Picot agreement, Palestine was to be placed under international control. In 1917 Britain issued the Balfour Declaration, promising to support the establishment of a national home for the Jewish people in Palestine.

Thus, by a stroke of the imperial pen, the Promised Land became twice-promised. Even by the standards of Perfidious Albion, this was an extraordinary tale of double-dealing and betrayal, a tale that continued to haunt Britain throughout the 30 years of its rule in Palestine. Of the three wartime pledges, the most curious, and certainly the most controversial, was the Balfour Declaration. Here, wrote Arthur Koestler, was one nation promising another nation the land of a third nation. Koestler dismissed the Declaration as an impossible notion, an unnatural graft, a 'white Negro'. C.P. Scott, the ardently pro-Zionist editor of the *Manchester Guardian*, played a significant part in persuading the British government to issue the Declaration. In an editorial article, Scott hailed the Declaration as an act of imaginative generosity. 'It is at once the fulfilment of aspiration, the signpost of destiny.'[1] Elizabeth Monroe in *Britain's Moment in the Middle East* conceded that to the Jews who went to Palestine, the Declaration signified fulfilment and salvation; but she also notes that to the British the Declaration brought much ill will, and complications that sapped their strength. 'Measured by British interests alone,' argued Monroe, 'it is one of the greatest mistakes in our imperial history.'[2]

On 2 November 1917, Arthur Balfour, Britain's Secretary of State for Foreign Affairs, addressed a letter to Lord Rothschild, one of the leaders of the British Jews, as follows:

I have much pleasure in conveying to you, on behalf of His Majesty's Government, the following declaration of sympathy which has been submitted to and approved by the Cabinet: His Majesty's Government view with favour the establishment in Palestine of a national home for the Jewish people, and will use their best endeavours to facilitate the achievement of this object, it being clearly understood that nothing shall be done which may prejudice the civil and religious rights of existing non-Jewish communities in Palestine, or the rights and political status enjoyed by Jews in any other country.

The statement was exceedingly brief, consisting of a mere 67 words, but its consequences were both profound and pervasive, and its impact on the subsequent history of the Middle East was nothing less than revolutionary. It completely transformed the position of the fledgling Zionist movement vis-à-vis the Arabs of Palestine, and it provided a protective umbrella that enabled the Zionists to proceed steadily towards their ultimate goal of establishing an independent Jewish state in Palestine. Rarely in the annals of the British Empire has such a short document produced such far-reaching consequences.

In view of its political impact, it is not surprising that the Balfour Declaration has attracted so much attention from historians of the Middle East. Nor is it surprising that, almost a century later, it remains such a contentious and controversial subject. There are several bones of contention in this debate, all of them revolving around the question of compatibility between the three wartime agreements. On the question of conflict between Britain's promises to Sharif Hussein and to the French, the most definitive study is by Elie Kedourie. Kedourie was the first scholar to bring together all the available evidence from British, French and Arabic sources to elucidate the meaning of the McMahon–Hussein correspondence and to examine its impact on British policy between the wars. His principal conclusion is that the Sykes–Picot agreement did not violate the commitments contained in the McMahon–Hussein correspondence. The Balfour Declaration, however, is only mentioned by Kedourie in passing because it falls outside the scope of his study.[3]

In 1916 the Sharif of Mecca proclaimed himself 'King of the Arab Countries', but the Allies recognised him only as King of the Hijaz. On the relationship between Britain's commitments to the Zionists and to King Hussein, the most recent study is *Palestine: A Twice-Promised Land?* by Isaiah Friedman.[4] Friedman's answer to the question posed in the title is that Palestine was not twice-promised inasmuch as McMahon's offer to recognise and uphold Arab independence after the war was conditional and non-binding and that, in any case, it did not include Palestine. Friedman argues not only that Sir Henry had definitely excluded Palestine from the prospective Arab kingdom but that this was understood by the Hashemite leader at the time. Hussein's silence following the publication of the Balfour Declaration is seen by Friedman as indicative of his attitude. Another piece of evidence cited by Friedman comes from the famous book by George Antonius, the spokesman and chronicler of the Arab national movement. From Antonius we learn that King Hussein 'ordered his sons to do what they could to allay the apprehensions caused by the Balfour Declaration among their followers [and] despatched an emissary to Faisal at Aqaba with similar instructions'.[5]

Friedman's conclusion is that the charges of fraudulence and deception levelled against the British after the war were largely groundless. Groundless or not, these charges acquired the status of dogma not only in the eyes of Arab nationalists but, more surprisingly, in the eyes of most British officials as well. In the case of King Hussein it is necessary to distinguish much more clearly than Friedman does between his initial response to the Balfour Declaration and his subsequent attitude. When news of the Declaration reached Hussein he was greatly disturbed by it and asked Britain to clarify its meaning. Whitehall met this request with the despatch of Commander D.G. Hogarth, one of the heads of the Arab Bureau in Cairo, who arrived in Jedda in the first week of January 1918 for a series of interviews with King Hussein. 'Hogarth's Message', as it came to be known, reaffirmed the Entente's determination that 'the Arab race shall be given full opportunity of once again forming a nation in the world'. So far as Palestine was concerned, Britain was 'determined that no people shall be subject to another'. Britain noted and supported the aspiration of the Jews to return to Palestine but only in so far as this was compatible with 'the freedom of the existing population, both economic and political'. Hussein voiced no disagreement with this policy, though we may be sceptical of Hogarth's report that he 'agreed enthusiastically' with it.[6]

Hogarth's Message is crucial for understanding King Hussein's attitude to the Balfour Declaration. Following the meetings in Jedda, Hussein thought he had Britain's assurance that the settlement of the Jews in Palestine would not conflict with Arab independence in that country. This explains his initial silence in public and his private efforts to allay the anxieties of his sons. Hussein had great respect for the Jews, seeing them, following the Koran, as 'the People of the Book', meaning the Bible. He was not opposed to the settlement of Jews in Palestine and even welcomed it on religious and on humanitarian grounds. He was, however, emphatically opposed to a Zionist takeover of the country. Hogarth gave him a solemn pledge that Britain would respect not only the economic but also the political freedom of the Arab population. When Britain subsequently refused to recognise Arab independence in Palestine, Hussein felt betrayed and accused Britain of breach of faith.[7]

If the disenchantment of Sharif Hussein and his sons with Britain was gradual, the hostility of the Arab nationalists towards Britain on account of the Balfour Declaration was immediate and unremitting. One valuable Arabic source on this period is the diary of Auni Abd al-Hadi. Abd al-Hadi was a Palestinian politician who served as one of Amir Faisal's secretaries at the Paris Peace Conference and during his short-lived administration in Damascus in 1920. He then served Amir Abdullah, Faisal's elder brother, in Transjordan. In 1924 he returned to Palestine and became one of the chief spokesmen of the Palestinian national movement. Abd al-Hadi's impression was that Faisal resented the Zionist intrusion into Palestine but was wary of upsetting the British. Faisal was also influenced, according to Abd al-Hadi, by the reassuring letters he received from his father in the early months of 1918 in his camp in Aqaba, on the subject of the Balfour Declaration.[8]

For his part, Abd al-Hadi did not believe in the possibility of cooperation with the Zionists in Palestine. He was therefore very critical in his diary of Faisal for signing an agreement on Arab–Jewish cooperation with Dr Chaim Weizmann at their meeting in Aqaba on 4 June 1919. Abd al-Hadi notes that Faisal signed the agreement without understanding its implications because it was in English, a language he did not know. But he also notes that Faisal added a hand-written codicil making the implementation of the agreement conditional on his demands concerning Arab independence being fulfilled.[9] As these conditions were not fulfilled, the agreement became null and void.

There are a number of other references to the Balfour Declaration in Auni Abd al-Hadi's diary, all of them highly critical of the British and of their Jewish protégés. His basic view, repeated on several occasions, was that the Declaration was made by an English foreigner who had no ownership of Palestine to a foreign Jew who had no right to it.[10] Palestine thus faced a double danger: from the British Mandate and from the Zionist movement. In December 1920 Abd al-Hadi participated in the Third Palestinian Congress in Haifa. The Congress denounced the actions of the British government and its plans for realising the Zionist goals. It also rejected Balfour's promise of a national home for the Jews in Palestine as a violation of international law, of wartime Allied commitments, and of the natural rights of the inhabitants of the country.[11] In 1932 Abd al-Hadi founded the Palestinian branch of the Pan-Arab Independence Party whose manifesto called for the cancellation of the Mandate and of the Balfour Declaration.[12] Arab hostility to the Balfour Declaration, as exemplified by Auni Abd al-Hadi, could have been predicted from the beginning. So why was it issued?

There are two main schools of thought on the origins of the Balfour Declaration, one represented by Leonard Stein, the other by Mayir Vereté. What later became the conventional wisdom on the subject was first laid out by Stein in 1961, in his masterly survey *The Balfour Declaration*.[13] This book provides a careful, detailed and subtle account of the decision-making process that led Britain to issue the Declaration, but it does not reach any clear-cut conclusions. The conclusion implicit in the narrative, however, is that it was the activity and the skill of the Zionists, and in particular of Dr Chaim Weizmann, that induced Britain to issue its famous statement of support for the Zionist cause.    Stein's book was subjected to an extended critique by Mayir Vereté of the Hebrew University of Jerusalem in a notable article he published in 1970, entitled 'The Balfour Declaration and its Makers'.[14] According to Vereté the Declaration was the work of hard-headed pragmatists, primarily motivated by British imperial interests in the Middle East. Far from the Zionists seeking British support, it was British officials who took the initiative in approaching the Zionists.

The definition of British interests in the Middle East began in 1915, leading to the Sykes–Picot agreement which reconciled Britain's interests with those of France, with a compromise over Palestine. On further reflection, however, the British felt that control over Palestine was necessary in order to keep France and Russia from the approaches to Egypt and the Suez Canal. In Vereté's account, it was the desire to exclude France from Palestine, rather than sympathy for the Zionist cause, that prompted Britain to sponsor a national home for the Jewish people in Palestine. It was also thought that a Declaration favourable to the ideals of Zionism was likely to enlist the support of the Jews of America and Russia for the war effort against Germany. Finally, rumour that Germany was courting the Zionists accelerated the pace at which Britain moved towards its dramatic overture. In contrast to Stein, Vereté concludes that Zionist lobbying played a negligible part in drawing Britain towards Palestine.

A similar though not identical argument was advanced by Jon Kimche in *The Unromantics: The Great Powers and the Balfour Declaration*. As the title suggests, the author believes that the driving force behind the Declaration was not sentimentality but hard-headed realism. Kimche, however, attributes this realism not only to the British but to the Zionists as well. Indeed, he maintains that the interests of the two sides were identical, and that by working for a Jewish Palestine they were working at the same time for a British Palestine. The Declaration provided the stepping stones: each partner used the same stones but later went his own way. 'This', argues Kimche, 'was the basic realism with which Balfour and Weizmann approached their compact; they understood that they would have to go together part of the way, but that a time would come when they would have to part'.[15] What is beyond question, as Kimche himself points out, is that there was little room for such sophistication in the heated politics of wartime Britain and postwar Zionism.[16]

The historiography of the Balfour Declaration took a step forward in 2000 with the publication of Tom Segev's book on the British Mandate in Palestine.[17] Segev's contribution lies in the interpretation he develops of the origins of British rule in Palestine. His 'revisionist account' is based on new source material as well as a new synthesis of earlier studies on the subject. In Segev's version, the prime movers behind the Balfour Declaration were neither the Zionist leaders nor the British imperial planners, but Prime Minister David Lloyd George. In his memoirs, written some 20 years after the event, Lloyd George explained his support for the Zionist movement during the First World War as an alliance with a hugely influential political organisation whose goodwill was worth paying for. The common wisdom in Britain at the time Lloyd George published his account was that the country had erred in supporting the Zionists and that he was probably trying to justify his wartime policy. Segev will have none of it. Lloyd George's support for Zionism, he argues, was based not on British interests but on ignorance and prejudice. In his own way Lloyd George despised the Jews, but he also feared them, and he proceeded on the basis of an absurdly inflated notion of the Zionists' power and influence. In aligning Britain with the Zionists, he acted in the mistaken – and anti-Semitic – view that the Jews turned the wheels of history. In fact, as Segev shows, the Jews were helpless, with nothing to offer – having no influence other than that generated by the myth of clandestine power. As for the Zionists, being a minority within a minority, they could not even speak in the name of world Jewry.

Lloyd George's misconceptions about the Jews were widely shared amongst the ruling class in Britain, as was his antipathy towards the French. In Segev's summary, the British entered Palestine to defeat the Turks; they stayed there to keep it from the French; and they gave it to the Zionists because they loved 'the Jews' even as they loathed them, at once admiring and despising them. The British were not guided by strategic considerations and there was no orderly decision-making process. The Balfour Declaration 'was the product of neither military nor diplomatic interests but of prejudice, faith, and sleight of hand. The men who sired it were Christian and Zionist and, in many cases, anti-Semitic. They believed the Jews controlled the world.'[18] Britain's belief in the mystical power of 'the Jews' overrode reality, and it was on the basis of such spurious considerations that Britain took the momentous decision to sponsor the Zionist cause.[19]

On one point there is a broad consensus among admirers as well as critics of the Balfour Declaration that it was a considered statement of policy, issued after prolonged deliberations, painstaking drafting and redrafting, and careful wording. Before the British government gave the Declaration to the world, it closely examined every word, and incorporated in the text countless changes and corrections. All these efforts did not, however, result in a clear or coherent text. On the contrary, they compounded its opaqueness, ambiguity and, worst of all, internal contradictions. The greatest contradiction lay in its supporting, however vaguely, the right to national self-determination of a minority of the inhabitants of Palestine while implicitly denying that right to the majority. At the time the proposed statement was under discussion in the War Cabinet, the population of Palestine was in the neighbourhood of 670,000. Of these, the Jews numbered some 60,000. The Arabs thus constituted roughly 91 per cent of the population, while the Jews accounted for 9 per cent. The proviso that 'nothing shall be done which may prejudice the civil and religious rights of existing non-Jewish communities in Palestine' implied that, in British eyes, the Arab majority had no political rights.

Part of the explanation for this peculiar phraseology is that the majority of the ministers did not recognise the Palestinians as a people with legitimate national aspirations, but viewed them as a backward, Oriental, inert mass. Arthur Balfour was typical of the Gentile Zionists in this respect. 'Zionism, be it right or wrong, good or bad,' he wrote in 1922, 'is of far profounder import than the desires and prejudices of the 700,000 Arabs who now inhabit that ancient land.'[20] The most charitable explanation that may be offered for this curious claim is that in an age of colonialism everyone was in some sense implicated in its ideology. Balfour may appear today like an extreme example of the colonial mentality, but he was not untypical of his era.

Yet Balfour's specific proposal to come out in favour of the establishment of a Jewish homeland in Palestine did not enjoy unanimous support round the Cabinet table. Edwin Montagu, the Secretary of State for India and the only Jewish member of the government, considered Zionism a threat to the Jews of Britain and other countries. He denounced Zionism as a 'mischievous political creed, untenable by any patriotic citizen of the United Kingdom'.[21] Montagu rejected the idea of the Jews as a nation and argued that the demand for recognition as a separate nation put at risk their struggle to become citizens with equal rights in the countries in which they lived.[22]

Lord Curzon, a member of the War Cabinet, was more troubled by the implications of the proposed move for the rights of the Arabs of Palestine. 'How was it proposed', he asked his Cabinet colleagues, 'to get rid of the existing majority of Mussulman inhabitants and to introduce the Jews in their place?' In a paper to the Cabinet he returned to the theme:

> What is to become of the people of the country? . . . [The Arabs] and their forefathers have occupied the country for the best part of 1,500 years, and they own the soil . . . They profess the Mohammedan faith. They will not be content either to be expropriated for Jewish immigrants or to act merely as hewers of wood and drawers of water for the latter.[23]

Montagu and Curzon were overruled. The three most powerful men in the Cabinet, Lloyd George, Balfour and Lord Milner, threw their weight behind the proposal. At the crucial meeting, on 31 October 1917, the Cabinet approved the final wording of the declaration of sympathy for a national home for the Jews in Palestine. Curzon restated his misgivings and his pessimism about the future of Palestine. Largely in deference to his anxieties, the final version of the Declaration contained the caveat about protecting the civil and religious rights of the non-Jewish communities in Palestine.[24] Chaim

Weizmann was waiting outside the room where the War Cabinet met. In the early afternoon, Sir Mark Sykes emerged, calling 'Dr Weizmann, it's a boy!'

While Chaim Weizmann's part in procuring the Balfour Declaration may have been exaggerated, his role in keeping Britain to its rash wartime promise was of critical importance. Weizmann went as the head of the Zionist delegation to the peace conference that convened at Versailles in January 1919. His aim was to ensure that the British would remain in Palestine. At the conference he pleaded for the international ratification of the Balfour Declaration. But at the San Remo conference, in April 1920, the French representative objected to the inclusion of the language of the Declaration in the text of the Mandate over Palestine. It took strong British pressure to persuade the League of Nations to incorporate the commitment to establish a Jewish national home in the terms of Britain's Mandate to govern Palestine.[25]

Even before the international ratification of the Balfour Declaration, violent protests broke out in Palestine against Britain's pro-Zionist policy and against Zionist activities. The Arabs emphatically refused to recognise the Declaration or anything done in its name, seeing it as the thin end of the wedge of an Anglo-Jewish plot to take over their country. Arab resentment towards the British and their protégés culminated in the Nebi Musa riots of April 1920. A court of inquiry appointed to investigate the riots noted that the Balfour Declaration 'is undoubtedly the starting point of the whole trouble'. The court also reached the conclusion that Arab fears were not unfounded.[26] The Nebi Musa riots were the first intrusion of mass violence into the Arab–Jewish conflict. The riots did nothing to advance the political aims of the Arab nationalists but they also boded ill for the Zionists' expectation of achieving their ends peacefully. In the words of Bernard Wasserstein, the riots and their aftermath 'created a gangrene of suspicion and mistrust in the British–Zionist relationship in Palestine which was to subsist throughout the three decades of British rule'.[27]

Throughout these three decades Britain was subjected to repeated criticism from Zionist quarters for reneging, or at least backsliding, on its wartime pledge to the Jews. In self-defence, the British pointed out that the Balfour Declaration committed them to support a national home for the Jews in Palestine, not a Jewish state. Not all British officials, however, adhered to this interpretation. Balfour and Lloyd George, for example, admitted in 1922 at a meeting with Winston Churchill and Chaim Weizmann that the Balfour Declaration 'had always meant a Jewish State'.[28]

The troubled and tangled history of the British Mandate in Palestine has been told many times before, recently by Joshua Sherman and Naomi Shepherd, among others.[29] Most historians of this period attribute to British policy a pro-Arab bias. Some Zionist writers go further: they accuse Britain not only of persistent partiality towards the Arabs, but of going back on its original promise to the Jews.

Tom Segev makes a major contribution to the existing literature on this issue by putting Britain's record as a mandatory power under an uncompromising lens. His verdict is that British actions considerably favoured the Zionist position and thus helped to ensure the establishment of a Jewish state. The evidence he presents of British support for the Zionist position is both rich and compelling. So is the evidence he adduces for the proposition that once the Zionist movement came to Palestine with the intention of creating a Jewish state with a Jewish majority, war was inevitable. From the start there were only two possibilities: that the Zionists would defeat the Arabs or that the Arabs would defeat the Zionists. British actions tended to weaken the Arabs and to strengthen the Zionists as the two national movements moved inexorably towards the final showdown. The Arab nationalists in Palestine, under the leadership of the Grand Mufti, Haj Amin al-Husseini, despaired of Britain and eventually threw in their lot with Nazi Germany. The Zionists, under the leadership of Chaim Weizmann, hitched a lift with the British Empire, advancing under its sponsorship to the verge of independence. The Zionists were not slow to grasp the importance for a weak national liberation movement of securing the sponsorship and support of a great power. Indeed, ensuring the support of the paramount Western power of the day remains to this day a basic tenet of Zionist foreign policy.

From the start, the central problem facing British officials in Palestine was that of reconciling an angry and hostile Arab majority to the implementation of the pro-Zionist policy that was publicly proclaimed on 2 November 1917. In general, British officials in Palestine had much more sympathy for the Arabs than did the policy-makers in London. Many of these officials had an uneasy conscience, even a feeling of guilt, as a result of their political masters' decision to honour Britain's wartime promise to the Jews while breaking its promise to the Arabs. Some suggested a revision of the policy because, in their opinion, it involved an injustice to the Arabs. But they constantly ran up against the argument that the Declaration constituted a binding commitment. Even Lord Curzon, who had originally opposed the Balfour Declaration, concluded in 1923 that the commitment to the Zionists could not be ignored 'without substantial sacrifice of consistency and self-respect, if not of honour'.[30]

Arab resentment and riots in Palestine persuaded the Lloyd George government to replace the military government with a civil administration, but not to reverse its pro-Zionist policy. And once the government resolved to continue to support a Jewish homeland in Palestine, it could not have chosen a more suitable man for the post of High Commissioner than Sir Herbert Samuel. Samuel's association with Zionism was intimate, and his attachment to the Zionist cause was perhaps the one passionate commitment of his entire political career.[31] Samuel was sent to Palestine not because of – or even despite – his Jewishness, but because he was a Zionist. The appointment pleased the Zionists but it destroyed the last vestiges of Arab faith in Britain's integrity and impartiality. Before Samuel took over from the military government, the chief administrative officer asked him to sign what became one of the most quoted documents in Zionist history: 'Received from Major General Sir Louis Bols, KCB – One Palestine, complete.' Samuel signed.[32]

Traditional British historians have tended to regard Herbert Samuel as an impartial administrator in the emerging conflict between Palestinian Arabs and Zionists. Sahar Huneidi, an Arab scholar living in London, challenges this claim in a major revisionist study of the early period of the Mandate. She argues that most of the measures Samuel took during his tenure in Palestine – in the political, economic and administrative spheres – were designed to prepare the ground not just for a Jewish national home but for a fully fledged Jewish state. Using a wide range of primary sources, both English and Arabic, Huneidi charts Samuel's career in Palestine against the complex background of British policy in the region.[33]

She argues convincingly that during Samuel's five years as High Commissioner in Palestine, from 1920 to 1925, he remained an ardent supporter of Zionism; but under the impact of fierce anti-Jewish riots, he began to doubt the practicality of a policy which seemed, as he put it, to be a recipe for 'a second Ireland'. He therefore devised endless schemes to draw the Arab notables into the political community of Palestine. These schemes all proved inadequate, however, to the task of reconciling the Arabs of Palestine to Zionism.[34]

The failure of his attempts to bring Arabs and Jews together within a unified political framework led Samuel to try to satisfy each community separately. His preferred method was the devolution of power to the increasingly separate Arabic and Jewish communal institutions. This policy encouraged the trend towards the internal partition of Palestine. Under Samuel's successors it gathered further momentum. While alleviating the inter-communal conflict in the short run, this process exacerbated the long-term problem by driving Arabs and Jews further and further apart. As the two communities built up the institutional strength required for the struggle ahead, the government of Palestine became little more than an umpire.[35]

Isaiah Berlin, an Anglo-Jewish supporter of Zionism and a prescient observer, was moved to compare the Palestine Mandate to a minor English public school:

> There was the headmaster, the high commissioner, trying to be firm and impartial: but the assistant masters favoured the sporting stupid boarders (Arabs) against the clever swot dayboys (Jews) who had the deplorable habit of writing home to their parents on the slightest provocation to complain about the quality of the teaching, the food, and so on.[36]

The role of umpire became increasingly difficult to sustain with the passage of time. High Commissioners came and went but their hands were tied by the pledge of 2 November 1917. Shortly after his arrival in Palestine, in December 1928, Sir John Chancellor reached the conclusion that the Balfour Declaration had been a 'colossal blunder', unfair to the Arabs and detrimental to the interests of the British Empire. In January 1930 he sent a long memorandum to London. He wanted to extricate Britain from the Balfour Declaration and to deal a blow to Zionism. His ideas were given a respectful hearing in London and the king asked for a copy.[37] On learning that the king would like to hear from him directly about the state of affairs in Palestine, Chancellor obliged with a 16-page letter explaining why, in Chancellor's view, Britain's national home policy in Palestine was misguided, unjust and impossible to carry out. It also repeated his earlier proposals for restricting Jewish immigration and land purchases in Palestine. The Jews took the view that the Arabs of Palestine were free to go to any part of Arabia and that they should be induced to move to Transjordan. Chancellor was strongly opposed to any such action on the grounds that it would be inconsistent with the part of the Balfour Declaration which laid down that in the establishment of a Jewish national home, nothing should be done to prejudice the rights of the non-Jewish communities in Palestine. Chancellor portrayed the Jews as an emotional people:

> What makes them difficult to deal with is that they are, regardless of the rights and feelings of others, very exacting in pressing their own claims. Even as a minority of the population of Palestine the Jews adopt towards the Arabs an attitude of arrogant superiority, which is hotly resented by the Arabs with their traditions of courtesy and good manners.[38]

Nor did the Jews cherish genuine sentiments of loyalty towards Britain. In spite of what they said on public occasions when it was in their interest to proclaim their devotion, 'the bulk of the Jewish population of Palestine have little feeling of gratitude or loyalty towards Great Britain for what she has done for the establishment of the Jewish National Home'.[39]

Having delivered his tirade against the Jews, Chancellor returned to the basic problem facing Britain and made a concrete proposal for dealing with it:

> The facts of the situation are that in the dire straits of the war, the British Government made promises to the Arabs and promises to the Jews which are inconsistent with one another and are incapable of fulfilment.
>
> The honest course is to admit our difficulty and to say to the Jews that, in accordance with the Balfour Declaration, we *have* favoured the establishment of a Jewish National Home in Palestine and that a Jewish National Home *in* Palestine has in fact been established and will be maintained and that, without violating the other part of the Balfour Declaration, without prejudicing the interests of the Arabs, we cannot do more than we have done.[40]

Chancellor's memorandum, along with number of other reports that also underlined the gravity of the situation in Palestine, contributed to a reformulation of the official line in London. In October 1930, after several discussions in Cabinet, Colonial Secretary Lord Passfield issued a White Paper, the premise and principal innovation of which was that the Balfour Declaration imposed on Britain a binary and equal obligation towards both Jews and Arabs. Accordingly, Jewish immigration to Palestine was linked to the Arab as well as the Jewish economy. In the past, Jewish immigration quotas were determined by the absorptive capacity of the Palestine economy. From this point on, Jews were to be allowed into the country only at a rate that would not put Arabs out of jobs. In the spirit of Chancellor's proposals, the White Paper assumed that the Jews would remain a minority. Chancellor and his officials were pleased by this redefinition of official policy, but their success was short-lived. Dr Weizmann succeeded in getting the new policy reversed within a few months. Once again the Zionists had won and the Arabs failed in London.[41]

As Chancellor had predicted, unrestricted Jewish immigration and land purchases in Palestine produced further unrest and periodic outbreaks of violence. The fundamental contradiction between Arab nationalist aspirations and Britain's 1917 undertakings to the Jews continued to render the Mandate inoperable. The influx of German Jews to Palestine following the Nazi rise to power in 1933 provoked deep anxieties among the Arabs. In 1936 the Arab Higher Committee declared a general strike with the aim of halting Jewish immigration, banning the sale of land to Jews, and establishing an independent national government. The general strike snowballed into a full-scale revolt that was to last three years. The British government's belated response to the outbreak of the Arab Rebellion consisted of appointing a Royal Commission, with Earl Peel as chairman, to investigate the underlying causes of the disturbances. The Peel Commission's report went to the heart of the problem:

> Under the stress of the World War the British Government made promises to Arabs and Jews in order to obtain their support. On the strength of those promises both parties formed certain expectations. . . . An irrepressible conflict has arisen between two national communities within the narrow bounds of one small country. . . . There is no common ground between them. . . . This conflict was inherent in the situation from the outset. . . . We cannot – in Palestine as it is now – both concede the Arab claim of self-government and secure the establishment of the Jewish National Home. . . . This conflict between the two obligations is all the more unfortunate because each of them, taken separately, accords with British sentiment and British interests.[42]

The Peel Commission proposed the partition of Palestine. The logic behind partition was unassailable. It was the only solution then and it remains the only solution today to the tragic conflict between the two national movements. In 1937 the Jews accepted partition but the Arabs rejected it; so the conflict continued and the violence escalated. The Arab Rebellion of 1936–9 demonstrated once again that there could be no compromise between the two rival communities in Palestine: only war could decide the issue. The Jewish community was militarily weak and vulnerable. It would have been easily defeated had Britain not intervened to restore law and order. The Jewish national home, in the last resort, had to be defended by British bayonets.

In November 1938 Major General Bernard Montgomery arrived in Palestine. His task was to crush the revolt. 'Monty' was a short-tempered professional soldier with no inclination to study the details of the conflict in Palestine. He gave his men simple orders on how to handle the rebels: kill them. This is what his men did; in the process they broke the backbone of the Arab national movement. When the struggle for Palestine entered its most crucial phase, in the aftermath of the Second World War, the Jews were ready to do battle whereas the Arabs were still licking their wounds.

The costs of the British presence in Palestine were considerable and the benefits remained persistently elusive. Palestine was not a strategic asset; it was a source not of power but of weakness. Field Marshal Sir Henry Wilson, the highest-ranking British soldier in the Middle East in the early 1920s, kept repeating that the British had no business being in Palestine, and the sooner they left, the better. 'The problem of Palestine is exactly the same . . . as the problem of Ireland', he wrote, 'namely, two peoples living in a small country hating each other like hell'. Wilson castigated the civilians – he called them the 'frocks' – for failing to understand that the Empire could not afford the luxury of spreading itself too thin. Again and again, he demanded that Palestine, or 'Jewland' as he called it, be abandoned.[43]

The logic of this position became irresistible after India's independence was declared in 1947. For if India was the jewel in the Empire's crown, Palestine was hardly more than an anemone in the king's buttonhole. Economic considerations reinforced the strategic arguments for withdrawal from Palestine. Hugh Dalton, the Chancellor of the Exchequer, deployed both arguments in a letter to Prime Minister Clement Attlee:

The present state of affairs is not only costly to us in manpower and money but is . . . of no real value from the strategic point of view – you cannot in any case have a secure base on top of a wasps' nest – and it is exposing our young men, for no good purpose, to abominable experiences and is breeding anti-Semites at a most shocking speed.[44]

In February 1947 the Labour government decided to hand the Mandate over Palestine to the United Nations, the League of Nations' successor. The Mandate was relinquished because it was unworkable. All of Britain's attempts to find a formula for peacefully reconciling the rival claims of Arabs and Jews to the country had finally failed. On 29 November 1947 the UN General Assembly voted for the partition of mandatory Palestine into two independent states, one Arab and one Jewish. The Arabs of Palestine, the Arab states and the Arab League rejected partition as illegal, immoral and impractical. The passage of the resolution was thus the signal for the outbreak of a vicious civil war between the two communities in Palestine, a war which was to end in a Jewish triumph and an Arab tragedy.

Britain refused to assume responsibility for implementing the UN partition resolution. It set a firm date for the end of the Mandate – 14 May 1948. As the Mandate approached its inglorious end, both sides felt let down by the British, accusing them of duplicity and betrayal. The manner in which the Mandate ended was the worst blot on Britain's entire record as the mandatory power. Britain left Palestine without an orderly transfer of power to a legitimate government. In this respect, the end of the Palestine Mandate has the dubious distinction of being unique in the annals of the British Empire.

The consequences of the Balfour Declaration were not confined to Palestine. The Declaration engendered anger towards Britain throughout the Arab world and at all levels of Arab society from the intellectual elites to the masses. Together with the Sykes–Picot agreement, Balfour's Declaration became a central point of reference for Arab intellectuals after the First World War. In *The Question of*

*Palestine*, for example, Edward Said dwells at great length on the unspoken assumptions behind the Declaration. For him it is a prime example of the moral epistemology of imperialism. The Declaration, he writes, was made:

> (a) by a European power, (b) about a non-European territory, (c) in flat disregard of both the presence and the wishes of the native majority resident in the territory, and (d) it took the form of a promise about this same territory to another foreign group, so that this foreign group might, quite literally, *make* this territory a national home for the Jewish people.[45]

At the other end of the spectrum there were popular demonstrations against the Balfour Declaration in the inter-war period by people whose grasp of its meaning was tenuous at best. One amusing example was a demonstration organised in al-Karak by Sulayman Al-Nabulsi, a schoolteacher who was later to become prime minister of Jordan:

> On the anniversary of the Balfour Declaration, he led his class into the streets, with the cry: *'Falyasqut wa'd Balfour!'*, which, figuratively translated, means: 'Down with the Balfour Declaration!'. The crowd in the streets was ignorant of its meaning, so started yelling: *'Falyasqut Karkur!'* ('Down with Karkur!'). Karkur was a local Armenian shoemaker and he ran out into the crowd, crying, 'Balfour, oh people, Balfour'. Others yelled *'Falyasqut wahid balkun!'* ('Down with a balcony!') and *'Falyasqut wahid min fawq!'* ('Down with one from the top!').[46]

In Britain itself, opinions about the Balfour Declaration remained sharply divided long after the end of the Palestine Mandate. Richard Crossman argued passionately that Balfour, Lloyd George and Milner all felt under an obligation, in the moment of Allied victory, to do something for oppressed world Jewry. Strategic calculations, Crossman believed, were at most secondary factors.[47] The opposite interpretation was advanced with equal passion and partisanship by

Arnold Toynbee. Toynbee believed that Balfour and his colleagues understood the consequences for the Arabs of fostering the equivalent of a white settler community but went ahead all the same for the sake of sustaining British influence in the eastern Mediterranean.[48] 'I will say straight out', Toynbee told an interviewer in 1973, 'Balfour was a wicked man'. He was wicked because he used the League of Nations Mandate to rob the Arabs of their right to self-determination. 'The Arabs had no political experience', Toynbee stated, 'and they were thrown into the most subtle and intricate political situation you can imagine. They were clearly unprepared for it. This is part of the monstrosity of the whole affair.'[49]

Britain's failure in Palestine can be at least partly attributed to the Balfour Declaration, for that was the original sin. In Arabic there is a saying that something that starts crooked, remains crooked. The Balfour Declaration was not just crooked – it was a contradiction in terms. The national home it promised to the Jews was never clearly defined and there was no precedent for it in international law. On the other hand, to refer to 90 per cent of the population as 'the non-Jewish communities in Palestine' was arrogant, dismissive and even racist. It was also the worst kind of imperial double standard, implying that there was one law for the Jews, and one law for everybody else.

With such a singularly inauspicious and murky beginning, British rule in Palestine was predestined to fail, as in a Greek tragedy. It was not just a policy failure, but an egregious moral failure. Britain had no moral right to promise a national home for a tiny Jewish minority in a predominantly Arab country. It did so not for altruistic reasons but for selfish and misguided ones. At no stage in this long saga did the Jews feel they were getting from their great power sponsor the support to which they felt entitled by virtue of the Balfour Declaration, and the end of the Mandate was accompanied by the most bitter recriminations. The Arabs were violently opposed to the Declaration from the start. They held Britain responsible for the loss of their patrimony to the Jewish intruders. By the end of the Mandate, there was no gratitude and no goodwill left towards Britain on either side of the Arab–Jewish divide. I can only agree with Sir John Chancellor that the Balfour Declaration was a colossal blunder – it has proved to be a catastrophe for the Palestinians and it gave rise to one of the most intense, bitter and protracted conflicts of modern times.

TWO

# The Civil War in Palestine

I n no other part of the world do the gales of nationalism blow as
hard as they do in Israel-Palestine. It may seem strange to refer
to the conflict between Israelis and Palestinians as a civil war,
but that is how it started almost a century ago and that is what, in
some respects, it still is today. Whereas inter-state wars are fought by
the regular armies of sovereign states, civil wars involve the whole of
society, civilians as well as soldiers. This is why civil wars tend to be
more complex, more bitter, more protracted and more intractable
than conventional wars between states. That is why they lend
themselves so easily, if that is the right word, to literary treatment.
And that is why they are so painful to watch, whether in Spain in the
1930s or in Israel-Palestine today.

In origin and in essence, the Arab–Israeli conflict is a clash between
two national movements: the Palestinian national movement and
the Jewish national movement, or Zionism. There were two peoples,
two distinct ethnic communities, and one land; hence the conflict.
Great Britain became the ruler and arbiter in this conflict when it
received the Mandate over Palestine from the League of Nations
after the First World War. From the beginning, nationalism lay at
the heart of the conflict, and the persistence of nationalist sentiment

on both sides has militated against reconciliation between the two communities. Each carried on its back the heavy baggage of history, ideology and distorted images of the other. 'A nation', said the French philosopher Ernest Renan, 'is a group of people united by a mistaken view about the past and a hatred of their neighbours.' The Jews and the Arabs are no exception. It is interesting to note how often the phrase 'to forge a nation' is used, because most nations are forgeries.

The narratives that the two communities have developed about their origins and causes are radically different. The Zionist narrative revolved around the right of the Jews to build an independent state for themselves on their ancestral land in Palestine, and to live there in peace and harmony with their neighbours. According to this narrative, Arab rejection of the right of the Jews to independent existence in Palestine is the principal cause of the conflict. In other words, the conflict is not about territory, but about the very right of the Jews to constitute themselves as a sovereign entity in the Land of Israel. The dominant Arab narrative, on the other hand, portrayed the Zionist movement not as an authentic national liberation movement of the Jews but as an outpost of Western colonialism, an inherently aggressive and expansionist movement bent on driving the native population out of its land. According to this view, Palestine is the patrimony of the Palestinians; and the dispossession and dispersal of the native population by the State of Israel is the real cause of the conflict.

Inevitably, as with all nationalist versions of history, both of these conflicting narratives are rather distorted, selective and self-justifying. The difference is that the Zionists have been much more effective than their opponents in putting across their side of the story. To make up for the military weakness of their movement, the early Zionists deployed traditional Jewish skills in advocacy and persuasion to the best possible effect. As a result, Zionism was one of the greatest public relations success stories of the twentieth century. And Palestinian nationalism was one of the greatest failures. The Palestinians had a strong case but poor advocates, notwithstanding some heroic exceptions such as Edward Said and Hanan Ashrawi.

The Zionists had a more problematic case but brilliant spokesmen like Chaim Weizmann and Abba Eban.

The Zionist leaders were firm about their goal – Jewish independence in Palestine – but shrewd and nimble in the tactics they employed in pursuit of it: at every juncture they accepted what was on offer and then came back for more. When a proposal was made that was not to their liking, they usually refrained from saying so loudly and waited for the Grand Mufti, Haj Amin al-Husseini, to let them off the hook. The Mufti was wrong-footed at every turn. Whichever way one looks at the Palestinian struggle for independence during the British Mandate, it is the story of how the Mufti muffed it.

The British government responded to the outbreak of the Arab Revolt of 1936 by appointing a Royal Commission, with Lord Peel as chairman, to investigate the causes of the disturbances and to recommend a solution. In its final report of July 1937, the Commission proposed a very small Jewish state of some 5,000 square kilometres, a large Arab state, and an enclave from Jerusalem to Jaffa under a permanent British Mandate. The reactions of the two communities to the Peel partition plan were in line with their basic strategies: rejectionist in the Arab case, gradualist in the Jewish. The Arab Higher Committee, headed by the Grand Mufti, promptly and vehemently rejected the Peel Commission's recommendations, insisting on full independence for Palestine and a ban on any further Jewish immigration and land purchases. It was a high-risk strategy of all or nothing that left no room for a compromise solution.

The Jewish response was more measured. At the twentieth Zionist Congress in Zurich the gradualists won the day and a decision was taken to support partition and the creation of a Jewish state in part of Palestine. Chaim Weizmann argued passionately for partition precisely because it involved the creation of a Jewish state. 'The Jews would be fools not to accept it,' he said, 'even if it is the size of a tablecloth.' Clearly, the small size of the proposed state did not dim his optimism. 'The Kingdom of David was smaller', he pointed out. 'Under Solomon it became an Empire. Who knows? *C'est le premier pas qui compte!*' David Ben-Gurion, much as he disliked the proposed borders, urged acceptance of the plan: 'Erect a Jewish state at once, even if it is not in the whole land. The rest will come in the course of time. It must come.'

A decade later, on 29 November 1947, the United Nations voted for the partition of Palestine into two states, one Arab and one Jewish. The resolution was greeted with jubilation and rejoicing on the Jewish side, rage and impotent defiance on the Arab side. Despite their reservations on the borders of the partition plan, the Zionist leaders, in keeping with their gradualist strategy, accepted it. It provided an invaluable charter of international legitimacy for the creation of an independent Jewish state. The Arab Higher Committee roundly denounced the UN partition resolution as 'absurd, impracticable, and unjust' and threatened to resist its implementation by force. It insisted on full sovereignty over the whole of Palestine and refused to accept a Jewish state of any shape or size in any part of it. By voting for partition the UN thus provided, unintentionally, the signal for a civil war in Palestine.

The first Arab–Israeli war is usually treated as one war. Israelis call it the War of Independence whereas Arabs call it al-Nakba or the catastrophe. In fact, it was two wars rolled into one. The war had two distinct phases, each of which had a different character and, on the Arab side, different participants. The first phase lasted from 29 November 1947, when the UN passed the partition resolution, until 14 May 1948, when the British Mandate expired and the State of Israel was proclaimed. The second phase lasted from the invasion of Palestine by the Arab states on 15 May 1948 until the termination of hostilities on 7 January 1949. The first and unofficial phase of the war was between the Jewish and Arab communities in Palestine, ending in triumph for the Jews and tragedy for the Palestinians. The second and official phase of the war involved the regular armies of the neighbouring Arab states and it ended in an Israeli victory and a comprehensive Arab defeat. Most of the literature on the first Arab–Israeli war relates to the official or inter-state phase of the war that began with the invasion of Palestine by the armies of seven Arab states upon expiry of the British Mandate. In many respects, however, the unofficial phase of the war was more important, and more fateful in its consequences. The first phase was, essentially, a civil war between the local communities. It was during this phase that the irregular Palestinian military forces were defeated, Palestinian society was pulverised, and the largest wave of refugees was set in motion. It was only after the collapse of Palestinian resistance that the neighbouring Arab states committed their own regular forces to the battle.

The defeat of the Arab armies by the newly born State of Israel sealed the fate of Arab Palestine. As a result of the war, Israel acquired considerably more territory and more contiguity than had been given to it by the UN cartographers. The name Palestine was wiped off the map. Over 700,000 Palestinians became refugees. Of all the Arab countries that participated in the invasion, Transjordan alone managed to save something from the dismal wreckage of Arab Palestine. Transjordan held on to the West Bank and in 1950 incorporated it into what became the Hashemite Kingdom of Jordan. The Palestinians were left out in the cold.

In the aftermath of the 1948 war the Arab–Israeli conflict persisted on two levels: the inter-state level and the Israeli–Palestinian level. Relations between Israel and the neighbouring Arab states were visible, volatile and violent, taking the form of a protracted border war and erupting periodically into full-scale wars. The Palestinian problem was much less prominent as an issue in world politics but it did not disappear, much as Israel wanted it to. What happened was that the international community, led by the UN, began to treat the Palestine problem not as a political problem requiring a political solution but as a refugee problem calling for repatriation, compensation and humanitarian assistance.

In the 1960s the Palestinians became more active in the struggle against Israel and renewed their demand to be recognised as a distinct nation with its own national 'entity'. In 1964 an Arab League summit decided to recognise a Palestinian 'entity' and to establish the Palestine Liberation Organisation. The PLO was committed to the liberation of the whole of Palestine by means of armed struggle. It thus gave the appearance of an independent Palestinian initiative to regain control over the destiny of the Palestinian people. In reality, however, the PLO was the creature of the Arab League and it continued to depend on individual Arab states for money, arms, training and, above all, bases from which to launch attacks against Israel. These attacks contributed to the tension and turmoil that plunged the Middle East into another full-scale war in June 1967.

The June 1967 war was a major watershed in the history of the Arab–Israeli conflict. It unleashed another wave of Palestinian refugees, some of whom became refugees for the second time. But at the same time it gave a powerful boost to the PLO in the struggle against Israeli occupation. By the end of the war, Israel had captured the Sinai peninsula from Egypt, the Golan Heights from Syria, and the West Bank from Jordan. The Arab states from now on had a direct stake in the conflict with Israel. They wanted to recover their land and they adopted the slogan that 'what was taken by force can only be regained by force'. The war thus intensified the conflict between Israel and its neighbours both on the inter-state front and on the Palestinian front.

For Israel itself the spectacular military victory in the Six-Day War had far-reaching consequences. Whereas the military outcome was clear-cut, the political consequences were much more complex. Before the war the essential goal of the Zionist movement had been achieved – there was an independent and viable Jewish state in Palestine. The war reopened the whole question of the territorial aspirations of the movement. On this question Israeli society was divided down the middle, and not necessarily along party lines. One half wanted to trade the occupied territories for peace with the neighbouring Arab states in line with UN resolution 242 of 22 November 1967. The other half, consisting of secular as well as religious nationalists, wanted to absorb the occupied territories into Greater Israel. For them, the West Bank in particular was not occupied territory but liberated territory. It was usually referred to by its biblical name – Judea and Samaria – and was treated as an integral part of the historic homeland that ought not to be subject to bargaining and compromise with foreign powers.

In the internal debate, the territorial maximalists gained the upper hand, and their victory was translated into an energetic policy of building Jewish settlements in the occupied territories. At first the government sponsored settlements only in areas that it intended to keep permanently, so as to preserve the option of a territorial compromise. But the religious nationalists, spearheaded by Gush Emunim, the Bloc of the Faithful, established settlements in cities with a religious resonance, such as Hebron, in defiance of the government. The rise to power of the right-wing Likud in 1977 changed the scope and the character of the settlement drive. Likud and Labour differed on foreign policy as markedly as they did on domestic policy. The Labour Party's attitude towards the West Bank was determined largely by security considerations, whereas the Likud's approach was determined largely by ideological factors. Likud built settlements not only in strategically important areas but across the entire length and breadth of the West Bank in order to foreclose the option of territorial compromise.

Regardless of which party was in power, Israel's behaviour in the matter of settlements after the June 1967 war suffered from a basic contradiction. Building settlements was a legacy of the pre-independence period when the borders of Palestine had not been settled. Accordingly, the Zionist movement pursued an energetic policy of purchasing land and establishing settlements in order to strengthen its claim to the land. This policy was called 'creating facts on the ground'. Its purpose was to stake a claim to the land and to pre-empt future negotiations. But in 1948 Israel became a sovereign state and the following year it signed armistice agreements with all its Arab neighbours – Egypt, Transjordan, Syria and Lebanon. These were the only internationally recognised borders that Israel ever enjoyed. Building settlements beyond these borders was an anomaly for a sovereign state and a flagrant violation of international law and, more specifically, of the Geneva Conventions.

Building Jewish settlements on Arab land inevitably exacerbated and further embittered the conflict, shifting the focus once again from the inter-state level to the inter-communal level. It meant the expropriation of Arab land and, more generally, the imposition of military rule over the civilian population, with all that that entailed. What had been a conflict between the Israel Defence Force (IDF) and the Palestinian guerrilla organisations increasingly involved civilians on both sides. The IDF was transformed from a first-rate regular army into an army of occupation or, to put it more strongly, into an instrument of colonial repression. Having gained independence from British colonial power in 1948, Israel became a latter-day colonial power itself. Holding on to the territories had at least as much to do with land-grabbing as with security. Moreover, the Israeli concept of security was completely one-sided. The IDF's duty was to protect the Jewish settlers; it had no parallel responsibility to protect the indigenous population. In the months and years after the 1967 war, Israel used to boast about the enlightened policies it claimed to be pursuing in the West Bank and Gaza. But an enlightened occupation is a contradiction in terms, like a quadrilateral triangle. By becoming an occupying power, Israel lost the moral high ground. As more and more settlers occupied more and more land, the Palestinians stepped up their resistance, and the IDF stepped up its repression.

Israelis look down on the Gaza Strip as a hotbed of political extremism and religious fanaticism. What Israelis tend to overlook is the part that they themselves have played in reducing the Gaza Strip to this sorry state. Only 146 square miles in size, Gaza is one of the most heavily populated areas on earth. It is home to a large number of refugees from the 1948 and the 1967 wars. Conditions in the refugee camps are an affront to civilised values. Yet side by side with this indescribable destitution and misery there existed affluent Jewish colonies, surrounded by barbed wire and heavily protected by the IDF. In 2005, there were 1.4 million Palestinians living in Gaza, and less than 8,000 Israelis. Yet the Israelis controlled 25 per cent of the territory and 40 per cent of the arable land. Not surprisingly, the Gaza Strip became a breeding ground for extremism, fanaticism and suicide bombers.

The first intifada or uprising erupted in Gaza on 9 December 1987, and from there it spread to the West Bank. Within days the occupied territories were engulfed in a wave of popular street demonstrations and commercial strikes on an unprecedented scale. Equally unprecedented was the extent of mass participation in these disturbances: tens of thousands of ordinary civilians, including women and children. Demonstrators burned tyres, threw stones and Molotov cocktails at Israeli cars, brandished iron bars, and waved the Palestinian flag. The standard of revolt against Israeli rule had been raised. The Israeli security forces used the full panoply of crowd control measures to quell the disturbances: cudgels, night sticks, tear gas, water cannons, rubber bullets and live ammunition. But the disturbances only gathered momentum.

The outbreak of the intifada was completely spontaneous. There was no preparation or planning by the local Palestinian elite or the Tunis-based PLO leadership. The PLO, however, was quick to jump on the bandwagon of popular discontent against Israeli rule and proceeded to play a leading role alongside a newly formed body, the Unified National Command. In origin the intifada was not a nationalist revolt. It had its roots in poverty, in the miserable living conditions of the refugee camps, in hatred of the occupation and, above all, in the humiliation that the Palestinians had had to endure over the previous 20 years. But it developed into a statement of major political import. The ultimate aim was self-determination and the establishment of an independent Palestinian state alongside Israel. In this respect the first intifada may be seen as the Palestinian war of independence.

One feature of the intifada was without precedent in Palestinian history: this was the first example of popular action, covering all social strata and groups. The whole population rebelled, which helped to raise the level of political awareness and to forge a common national experience. In a remarkable demonstration of national cohesion, urban as well as rural areas participated in the uprising. As a result of this inclusiveness, the intifada accomplished more in its first few months than had decades of PLO military operations. At least some of Israel's leaders began to concede that military power has its limits, and that there could be no military solution to what is essentially a political problem. An army can beat an army, but an army cannot beat a people.

On the Palestinian side political success promoted political moderation. On the one hand, the intifada raised the morale and boosted the pride and self-confidence of the Palestinian community.

On the other hand, it did not bring an end to Israeli occupation, and living conditions deteriorated rapidly in the course of the struggle. Local leaders realised that a Palestinian peace initiative was essential. They were worried that the intifada would come to an end without yielding any concrete political gains. Consequently, they started putting pressure on the PLO chiefs in Tunis to meet the conditions that would enable them to enter into negotiations with Israel. Over the years the PLO mainstream had moved towards more moderate positions, but it avoided a clear-cut statement of these positions for fear of alienating the militant factions of the organisation. Now the moment of truth had arrived.

Yasser Arafat, the chairman of the PLO, took the lead in moderating its political programme. At the meeting of the Palestine National Council in Algiers in mid-November 1988, Arafat won a majority for the historic decision to recognise Israel's legitimacy, to accept all the relevant UN resolutions going back to 29 November 1947, and to adopt the principle of a two-state solution. The claim to the whole of Palestine, enshrined in the Palestinian National Charter, was finally laid to rest and a declaration of independence was issued for a mini-state in the West Bank and Gaza with East Jerusalem as its capital. This revolution in Palestinian political thinking coincided with the rise to power in Israel of a hardline Likud government headed by Yitzhak Shamir. Just as the Palestinians were moving towards territorial compromise, Israel was moving away from it. Its rejection of the PNC declaration was absolute and unconditional. There was no one to talk to on the Israeli side.

Israel's position on the PLO changed only after the Labour Party returned to power in 1992 under the leadership of Yitzhak Rabin. Rabin was the first Israeli leader to move forward towards the Palestinians on the political front. Nine months of secret negotiations in the Norwegian capital culminated in mutual recognition between the government of Israel and the PLO, and in a Declaration of Principles for Palestinian Self-Government in Gaza and Jericho. The Oslo Accord, as it became known, was signed in the White House on 13 September 1993 and was clinched with the famous handshake between Rabin and Arafat. By signing the Accord, Israel recognised the PLO as the representative of the Palestinian people, the PLO renounced violence, and the two parties undertook to resolve all their outstanding differences by peaceful means. To be sure, the Oslo Accord represented only a modest start in dealing with these differences. All the really difficult issues – the status of Jerusalem, the rights of the 1948 refugees, the borders of the Palestinian entity – were kept on hold for the 'permanent status' negotiations at the end of the transition period of five years. At the Camp David summit in July 2000, all these issues were discussed but no agreement was reached. The summit thus marked the breakdown of the Oslo peace process. Conflicting explanations have been suggested for the failure, with each party trying to pin the blame on the other. In my opinion, the most fundamental cause was Israel's violation of the spirit of Oslo by continuing to expand settlements on the West Bank. There was something deeply dishonest in the Israeli position. Israel's rhetoric was the rhetoric of peace, but its actions revealed its hidden agenda, which was territorial expansion at the expense of the Palestinians.

Under these circumstances, a major explosion was only a matter of time. The explosion occurred on 28 September 2000 when Ariel Sharon, the leader of the opposition, paid a deliberately provocative visit to the Muslim holy places in the Old City of Jerusalem. Muslim worshippers began to riot and to throw stones. The Israeli security forces reacted with overwhelming force, firing rubber bullets and live ammunition and causing a high number of casualties. In the first month alone, the IDF fired 1,300,000 bullets at fewer than 100,000 demonstrators in various locations. The Palestinian police returned some of the fire and the situation quickly got out of hand. The al-Aqsa intifada had begun.

The Palestinians may have been provoked beyond endurance by the brutality of Israeli power. Nevertheless, resorting to firearms was a mistake of historic proportions. The key to the success of the first intifada lay in its non-violent nature. By resorting to violence in 2000, the Palestinian leadership reneged on its principal pledge under the Oslo Accord. Palestinian violence destroyed the Israeli peace camp; it persuaded Israelis from all points along the political spectrum that there is no Palestinian partner for peace; and it paved the way for Ariel Sharon's victory in the elections of 6 February 2001. Sharon had always been a champion of violent solutions and the practitioner of the most savage brutality towards Arab civilians. With him at the helm, Israel's war against the Palestinian people was predictably pursued, with no holds barred.

Both societies paid a heavy price for this latest round of violence, especially the Palestinians. In the first four years of the intifada, according to the facts and figures of the Palestinian NGO Miftah, the total number of Palestinian dead was 3,747, of whom 819 were children and 250 were women. The total number of Israeli dead was 973, of whom 112 were children and 289 were women. 27,484 Palestinians were injured. Israel demolished 7,440 Palestinian homes, uprooted 1,167,913 trees, confiscated 224,415 dunums of land, and razed 72,591 dunums. Do these facts and figures indicate a civil war in Palestine? Whatever the answer, there is no denying the scale of the human tragedy involved. The two societies are clearly caught up in an inferno of mutual carnage and self-destruction.

# THREE

# The Rise and Fall of the All-Palestine Government in Gaza

T he All-Palestine Government established in Gaza in September 1948 was short-lived and ill-starred, but it constituted one of the more interesting and instructive political experiments in the history of the Palestinian national movement. Any proposal for an independent Palestinian state inevitably raises questions about the form of government that such a state would have. In this respect, the All-Palestine Government is not simply a historical curiosity, but a subject of considerable and enduring political relevance in so far as it highlights some of the basic dilemmas of Palestinian nationalism and above all the question of dependence on the Arab states.

In the aftermath of the Second World War, when the struggle for Palestine was approaching its climax, the Palestinians were in a weak and vulnerable position. Their weakness was clearly reflected in their dependence on the Arab states and on the recently founded Arab League. Thus, when the Arab Higher Committee (AHC) was reestablished in 1946 after a nine-year hiatus, it was not by the various Palestinian political parties themselves, as had been the case when it was founded in 1936, but by a decision of the Arab League. Internally divided, with few political assets of its own, the new AHC was unable to pursue an independent policy or to act decisively. Consequently, the Arab League became the principal forum for determining the all-Arab policy on the political disposition of Palestine.

Within the Arab League, however, there was no consensus on the future of Palestine. Most members, at least at the declaratory level, backed an uncompromising policy in the fight against Zionism, and denounced the United Nations partition plan of 29 November 1947 as illegal, impracticable and unjust, as did the AHC. The Arab League was fully behind the Palestinians in opposing partition and, from the time it was founded in March 1945 until Britain confirmed its decision to withdraw from Palestine in the autumn of 1947, there was consistent support for creating a unitary and independent Palestinian state. After that, however, there were conflicting views concerning the positive policy to adopt on the future of Palestine. On the one hand there was Haj Amin al-Husseini, the Mufti of Jerusalem, who pursued a maximalist programme for an independent and sovereign Palestinian state over the whole of Palestine.[1] On the other hand there was King Abdullah of Transjordan, whose undeclared aim was to partition Palestine with the Zionists and to annex the Arab part to his kingdom.[2]

After Britain's September 1947 announcement of its intention to withdraw from Palestine, the AHC appealed to the Arab League for support in setting up a Palestinian government to fill the power vacuum that was going to be created.[3] But most members of the League were reluctant to extend active support to a government that would be headed by the Mufti, or to entrust him with the leadership of the Arab war effort in Palestine. At the meetings of the Arab League Council in Aley, Lebanon, in October 1947 and in Cairo that December, the Mufti pleaded passionately for the establishment of a shadow government under the aegis of the AHC. His pleas fell on deaf ears, however, as did his warnings against deploying in Palestine the armies of the neighbouring Arab states. In February 1948, the League not only rejected the Mufti's demand for the establishment of a Palestinian government-in-exile and for the appointment of

Palestinian military governors for the country, but declined even to extend a loan to the AHC to cover its administrative expenses. During March, April and the first half of May, the AHC kept up the pressure for the establishment of a government to manage the affairs of the country, but the Arab League persisted in its negative stance. The Mufti and his colleagues were progressively marginalised during this unofficial but critical phase of the struggle for Palestine. By 15 May 1948, when the State of Israel was proclaimed, only one solitary member of the AHC, Ahmad Hilmi Abdul Baqi, remained in Palestine.[4]

Thus, when the regular Arab armies marched into Palestine the following day and the official phase of the war began, the Arabs of Palestine – in sharp contrast to the Israelis – did not have a responsible government, an administrative regime, or a unified military command. The Palestinian community was decimated and pulverised in the course of the fighting, and successive waves of refugees were expelled or left the country. By the time the first truce was declared on 11 June, the Israel Defence Force was in control of areas beyond what had been assigned to the Jewish state under the partition plan; the Egyptian army held onto the coastal strip to roughly 14 miles north of Gaza; the Iraqi forces held the mountainous region constituting the northern part of central Palestine; and King Abdullah's forces were in control of the central part of Palestine including East Jerusalem, the Hebron hills and Lydda and Ramle in the coastal plain. When Count Bernadotte, the UN mediator, recommended in his initial proposals on 27 June that the Arab parts of Palestine be attached to Transjordan, King Abdullah's opponents within the Arab League decided to act.

On 8 July 1948, the Political Committee of the Arab League met in Cairo and reached a decision to set up a temporary civil administration in Palestine that would be directly responsible to the League. This decision, which marked a partial reversal of the League's previous policy of rejecting any solution that would give a prominent place to the Mufti, was based on a compromise that failed to satisfy either of the two principal claimants. Out of deference to King Abdullah, the decision spoke not of a Palestinian government but of a temporary administration with jurisdiction only in civic affairs. Nevertheless the king, with British encouragement, remained implacably hostile to the whole idea. The AHC, on the other hand, had serious reservations about the proposed body both because it would be dependent on the Arab League and because of the threat it was expected to pose to its own position.[5] With strong opposition from King Abdullah, and only half-hearted support from the AHC, the new body never got off the ground.

King Abdullah's increasingly overt use of the Arab Legion to make himself master of Arab Palestine and his claim that the Transjordanian delegates rather than the AHC represented the Palestinians inside the Arab League antagonised the other member states, especially Egypt, Syria and Saudi Arabia. Britain's support of Abdullah's claims further fuelled the Arab League's anti-Abdullah forces. Led by Egypt, these Arab states began to manoeuvre for the creation of an Arab government for Palestine. The proposal for turning the 'temporary civil administration' that had been agreed upon in July into an Arab government for all Palestine was placed at the top of the agenda of the Arab League's Political Committee meeting, which opened in Alexandria on 6 September and lasted for ten days. Jamal al-Husseini, the Mufti's cousin and a prominent member of the AHC, visited several Arab capitals, including Amman, to mobilise support for this proposal. After a series of meetings, the Political Committee, despite the doubts expressed by the Transjordanian delegates, reached an agreement on the establishment of an Arab government for Palestine with a seat in Gaza. A formal announcement of this decision was issued on 20 September. To forestall Transjordanian objections that the decision implied Arab acceptance of partition and of the State of Israel, the new body was called the Government of All-Palestine, or the All-Palestine Government (APG).[6]

The motives for this major Arab League decision were diverse and contradictory, and in more than one way they were antagonistic to Transjordan. The desire to placate Arab public opinion, critical of governments for failing to protect the Palestinians, was one consideration. Another was the determination to safeguard the Arab claim to sovereignty over the whole of Palestine by providing an alternative to international recognition of Israel and by preventing any Arab government from recognising the Jewish state. But at the same time, the decision to form an Arab government of Palestine and the attempt to create armed forces under its control furnished the Arab League members with the means for divesting themselves of direct responsibility for the prosecution of the war and of withdrawing their armies from Palestine with some protection against popular outcry.[7] Whatever the long-term future of the proposed Arab government in Palestine, its immediate purpose, as perceived by its Egyptian sponsors, was to provide a focal point of opposition to Abdullah and to serve as an instrument for frustrating his ambition to federate the Arab regions of Palestine with Transjordan.

Britain had been lending discreet support to King Abdullah's plan for a Greater Transjordan because this held out the best hopes of safeguarding its own strategic interests following the termination of the Mandate over Palestine. Hostility to the Mufti and to the idea of a Palestinian state under his leadership was a constant and important feature of British policy in 1948, and it goes a long way to explain Britain's attitude towards the Egyptian-led initiative. In British eyes a Palestinian state was equated with a Mufti state, and the rationale against a Mufti state was that it would be 'a hotbed of ineffectual Arab fanaticism' that would very likely be taken over by the Jewish state.[8] The Foreign Office therefore exerted heavy pressure in Arab capitals to prevent the proclamation of the All-Palestine Government, arguing that such a move would be ill-timed and likely to serve the interests of the Mufti. Azzam Pasha, the Secretary General of the Arab League, downplayed the significance of the Mufti issue and told a senior British diplomat that if the Palestine problem could be solved within six months, he would join those who wanted to 'cut the Mufti's throat', but since it would not be solved for at least ten years, the Mufti could still be useful. Azzam added that the Mufti would remain in Egypt and would be able to exercise influence over Palestine only indirectly, from Cairo.[9]

Although Britain's concern about the role of the Mufti was widely shared in Arab political circles, he and the AHC in fact played a major part in the formation of the new government. The government was headed by Ahmad Hilmi Abdul Baqi, who had recently left the AHC by accepting King Abdullah's offer to become military governor of Jerusalem, but was now being lured away from the king by the Mufti and the Egyptians.[10] Hilmi's Cabinet consisted largely of followers of the Mufti but also included representatives of the other factions of the Palestinian ruling class and a number of prominent Palestinians who had previously supported Abdullah. Jamal al-Husseini became foreign minister, Rajai al-Husseini (the former head of the Arab Office in Jerusalem) became defence minister, and Michael Abcarius (a senior civil servant in the British Administration) finance minister, while Anwar Nusseibeh (a former judge) became secretary of the Cabinet. There were 12 ministers in all, most of whom had also been members of the 'temporary civil administration' of the previous July. They were living in various Arab countries and now headed for Gaza to take up their new positions.

On 22 September a communiqué about the formation of the All-Palestine Government was issued in the name of the AHC. Whereas the Arab League announcement had spoken modestly of the decision to turn the Palestinian civil administration into a Palestinian government, the AHC resoundingly stated that 'the inhabitants of Palestine, by virtue of their natural right to self-determination and in accordance with the resolutions of the Arab League, have decided to declare Palestine in its entirety . . . as an independent state under a government known as the All-Palestine Government which is based on democratic principles.'[11] In addition to this official communiqué, an appeal was broadcast to the Arabs of Palestine calling on them to rally around their national government and help with the liberation of their homeland.[12] Word was sent out to the supporters of the Mufti to assemble in Gaza, while Egyptian troops were sent to Bethlehem to distribute small arms to anti-Hashemite elements. Most Palestinians, and especially the refugees, received the news with great joy. For the first time in their lives they had heard of a Palestine government, and it sparked in them a ray of hope amidst all the gloom and doom of the previous year. When the Mufti – who had been living in Cairo, the most recent stop in his 11-year exile – defied the Egyptian authorities and turned up in Gaza, he was welcomed by local inhabitants in a display of great excitement and jubilation.

The sporadic displays of popular support did not blind the Mufti and his colleagues to the need to endow the new government with real legitimacy and substance. During the first week of its life in Gaza, the All-Palestine Government revived the Holy War Army (*Jaish al-Jihad al-Muqaddas*), the Mufti's irregular forces, which had played a major part during the unofficial phase of the Palestine war, and began to mobilise with the declared aim of liberating Palestine. On the diplomatic front, the new government sought international recognition, even designating a delegation to represent it at the United Nations, although the world body had not acknowledged it. Finally, any member of the Palestinian people was declared eligible for a Palestinian passport, and within a short period some 14,000 of these documents were issued, mostly to notables and businessmen from the Gaza Strip.

Given the Arab League's increasingly ambiguous stand and King Abdullah's repeated claims that the APG had been set up against the will of the Palestinian people, the new government decided to convene a constituent assembly aimed at securing a more broadly based and legitimate source of authority, and at refuting Abdullah's claims. Accordingly, invitations were sent to Palestinian representatives from all parts of the country, including the members of the AHC, the mayors and heads of local councils in Palestine, heads of chambers of commerce and trade unions, Palestinian members of the National Committees, leaders of political parties, and military commanders.[13] The Palestinian National Council convened under the chairmanship of the Mufti in a semi-derelict school building in Gaza on 30 September 1948. Only half of the 150 delegates who had been invited made it to Gaza, partly because of the restrictions on travel imposed by the Transjordanian and Iraqi armies which were in control of central Palestine. Nevertheless, a mood of elation and euphoria permeated the deliberations of the Council. First, Haj Amin al-Husseini was unanimously elected as President of the Council. Second, the

Council passed a vote of confidence in the government headed by Ahmad Hilmi and endorsed its plans for the liberation of Palestine. Then a long series of resolutions was passed, including the adoption of a provisional constitution, the original flag of the Arab Revolt of 1916, and Jerusalem as the capital. Finally, a declaration of independence was signed by the delegates and issued to the press. It asserted the right of the Palestinian people to a free, sovereign and democratic state with its borders defined as 'Syria and Lebanon in the north, Syria and Transjordan in the east, the Mediterranean in the west, and Egypt in the south'.[14]

However, the contrast between the pretensions of the All-Palestine Government and its capability quickly reduced it to the level of farce. It claimed jurisdiction over the whole of Palestine, yet it had no administration, no civil service, no money and no real army of its own. Even in the small enclave around the town of Gaza its writ ran only by the grace of the Egyptian authorities. Taking advantage of the new government's dependence on them for funds and protection, the Egyptian paymasters manipulated it to undermine Abdullah's claim to represent the Palestinians in the Arab League and in international forums. Ostensibly the embryo for an independent Palestinian state, the new government was thus, from the moment of its inception, reduced to the unhappy role of a shuttlecock in the ongoing power struggle between Cairo and Amman.

From Amman, King Abdullah pursued his campaign against the All-Palestine Government with renewed vigour. At the time of its proclamation, he had not only refused to recognise it, but had sent angry telegrams of protest to Ahmad Hilmi and Azzam Pasha. Abdullah soon served notice that the All-Palestine Government would not be allowed to operate in any of the areas occupied by the Arab Legion. To Mahmud Nuqrashi, the Egyptian prime minister, he said quite bluntly that he had no intention of allowing a weak Palestinian government to take charge of the Arab part of Palestine when it had no army to protect it from Jewish attacks.[15] While waging this open campaign, King Abdullah also took practical steps to formalise Transjordan's authority over the areas it held to the west of the Jordan river and to organise his own Palestinian supporters in opposition to the government in Gaza.[16]

Thus, on 30 September 1948, the very same day that the Mufti's Palestinian National Council issued its declaration of independence in Gaza, the rival 'First Palestinian Congress' convened in Amman, its several thousand participants swearing allegiance to the Hashemite monarch. The Amman Congress denounced the formation of the Gaza government as being contrary to the wishes and interests of the Arabs, declared that Transjordan and Palestine constituted a single territorial unit, and resolved that no Arab government should be set up for Palestine until the entire country had been liberated.[17]

Popular support for the high-sounding but largely illusory All-Palestine Government had never developed into a groundswell; after the two rival Congresses were held it began to dwindle. Many of the Arab towns and villages in Palestine sent delegations to Amman to pledge their loyalty to the king and to give him power of attorney to solve the Palestine problem as he saw fit. In some cases these delegations were the result of local political initiative; in others it was the Transjordanian military governors who helped to collect the signatures and despatch the delegations to Amman.[18] The Transjordanian regime also used bribery to induce some supporters of the Mufti's government to transfer their loyalty to King Abdullah. Outside Palestine, the Gaza government was largely unsuccessful in its efforts to gain international recognition as the representative of the Palestinian people. London, of course, had no intention of recognising 'this so-called government', and most other members of the United Nations followed the British example in ignoring it.

Meanwhile, within the Arab camp intense negotiations were taking place concerning what stance to adopt on the All-Palestine Government. On the one hand, the Arab leaders almost without exception were prepared to sacrifice Arab interests in Palestine for purely local ends. The Arab reluctance fully to back the new body was increased by the continuing and general aversion to the Mufti; indeed, the prominence of his role in directing events in the APG had given them second thoughts concerning the entire process leading up to the All-Palestine Government, which they themselves had unleashed to check King Abdullah's annexation of Arab Palestine. As events progressed, they were anxious not to escalate the conflict with Abdullah and risk the breakup of the Arab League. Azzam Pasha had even tried, unsuccessfully, to stop the proclamation of the government.[19]

On the other hand, the Arab regimes had to consider domestic public opinion, which across the Arab world cared passionately about Palestine and was adamant in its opposition to partition. At the same time, opposition to Abdullah ran high, and preventing the expansion of his kingdom was almost on a par with opposition to partition, as one of the few goals behind which nearly all the Arab states could rally. Abdullah's loyalty to Britain was increasingly equated with disloyalty to the Arab cause. The knowledge that he had been in contact with Jewish leaders added to suspicions that he had from the outset been prepared to compromise the Arab claim to the whole of Palestine in order to acquire part of it for himself. Abdullah's position in the Arab world was not helped by the mismanagement that characterised his handling of the Palestinian population that came under his control. A few months earlier, Abdullah had been a hero for heeding Palestinian calls for help and going to the rescue; now, he had sunk almost to the level of pariah among his brother Arabs. A more pragmatic reason for the other Arab regimes' opposition to Abdullah was his usefulness as a scapegoat for the failure of their own Palestine policy. Thus, the need to protect their Arab nationalist credentials combined with their antipathy to Abdullah ultimately took precedence over their misgivings regarding the Mufti. Once the APG was declared, the Arab states began, however half-heartedly, to rally behind it. Predictably enough, Egypt, which after all had sponsored the new government, was its chief backer. Riad al-Sulh, the Lebanese prime minister who was savagely critical of King Abdullah, also played a leading role in pressing the Arab League's Political Committee to give its blessing to the All-Palestine Government.[20]

Much of the diplomatic activity concerning the All-Palestine Government centred on Iraq, whose position was particularly crucial, since it held the northern half of central Palestine (the West Bank).

Iraqi cooperation with the Egypt-sponsored body would have made Transjordan's position very difficult. King Abdullah therefore called his nephew Abd al-Illah, the Regent in Baghdad, to ensure that this did not happen, but was not given a clear reply.[21] Less than a week later Jamal al-Husseini – soliciting Iraqi support for the All-Palestine Government on a visit to Baghdad, and in an effort to circumvent opposition deriving from the Mufti's prominence in the project – suggested that the Mufti might be got rid of later, and went so far as to suggest that if Palestine were saved for the Arabs the throne could be offered to King Abdullah.[22]

Despite the dynastic considerations that generally allied Iraq with Abdullah to form the Hashemite bloc within the Arab League, and despite a deep aversion to the Mufti stemming from his involvement in the anti-Hashemite Rashid Ali coup in 1941, Iraq had good reason to support the APG. The Palestine problem was the litmus test of its commitment to pan-Arabism, and the Regent had worked hard to establish his Arab nationalist credentials by taking a strong stance against partition and by sending troops to Palestine. Siding with Abdullah, whose prestige among the masses in Iraq and elsewhere in the Arab world was at a low ebb, could compromise the measure of domestic credibility the regime had thus acquired. For various reasons, then, the Regent of Iraq joined in the general campaign of vilification against his uncle. His criticisms were heartily reciprocated, and the relationship between them became so sour that they could no longer have a sensible discussion about Palestine.[23]

But Iraq, mindful of the risks Abdullah was running vis-à-vis his own public opinion, continued to exert efforts to bring Abdullah into line with the common Arab stance. The Iraqi prime minister, Muzahem al-Pachachi, advised Abdullah to go slowly,[24] and with the tacit support of the Regent did his utmost to induce the king to recognise 'temporarily' the All-Palestine Government. Unable to declare open antagonism towards the Mufti, al-Pachachi used the argument that the new government would fail and Arab Palestine would ultimately be bound to go to Transjordan. The king countered that recognition would merely implement the partition of Palestine before it was known what the United Nations was going to decide.[25]

Meanwhile, the British Foreign Office pointed out to the Iraqi prime minister and the Regent the dangers of going along with Egypt in encouraging the Mufti to extend his influence in Palestine. To the Regent in particular, it was emphasised that any growth of the Mufti's influence would necessarily be dangerous to the Hashemite house. The Regent was told, in what amounted to a rebuke, that he could not sit back and allow attacks on the position of King Abdullah without danger to himself. Whatever the Regent's own views on the matter, the British view was that a strong and enlarged Transjordan was in the interest of the maintenance of stability in Iraq, and of the position of the Regent and the royal family.[26]

Arab resistance both to Transjordan's enlargement and to appearing to endorse partition was so overwhelming that the British argument – that a weak Palestinian government would facilitate Jewish expansion over the whole country – made no impression. A major stumbling block in the way of Britain's policy, following Bernadotte's suggestion of assigning the West Bank and the Negev to Abdullah, was thus Arab opposition to a plan that would reduce Arab Palestine to nothing. Paradoxically, as one British official observed, 'although the primary Arab objection to the Bernadotte plan is that its acceptance would involve partition, there are clear signs that, in their hearts, all but the most rabid fanatics, like Haj Amin, realise that the existence of the State of Israel will have to be accepted sooner or later'. What the Arabs could never agree upon was the partition of what was left of Palestine.[27]

While the Arab states were prevaricating over whether or not to recognise the APG and to what extent they should support it, events on the ground conspired to make all these debates meaningless.[28] First came the dismantling of the Mufti's Holy War Army by Glubb Pasha, the fiercely anti-Palestinian British commander of Transjordan's Arab Legion. The Mufti's forces had been carrying out attacks on UN observers[29] and Israeli troops which seemed designed to embroil the Arab Legion in the fighting, and which gave the impression of attempting to create disturbances in the areas occupied by Transjordan, especially in and around Jerusalem. Glubb and King Abdullah feared that these activities would endanger their own control in Arab Palestine and decided to nip in the bud the growth of the Mufti's army.[30]

Towards the end of September, then, Glubb instructed colonel Abdullah al-Tall to disband the Holy War Army and seize its arms, but al-Tall balked. His reasons, enumerated in his memoirs, are probably fairly representative of Arab sentiments at the time and hence worth mentioning here: the Jerusalem area was in a state of war with the Jews, and the Arabs needed every man who could bear arms to defend the Holy City; the Holy War Army consisted of Palestinians who had defended their country before the entry of the Arab armies, and thus should not be demobilised and disarmed when the Arab states had failed to save their country; and there was need for cooperation among all the armed forces in Palestine against the common enemy.[31]

Given al-Tall's refusal and the likelihood that other Arab officers would be similarly unwilling to carry out so unpatriotic a task, when on 3 October 1948 Glubb received a written order from Transjordan's defence minister laying down that all armed bodies operating in the areas controlled by the Arab Legion were either to come under its orders or be disbanded,[32] he turned to British officers. The order was carried out promptly and ruthlessly. The various units of the Holy War Army were surrounded and forcibly disarmed. The operation brought the Arabs to the brink of internecine war when they were supposed to be cooperating against the common enemy. But it effectively neutralised the military power of Abdullah's Palestinian rivals and checked the growth of public sentiment in favour of an autonomous Palestine state.

Shortly thereafter, on 15 October, Israel broke the second truce by launching a fierce offensive against the Egyptian army in the south, splitting it in three and forcing it to retreat along the coast down to Gaza. Such was the hostility between Transjordan and Egypt that the Arab Legion remained neutral when hostilities were renewed. Glubb Pasha privately expressed the hope that the Jewish offensive 'may finally knock out the Gaza government and give the gyppies [*sic*] a lesson!' In a letter to the British commander of his First Brigade, he explained that 'if the Jews are going to have a private war with the Egyptians and the Gaza government, we do not want to get involved. The gyppies and the Gaza government are almost as hostile to us as the Jews!'[33]

Ironically, it was at about this time, mid-October, that the Arab states finally got around to recognising the All-Palestine Government, with Egypt being the first to grant formal recognition, Iraq coming next, and Syria, Lebanon and Saudi Arabia following suit three days later. Nothing is more indicative of their half-hearted support than the fact that by the time they gave formal recognition the game was over and the government was but an empty shell.

It was Israel's victory in the war with Egypt that in essence marked the end of the Gaza government. Destroying the embryo of a Palestinian state had not been the primary aim of the operation, but it was the effect. This was a classic example of the politics of unintended results. Until this war had broken out, the Palestinians were divided, some looking to King Abdullah for protection and others looking to the Mufti for a lead. Although the Arab Legion controlled the West Bank, some Palestinians still pledged their loyalty to their traditional leader. As a result of the Egyptian defeat, however, the Mufti's government lost its last and exceedingly tenuous physical toehold on Palestinian soil, its weakness was exposed for all to see, its prestige slumped and its authority was undermined.

Indeed, by the end of October no members of the All-Palestine Government remained in Gaza. The Mufti himself, who had greatly annoyed Egypt's King Farouk when he went to Gaza on 27 September without royal permission after having entered the country as a political refugee,[34] had been ordered back to Cairo by Mahmud Nuqrashi, the Egyptian prime minister, on 6 October. When he refused, an officer was despatched to bring him back by force. In Cairo the Mufti was kept under a strict police supervision that fell just short of house arrest; his freedom of action was so curtailed that he was not even allowed to visit the Palestinian refugee camps in Gaza.[35] Ahmad Hilmi and the members of his Cabinet had remained in Gaza beyond the Mufti's forced departure, but following the renewal of hostilities in mid-October the Egyptians insisted that they move to Cairo as well, on the pretext that the Gaza Strip was a military zone in which there was no room for a government to operate. Once in Cairo, the ministers held a number of talks with the Mufti but were unable to carry out their duties, especially in the political realm. In fact, as Anwar Nusseibeh later recalled, there was very little for them to do and their stay in the Egyptian capital was both boring and frustrating.[36] The secretariat of the Arab League also cold-shouldered them, thereby accentuating their sense of isolation and helplessness. Symptomatic of this attitude on the part of the original sponsors of the All-Palestine Government was the refusal to extend to it any financial assistance or even to pass on contributions from Arab and Islamic countries, leaving the government-in-exile without funds to pay salaries or defray its administrative expenses.[37]

Even without these humiliations, after its departure from Palestine the All-Palestine Government ceased to be a political force. Palestinian opinion shifted perceptibly in favour of merging the Arab parts of Palestine with Transjordan. Among the more educated Palestinians, dislike and mistrust of King Abdullah persisted. But the political trimmers in Palestine concluded that the prospects of an independent Arab state were receding, while union with Transjordan appeared more probable and perhaps more profitable.[38]

Indeed, the situation was such that the Palestinian ministers, led by Ahmad Hilmi and Jamal al-Husseini, were led to seek a rapprochement with their greatest opponent, King Abdullah. Jamal al-Husseini made the extraordinary statement that 'the Palestinian government is willing to transfer its territory to Transjordan if Abdullah will cooperate with the other Arab states in ridding Palestine of the Zionists'.[39] With the approval of their colleagues, the foreign minister accompanied the prime minister on a visit to Amman to talk with the king, but no progress was made in reaching an understanding. The following weeks witnessed the resignation of some of the ministers; others simply ceased to take part in its meetings.[40] Hilmi, a banker by profession, devoted more time to his business affairs than to the Shadow Cabinet of which he remained the nominal head. Other members of his Cabinet gradually drifted to various Arab capitals; some going to Amman in response to royal gestures of pardon or to take up lucrative positions, openly switching their allegiance to King Abdullah.[41]

The high-sounding Government of All-Palestine thus slowly fell apart under the weight of its own impotence, ending up four years later as a 'department' of the Arab League. Formally it retained its shadowy existence, but politically it went into steep decline and even its petitions and publications began to appear under the name of the Arab Higher Committee. The All-Palestine Government continued to exist in name only, issuing the occasional statement from its headquarters in Cairo, until President Nasser finally closed its offices in 1959. Power to represent the Palestinians had long passed to the Arab states and their leaders.[42]

With the All-Palestine Government reduced to powerlessness, King Abdullah was in a much stronger position to proceed with his plan to annex what was left of Arab Palestine. The second Palestinian Congress, held in Jericho on 1 December 1948, was an important landmark on the road to annexation. Attended by some 3,000 delegates, including the mayors of Hebron, Bethlehem and Ramallah, military governors of all the districts controlled by the Arab Legion, and former supporters of the Mufti, the Congress purported to reflect the will of the people, but the initiative and direction had clearly come from the king. The assembled notables duly proclaimed the union of Palestine and Transjordan and acknowledged Abdullah as king of the united country.[43]

In retrospect, the experience of the Government of All-Palestine appears interesting and instructive, but it was in the final analysis a cul-de-sac of political evolution that led the Palestinians nowhere. The government's fall was no less swift than its rise had been. The government's origins go a long way towards explaining its ultimate failure. For although it was projected as the nucleus of Palestinian self-government, it was a phantom deliberately created by the Arab states, with Egypt at their head, in order to meet their publics' opposition to partition and to challenge Transjordan's claim to the residue of Arab Palestine. It was for their own selfish reasons that the Arab states created the All-Palestine Government and it was for their own selfish reasons that they abandoned it. True, in the first three weeks of its short life this fledgling government did represent a genuine attempt by the Palestinians to assert their independence from their dubious sponsors and to assume firm control of their own destiny. But time had run out on it. Born of inter-Arab rivalries, it rapidly and inexorably foundered on the rocks of inter-Arab rivalries. For the Palestinian cause, the Arab states, individually and collectively, turned out to be a broken reed. Consequently, if there is one lesson that stands out from this calamitous phase of Palestinian history, it is the need for self-reliance and, above all, for defending the Palestinian cause against control and manipulation by the Arab states.

FOUR

# *Did They Leave or Were They Pushed?*

O f all Zionist slogans, the most persuasive has always been Israel Zangwill's 'a land without a people for a people without a land'. Had this slogan been true, there would have been no conflict; the Jews could have peacefully realised their dream of statehood in their Biblical homeland. Unhappily, an Arab community had lived on the land for centuries and its refusal to share it with the Jewish immigrants from Europe spawned the conflict which reached its climax in 1948 with the creation of the State of Israel and the uprooting and dispersal of some 730,000 Palestinians.

The causes of the Palestinian exodus of 1948 have been hotly debated ever since. Arab spokesmen have consistently claimed that it was the result of a premeditated, pre-planned and ruthlessly executed Zionist policy of expulsion. Palestinian writers in particular have stressed the link between Zionist theory and Zionist practice, seeing the exodus of the indigenous population as the inevitable accompaniment of the drive to establish a Jewish state in Palestine. Israeli spokesmen have maintained with equal consistency that the Palestinians were not pushed out but left of their own accord, in response to orders from their own leaders or Arab broadcasts and in the expectation of a triumphal return. This explanation absolved

Israel of any responsibility for the creation of the Palestinian refugee problem, and underpinned its refusal to allow the refugees the right of return or even to offer compensation for the property they left behind.

More recently, a group of revisionist Israeli historians, using official documents released under the 30-year rule, have challenged the standard Zionist version of the 1948 war in general and the origins of the Palestinian refugee problem in particular. The first and most comprehensive attack on the official version came in 1988 with Simha Flapan's *The Birth of Israel: Myths and Realities.* That same year saw the publication of Benny Morris's *The Birth of the Palestinian Refugee Problem, 1947–1949.* Morris describes the flight of the Palestinians wave after wave, town by town, and village by village. He gives numerous specific examples of psychological warfare, of intimidation, of expulsion by force and of atrocities committed by the armed forces of the infant Jewish state. But he found no evidence of a Jewish master plan or of a systematic policy dictated from above for the expulsion of the Palestinians. He therefore rejects both the Jewish robber state and the Arab order explanations. His much-quoted conclusion is that 'the Palestinian refugee problem was born of war, not by design, Jewish or Arab'.

Some reviewers felt that the evidence presented by Benny Morris supports a somewhat different conclusion. While accepting that various causes contributed to the flight of the Palestinians, they think that the evidence points most directly to Jewish military pressure as by far the most important precipitant. One critic of Morris's conclusion is Nur Masalha, an Israeli Arab and a graduate of the Hebrew University of Jerusalem. The subject of Masalha's book,* more accurately conveyed by its subtitle than its title, is the concept of 'transfer' in the Zionist movement until the birth of the State of Israel. 'Transfer' is a euphemism for the expulsion or organised removal of the indigenous population of Palestine to the neighbouring Arab countries. In today's world, the closest equivalent to 'transfer' is the ethnic cleansing practised by the Serbs

* Nur Masalha, *Expulsion of the Palestinians: The Concept of 'Transfer' in Zionist Political Thought, 1882–1948* (London: I.B. Tauris, 1994).

in the former Yugoslavia. There are also of course extreme right-wing Israeli political parties, like Moledet, that openly advocate the mass expulsion of Palestinians.

The history of Zionism, from the earliest days to the present, is full of manifestations of deep hostility and contempt towards the indigenous population. On the other hand, there have always been brave and outspoken critics of these attitudes. Foremost among them was Ahad Ha'am (Asher Zvi Ginsberg), a liberal Russian Jewish thinker who visited Palestine in 1891 and subsequently published a series of articles that were sharply critical of the aggressive behaviour and political ethnocentrism of the Zionist settlers. They believed, wrote Ahad Ha'am, that 'the only language that the Arabs understand is that of force'. And they 'behave towards the Arabs with hostility and cruelty, trespass unjustly upon their boundaries, beat them shamefully without reason and even brag about it, and nobody stands to check this contemptible and dangerous tendency'. Little seems to have changed since Ahad Ha'am wrote these words a century ago.

That most Zionist leaders wanted the largest possible Jewish state in Palestine with as few Arabs inside it as possible is hardly open to question. As early as 1919, at the Paris Peace Conference, Chaim Weizmann called for a Palestine 'as Jewish as England is English'. And Chaim Weizmann was one of the moderates. What Masalha sets out to do is to explore the link between the goal of Jewish statehood and the advocacy of transfer by the leaders of the Zionist movement. His aim is to demonstrate that Zionist thought was translated into action and culminated in the mass expulsion of the Palestinians in 1948. In short, he seeks to prove that the Palestinians did not leave Palestine of their own free will, but were pushed out.

Masalha's study is based on extensive research in Israeli state, party and private archives, supplemented by material from British and Arab sources. He makes very full use of the diaries and memoirs of prominent as well as obscure Zionist leaders from Theodor Herzl onwards. The notion of transfer, says Masalha, was born almost at the same time as political Zionism itself, with Herzl's hope to 'spirit the penniless population across the border'. Zangwill's slogan about 'a land without a people' was useful for propaganda purposes, but from the outset the leaders of the Zionist movement realised that they could not achieve their aim without inducing, by one means or another, a large number of Arabs to leave Palestine. In their public utterances the Zionist leaders avoided as far as possible any mention of transfer, but in private discussions they could be brutally frank. So it is from private rather than public sources that Masalha draws the bulk of his incriminating evidence. He goes to some length to demonstrate that support for transfer was not confined to the extremists or maximalists but was embraced by almost every shade of Zionist opinion, from the Revisionist Right to the Labour Left. Transfer, he argues, occupied a central position in the strategic thinking of the Jewish Agency as a solution to what was coyly referred to as the 'Arab question'. Virtually every member of the Zionist pantheon advocated it in one form or another.

In 1930, against the background of disturbances in Palestine, Weizmann tentatively advanced the idea of an Arab transfer in private discussions with British officials, but met with no support for this idea. It was not until November 1936, when the British government sent the Peel Commission in to investigate the causes of unrest in Palestine, that Weizmann and his colleagues began to lobby actively, but still discreetly, for a 'voluntary' transfer of displaced Arab farmers to Transjordan. The commission's report was the first official endorsement of the principle of partition and the creation of a Jewish state. In this respect, it was a turning point in the search for a solution to the conflict between the Arab and Jewish communities in Palestine. Weizmann and his colleagues welcomed the idea of partition but were deeply concerned about the prospect of a large Arab minority remaining inside the borders of the proposed Jewish state. From now on, Masalha observes, partition and transfer became closely linked in Zionist thinking.

David Ben-Gurion, the chairman of the Jewish Agency, was one of the earliest converts to the idea of transfer as the best way of dealing with the problem of an Arab minority. Masalha argues convincingly that around the time of the Peel Commission inquiry, a shift occurred in Ben-Gurion's thinking, from the notion of a

voluntary to that of a forcible transfer. While the ethics of transfer
had never troubled Ben-Gurion unduly, the growing strength of the
Jewish Agency eventually convinced him of its feasibility. On 12
July 1937, for instance, he confided to his diary: 'The compulsory
transfer of the Arabs from the valleys of the proposed Jewish state
could give us something which we never had . . . a Galilee free from
Arab population . . . We must uproot from our hearts the assumption
that the thing is not possible. It can be done.' The more he thought
about it, the more convinced he became that 'the thing' not only
could be done, but had to be done. On 5 October 1937 he wrote to
his son with startling candour: 'We must expel Arabs and take their
places . . . and, if we have to use force – not to dispossess the Arabs
of the Negev and Transjordan, but to guarantee our own right to
settle in those places – then we have force at our disposal.' The letter
reveals not only the extent to which partition became associated in
Ben-Gurion's mind with the expulsion of the Arabs from the Jewish
state, but also the nature and extent of his territorial expansionism.
The letter implied that the area allocated for the Jewish state by the
Peel Commission would later be expanded to include the Negev
and Transjordan. Like Vladimir Jabotinsky, the founder and leader
of Revisionist Zionism, Ben-Gurion was a territorial maximalist.
Unlike Jabotinsky, he believed that the territorial aims of Zionism
could best be advanced by means of a gradualist strategy.

When the UN voted in favour of the partition of Palestine on
29 November 1947, Ben-Gurion and his colleagues in the Jewish
Agency accepted the plan despite deep misgivings at the prospect of
a substantial Arab minority, a fifth column as they saw it, in their
midst. The Palestinians, on the other hand, rejected partition, some
vehemently and violently. By resorting to force to frustrate the UN
plan, they presented Ben-Gurion with an opportunity, which he was
not slow to exploit, to extend the borders of the proposed Jewish
state and to reduce the number of Arabs inside it. By 7 November
1949, when the guns finally fell silent, 730,000 people had become
refugees.

For Masalha this mass exodus was not an accidental byproduct of
the war but the inevitable accompaniment of the birth of Israel: 'the

result of painstaking planning and an unswerving vision . . . stated and restated with almost tedious repetitiveness for almost fifty years'. Chaim Weizmann, who became Israel's first president, hailed the Arab evacuation as 'a miraculous clearing of the land: the miraculous simplification of Israel's task'. For Masalha it was less of a miracle than it was the result of over half a century of sustained effort and brute force. The main strength of his book derives from the new material he has unearthed about Zionist attitudes to transfer during the pre-1948 period. But he spoils a good case by overstating it. In the first place, he focuses very narrowly on one aspect of Zionist thinking and neglects the broader political context in which this thinking crystallised. Secondly, he portrays the Zionist movement as monolithic and single-minded in its support for transfer, ignoring the reservations, the doubts, the internal debates and the opposition. Thirdly, he presents transfer as the cornerstone of Zionist strategy, when it was in fact only one of the alternatives under consideration at various junctures in the conflict over Palestine. Fourthly, while sharply critical of the Zionist design and of the means by which it was achieved, he completely ignores the part played by the Palestinians themselves in the disaster that eventually overwhelmed them, or the part played by their leader, Haj Amin al-Husseini, who had about as much political sense as the Good Soldier Schweik.

The end result of Masalha's selective use and tendentious interpretation of the evidence is an account which posits a straightforward Zionist policy of transfer and lays all the blame for the flight of the Palestinians in 1948 at the door of the wicked Zionists. If Benny Morris does not go as far in his critique of the Zionists as his evidence would seem to warrant, Nur Masalha goes way beyond what his evidence can sustain. If Morris carries his multi-phase and multi-cause explanation to the point of obscuring the primary responsibility of the Zionists for the displacement and dispossession of the Palestinians, Masalha ends up with a monocausal explanation which absolves everybody other than the Zionists.

For a broader, more balanced and more searching analysis of the causes of the Jewish triumph and the Arab defeat in the struggle for Palestine one must turn to Ilan Pappé. Pappé is an Israeli academic from the University of Haifa who joined the ranks of the revisionists in 1988 with a highly original study of *Britain and the Arab–Israeli Conflict, 1948–51*. His second book, *The Making of the Arab Israeli Conflict 1947–1951*, was the product of five further years of research and reflection.* Based on deep knowledge of the primary and secondary sources in English, Arabic and Hebrew, it provides a powerful synthesis of the revisionist literature on the causes and consequences of the first Arab–Israeli war. Pappé sets out to investigate the way the two communities, the Jews and the Arabs of Palestine, prepared themselves for the trial of strength which was bound to occur sooner or later in the absence of a peaceful settlement. He is much more interested in the politics of the 1948 war than in its military aspects. Indeed, he believes that the outcome of the war had been determined by the politicians on both sides before the first shot was fired. Jewish success in building the infrastructure of a state and then in winning the diplomatic campaign, Pappé argues, decided the outcome of the war before the actual confrontation took place. The inadequacy of the Palestinian leadership and division within the ranks of the Arab League are presented as further reasons for the Arab defeat.

Pappé examines every claim and counterclaim against the available evidence, and discards all those which fail to stand up to his critical scrutiny. On the question of whether the expulsion of the Palestinians was pre-planned, for example, he is much closer in his views to the Palestinian historian Walid Khalidi than he is to his compatriot and co-revisionist Benny Morris. Morris regards Plan D, the Haganah plan of early March 1948, as a military plan for coping with the anticipated Arab invasion. Pappé agrees with Khalidi that Plan D was also, in many ways, a master plan for the expulsion of as many Palestinians as could be expelled. In the final analysis, he argues, if you have a plan to throw someone out of his house, and the person leaves before you carry out your plan, that does not in any way alter your original intention. For all the trouble he took to cover his traces, David Ben-Gurion emerges from Pappé's book, as

---

* Ilan Pappé, *The Making of the Arab Israeli Conflict 1947–1951* (London: I.B. Tauris, 1992).

he does from the books by Morris and Masalha, as the great expeller of the Palestinians in 1948.

The failure of the parties to reach a settlement at the end of the war ensured the perpetuation of the Arab–Israeli conflict. Traditional Israeli historians explain this failure exclusively in terms of Arab intransigence; Pappé explains it essentially in terms of Israeli intransigence. He shows that at the conference convened at Lausanne in April 1949 by the Palestine Conciliation Commission, the Arabs were prepared to negotiate on the basis of the UN partition resolution which they had rejected 18 months earlier. Israel, however, insisted that a peace settlement should be based on the status quo without any redrawing of the borders or readmission of the Palestinian refugees. It was therefore Israeli rather than Arab inflexibility which stood in the way of a peaceful settlement.

Morris's aim was to describe how, and try to explain why, so many Palestinians became refugees in 1948. Masalha set out to prove that the expulsion of the Palestinians was implicit in Zionist thinking from the very beginning. Pappé's aim is neither to provide a narrative of events nor to buttress one national version against another, but to explore the dynamics of the conflict. In so doing, he has added significantly to our understanding of a formative period in the Arab–Israeli conflict.

# FIVE

# *Husni Zaim and the Plan to Resettle Palestinian Refugees in Syria*

T he chief of staff of the Syrian army, Colonel Husni Zaim, overthrew the civilian government headed by President Shukri al-Quwatli in a bloodless coup on 30 March 1949. On 14 August 1949, Zaim himself was deposed and then executed by some of the disgruntled officers who had helped him to plan and carry out his own coup. Although he remained in power only four and a half months, Zaim radically changed the pattern of Syrian politics. In the aftermath of the Arab defeat at the hands of Israel in 1948, there was mounting popular discontent with the old order, which was held responsible for the defeat and its bitter consequences. But it was Zaim who carried out the first coup and thereby set the regional trend for military intervention in politics. In the context of the Arab–Israeli conflict, the Zaim episode is intriguing and instructive, though it did not make such a lasting mark abroad. One of Zaim's top priorities on coming to power was to make peace with Israel, and as part of an overall settlement he even offered to resettle in Syria 300,000 of the total of 700,000 Palestinian refugees created by the war.

In his early career, Husni Zaim did not distinguish himself as a natural populist leader, social reformer, peacemaker, or champion of the Palestinian refugees. His critics saw him as a mercurial and mentally unstable individual, a military adventurer without any ideals, an opportunist who sought power for its own sake and for the material benefits it could bring him. There were a number of episodes in Zaim's career prior to 1949 which lend credence to this unflattering view of him, notably his embezzlement of a large sum of money given to him by the Vichy Administration in 1941 to organise guerrilla operations against the Free French and the British forces. For this offence he served a two-year prison sentence, and was exiled to Lebanon. On his return to Syria in 1946, he was appointed inspector general of the police and, in May 1948, chief of the general staff of the army. Nobody doubted Zaim's courage, and his war record was impressive, but after the war he became implicated once more in a corruption scandal. According to one theory he staged his coup not to save the country from the politicians but to save his own skin.[1] Whether true or not, Zaim does not stand out as a shining example of integrity or altruism, nor was he above exploiting public positions to line his own pockets.

Yet, despite all Zaim's defects of character and shortcomings, he does appear to have been motivated by a genuine desire to sweep away the old order and lay the foundations for a more just, egalitarian, enlightened and above all a more prosperous society. Modelling himself on Mustafa Kemal Atatürk, the father of modern Turkey, Zaim aspired to separate religion and state and to introduce far-reaching social and political reforms. During his brief tenure he introduced one reform – the enfranchisement of women – which represented a clear departure from Islamic tradition. To pave the way for agrarian reform, he abolished the private administration of family *waqfs* (religious endowments).[2] The offer to settle 300,000 Palestinian refugees in Syria, if enough outside economic assistance could be provided, must be viewed in the context of this general drive to develop and modernise the country. It was the desire for foreign capital to generate nationwide economic development, rather than a purely humanitarian concern to alleviate the suffering of the refugees, that constituted his primary consideration. Of all the Arab states, Syria had, potentially, the greatest absorptive capacity.

The Jazirah region in northern Syria, with its sparse population and fertile land, provided ideal conditions for large-scale resettlement. Zaim reasoned that apart from helping to solve the refugee problem, an externally financed project on this scale would also carry manifold advantages for Syria, such as building infrastructure, extending the land area under cultivation, modernising agricultural production and raising the living standards of the inhabitants of the Jazirah. It may well be, as his first foreign minister, 'Adil Arslan, later hinted, that some of the money Zaim hoped to obtain from the Americans was intended for his private pocket.[3] But this kind of corruption did not make Zaim unique among politicians in the Middle East or elsewhere. His policy towards the Palestinian refugees is best summed up as one of enlightened self-interest.

Zaim's ascent to power gave rise to extravagant hopes among Syrians, some Arab rulers, and among the great powers. At home he was supported not just by the army but by the opposition parties, important social groups and the mass of the people. Jordan and Iraq welcomed the revolution, but, suspecting them of expansionist designs, Zaim quickly abandoned his pro-Hashemite orientation in favour of a close alliance with Egypt and Saudi Arabia. All the Western powers, for different reasons, looked with favour on the new regime in Damascus. The French saw in it an opportunity to consolidate their influence in the Arab East and spared no effort in persuading other countries to recognise the new regime. One of Zaim's first acts as prime minister was to sign a currency agreement which ushered in a new era of improved understanding and close economic cooperation between Syria and France. The British, who were widely but mistakenly thought to be the secret backers behind Zaim's bid for power, believed the new regime might be instrumental in restoring the regional equilibrium that had been shattered by the termination of the Mandate over Palestine. The prospect of a military dictatorship did not trouble the British unduly. On the contrary, their contempt for Syrian politicians was such that they were disposed to regard any form of government as an improvement, especially if it could instil the sense of discipline necessary for economic and social progress.[4] Viewing the refugee problem as a source of political instability, the British were anxious to move from the stage of relief to the stage of permanent resettlement. Consequently, the Foreign Office was greatly attracted to the Jazirah scheme as a way of combining economic development with a political solution to the refugee problem.[5]

It was from America, however, that Zaim received his most enthusiastic and most consistent support. The precise nature and extent of this support is far from clear, while the reasons behind it are rather complex. Some of Zaim's domestic opponents denounced him as an American stooge and the spearhead of American economic penetration into the Arab East. Shortly before the coup, in February 1949, the Syrian government concluded an agreement with the American oil company ARAMCO, granting the latter the concession to construct a large-gauge pipeline linking its oil fields in Saudi Arabia to the port of Sidon in Lebanon; but the agreement still required parliamentary ratification. According to Khalid al-'Azm, who signed the agreement in his capacity as prime minister, the Americans concluded that ratification was unlikely in the face of strong parliamentary opposition and decided to pre-empt defeat by encouraging Zaim to seize the initiative. The facts speak for themselves, argued al-'Azm: shortly after Zaim seized power he ratified the agreement.[6] It was left to Miles Copeland to reveal that the CIA had in fact engineered the coup for Zaim, though he makes no mention of the Tapline agreement.[7] Zaim certainly conformed to the ideal, popular in the Truman Administration, of a patriotic and reforming military officer who represented the wave of the future in the Middle East, and the best answer to the kind of semi-feudal rulers who had traditionally served the interests of the British Empire in the region.

But whether or not he was 'the Americans' boy' from the start, Zaim rapidly gained the confidence and support of the Truman Administration by offering to accept a quarter of a million refugees for resettlement in Syria, and by promising to work for a speedy settlement of the dispute with Israel. This offer neatly dovetailed with the Administration's thinking on the need to secure a permanent solution to the Palestinian refugee problem, with American financial and technical aid to create employment opportunities, build transport facilities, improve the local economy, increase agricultural productivity and develop new industry. George McGhee, then coordinator for Palestinian refugees, recalls that he and his colleagues in the State Department were elated when Zaim's offer was reported to them, and that they tried to pin him down. In retrospect, McGhee considered the offer as one of the three best opportunities for solving the refugee problem, and he often thought how drastically the course of Middle East history would have been changed if one of these possibilities had materialised. Responsibility for missing this particular opportunity is attributed by McGhee to Israel: 'Zaim had great difficulties in working out a ceasefire with Israel and felt he could not make concessions on refugees without a quid pro quo from Israel. These were not forthcoming and time ran out on him.'[8]

What the Americans did not know is that in the course of his highly chequered career, Colonel Zaim had also had some contacts with Israeli secret agents. The existence of these contacts remains a closely guarded secret and there is no reference to them in any of the recently declassified official Israeli documents. But from fragmentary pieces of evidence, and more particularly from interviews with former Israeli officials, the following picture emerges. Tuvia Arazi, an intelligence agent with a rich record of operations in Syria and Lebanon, made the contact with Zaim. Arazi was working under the supervision of Elias Sasson, the Syrian-born head of the Middle East Department in the Israeli Foreign Ministry, who set up a base in Paris in August 1948 to initiate and orchestrate contacts with numerous Arab politicians and groups. Towards the end of 1948, Zaim came up with a plan for which he requested a million dollars to topple the Syrian government, put an end to the war, and bring about a change in Syria's policy towards Israel. Arazi and Sasson thought the risk worth taking, but their superiors were more sceptical. Whether any payment was made to Zaim in the end cannot be established with any certainty; but if payment was made, it would probably have been well below his initial asking price. Ezra Danin, a senior intelligence officer in the Haganah, told the author that they used to refer to Zaim jokingly as 'Tuvia's employee', and that he himself assumed that Zaim was on Tuvia Arazi's payroll until his rise to power. Yehoshua Palmon, another member of the intelligence community, considered it not unlikely that Arazi would have sent Zaim 'financial aid' from Europe, but he did not know what kind of a budget Arazi had at his disposal or whether he was in a position to extend more than token assistance.[9] So it appears virtually certain that Zaim did have some clandestine exchanges with secret agents of the Israeli government and it is probable, but not certain, that he received some modest payment towards the coup he proposed to carry out.

Once in power, Zaim acknowledged no commitment to Israel, nor did the Israelis have any commitment towards him. Any evidence of their association would have been used to denounce Zaim for treason and collaboration with the Zionist enemy, so he had every reason to put a dark veil over the past and address the problems of the present. Yet he also had some powerful reasons for wanting to make peace with Israel. First, after the defeat of Egypt on the southern front and of Jordan on the eastern front, the full might of the victorious Israeli army could be turned against Syria, and Zaim wanted to neutralise this threat by means of a peace agreement with Israel. Second, he urgently needed to end the war in order to be able to withdraw his army from the front, use it to consolidate his precarious hold over power, and deal with the new threat posed by Jordan and Iraq. Third, Zaim's strong pro-French orientation and his lack of any ideological or practical commitment to pan-Arabism reinforced his desire to resolve his differences with Israel in the interests of both Syria and France. But perhaps the most important incentive for modifying Syria's hostile attitude towards Israel was Zaim's expectation of winning American goodwill and support. Like many Arab politicians, he had an exaggerated notion of Israel's influence in the United States, in the United Nations, and in international banking. He looked to the Israelis to use their influence to persuade the US government and international agencies to finance his project for settling the Palestinian refugees in Syria.[10]

Zaim used the armistice talks, which opened under UN auspices near the Israeli–Syrian border on 5 April, as a channel for communicating his proposals to the Israeli leaders. Major-General Mordechai Makleff and Yehoshua Palmon reported that in an informal conversation, at which the UN men were not present, the Syrian representatives were full of admiration for Zaim. They wanted to skip the armistice talks altogether and proceed directly to the conclusion of a peace agreement, with an exchange of ambassadors, open borders and normal economic relations. They also reported that Zaim had wider regional ambitions; he calculated that Syria and Israel together could field 500,000 soldiers, and that by forming a united front they could dominate the entire Middle East. But since they were offering a separate peace agreement to Israel, they wanted a modification of the border, giving Syria half the Lake of Tiberias.[11] Prime Minister David Ben-Gurion, who also held the defence portfolio, instructed Makleff and Palmon to tell the Syrians bluntly that they must first sign an armistice agreement on the basis of the existing international border, and only then might they discuss peace, adding that Israel would be ready for full cooperation.[12]

To resolve the deadlock, the Syrian representative intimated that a return to the international border might be possible, but only within the framework of a peace agreement. He also conveyed Zaim's offer to meet directly with Ben-Gurion. Ben-Gurion was unwilling to meet Zaim and was at that time actively examining Israel's military options for liquidating the bridgehead established by the Syrian army on the Israeli side of the Jordan river.[13] This negative response was characteristic of Ben-Gurion's general preference for force over diplomacy as a means of resolving disputes between Israel and the Arabs. On this occasion, however, Ben-Gurion came under strong pressure from the UN mediator, Dr Ralph Bunche, and from the US government, to agree to a personal meeting with the Syrian leader to resolve outstanding issues.

The American ambassador in Damascus, James Keeley, reported to the State Department that Zaim repeated his willingness to accept, as part of a comprehensive settlement of the Palestine conflict, 250,000 or more Arab refugees for resettlement provided they were compensated for their losses and Syria was given adequate financial aid to resettle them. He cited the concessions already made to Israel as proof of his sincerity but emphasised that unless Israel also manifested a spirit of compromise, the stalemate would continue.[14] Under strong American pressure, Ben-Gurion agreed to meet Zaim but only if the latter committed himself prior to the meeting to withdraw all his forces from Israeli territory and to return to the international border.[15] This condition, of course, nullified the whole point of the proposed high-level meeting. But laying down his maximum demands and insisting that they be accepted in full as a condition for negotiations was in fact the essence of Ben-Gurion's peculiar bargaining style. Dean Acheson, the American Secretary of State, was dumbfounded. He wondered whether Zaim's offer had been brought to Ben-Gurion's attention and urged him to respond positively.[16]

Major-General William Riley, the UN chairman of the Syrian–Israeli armistice talks, also made representations on behalf of the Syrian ruler in a private conversation with Shabtai Rosen of the Israeli Foreign Ministry. Riley intimated that Zaim wanted to solve the Syrian–Israeli problem by peaceful and honourable means so he could devote himself entirely to the task of reviving and rebuilding Syria. However, he was afraid of a revolution that would restore to power politicians who would criticise all his activities, including the negotiations with Israel. He was, therefore, looking for an honourable way out and asked Riley to find out what the Israeli response might be to the following proposal: within the framework of the Lausanne talks (convened by the UN's Palestine Conciliation Commission), Syria would undertake to settle within its borders 300,000 Arab refugees, and the problem of borders would also find its solution within the same framework. Ben-Gurion's response, as Rosen had anticipated, was entirely negative.[17] His preoccupation with the territorial issue and his insistence that the Syrians sign the armistice agreement on the dotted line were so emphatic that he did not even address the refugee aspect of the problem.

Abba Eban, the Israeli ambassador to Washington, tried to counter this fixation on the territorial question. He wanted to know

why his government was unimpressed by the prospect that Syria
would absorb 300,000 refugees. It seemed to him highly significant
that the proposal was made through Riley and that Washington was
informed of Syria's readiness to accept large-scale resettlement.[18] The
State Department heard from its representative in Damascus that:[19]

> Everyone who has discussed that matter with Zaim is impressed
> by his sincerity and broadminded attitude towards Israel (far cry
> from stubborn intransigence of previous Syrian Government) but
> his ardour is cooling in face of evident Israeli insatiability. While
> Zaim is at least trying to measure up to Kemal Atatürk's stature
> and is susceptible to moderating influence, it is unfortunately
> becoming increasingly evident that Ben-Gurion is no Venizelos.[20]
> Yet unless Israel can be brought to understand that it cannot
> have all of its cake (partition boundaries) and gravy as well (areas
> captured in violation of truce, Jerusalem and resettlement of Arab
> refugees elsewhere) it may find that it won the Palestine war but
> lost the peace.[21]

One of the few Israeli leaders who did understand this was the
moderate foreign minister, Moshe Sharett. Sharett readily agreed to
meet with Zaim himself and planned to cut through the Gordian
knot of the armistice and explore the reality behind his alleged
proposal to settle 300,000 refugees. He attached 'tremendous
importance' to this latter point and was greatly impressed when he
first learnt of it in Geneva.[22] At a meeting of departmental heads
in the Foreign Ministry he singled out the refugee problem as the
principal bone of contention between Israel and the Arabs at the
Lausanne conference. There was one school of thought, said Sharett,
in an indirect reference to the prime minister, which argued that
Israel would not be the loser if matters dragged on inconclusively,
because formal peace with the Arab states was not a vital need
for Israel. The other school of thought, to which Sharett himself
belonged, maintained that Israel ought to accelerate the search for
a solution because it needed to know whether some of the refugees
would be returning before deciding what to do with the Arab villages

in its possession; because the absence of formal peace harmed Israel economically and militarily; and because international loans would probably be conditional on the attainment of peace. Zaim's specific proposal, Sharett observed, showed that he was bolder and more far-sighted than the other Arab leaders, and that he better understood the importance of the revenue which would accrue to the state and the benefit which all parties concerned would derive from the flow of capital. From Israel's point of view, Zaim's suggestion had enormous significance because it meant that he was prepared to absorb three times the number of refugees currently living in Syria and Lebanon. In any case, added Sharett, if there was one country prepared to do that, it would break the united Arab front, and that is why he thought it well worth meeting with Zaim, especially to explore the refugee resettlement idea.[23]

Sharett communicated to Bunche his willingness to meet either Zaim or his foreign minister, 'Adil Arslan, and suggested a two-point agenda consisting of armistice and peace. Zaim, however, considered it imperative that he meet with Ben-Gurion because none of his own subordinates would dare commit the Syrian government, and only a meeting between heads of state would produce results.[24] The Syrian reply stated that they could not meet with Sharett because the armistice conference was the proper place to discuss the first item on his proposed agenda, whereas peace relations could only be discussed together with other Arab states. Sharett angrily charged the Syrians with prevarication and deceit and demanded that Bunche put an end to the farce. When the Syrians suggested the meeting, Sharett sarcastically remarked that perhaps they had in mind subjects such as medieval Arab poetry, Bedouin lore, or maybe Cartesian philosophy or Japanese art.[25]

While the negotiations with Israel remained deadlocked, Zaim achieved his ambition of climbing from the prime ministership to the presidency of the republic, and had his appointment confirmed by a plebiscite held on 25 June. Feeling more firmly in the saddle, Zaim dismissed his nationalistic and fiercely anti-Israel foreign minister, 'Adil Arslan, who was later to claim credit for sabotaging

Zaim's efforts to have direct talks with the Israeli leaders.[26] To replace
Arslan and to form a new government Zaim chose Dr Muhsin
Barazi, with whom he shared not only Kurdish origins but a more
flexible attitude towards Israel and a commitment to social reform
and economic reconstruction. In general, the new government was
designed to give the newly elevated president – who was showing
increasing signs of megalomania – a freer hand and to enable him to
go about implementing the grandiose plans he had promised.

Unfortunately for Zaim, the Lausanne conference, which got
under way when he was at the peak of his power, turned out to be
an exercise in futility. Syria's agreement to embark on peace talks
before a solution to the refugee problem was found did not have
the intended effect of opening the road to progress. Between the
Arab and Israeli delegations there was no real meeting of minds and
no serious negotiations took place. The official Israeli line, as Elias
Sasson privately conceded, was absurd:

> The Jews think they can achieve peace without paying any price,
> maximal or minimal. They want to achieve (a) Arab surrender
> of all the areas occupied today by Israel; (b) Arab agreement to
> absorb all the refugees in the neighbouring countries; (c) Arab
> agreement to border modification in the centre, the south and
> in the Jerusalem area to Israel's exclusive advantage; (d) the
> relinquishment by the Arabs of their assets and property in Israel
> in exchange for compensation which would be evaluated by the
> Jews alone and which would be paid, if at all, over a number
> of years after the attainment of peace; (e) *de facto* and *de jure*
> recognition by the Arabs of the state of Israel and its new frontiers;
> (f) Arab agreement to the immediate establishment of diplomatic
> and economic relations between their countries and Israel, etc.,
> etc. . . .[27]

All the reports and assessments reaching Ben-Gurion confirmed
that Zaim was outspoken in declaring his desire for peace with Israel,
and seriously committed to negotiating a solution to the refugee
problem as a first step in the search for a comprehensive solution

to the Arab–Israeli conflict. Sasson reported that at Lausanne the representatives of the refugees were putting pressure on the representatives of the Arab states to make peace with Israel so that their own problem might be resolved, but that no other country except Syria was willing to take the initiative. Dr Walter Eytan, head of the Israeli delegation to Lausanne, also thought that the first peace agreement was possible with Syria, and that Zaim had the ambition to be the first Arab leader to meet the Israelis face to face. Ben-Gurion himself noted in his diary that the fact that Zaim was prepared to settle for an armistice agreement which entailed a total withdrawal to the border proved that for some reason he wanted good relations with them.[28] Why then not reward Zaim for his courage, reciprocate his concessions with Israeli concessions, and let real peace negotiations get under way? The answer is to be found in Ben-Gurion's belief that the armistice agreements were sufficient for Israel's purposes and that it need not strain itself unduly in the pursuit of peace. If Israel appeared over-eager, the Arabs might demand a price – on the territorial front, on the refugee front, or on both. It was best, therefore, to wait a few years and deflect American and British pressures to promote a solution to the refugee problem.[29] As Ben-Gurion told Kenneth Bilby – an American journalist who opined that Zaim openly declared his desire for peace because he wanted to create a good impression and because he felt strong enough to say anything he chose – 'Although I am prepared to get up in the middle of the night and sign a peace agreement, I am not in a hurry and I am prepared to wait ten years. We are under no pressure to do anything.'[30] Once Ben-Gurion had said that, he had said everything.

Small wonder then that Zaim, who was interested in action rather than in the vacuous protestations of good intentions, was becoming restive, and that the Americans were growing increasingly impatient with Israeli stonewalling. Zaim summoned the American ambassador, James Keeley, on 14 July, to express his anxiety over the refugee problem and to stress that unless the refugees could be speedily resettled, their deteriorating situation and morale would make them increasingly amenable to communist propaganda.

Unlike most Syrians, Zaim lost no time in criticising Israel for its failure to implement the repatriation provisions of the UN resolution of 11 December 1948, but he made an earnest plea for US aid in resettling the refugees, implying that resettlement was the only realistic solution to the problem. Explaining that he could not openly take the initiative because the opposition would attack him for selling out to the Jews and their backers, Zaim pledged his wholehearted cooperation if the US would take the lead. Referring to numerous economic development projects which Syria was anxious to implement, and concerning which detailed studies had already been made, he asked for funds and technical assistance as a means of absorbing refugee labour. To Keeley, Zaim's sincerity was beyond question, if for no other reason than his awareness that the problems spawned by the Palestine conflict stood in the way of realising many of his dreams. Keeley and his colleagues were also of the opinion that it was in the interest of peace in the Middle East to capitalise on Zaim's cooperation by recognising the delicacy of his position and by giving him encouragement, support and technical assistance.[31]

It was largely due to Zaim's flexible and conciliatory attitude in the face of unremitting Israeli intransigence that the armistice agreement between Israel and Syria was eventually signed on 20 July 1949 – the last in the series of agreements between Israel and the neighbouring Arab states. But the hopes that this necessary first step would pave the way for comprehensive peace agreements were soon dashed. The Palestine Conciliation Commission continued its deliberations, but the Israeli contention that the refugee problem was created by the invasion of the Arab states, who should solve it by resettlement, and the Israeli rejection of repatriation as tantamount to committing suicide, left very little scope for compromise.[32]

The Israeli officials in charge of refugee affairs, like Ezra Danin and Yehoshua Palmon, recognised the importance of Zaim's offer and were greatly impressed with the potential of the Jazirah for accommodating a large number of refugees.[33] Danin paid Zaim the compliment of calling him a Zionist, meaning not that he was pro-Israeli but that he aspired to bring to Syria the kind of revolution that the early Zionists had effected in Palestine through the injection of outside capital and the settlement of the land.[34] One of Danin's pet schemes was to persuade ARAMCO to employ Palestinian refugees in building the Tapline with the help of a subsidy from the Israeli government as an alternative to the UNRWA[35] method of providing relief to the camps. The attitude of Danin's superiors was at best indifferent, and the possibility of using Israeli money, even in modest amounts, was firmly ruled out. In the middle of these low-level but apparently promising negotiations which Danin conducted with various parties in London came the news of Zaim's assassination at the hands of his disaffected co-conspirators.[36] Ben-Gurion's reaction on learning of Zaim's overthrow was one of calm indifference.[37] On the other hand, Elias Sasson, who was the most outstanding exponent of the opposite, or Sharettist, school of thought in relation to the Arab world, gave out such a heart-rending scream on hearing the news that a colleague thought that a member of Sasson's own family had died.[38]

Despite rumours and claims to the contrary, Husni Zaim was not overthrown because of his readiness to make peace with Israel. Nor is there any reason to suppose that agreement by Ben-Gurion to meet him, had it been forthcoming, would have done anything to save Zaim from his fate. The principal reason for Zaim's fall was internal: he progressively antagonised all the major groups who had supported his initial rise to power.[39]

In retrospect, it may be tempting to dismiss Zaim as an unstable and unpredictable military dictator, as a corrupt and unprincipled opportunist, and as a megalomaniac whose removal from the scene made very little difference to the prospects of solving the Arab–Israeli problem in general or the refugee problem in particular. I have tried to show that despite Zaim's undeniable defects of character, he was a serious and consistent proponent of social reform and economic development, and regarded peace with Israel and the resettlement of the refugees as essential for the attainment of these greater goals. There is, of course, no way of knowing what might have happened if Zaim had managed to prolong his hold on power. But during his brief tenure he gave Israel every opportunity to bury the hatchet and lay the foundations for peaceful coexistence in the long term. If his overtures were spurned, if his constructive proposals were not put to the test, and if an historic opportunity was frittered away through lack of vision and obsession with minutiae, the fault must be sought not with Zaim but on the Israeli side. And the fault can be traced directly to that whole school of thought, of which Ben-Gurion was the most powerful and short-sighted proponent, which maintained that time was on Israel's side and that Israel could manage perfectly well without peace with the Arab states and without a solution to the Palestinian refugee problem.

# SIX

# All the Difference

T he fortieth anniversary of the establishment of the State of Israel in 1988 was accompanied by the publication of a number of books which critically re-examined various aspects of what Israelis call their War of Independence. The authors of these books – Simha Flapan, Benny Morris, Ilan Pappé and myself – are sometimes collectively referred to as the 'new historians' or the 'Israeli revisionists'. Revisionist historiography challenged the traditional Zionist version of the birth of Israel on a number of points: Britain's policy towards the end of the Mandate; the causes of the Palestinian refugee problem; the Arab–Israeli military balance in 1948; Arab war aims; and the reasons for the political deadlock after the guns fell silent.

Itamar Rabinovich's *The Road Not Taken*\* concerns the last but not least contentious point in this debate: the attempts to resolve the dispute between Israel and its neighbours in the aftermath of the 1948 war, and their eventual failure. Itamar Rabinovich is one of Israel's leading Middle Eastern experts and the Rector of Tel Aviv University. In 1989, when he was the director of the Dayan Centre

\* Itamar Rabinovich, *The Road Not Taken: Early Arab–Israeli Negotiations* (Oxford: Oxford University Press, 1991).

for Middle Eastern and African Studies at Tel Aviv University, he organised a conference on the new sources for and approaches to the study of the 1948 war. The conference turned into a fierce, frequently acrimonious confrontation between the 'old' and the 'new' historians, a confrontation which generated rather more heat than light. Professor Rabinovich himself was one of the most dispassionate, well-informed and open-minded participants in this debate. His book is the product of the same balanced and scholarly approach displayed at the conference. His aim is not to defend any of the actors or to allocate blame but to re-examine Arab–Israeli relations in the light of new archival and other sources.

The book focuses on the three sets of bilateral negotiations that Israel held between 1949 and 1952 with Syria, Jordan and Egypt respectively. The title of the book, like the poem by Robert Frost which inspired it, is rather ambiguous, perhaps deliberately so. Rabinovich declines to identify those who decided not to take the road towards peace. He may be intrigued by Frost's suggestion that the choice when reaching the fork in the road 'makes all the difference', but all he will finally say is that 'the choices of 1948–9 were made by Arabs, Israelis, Americans and others. And credit and responsibility for them belongs to all'.

Although Rabinovich does not openly take sides in the debate between traditionalists and revisionists, he does concede, at least by implication, that during this critical period Israeli leaders had some freedom of choice and that the choices they made affected the subsequent course of Israel's relations with the Arabs. Implicitly, he rejects the notion of *ein breira* – that Israel had no alternative but to stand up and fight – which lies at the core of most traditionalist accounts. Another claim which has always featured in traditionalist accounts, and in Israeli propaganda over the last four decades, is also conspicuous in its absence from Rabinovich's book. This is the claim of Arab intransigence, the claim that the Arabs rejected Israel's very right to exist and that there was no one to talk to on the other side.

Rabinovich's book reveals an astonishing readiness on the part of the Arab rulers to negotiate with the newly born state of Israel, even though some of them insisted on keeping these negotiations secret. Indeed, his book is essentially a record of the Arab–Israeli negotiations that took place in different places and at different levels between the conclusion of the armistice agreements in the first half of 1949 and the Egyptian revolution of July 1952. Of the three sets of bilateral negotiations surveyed in this book, those between Israel and Syria's first military dictator, Colonel Husni Zaim, are the most instructive.

Zaim openly proclaimed his desire to be the first Arab leader to make peace with Israel. He also asked for a face-to-face meeting with David Ben-Gurion, Israel's first prime minister, in order to break the deadlock in the negotiations. Rabinovich finds Israel's response to Zaim's initiatives puzzling and is critical of Ben-Gurion for refusing to meet with him. But he also dwells on Zaim's defects of character, on the questionable legitimacy of his regime, and on the strong opposition to his policy of accommodation with Israel from the nationalist political establishment he had overthrown. Against this background, it seems to Rabinovich that Ben-Gurion didn't miss an opportunity to reach an agreement that would have transformed Arab–Israeli relations.

There can, of course, be no definitive answer to the question of whether Israel missed a historic opportunity to come to an arrangement with Syria. All we can say with certainty is that in the spring of 1949 Zaim offered direct high-level talks and that Ben-Gurion spurned his offer. What might have happened if the meeting had taken place there is no way of telling – history does not disclose its alternatives. The Zaim episode is nonetheless significant. First, as Rabinovich notes in his conclusion, it calls for a revision in the traditional perception of the Syrian–Israeli conflict, which has always been seen as bitter and hopeless. Syria, though committed to pan-Arab nationalism and the Palestinian cause, was willing to be influenced by pragmatic considerations. Second, the episode reveals that Israel was nowhere near as flexible, on either procedure or substance, as the traditionalist historians would have us believe. Various arguments can be advanced to explain Israel's inflexibility, but they only serve to underscore the central point, which is that in the spring of 1949 the leader of an important Arab state wanted to embark on the road to peace but found no one from the other side with whom he could speak.

Greater tactical flexibility but a similar reluctance to pay a significant price emerge from the survey of Israel's negotiations with Jordan. That King Abdullah, the grandfather of King Hussein, dealt with the Jewish Agency was an open secret. These contacts were maintained from the establishment of the emirate of Transjordan in 1921 until Abdullah's assassination in 1951. Rabinovich's chapter focuses on the period from November 1949 to March 1950, when first a comprehensive settlement and then a less ambitious non-aggression pact were on the agenda. He gives a very full account of these negotiations before broaching the question of why they failed.

Rabinovich does not doubt that Abdullah was motivated by a genuine desire for peace, despite widespread opposition to his policy both at home and in the Arab world. On the other hand, as he points out, Abdullah was not interested in piecemeal arrangements on minor issues: what he wanted was a general settlement in which he would regain enough Arab land to counter the criticism that a separate peace with Israel was bound to arouse in the Arab world. Since a concession of this magnitude was unacceptable to Israel, Rabinovich concludes that the negotiations for a comprehensive settlement were doomed from the start.

True to his general rule, Rabinovich seeks to explain the positions of the parties and the objective obstacles on the road to peace rather than to apportion credit and blame. He follows an Israeli Foreign Ministry paper which enumerates the principal actors other than Israel who shaped the negotiating process. Israel's role, he notes, was rarely scrutinised by the Israeli Foreign Ministry. In his account of the forces at work he has sections on the Arab system, Abdullah, Britain and the United States, but he does not have a section on Israel. This omission is highly significant given the historical perspective available to us today. There is a good deal of new material on Israel here but it is left to speak for itself. Rabinovich tells us what Israel's stand was: he does not tell us whether he thinks its stand was justified or not. One is left with the impression that he regards the price demanded by Abdullah as exorbitant and Israel's refusal to pay as only natural, but he does not explicitly say so.

What governed Egypt's position on the Palestine conflict was the quest for regional hegemony. It was to assert this hegemony that King Farouk ordered his army into Palestine, and it was to preserve this hegemony that he began to issue peace feelers in September 1948. Farouk acted in total disregard of Palestinian rights, the ostensible reason for Arab intervention in the conflict. With military defeat staring him in the face, his primary concern was to extricate himself from the conflict and to pre-empt his great rival, King Abdullah, in coming to terms with the Jewish state.

Farouk's price for a *de facto* recognition of Israel was Israeli agreement to Egypt's annexation of southern Palestine. Ben-Gurion rejected the price as too stiff, even when taken as merely the opening bid in a bargaining process. He wanted to establish Israeli control over the entire Negev and since the military balance favoured Israel, he decided to end the war with a clear-cut military victory against Egypt. Israel's victory on the battlefield enabled it to conduct the armistice negotiations with Egypt from a position of strength. The agreement that was reached, however, marked the formal end of the war rather than the beginning of the journey towards peace. The road to peace was not taken, not because Egypt was ideologically opposed to a separate deal with Israel, but because no agreement could be reached on the terms of a deal. Egypt continued to claim the Negev, while Israel wanted a peace settlement based on the territorial status quo, and the gulf between the positions remained unbridgeable.

The picture which emerges from the detailed chronicle of the three sets of bilateral negotiations is one of remarkable pragmatism on the part of all the Arab rulers in the aftermath of the Palestine disaster. After the sobering experience of military defeat at the hands of the infant Jewish state, the rulers of the neighbouring Arab states were prepared to recognise Israel, to negotiate with it directly, and even to make peace. Each of these rulers asked in return for far-reaching territorial concessions which Israel was unable or unwilling to make. While the Arab rulers themselves were pragmatic, at the popular level there was growing hostility towards Israel. And as this book clearly demonstrates, the rulers encountered enormous difficulties in their efforts to mobilise political support for their policy of accommodation with Israel.

On the Israeli side the picture is also complex. Rabinovich analyses Israel's conduct in terms of a spectrum of views, but his focus is always on Ben-Gurion's choices. Many insights into Ben-Gurion's thinking are gleaned from his diary and the documents, but no attempt is made to define his basic position or to relate it directly to the deadlock in the peace talks. Ben-Gurion probably considered that the armistice agreements met Israel's essential needs for recognition, security and stability. He knew that for formal peace agreements Israel would have to pay by yielding territory to its neighbours and by agreeing to the return of a substantial number of Palestinian refugees, and he did not consider this a price worth paying. Whether Ben-Gurion made the right choice when he reached the fork in the road is a matter of opinion. That he had a choice is undeniable.

One gets the impression that Rabinovich believes that Ben-Gurion made the right choice, but he never says so outright. Ben-Gurion is mildly criticised for his tactical rigidity, but there is no suggestion that his policy towards the Arabs was unsound or that he missed any real opportunities for a settlement. In the concluding chapter, Rabinovich quotes just about everybody's verdict on the early Arab–Israeli talks except his own. Nor does he engage directly in the debate between the traditional Zionist historians and the new historians. He notes that the source material that became available in the 1980s enabled the new historians to bring new facts to the surface and thereby to present a fuller, less schematic picture of the early years, but he is also critical of the revisionist school because 'its point of departure is political and moralistic rather than academic; it relied almost exclusively on Israeli and Western rather than Arab sources, thereby presenting an unbalanced picture; and it introduced emotional issues that were not always the most important ones'. Itamar Rabinovich has evidently tried to avoid these pitfalls. He has chosen an extremely important issue for his book, he has made full use of all the available sources, the picture he presents is a balanced one, and no one could possibly accuse him of being emotional. But he is evasive. The Hebrew title of his book is *The Evasive Peace*. And the author might be called the evasive historian.

# SEVEN

# Israel's Dirty War

Benny Morris is one of the most original and prolific contributors to the revisionist Israeli historiography of the Arab–Israeli conflict. From the outset, the new historiography focused mainly on the 1948 Arab–Israeli war and on the 'missed opportunity' for peace in its immediate aftermath. In two earlier works, *The Birth of the Palestinian Refugee Problem, 1947–9* and *1948 and After: Israel and the Palestinians*, Morris drove a coach and horses through the official version, which denied any Israeli responsibility for the Palestinian exodus. *Israel's Border Wars* is an impressive sequel bringing the story up to the 1956 Suez War.* It is an account of what might be termed Israel's dirty war, because the violence was directed largely against civilians, many of whom were refugees from the 1948 conflict.

Almost as soon as the guns fell silent and armistice agreements were concluded between Israel and its neighbours in 1949, voices began to be heard in the Arab world calling for a second round against the newly born Jewish state. Faint echoes of these voices were also heard on the Israeli side of the divide. Some generals,

---

* Benny Morris, *Israel's Border Wars, 1949–1956: Arab Infiltration, Israeli retaliation and the Countdown to the Suez War* (Oxford: Clarendon Press, 1993).

notably Moshe Dayan, were dissatisfied with the outcome of the
first round and they too advocated a second – to crush the Arab
armies and 'rectify' Israel's borders. After he became chief of staff
in December 1953, Dayan actively, deliberately and deviously
pushed for war. For nearly three years he was eager for another go
at the Arabs. The long-awaited second round broke out in October
1956. It was initiated not by the Arabs but by Israel, in collusion
with Britain and France, against Egypt, now the standard bearer of
radical Arab nationalism.

The period 1949–56 may be seen simply as an interval between
the first and second rounds. But it was a critical phase in the history
of the Arab–Israeli conflict, a period of increasing hostility leading to
violence and then to full-scale war which set the pattern for decades
to come. *Israel's Border Wars*, as its subtitle indicates, is a study of Arab
infiltration into Israel across the armistice lines, of Israeli military
retaliation, and of the preamble to the Suez War. As in his previous
books, Morris subjects the official versions of events, Arab as well as
Israeli, to the most exacting historical scrutiny: important elements
of the official versions, especially the Israeli one, do not survive. A
fuller, more nuanced and more convincing picture emerges from
this book than from any previous account of the endless chain of
action and reaction which culminated in the tripartite attack on
Egypt in 1956.

The conventional (Israeli) view is that Palestinian infiltration
into Israel was aided and abetted by the Arab governments,
following the defeat of their regular armies on the battlefield; that
it was a form of undeclared guerrilla warfare designed to weaken
and even destroy the infant Jewish state; that Israel was thus the
innocent victim of Arab provocation and Arab aggression; and
that its military reprisals were legitimately undertaken in self-
defence. The evidence gleaned by Morris from Israeli, British,
American and UN archives – Arab governments do not, as a
rule, open their archives to research – suggests that infiltration
into Israel was a direct consequence of the displacement and
dispossession of over 700,000 Palestinians in the course
of the Palestine War, and that the motives behind it were

largely economic and social rather than political. Many of the infiltrators were Palestinian refugees whose reasons for crossing the border included looking for relatives, returning to their homes, recovering possessions, tending their fields, harvesting and, occasionally, exacting revenge. Some of the infiltrators were thieves and smugglers; some were involved in the hashish convoys; others were nomadic Bedouins, more accustomed to grazing rights than to state borders. There were acts of terror and politically motivated raids, such as those organised by the ex-Mufti, Haj Amin al-Husseini, and financed by Saudi Arabia, but they did not amount to very much. In the period 1949–56 as a whole, 90 per cent or more of all infiltrations, in Morris's estimate, were motivated by economic and social concerns.

As the years went by, a certain overlap developed between economic infiltration and political infiltration geared to killing and injuring Israelis. The 'free-fire' policy adopted by the Israeli army, border guard and police in dealing with suspects – a policy of shooting first and asking questions later – contributed to this overlap. Faced with trigger-happy Israeli soldiers, infiltrators started coming in organised bands and responding in kind. Altogether between 2,700 and 5,000 infiltrators were killed in the period 1949–56, the great majority of them unarmed.

Morris also shows that the governments of the neighbouring Arab states were opposed to the cross-border forays into Israel for most of the period under discussion. Arab governments were caught on the horns of a dilemma: if they openly intervened to stop infiltration, they risked alienating their own passionately pro-Palestinian publics; if they were seen to condone it, they risked clashes with the Israeli army and the possible loss of more territory. Each government dealt with this problem in its own way, with varying degrees of success. The Lebanese authorities transferred many of the Palestinian refugees northwards, to camps in Beirut, Tyre and Sidon, and effectively sealed the border with Israel. Consequently there were no large-scale Israeli raids into Lebanon in these years. The Syrian authorities also exercised strict control over their border with Israel and infiltration was rare. But the Syrian army was allowed to cultivate the demilitarised zones along the border and this provoked recurrent clashes with the Israeli army.

Jordan had the longest and most complicated border with Israel, with the largest number of civilians on both sides. The upshot was massive infiltration, Israeli reprisals, countless Jordanian proposals to improve the situation in the border areas, and a singular failure to stem the tide of infiltration. Until his dismissal in March 1956, the British officer Glubb Pasha commanded Jordan's small army, the Arab Legion. Glubb did his utmost to persuade the Israelis that Jordan opposed infiltration and was trying hard to curb it. The Israelis did not doubt his sincerity but they piled the pressure on Jordan to do more. Glubb suspected that the Israeli authorities were crying wolf in order to persuade their own public to accept the rigours of Israeli life. He also believed that the Israelis had a psychological need to bully their weaker neighbours.

Whether or not from psychological need, they did play the bully in Jordan with a series of well-planned ground raids against villages in the West Bank, beginning in January 1951. The largest and most notorious of these was directed against the village of Qibya in October 1953. The raid was carried out by Unit 101, a commando force designed to sharpen the policy of reprisals. This unit was commanded by an unusually aggressive and devious young major named Ariel Sharon. Sharon and his men blew up 45 houses and killed 69 Jordanians, the majority of them women and children. Sharon was apparently well pleased with the operation, which in some quarters earned him the title 'the murderer of Qibya'.

The Qibya raid triggered serious civilian unrest in Jordan and a storm of international protest against Israel. The Israeli claim that the infiltrators from Jordan who provoked the raid were sponsored and guided by the Arab Legion did not fool anybody. When Arye Eilan, an official in the Foreign Ministry, asked Yehoshafat Harkabi, the Deputy Director of Military Intelligence, for some clear documentary proof of the Arab Legion's complicity, Harkabi answered that 'no proof could be given because no proof existed'. Harkabi added that having personally made a detailed study of infiltrations, he had arrived at the conclusion that 'Jordanians and especially the Legion were doing their best to prevent infiltration, which was a natural, decentralised and sporadic movement.' To this clear-cut message Eilan reacted by insisting that, whatever the truth of the matter, as Israel's leaders had repeatedly gone on record asserting Jordan's official complicity, Israeli spokesmen must continue to support them: 'If Jordanian complicity is a lie, we have to keep on lying. If there are no proofs, we have to fabricate them.'

The charge of instigating and encouraging Palestinian infiltration from the Gaza Strip and Sinai was also pressed by Israel against the Egyptian authorities, again as part of the propaganda war and without any documentary evidence. The documents of the Egyptian military and civilian authorities in Gaza, captured by Israel during the 1956 and 1967 wars, tell a very different story. In 1975, Ehud Ya'ari, who was given access to these documents, published a short but highly important pamphlet in Hebrew entitled *Egypt and the Fedayeen, 1953–6*. Ya'ari found that the Egyptian authorities had a clear and consistent policy of curbing private incursions into Israel until February 1955, when Ben-Gurion ordered the famous raid on the Egyptian army camp in Gaza City, in which 38 Egyptian soldiers were killed and many others wounded.

Morris agrees with Ya'ari that the Gaza raid marked a watershed in Egypt's relations with the Palestinian *fedayeen* or 'self-sacrificers'. Before the raid, Egyptian policy, with some minor exceptions, had been to oppose and restrict infiltration: after the raid, while continuing to oppose private initiatives, the Egyptian authorities organised *fedayeen* units within the regular army and employed them as an official instrument of warfare against Israel. Morris is more critical than Ya'ari of the Egyptian authorities, especially for sending *fedayeen* squads into Israel in 1954 to gather military intelligence or commit acts of sabotage, but both men recognise that Israel's policy of reprisals played a major part in escalating the border war with Egypt.

To absolve the Arab governments of responsibility for sponsoring infiltration into Israel in the pre-1955 period is not to deny that infiltration posed a very serious problem for Israel in general and the border settlements in particular. Many of the border settlers were new immigrants from Muslim countries. Infiltration from across the border placed their lives at risk, exacted a heavy economic toll, and raised the possibility of mass desertion. There was also the threat that the infiltrators would try to re-establish themselves in their former homes inside Israel. Infiltration, in short, posed a danger not only to the country's day-to-day security but also to its territorial integrity. To cope with this threat Israel established new settlements along the borders and razed abandoned Arab villages. Israeli units began patrolling the borders, laying ambushes, sowing mines and setting booby-traps. The 'free-fire' policy towards infiltrators was adopted. Periodic search operations were also mounted in Arab villages inside Israel to weed out infiltrators. Intermittently, the soldiers who carried out these operations committed acts of brutality, among them gang rape, the murder of civilians, and the dumping of 120 suspected infiltrators in the Arava desert without water.

Until the Qibya raid, military retaliation was directed mainly against civilian targets, and thereafter mainly against military targets. Throughout the 1950s, Israeli governments came under pressure from the public to respond forcefully to Arab provocations. The political climate was thus generally conducive to the use of force. David Ben-Gurion, a peppery and combative little fellow, personified this militant national mood. His instinct was to let the military have their head and to sidestep the slow-moving machinery of the United Nations. In Hebrew the UN is called *Oom*, and Ben-Gurion showed his contempt for it by calling it *Oom-shmoom*.

Military retaliation was, however, a controversial policy inside Israel. Major-General E.L.M. Burns, the chief of staff of the United Nations Truce Supervisory Organisation, divided the Israeli leaders into the school of retaliation and the school of negotiation. Benny Morris divides them into activists and moderates. The activist school was led by Ben-Gurion, prime minister and defence minister until his 'temporary' retirement to the settlement of Sedeh Boker in the Negev at the end of 1953. It included Moshe Dayan and Pinhas Lavon – who were appointed chief of staff of the IDF and defence minister respectively, just before Ben-Gurion's retirement – and the great majority of Israel's powerful defence establishment. The moderate school was led by Moshe Sharett, foreign minister from 1948 until his forced resignation in June 1956 and prime minister from December 1953 until November 1955. It included most of the officials in Israel's largely powerless Foreign Ministry.

Military retaliation was the central issue in the debate between the activists and the moderates. The activists believed that the Arabs were interested only in Israel's destruction, that they understood only the language of force, that Israel could not rely on the UN or great power guarantees for its own security, and that in order to survive the state of Israel had to give repeated demonstrations of its military power. The moderates were more sensitive to Arab feelings and to world opinion; they wanted to create a climate that would favour the possibilities of peaceful coexistence in the Middle East; they feared that frequent and excessive use of force would further inflame Arab hatred of Israel and set back the prospects of peace. Put starkly, 'it was a struggle between hardliners and softliners, security-centredness and diplomacy, intractability and conciliation, the certainty of war and the chance for peace'.

Once in the saddle, Sharett tried to put his moderate views into practice. He rejected the policy of automatic, massive retaliation but reluctantly authorised certain limited reprisals when pressure from the public and the army proved too powerful to contain. Sharett also initiated a secret dialogue with President Gamal Abdel Nasser through personal emissaries who met in Paris. Nasser apparently respected Sharett, for he referred to him as 'an honest and moderate man'. Morris mentions these secret contacts only in passing and grossly underestimates their importance. About the content of the talks he says next to nothing, ignoring the material that is available in the files of the Israeli Foreign Ministry and in the detailed and revealing diary which Sharett wrote from 1953 to 1957, published in eight volumes in 1978. Nor does Morris shed any light on the part played by the activists in sabotaging Sharett's diplomatic efforts.

As prime minister, Sharett experienced the greatest difficulty controlling the activists. Ben-Gurion had handed him a stacked deck before taking to his desert retreat. His chief of staff was an expansionist and a hawk, with nothing but contempt for what he called 'Mr Sharett's policy of appealing here and complaining there'. Pinhas Lavon, as defence minister, pushed the activist line to such extremes that even the army officers came to regard him as a dangerous man. The one thing that the minister and army officers did agree on was the need to reverse the prime minister's policy of moderation.

Without informing Sharett, in July 1954 the defence establishment activated a Jewish spy ring in Cairo in an attempt to make bad blood between Egypt and the Western powers. The attempt backfired, with disastrous consequences for Israeli–Egyptian relations. Towards the end of February 1955, in the wake of 'the mishap', Ben-Gurion re-emerged from his desert retreat to assume the defence portfolio in the Cabinet, which was still headed by the hapless Sharett. A week later he authorised the Gaza raid. The raid sent a signal that the activists were back in charge, and served to boost Israeli morale. But it also put an end to the covert Israeli–Egyptian peace contacts and launched the two countries on the road to war. Badly shaken by the raid, Nasser retaliated with *fedayeen* attacks and by negotiating a major arms deal with the Soviet Union to offset Israel's military superiority.

Ben-Gurion failed to understand the impact of the Gaza raid on Egypt and on Nasser. At a caucus meeting of ministers from the left-wing Mapai party held on 17 May, with a general election in the offing, the diminutive Ben-Gurion, raising his voice, said that Nasser had to be taught a lesson or be overthrown: 'It is certainly possible to overthrow him and it is a blessed obligation [*mitzva*] to do so.' Who did this Nasser Shmasser think he was?

After the Gaza raid it was downhill all the way. Israel resorted to force along its borders ever more frequently and on an ever-increasing scale. All it achieved was an escalation of the border war on the Egyptian, Jordanian and Syrian fronts. In September 1955, Nasser obtained the Soviet arms he had been asking for through the so-called Czech arms deal, which threatened to tip the military balance against Israel. The activists resolved to confront and defeat the Egyptian army before it had a chance to absorb the Soviet weapons. By gradually escalating the level of violence along the borders, Ben-Gurion and Dayan hoped to provoke an Egyptian counterattack which would provide the excuse for an all-out war. This was the thinking behind the major retaliatory strikes between October and December 1955, on Kuntilla, al-Sabha and Kinneret.

The Kinneret raid was directed with devastating force against Syria, which had recently signed a defence pact with Egypt, in order to draw Nasser into war. It was launched on 11 December 1955 while Sharett, by now only foreign minister, was in Washington, waiting for a reply to his request for American arms, which was promised for the following day. The reply he got, after the Kinneret raid, was emphatically negative. Sharett was dumbfounded. To his colleagues on Mapai's Political Committee on 27 December, Sharett remarked that the devil himself could not have thought up a better way to harm Israel. He also came down firmly against the option of a pre-emptive war, which was rapidly gathering momentum within the defence establishment.

To clear the decks for what was always referred to as 'pre-emptive war' against Egypt – never simply as 'war' – Ben-Gurion ousted Sharett from his post as foreign minister in June 1956. Sharett's successor was Golda Meir – the only man in the Cabinet, as Ben-Gurion liked to point out. With the help of his new foreign minister, Ben-Gurion overcame the remaining obstacles along the road and in October 1956 the Sinai campaign against Egypt was launched, in cahoots with France and Britain. This campaign was the biggest reprisal raid of them all. Its declared aims were to destroy the *fedayeen* bases and to open the Straits of Tiran to Israeli shipping. Its undeclared – and unachieved – aims were territorial expansion and the overthrow of Nasser Shmasser. Israel's dirty little war thus culminated in a very big war, which involved two big colonial powers who had their own reasons for wanting to knock Nasser off his perch. Nasser not only survived the tripartite aggression but snatched a resounding political victory from the jaws of military defeat. Israel, on the other hand, only succeeded in stoking the fires of Arab hatred. Force turned out, in the final analysis, to be the only language that the activists knew how to use in dealing with the Arabs. But it was a language which the Arabs did not seem to understand.

# EIGHT

# The Struggle for Jordan

During the 1948 Arab–Israeli War, King Abdullah of Jordan gained control over the West Bank. After the war relations between the Jordanian regime and its large Palestinian population were characterised by difficulties, conflicts and political confrontations. There was also mutual suspicion between Jordan and the Palestine Liberation Organisation (PLO), created by the Arab League in 1964. Each of the two sides strove to ensure its own superiority within this large entity. At different times, and in the light of changing circumstances and constraints, they reached a certain degree of mutual understanding. But even when the relations assumed a more cooperative form, the basic conflict between the interests of the two sides remained.

The relationship between the Hashemite regime and the Palestinian population in Jordan is thus a key issue in the political history of the country. In his book *Between Jordan and Palestine*, Asher Susser examines this question in its critical years – from the beginning of the 1960s to the beginning of the 1970s – through a political biography of a prominent Jordanian figure, Wasfi al-Tall.*

---

* Asher Susser, *On Both Banks of the Jordan: A Political Biography of Wasfi al-Tall* (London: Routledge, 1994). First published as *Bein Yarden Lefalastin: Biografia Politit Shel Wasfi al-Tall* (Tel Aviv: Hakkibutz Hameuhad, 1983).

In the Jordanian–Palestinian confrontation, it is difficult to point to a more central figure than Wasfi al-Tall, whose political career was involved from beginning to end in the Palestinian question and its repercussions in Jordan. Al-Tall was one of the principal pillars of the Jordanian political elite which constitutes the backbone of the Hashemite regime and is the secret of its vitality and longevity. This elite was short of leaders of stature capable of sharing with the king the burden of preserving the regime under conditions of pressure and permanent crisis. Within this small group of authoritative leaders, a special place is reserved for Wasfi al-Tall, alongside Tawfiq Abu al-Huda, Samir Rifa'i , Zaid Rifa'i and Sharif Abd al-Hamid Sharaf.

Susser's book draws a portrait of al-Tall and describes his political career against the background of contemporary Jordanian history. Wasfi al-Tall was a practical politician and not a philosopher, hence there are no special chapters in this book on his world of ideas. They are noted in the book only at those places where they have a direct bearing on his political activity. In his strong personality, his unshakable loyalty to the Hashemite dynasty, and his uncompromising stand against the opponents of the regime, al-Tall epitomised the vitality of the Jordanian entity. All the fundamental characteristics of the Hashemite regime in Jordan became an inseparable part of al-Tall's political consciousness.

From the beginning of his political career al-Tall identified completely with the monarchical regime and tied his own fate to that of the regime. Even if he chose this path out of opportunistic considerations, he clung to it with unusual consistency and resolution. He was, in Susser's view, an example and a symbol of that Jordanian establishment which is jealous of the country's independence and fearful of the forces of pan-Arabism. He belittled the value of revolution in the Nasserist or Ba'thist style. As a pragmatist he strove consistently towards clearly defined political objectives without any inclination to a particular ideology. By temperament al-Tall was a fierce polemicist, with a blunt and belligerent style, who treated his critics with contempt. He was a quarrelsome man who brooked no compromise and struggled indefatigably to ensure what he saw as the supreme interests of Jordan. The use of force against those who challenged the Hashemite regime had been accepted by the Jordanian political establishment since the founding of the emirate; in Wasfi al-Tall King Hussein found a zealous executor of this basic feature in the Hashemite policy.

Al-Tall had no 'philosophy of government' to distinguish him from the norms prevalent in the Arab East. His outlook, says Susser, was anchored in the authoritarian political tradition of Islam that leaves little room for the concepts and institutions that are central to Western political experience, such as parliamentary government or 'loyal opposition'. Though al-Tall enjoyed Western education and graduated from the American University in Beirut, he did not regard political freedom and the right to participate in government as something that citizens should take for granted. In his view, it was the government that conferred freedom and it was up to the government to determine the limits of that freedom. Like Hussein, al-Tall believed that Jordan could be turned into a success story through economic development, efficient administration and the strengthening of the legitimacy of the regime. And like Hussein, al-Tall believed in no reform except that carried out from above. His outlook reflected intolerance of any real opposition.

If in this respect al-Tall merged very well with the political culture dominant in the region, in another respect he was exceptional. He rejected with vehemence all the conspiracy theories used to explain and justify Arab failures. For example, he described the defeat in the 1948 war against Israel very frankly as the result of the shortcomings of the Arabs themselves. Wasfi al-Tall's attitude towards Israel was as complex as it was sober. On the one hand he fought for the Palestinian cause and described Zionism as 'an aggressive, racist, expansionist and fascist movement, a base for imperialism and a bridgehead for the war against liberation'. On the other hand he estimated realistically the strength of Israel and the balance of forces between it and the Arab world. Towards the other Arab states al-Tall displayed distrust and suspicion and he did not rate the Palestinian National Movement highly. In order to avert a war with Israel, he was prepared to deal very firmly with those who intended to upset the peace along Jordan's border and to drag the country into a confrontation with the Israeli army. While al-Tall's attitude towards Israel was negative, the overriding goal of preserving the Hashemite regime dictated accommodation and recognition of the common interests of Israel and Jordan on the Palestinian question. Basic hostility towards Israel thus coexisted uneasily with a policy of compromise.

Al-Tall served three times as prime minister: January 1962 to March 1963; February 1965 to March 1967; and October 1970 to November 1971. All these periods were marked by difficulties stemming from the complex relations between the Hashemite regime and the Palestinians. During al-Tall's first term in office, Jordan worked to prevent the attempts to revive the Palestinian entity. This action was taken in the context of the consistent Hashemite strategy of absorbing the Palestinians into the Jordanian state, and blurring the distinctive Palestinian identity in order to deprive them of the capacity to organise a power base independent of the central government in Amman.

Previously Jordan's policy had been one of reacting defensively to moves initiated by Egypt and Iraq. Al-Tall's government, on the other hand, seized the initiative by formulating a plan of its own for the liberation of Palestine. It also published a White Paper in July 1962 on the Palestine question and inter-Arab relations. Through this document al-Tall wanted to clarify three points: first, that the Arabs needed to act cautiously with regard to the West Bank because of Israel's possible reactions; second, that in any action against Israel Jordan would constitute a major factor and should therefore be brought into the Arab plans; and third, that the mobilisation of the Palestinian potential should be made within the framework of a Jordanian effort because the Jordanian entity and the Palestinian entity were one and the same. The last point stood in sharp contrast to the Arab consensus, which strove to preserve a Palestinian identity and even to give it a separate organisational expression. It was this concept which lay behind the establishment of the Palestine Liberation Organisation in 1964.

During his second term of office al-Tall fought against the PLO's efforts to strike roots among the Palestinian population of the kingdom. He saw the PLO as a dangerous challenge from the very start. The danger was that the PLO would erode the power base of the regime, undermine its stability, and ultimately topple it. Al-Tall firmly rejected the PLO's demands to organise the Palestinian population of the kingdom under its authority or to station units of the Palestine Liberation Army on the West Bank. King Hussein warned against any ill-considered action that could prematurely push the Arabs into war. 'We shall cut off any hand', he said, 'which is raised malevolently against this united and struggling nation.' The offensive by Hussein and his government met with a firm response from Ahmad al-Shuqayri, the chairman of the PLO. Shuqayri denied Jordan's right to exist in its present form: 'The final conclusion that we have reached is that Jordan, with both its banks, is under the colonial rule of the Hashemite family and that the Jordanian people with the help of the Arab people must therefore liberate Jordan from this colonialism as a necessary step towards the liberation of Palestine.'

Parallel to the deterioration in relations between Jordan and the PLO, there was a reversal of the trend towards inter-Arab reconciliation which had begun with the Cairo summit of January 1964. Gamal Abdel Nasser's assertion that only the revolutionary Arab forces could confront the Zionist danger caused a polarisation in 1966 between the radical and the conservative Arab regimes. Given his outlook and experience, al-Tall was a natural candidate to carry out the new policy of moving closer to Saudi Arabia and conducting an unceasing propaganda war against Nasser and the Syrian Ba'th.

One of the symptoms of the renewal of the Arab cold war was Egyptian and Syrian encouragement of guerrilla raids against Israel launched from Jordanian territory. The efforts of the Jordanian authorities to curb such activities were only partially successful. After an incident in which three Israeli soldiers were killed, the IDF retaliated on 13 November 1966 with a raid against the Jordanian village of al-Samu', south of Hebron. This was the largest reprisal raid carried out by the IDF since the Suez War. Instead of striking the *fedayeen* organisations, the operation destabilised the regime in Jordan and exposed it to a combined propaganda offensive by Egypt, Syria and the PLO. Since the annexation of the West Bank by the Kingdom of Jordan in 1950, the policy towards Israel had been one of the main sources of tension between a large part of the Palestinian public and the Jordanian regime. The latter, out of a sober appraisal of the balance of forces, preferred to preserve the status quo with Israel, which required peace along the border. It was a policy derived from the regime's weakness; reprisal raids from Israel underlined the impotence of the regime, and in the event of a full-scale confrontation had the potential to culminate in the Israeli capture of the West Bank. The Palestinians, on the other hand, demanded that Jordan be turned into a base for launching the war for the liberation of Palestine. The raid on al-Samu', as Susser shows, exposed this latent tension. It presented the regime as incapable of defending the West Bank and unwilling to turn Jordan into the vanguard in the struggle against Israel.

Wasfi al-Tall's frank comments after the raid on al-Samu' against the entry of Arab forces into Jordan and *fedayeen* operations against Israel, and his tough handling of the opposition, turned him and his government into the object of criticism by militant Palestinian forces. Al-Tall's government succeeded in stabilising the internal situation, but Hussein thought that in the sphere of relations with Egypt al-Tall had gone too far. Al-Tall's replacement thus came to pave the way for an improvement in relations both internally and in the inter-Arab sphere. It was neither the first time nor the last that Hussein would resort to a government reshuffle in order to overcome a crisis. The events following the raid on al-Samu' were a typical example of that phenomenon in Jordanian politics in which the government and its head are used as a kind of shock absorber designed to draw criticism which is in fact directed at the king's policies.

Al-Tall's appointment as Chief of the Royal Court left him within the inner circle. During the crisis of May–June 1967, however, his efforts to persuade Hussein not to join the Egyptian camp in the war against Israel were unsuccessful. Al-Tall was opposed to Hussein's entry into the war and was the only Jordanian politician who dared criticise publicly the cooperation between Jordan and Egypt in June 1967. Hussein was very concerned with the perception of his regime's legitimacy in the eyes of the Arab world in general, and among Palestinians in particular. He was therefore prepared to make compromises and concessions, even costly ones, to the Egyptians and Palestinians for the sake of his long-term goal of strengthening his regime at home and abroad. Al-Tall, on the other hand, was prepared to pay the price of confrontation with the Palestinians and the price of isolation within the Arab world. He was much less troubled by considerations of prestige, honour and legitimacy.

Al-Tall was no less hostile towards Syria than he was towards Egypt. Susser argues that in the middle of the June War, when the Arab defeat was imminent, al-Tall participated in a plot to topple the Ba'th regime in Syria. The source for this startling revelation was the trial in Damascus of 77 officers and civilians who were accused of involvement in the abortive coup of Salim Hatum in June 1967. One of the witnesses spoke of the contacts they had had with Jordan and of meetings at which al-Tall was present and gave his backing to the activities of the conspirators. According to the witness, al-Tall sent a signed cheque for over 40,000 Lebanese pounds to Salah al-Din al-Bitar, the old leader of the Ba'th, who was in exile in Lebanon and a co-conspirator with Hatum. During the June War, said the witness, there were a number of meetings with al-Tall in Amman at which he urged the conspirators to seize the opportunity presented by the war. Indeed, on 10 June, at the meeting between al-Tall and Hatum, it was decided to launch the coup under the pretext of saving the country from Israel. Hatum and his supporters, who were in a military camp in Mafraq in northern Jordan, crossed the Jordanian–Syrian border the next day, but the bid for power was unsuccessful as they were unable to make contact with their supporters in Syria. The Syrian security forces caught Hatum and his men trying to escape back to Jordan and placed them on trial in September 1968.

On 14 June, a few days after the end of the war, al-Tall resigned from his position as Chief of the Royal Court. On 31 October 1967, Hussein appointed a new Senate. Al-Tall was a member of this Senate, but in fact he remained outside the small political group that ran the government. This freezing out of al-Tall was not accidental: after the June War there was Jordanian–Egyptian cooperation in the inter-Arab sphere, and cooperation between the Hashemite regime and the *fedayeen* inside Jordan. Under these circumstances there was no room for al-Tall within the inner circle of policy-makers.

In August 1967, al-Tall submitted to the king a plan for far-reaching action to contain the PLO and to stop the *fedayeen* organisations from continuing to erode the authority of the central regime in Jordan. The plan included strengthening the Jordanian front with air and armoured forces, establishing a popular militia, reorganising the regular army into small and independent units, and integrating the *fedayeen* operations into the general military effort. This effort was intended to lead to a real guerrilla war that would exhaust Israel and force it to overextend itself, thus bringing about its eventual collapse. Al-Tall made his plan conditional on the rejection of any political settlement that would recognise Israeli sovereignty over part of Palestine. In order to ensure success, al-Tall demanded the transformation of Arab society into a fighting society in which everyone contributed to the national effort. But another condition for the implementation of his plan was that the *fedayeen* be subordinated to the Jordanian army. Hussein did not accept the plan and preferred for the time being to continue with his policy of restraint. But when his authority continued to be flouted, the king opted for full-scale confrontation and launched the army offensive which became known as 'Black September'. Once he had decided to fight, Hussein's aim was to destroy completely the *fedayeen* organisations in Jordan. The road was thus opened for the return of Wasfi al-Tall as the most suitable candidate to implement this tough and uncompromising policy.

During his third term as prime minister, from October 1970 to November 1971, al-Tall restored law and order, conducted a policy of permanent pressure on the *fedayeen*, presided over their final expulsion from Amman and Irbid, and prevented them from re-establishing their presence in the Jordan valley. The government sought to thwart any attempts to carry out operations against Israel for fear that Israeli reprisals would upset the plans to redevelop this important agricultural area, and perhaps even lead to war. Under the leadership of al-Tall, the effort to liquidate the PLO presence was systematic, resolute and uncompromising. Moreover, ending the *fedayeen* presence in Jordan weakened the other sources of opposition in the kingdom and restored the authority of the central government.

Al-Tall had few inhibitions and hesitations when it came to taking measures against the Palestinians. That is why Susser identifies him with the group inside the Jordanian political elite that included Prince Hassan, the Queen Mother Zain, and Hussein's uncle, Sharif Nasser bin Jamil. This group allegedly wanted to disengage from the West Bank and from Jordan's commitment to the Palestinian cause. But it would be an exaggeration to speak of two rival schools of thought within the Jordanian political elite. The picture drawn by Susser is much more complex. Hard evidence about the differences in approach between the king and the anti-Palestinian group are not easy to come by. Susser therefore presents a series of assumptions which, together, amount to a persuasive explanation of the thinking and aims of the king and those close to him.

Al-Tall's policy of liquidating the *fedayeen* presence in Jordan was not intended to weaken Jordan's link with the West Bank. His government even took some steps to maintain this link, notably with the creation of the 'Jordanian National Union' in September 1971. The ideological basis for rallying the public behind the regime found expression in the covenant of the National Union drafted by Wasfi al-Tall together with Ibrahim Habashna and two Palestinians, Adnan Abu Odeh and Mustafa Dudin. In its ideas, content and goals the covenant closely resembled the White Paper published by al-Tall's government in 1962 on Jordan's position on the Palestinian question and inter-Arab relations. The covenant, like the White Paper, emphasised Jordan's commitment to unity with the Palestinians and the interdependence of the two banks of the river Jordan.

During al-Tall's last term as prime minister there were rumours of friction between him and King Hussein. His arrogant and cynical behaviour, blunt manner, and scornful dismissal of his critics created the impression that he was not just the executor but the architect of the tough policy towards the *fedayeen*. But the claim that al-Tall and members of the royal family dictated policy to Hussein is not convincing. Despite his soft manner, Hussein was no more compromising than al-Tall. And in any case there was no fundamental difference between his policy and that of al-Tall. The difference was one of temperament, style and tactics. It stemmed from the different weight attached by the two leaders to the constraints of diplomacy and legitimacy. Whereas Hussein was greatly preoccupied with these considerations, to al-Tall they appeared of only limited consequence. Hussein's vision was broader, more sober and more long-term than al-Tall's; he was more adept at political manoeuvres and less dogmatic. Occasionally Hussein had reservations about steps taken by al-Tall and had to cover up for his mistakes and excesses. Al-Tall had considerable influence and shared the burden of governing the country, but he did not act in opposition to the basic interests of the Hashemite king. Hussein remained the principal policy-maker, the central axis around which the entire political system revolved, and when he handed the reins of power to al-Tall, as with other politicians before and after him, it was understood that the incumbent would carry out to the best of his ability the policy favoured by the king at that particular time.

On 28 November 1971, at the peak of his political career and in the middle of a process of reinvigorating the Jordanian regime, al-Tall was assassinated in Cairo by an offshoot of Fatah called 'Black September'. The killers were defended at their trial by none other than Ahmad al-Shuqayri, the former PLO chairman; all four were freed. Shuqayri argued that al-Tall had been killed not just because of his direct responsibility for the events of September 1970, but because he was a target symbolic of the Hashemite regime, which was responsible for all the disasters that had befallen the Arab nation. For the *fedayeen* and for the followers of Gamal Abdel Nasser – like Muhammad Hasanayn Heikal, who also justified the murder – al-Tall was indeed a symbol of the Hashemite regime and a reminder of the failure to remove that regime from the political scene. The great irony is that al-Tall's political career, which began by his joining the Palestinian fight against the Zionists in the 1940s, came to its sudden end when he was murdered by Palestinians who saw in him the real force behind their expulsion from Jordan.

An irony of a different kind lies in the fact that al-Tall's first biographer is an Israeli, and that the only full-scale study of his political career appears in Hebrew. Asher Susser is well aware of the disadvantages of writing about a major Jordanian public figure without having had the opportunity to visit Jordan or to talk to the people who worked with him. Nevertheless, Susser believes that the primary sources at his disposal – al-Tall's writings, speeches and interviews, articles in the press, and transcripts of radio broadcasts – as well as the secondary literature, makes it possible to draw an authentic picture of the man and his place in Jordanian politics in the 1960s and early 1970s. This belief is fully borne out by the final product. The author has not only carried out extensive and in-depth research, he also presents his material in an admirably clear, orderly and coherent manner. The result is a fine book which sheds a great deal of new light on the troubled relationship between Jordan and the Palestinians.

# NINE

# Abu Nidal, Abu Shmidal

In March 1954 Isser Harel made his first official visit to the
United States as head of Mossad. Warmly received by Allen
Dulles, the director of the CIA, he presented his American
opposite number with an ancient dagger inscribed with the words
from the Psalms: 'The Guardian of Israel neither slumbers nor
sleeps.' Like the celestial guardian, Mossad was expected to uphold
a high standard of morality, to show integrity and commitment in
the service of a noble cause. The contrast between Mossad and the
secret services of other states was deliberately emphasised, just as the
Israeli army was designated the Israel Defence Force to suggest that
its role was purely defensive. With the passage of time a popular
image developed of Mossad, based partly on fact and partly on
fantasy, as the best intelligence service in the world – an image
reinforced by novels like John le Carré's *The Little Drummer Girl*
and *Agents of Innocence* by the American writer David Ignatius. In
recent years, however, a number of scandals have badly tarnished
the reputation of Israel's security services and stimulated calls for
greater public accountability. One of the most damaging blows was
struck by Victor Ostrovsky, a disgruntled former insider, in a book
which the Israeli government unsuccessfully tried to suppress, *By*

*Way of Deception: The Making and Unmaking of a Mossad Officer.*
Interestingly, the title of Ostrovsky's book was inspired by another
Biblical injunction, which Mossad adopted as its motto: 'By way of
deception, thou shalt do war.'

Ian Black and Benny Morris's *Israel's Secret Wars*\* is a long, lively
and comprehensive account of Israeli intelligence. It deals in some
detail with the pre-state period when Palestine was under the British
Mandate, and covers all three branches of the Israeli intelligence
community: the Shin Bet, in charge of internal security and counter-
espionage; Aman, the corps within the IDF charged with the
assessment of enemy capabilities and intentions; and Mossad, whose
brief is espionage and special operations abroad. It is something of
an exaggeration to claim that the book tells an 'untold' story, since
the story of Israeli intelligence has been told many times before.
Where *Israel's Secret Wars* does differ from most of its forerunners
in this crowded field is that it is based on thorough research, the
material is handled in an intelligent and responsible manner, and the
judgements are for the most part sober. The book's authors are both
trained historians and close observers of the Israeli political scene
who share a special interest in Israeli–Arab relations.

The performance of the pre-state intelligence services during what
Israelis like to call their War of Independence in 1948 turns out to
have been little short of abysmal. The Shai, the intelligence branch
of the Haganah, was a part-time and essentially amateur service
which retained a political rather than a military focus. It persistently
misread the intentions of the British government during the twilight
of British rule in Palestine, and kept feeding the policy-makers with
false reports about British plots against the Jewish community
long after the British had resigned themselves to the emergence of
a Jewish state. The Shai's information about Arab plans to invade
Palestine when the Mandate expired was both too vague and at least
in part inaccurate: broadly speaking, the intelligence community
of the Yishuv failed to meet its first critical challenge. Despite this
intelligence failure, the armed forces of the newly born state went on

\* Ian Black and Benny Morris, *Israel's Secret Wars: The Untold History of Israeli Intelligence*
(London: Hamish Hamilton, 1991).

to win a major victory on the battlefield against the regular armies of the neighbouring Arab countries. In this respect 1948 set a pattern which was to be repeated in Israel's subsequent wars.

The history of Israeli intelligence since 1948 has oscillated between spectacular successes and terrible failures. It is one of the paradoxes of intelligence, and to its practitioners one of the disappointing aspects of their profession, that its greatest successes are never disclosed to the outside world or are only disclosed involuntarily when disaster strikes. An example of this is Eli Cohen, 'our man in Damascus', the legendary spy who gained acceptance in the highest echelons of the Syrian government, and was consequently able to supply his bosses in Tel Aviv with priceless information – until, that is, he was caught and hanged.

Even without making allowance for the secrets that will for ever remain secret, Israel's intelligence services can boast some astonishing successes. The list of world-class coups includes the acquisition of Nikita Khrushchev's de-Stalinisation speech, the abduction of Adolf Eichmann, procuring the defection of an Iraqi pilot with his MiG, the raid to rescue the hostages at Entebbe, and the destruction of the Iraqi nuclear reactor in 1981. For sheer chutzpah, the theft of the Mirage production plans and the stealing of five missile boats from Cherbourg harbour following the suspension of French arms supplies to Israel take some beating. In addition, there have been the covert airlifts to bring to Israel the Jews of Iraq, Morocco, Ethiopia and, more recently, the entire Jewish population of Albania.

The list of failures is also long, however; and, when it has come to reading the political and strategic map of the Middle East, and providing the policy-makers with advance warning of enemy intentions and capabilities, very costly. In the mid-1960s, for example, the prevailing assessment was that Egypt would not be ready for war until at least the end of 1970. During the crisis of May 1967, intelligence chiefs completely misread the meaning of the Egyptian and Jordanian moves. The draft of the 1967 annual intelligence evaluation, prepared in May, explicitly stated that there was no chance that war would break out in the coming years. On the other hand, immaculate intelligence preparation at the tactical level paved the way for the pre-emptive air strike which within hours determined the outcome of what the Arabs had long been hailing as the imminent battle of destiny. As so often in Israel's history, tactical virtuosity went hand in hand with strategic blindness.

A much more serious failure occurred six years later when Egypt and Syria launched their surprise attack against Israel on Yom Kippur, the holiest day in the Jewish calendar. This time it was the IDF which was caught with its pants down. On 5 October 1973, a day before the onslaught, the intelligence estimate remained that war was 'highly improbable'. This assessment was not the result of inadequate information. The IDF had first-class information at its disposal, including a report from a secret agent which predicted almost exactly when the attack would begin. Rarely in the annals of war did the intelligence chiefs of one army know more about the plans and preparations of their enemies than the Israelis did on the eve of the Yom Kippur War. The root cause of the surprise was not inadequate or inaccurate information but faulty evaluation. It was a remarkable instance of the stupidity of intelligence.

This time heads rolled. A commission of inquiry was appointed which recommended the removal of some senior officers from their posts, and far-reaching reforms of the intelligence system. The Agranat Commission traced the mistake in evaluation to a set of interlocking assumptions which held that the Arabs were not prepared to go to war. All incoming signals were filtered through and distorted by these assumptions, which were themselves the product of a general contempt for the Arabs and a mood of complacency that spread from top to bottom of Israeli society in the aftermath of victory in the 1967 War. Whether it was the self-assurance of the military which infected the politicians, or the politicians' commitment to the status quo which subtly influenced the outlook of the military, is not easy to determine. What is clear is that when the country was about to confront a challenge of supreme magnitude, the guardians of Israel, both political and military, were fast asleep.

If the primary function of the intelligence experts is to provide advance warning of attack, they also have the function of anticipating major political and strategic changes. Of special significance in this context is the ability to detect subtle changes of attitude on the other side, small cracks in the wall of Arab hostility surrounding Israel which might provide an opening for accommodation and peace. As Yehoshafat Harkabi, the outspokenly dovish former head of military intelligence, observed, 'knowing your enemy' must include the ability to know when the enemy is in the process of becoming less intransigent.

In this respect, too, the performance of Israel's terrestrial guardians has not been distinguished by alertness or perspicacity. Only four years after the disaster of 1973, they failed to foresee President Sadat's peace initiative which resulted, in 1978, in the signing of the Camp David accords and, in 1979, in the signing of the Israel–Egypt Peace Treaty. Israel's basic conception of the attitude of the Arabs towards it more or less ruled out the possibility of reconciliation, and any move in that direction from the Arab side was liable to be dismissed as a purely tactical ploy. When Sadat announced his readiness to come to address the Knesset in Jerusalem, the head of military intelligence told the chief of staff: 'This is the deception of the century.' When Sadat was addressing the Knesset, Defence Minister Ezer Weizman sent the chief of staff a note saying: 'Start preparing for war'. The failure of the entire Israeli intelligence community to predict the Sadat peace initiative called into question, not for the first time, its capacity to look beneath the surface and detect the underlying political and strategic trends in the Middle East.

Israel's invasion of Lebanon in 1982, preposterously named 'Operation Peace for Galilee', revealed the same limitations in reading the Middle East political map and inevitably ended in egregious failure. The authors trace in fascinating detail the process by which Israel sank deeper and deeper – or rather pushed itself into – the Lebanese quagmire. It is Mossad which emerges as the chief advocate of a full alliance with the Phalange, the main party of the Maronite Christian Right. Aman, by contrast, was unenthusiastic from the start about the Christian connection and regularly pointed out the shortcomings of the Phalange. The fateful alliance received its most powerful boost, however, when Ariel Sharon, the fiercely aggressive advocate of Greater Israel, succeeded Ezer Weizman as defence minister in Menachem Begin's second Likud government and vowed to 'solve the problem of Lebanon once and for all'. Banking on the Christians in his ill-conceived plan to destroy Palestinian and Muslim power in Lebanon, he brushed aside Aman's warnings that the Christians were a broken reed. He even pushed Mossad to the sidelines in his usual pig-headed way. 'Mossad's involvement lost importance as soon as the Christians found their way directly to Sharon's ranch', one senior executive said bitterly.

An attempt on the life of the Israeli ambassador to London was seized upon by Sharon and the militants to obtain the sanction of a wavering Cabinet for a war against the PLO in Lebanon. The assassination attempt had been carried out by the breakaway group led by Abu Nidal, which was opposed to Yasser Arafat's 'capitulationist' leadership of the PLO, and was probably designed to provoke an Israeli attack on Arafat's stronghold in southern Lebanon. The experts tried to explain these factional rivalries to the Cabinet, but Begin cut them short, saying: 'They are all PLO.' 'Abu Nidal, Abu Shmidal', said another senior official. 'We have to strike at the PLO.'

After Israel became bogged down in Lebanon and the Christians were exposed as weak and unreliable, some Israeli officers tried to forge a new alliance with the Shiite Amal militia. Aman maintained that Amal could not be trusted because of the presence within its ranks of radical, fundamentalist and pro-Iranian elements. Israel therefore encouraged Major Sa'ad Haddad to recruit Shiite soldiers into his predominantly Christian militia. Traditional divide-and-rule tactics were used, supplemented by psychological warfare, in an attempt to exploit factional, religious and communal rivalries to Israel's advantage. But it was all to no avail.

Black and Morris see the 1982 invasion of Lebanon as 'Israel's greatest intelligence failure'. It was unquestionably a failure, but the failure was primarily one of policy rather than of intelligence. Politics and intelligence do not always make comfortable bedfellows, but it is the elected politicians and not the intelligence professionals who must bear the ultimate responsibility for national policy. It is all the more unfair to blame the experts when their advice was ignored and sometimes deliberately suppressed because it did not fit in with the defence minister's wild designs. It is true that some of the intelligence on Lebanon was faulty, but it is also true, as the authors themselves make abundantly clear, that the intelligence facts were selectively marshalled by hawkish politicians in order to push the country into a savage, unnecessary and unwinnable war.

One of the merits of Black and Morris's book is that it covers not only Israel's wars against the Arab states but also the secret war it has conducted against the Palestinians, especially following the occupation of the West Bank and Sinai in 1967. It shows how Aman, the Shin Bet and Mossad, while maintaining their pre-war functions, greatly expanded their regular activities to meet the security requirements of Greater Israel. Aman retained its overall responsibility for national intelligence, the Shin Bet was given control over operational intelligence in the occupied territories, and Mossad was ordered to step up its targeting and penetration of Palestinian organisations abroad.

The authors recognise that there have been mistakes and excesses, and that the massive expansion in the size of the security services involved some dilution in quality, but the balance sheet they draw is overwhelmingly positive. The Shin Bet, they write, was 'deployed quickly and imaginatively to crush the *fedayeen* before they had a chance to strike roots and acquire operational experience'. It was 'relentless, fast and ruthless, sowing uncertainty by its massive use of informers and giving no quarter in the struggle'. We are told that the Israelis constructed a security system based on the 'carrot' of inducements combined with severe punishments, and that it was a system which worked surprisingly well. But even if the system worked well, which is questionable, it was hardly imaginative. The carrot and stick are as old as the Judean hills.

The IDF's attacks on PLO bases and refugee camps in Jordan and Lebanon are described as 'preventative and retaliatory', but at least it is admitted that they encouraged a response which did nothing but perpetuate and deepen the conflict. The other two services get much higher marks for the part they played in the war to crush Palestinian resistance. 'The Shin Bet and the Mossad', the authors conclude, could 'be justly proud of their achievements in making the status quo tenable – for their own countrymen at least.' But the whole point about the post-1967 status quo is that it was unacceptable to the Arabs and therefore untenable. That is why they went to war in 1973. The most that can be said for the security services is that it is not they but Golda Meir and her ministers who were primarily to blame for the rigid and unimaginative policy pursued by Israel in the inter-war period.

On the ill-treatment and torture of Palestinians and other human rights abuses by the Shin Bet, Black and Morris have surprisingly little to say, and the little they do say is presented in an exceedingly coy fashion. Thus they mention that in June 1977 the *Sunday Times* published 'a lengthy and well-documented report about the alleged torture of Palestinian detainees' but they tell us nothing about its substance. Nor do they report the mounting body of evidence from former prisoners as well as organisations like Amnesty International and the Red Cross, which proves conclusively that human rights abuses are routine under Israeli occupation.

The only report Black and Morris choose to quote is that of the Landau Commission appointed in 1987 to investigate the Shin Bet's techniques in dealing with cases of 'hostile terrorist activities'. The commission found that for 16 years Shin Bet agents had regularly fabricated evidence and lied to the country's courts about confessions obtained under physical pressure from Palestinian suspects, but the practice of giving false evidence to the courts seemed to worry them more than the actual torture and ill-treatment of detainees. In its final report the Commission set down detailed guidelines on the use of force – 'limited and clearly delineated psychological and physical pressures' – and recommended that these be reviewed annually. A wide range of reactions to these findings and recommendations is recorded, but not Black and Morris's own reactions.

Another subject on which the authors barely scratch the surface is that of the intelligence relationship between Israel and the United States, and the secret wars these unequal partners have fought together. Black and Morris do touch on this relationship at various points in their story, but their approach is largely anecdotal and unsystematic. What is missing is any serious analysis of the nature and significance of the relationship. There are also some glaring omissions which cast doubt on the authors' objectivity, the most serious being their failure even to mention Israel's bombing of the American intelligence ship, the *USS Liberty*, during the war of June 1967, ostensibly because it was known to be monitoring Israeli radio communications. This episode is treated in a number of books – among them, Anthony Pearson's *Conspiracy of Silence: The Attack on the USS 'Liberty'* (1978) and Stephen Green's *Taking Sides: America's Secret Relations with a Militant Israel* (1984). It is easy to see why the Israeli authorities would be anxious to avoid any further exposure of this episode, but it is not easy to see why the authors would want to run the risk of being regarded as accomplices in a conspiracy of silence.

From the very beginning Israel saw itself as part of the West and not of the Middle East, and set about making itself useful to the United States in order to gain American patronage. One of the principal ways in which Israel tried to turn itself into a strategic asset to the US was by acting as a clandestine channel of information about other countries. The first US–Israel agreement on intelligence cooperation was signed in 1951. By building up such extensive and expert intelligence services, the Israelis hoped not only to meet their own unique security needs but also to hold up their end of what slowly developed into a fully fledged strategic partnership with the US. The text of Khrushchev's de-Stalinisation speech, for example, was of little interest to Israel but of considerable value to the US – and one good turn deserves another.

In addition to intelligence cooperation, Israel has acted as a proxy for the US in the Middle East, Africa and Latin America (while at the same time furthering its own interests). Among the services provided by Israel are the subversion of anti-Western regimes in the Third World, and the supply of arms and military support and training to regimes and other groups which the US is unable or unwilling to help directly. The Iran–Contra affair is only one of the more intriguing instances of Israel's versatility and global reach as a proxy. These shadowy activities around the world are not, strictly speaking, part of the job description of the guardian of Israel. But in what purports to be a serious study of Israel's secret wars, they deserve much closer attention than they receive in Black and Morris's book.

Black and Morris's outlook, and the unspoken assumptions which colour their narrative, are not basically at odds with the outlook and assumptions of the Israeli defence establishment. Thus the secret wars between Israel and the Arabs are presented here not as a continuous chain of action and reaction but usually as Israeli responses to Arab threats and Arab provocations. On the other hand, the book is entirely free of the hyperbole, sensation-mongering and sheer fantasy that one has come to expect from books on Israeli intelligence in general and Mossad in particular. The non-expert will find this book interesting, instructive, up-to-date and highly readable. The expert in search of a revisionist history of Israeli intelligence and covert operations is likely to be disappointed.

TEN

# *Sleepless Afternoons*

I n his farewell address in 1796 George Washington counselled the new nation to refrain from 'passionate attachment' to or 'inveterate hatred' of any other nation, and to cultivate instead peace and harmony with all. Such an attachment to another nation, he warned, could create the illusion of a common interest where no common interest exists. To speak – as George Ball and his son do in their book *The Passionate Attachment: America's Involvement with Israel* – of America's passionate attachment to Israel involves a slight exaggeration for, as Charles de Gaulle once remarked, there are no love affairs between states.* Even the love affair between American Jews and Israel is only skin deep: American Jews admire Israel for her body, while Israelis are attracted to American Jews for their money.

Nevertheless, Washington's farewell address does serve to spotlight the two central themes of this wide-ranging and rather rambling book. The first is that in this relationship the US has been the loser in political and moral terms, as well as financially. The second and related theme is that America's over-indulgent attitude towards Israel has not been an unmixed blessing: 'If a passionate

* George Ball and Douglas Ball, *The Passionate Attachment: America's Involvement with Israel* (New York: W.W. Norton, 1992).

attachment harms the infatuated country, it can equally injure the nation that is the object of its unrequited affection.' Even some of Israel's most devoted friends in the US would admit that it is not the most gracious or grateful of partners. Henry Kissinger, a leading advocate of the strategic partnership with Israel, had this to say on Israeli negotiating tactics: 'In the combination of single-minded persistence and convoluted tactics, the Israelis preserve in the interlocutor only those last vestiges of sanity and coherence needed to sign the final document.' No less revealing is Kissinger's comment on Yitzhak Rabin, the prime minister who had served as ambassador to Washington in the early 1970s:

> Yitzhak had many extraordinary qualities, but the gift of human relations was not one of them. If he had been handed the entire United States Strategic Air Command as a free gift he would have a. affected the attitude that at last Israel was getting its due, and b. found some technical shortcoming in the airplanes that made his accepting them a reluctant concession to us.

A typical example of the way Israel exploits America is provided by the saga of the Lavi aircraft. To secure American agreement to this hare-brained project in 1982, Israel assured the US that the planes would be solely for Israeli use. Yet early the following year the Israeli Aircraft Industries issued a marketing brochure entitled 'Lavi – the affordable fighter'. The Pentagon opposed the Lavi from the beginning, as did the State Department. One State Department official remarked that 'they were going to build this airplane. All they needed was American technology and American money.' By the time the project was finally killed, America had provided more than 50 per cent of the technology and 90 per cent of the funding.

Moshe Dayan summed up the Israeli view of the special relationship when he said: 'Our American friends give us money, arms and advice. We take the money, we take the arms, but we decline the advice.' As well as pursuing single-mindedly their own national interests, Israelis, with characteristic chutzpah, tend to assume that they know better than American leaders what is in the

American interest. Often in this highly unequal relationship, it has been the tail that wags the dog.

For America the relationship with the Jewish state has always been a deeply sensitive, complex and controversial issue. At the outset, American economic aid for Israel was justified on humanitarian and idealistic grounds. As the only authentic democracy in the Middle East, it used to be argued, Israel deserved American encouragement and support. After Israel's resounding military victory in the June 1967 war, however, support for Israel was increasingly justified on the grounds that it was in America's interest. Israel came to be seen not simply as an economic mendicant, but as a military giant. Israel, it was argued, was a strong, stable and reliable ally whose presence in the region served to check the influence of the Soviet Union and of the radical Arab regimes allied to Moscow. In short, Israel was not just a democracy worthy of support but a strategic asset for the United States.

The development of the strategic partnership with Israel was bound to affect America's entire policy towards the Middle East. US policy-makers were divided into two broad schools of thought, the even-handed school and the Israel-first school. The even-handed school, of which George Ball was a leading member, argued that America should not identify too closely or exclusively with Israel because this could jeopardise America's other vital interests in the Middle East, such as the friendship of the moderate Arab countries and access to oil. The rival school, which gained the upper hand in the Nixon Administration, maintained that Israel was America's only reliable ally in the region and that it should be given all the material support and political backing it needed to preserve the regional status quo, which was favourable to US interests. If this support antagonised the Arabs, it did not matter since they needed America more than America needed them.

Another way of dividing American policy-makers is into regionalists and globalists. The regionalists, of which George Ball was again a leading example, maintained that the problems of the Middle East were homegrown rather than instigated by the Soviet Union and that American policy should be directed at solving or alleviating them. Unqualified support for Israel, according to this school, was emphatically not the way to go about solving these problems, above all the Palestinian problem. The globalists, on the other hand, like Richard Nixon, Henry Kissinger, Ronald Reagan and Alexander Haig, looked at the Middle East as just one arena in their global fight against the Soviet Union. For them Israel was not part of the problem, but part of the solution.

The State Department, where George Ball had served as under-secretary in the Johnson Administration, is the natural stronghold of the regionalists. The White House, especially when inhabited by a Republican President, has tended to be the stronghold of the globalists. American policy towards the Middle East consists of frequent swings of the pendulum between the pro-Arab State Department and the usually pro-Israeli White House. AIPAC, the America–Israel Public Affairs Committee, popularly known as the Jewish lobby, is also an actor in the policy-making process, although it receives surprisingly little attention in the Balls' book. AIPAC was established, in the words of its founder, I.L. Kenen, 'to lobby the Congress to tell the President to overrule the State Department'.

During the Reagan presidency, AIPAC amply fulfilled its original mission. Of all American presidents since 1945, Ronald Reagan has been the most globalist in outlook and the most pro-Israeli. Reagan spent many sleepless afternoons in the White House worrying about the Soviet threat. This worry powerfully reinforced his sentimental attachment to Israel. As the authors point out, because the Cold War supplied the coordinates by which Reagan charted all aspects of foreign policy, he warmly embraced the doctrine that Israel was an important US strategic asset. In a sharp break with a bipartisan American policy that went back to 1967, Reagan declared that the Israeli settlements on the West Bank were not illegal. Unlike Jimmy Carter, he had no sympathy whatever with Palestinian claims to national self-determination. On the PLO, Reagan also followed the Israeli line that it was a terrorist organisation and that negotiating with it was totally out of the question. He even adopted the Israeli position towards the Camp David accords, stating that he would 'continue to support the process as long as Israel sees utility in it'.

This undiluted 'Israel first' policy encouraged Israel both to persist in its diplomatic intransigence just when its Arab neighbours seemed prepared to make peace, and, worse still, to embark in 1982 on its ill-fated invasion of Lebanon. Reagan and his Secretary of State, Alexander Haig, were sufficiently ignorant and gullible to believe that Israel could create a new political order in Lebanon and that this would serve to undermine the Soviet position in the region. During the war, America was drawn ever more deeply into the Lebanese quagmire and ended up as a co-belligerent with Israel in its war with the Arabs. When Reagan, or rather the State Department regional experts, belatedly came up with the sensible and even-handed peace plan which bore his name, Prime Minister Menachem Begin summarily rejected it as a threat to Israel's existence and declared it 'a lifeless stillborn'. The old pattern of Israel taking American money and American arms but declining American advice reasserted itself with a vengeance. The Balls are critical of Reagan for his handling of the crisis in Lebanon but not as critical as one would expect them to be, possibly because the senior author had devoted a whole book to this subject, appropriately entitled *Error and Betrayal in Lebanon*.

George H.W. Bush did not share Reagan's sentimental attachment to American Jews or the Jewish state. In private, Bush would point out that he had been vice-president for eight years in the most pro-Israeli Administration in US history but got only 5 per cent of the Jewish vote when he ran for president in 1988, so he owed nothing to American Jewry. Nor was Bush, a former oil executive, particularly sympathetic to Israel. But it took the ending of the Cold War, and then the First Gulf War, to bring about a decisive change in American policy towards Israel. With the collapse of the Soviet Union and the orphaning of its Arab clients, Israel was no longer needed to safeguard American interests in the Middle East, if that is what it had been doing. During the Gulf War the best service that Israel could render its senior partner was to sit tight, keep a low profile and do nothing.

Characteristically, the Likud government headed by Yitzhak Shamir tried to extract from Washington the highest possible price for its passive cooperation in defeating Saddam Hussein. But when the Bush Administration tried to promote a peaceful solution to the Arab–Israeli conflict it met with a singularly uncooperative attitude in Jerusalem. Even when the Shamir government reluctantly agreed to participate in the US-sponsored peace process, it rejected the principle of trading land for peace and continued to build settlements in the occupied territories. The straw that broke the camel's back, however, was Shamir's request for a $10 billion loan guarantee to finance the absorption of Soviet Jews in Israel. Shamir pushed AIPAC to wage a battle against the Bush Administration on the issue. Bush won this fight hands down, weakening AIPAC and discrediting Shamir in the process. Indirectly, but consciously and skillfully, Bush also helped to bring about a Likud defeat and a Labour victory in the June 1992 general election. What Bush in effect told the Israelis was that they could not have American money if they chose to disregard American advice. The battle over the loan guarantee thus marked something of a turning point in the history of the relations between the US and Israel.

Throughout this far from dispassionate study, the Balls emphasise the cost of 'the passionate attachment'. They calculate that between 1948 and 1991, America subsidised Israel to the tune of $53 billion. This exceeds the aggregate assistance the US gave Western Europe under the Marshall Plan. Rarely in the annals of human history have so few owed so much to so many. Nor can the cost be measured in financial terms alone. The political and moral cost of the passionate attachment has been considerable. Israel's disdain for international norms involves America in a pattern of hypocrisy and makes a mockery of its claim to moral leadership. Two examples are used to illustrate this point. First, America poses as the champion of human rights yet stands silently by while the Israeli army systematically violates the human rights of the Palestinians in the occupied territories. Second, America declares its opposition to the spread of nuclear, biological and chemical weapons, then turns a blind eye to Israel's activities in all these areas. True, the Bush Administration did put forward a plan for halting the production of nuclear weapons in the Middle East, but the Israelis took the view that a bomb in the hand is worth ten in the Bush. From both the financial and the moral aspects, the fundamental question posed by the authors is: 'Are we getting anything faintly resembling a reasonable return from the costs we are incurring?' The evidence presented here points to an emphatically negative answer.

Throughout their book, the Balls, father and son, remain on solid ground in their critique of Israel and their critique of uncritical US support for Israel. Where they are on much shakier ground is in depicting Israel as almost exclusively responsible for all the errors and betrayals committed by the two countries since 1947. If America is not her brother's keeper, nor is Israel; and America's sins should therefore not be visited upon Israel. The US must bear the full responsibility for its own actions, and for the unfortunate consequences of these actions in perpetuating and exacerbating the problems of the Middle East. As between the two allies, the authors are decidedly not even-handed. They portray Israel as the chief culprit and an evil influence, while America emerges as a noble and altruistic great power committed to the highest moral standards in world affairs. America's postwar record in the Middle East, with the exception of Eisenhower's stand on Suez, does not support this view. As for George H.W. Bush's claim to have established a New World Order in the aftermath of the First Gulf War, the authors would surely agree that that was the mother of all prattles.

# PART II

*To Oslo and Beyond*

ELEVEN

# The Face that Launched a Thousand MiGs

Golda Meir was the only woman among the founding fathers of the State of Israel. In many ways, her personal story reflects the story of Israel itself. A working-class girl from pogrom-ridden Russia, she had a stormy adolescence in Milwaukee, emigrated to Palestine in 1921, and rose steadily through the ranks of the Labour Party to become Israel's labour minister, foreign minister, and finally prime minister. Even at the height of her power 'Golda', as she was affectionately called, retained her warmth and informality. Except for the omnipresent Chesterfield cigarettes and the nicotine-stained fingers, she looked like a kindly Jewish grandmother with her craggy face, baggy suits, swollen ankles, orthopaedic shoes, and old-fashioned handbag. But this homely exterior masked a pugnacious personality, a burning ambition, monumental egocentrism and an iron will.

The subtitle of Elinor Burkett's biography of Golda Meir, 'The Iron Lady of the Middle East', is problematic.* She may have been 'the iron lady' of Israel but she was most emphatically not a lady of the Arab people. Indeed, far from being a regional icon, Golda Meir

* Elinor Burkett, *Golda Meir: The Iron Lady of the Middle East* (London: Gibson Square, 2008).

personified the most paranoid, aggressive and racist attitudes of the Zionist movement when it came to dealing with the Arabs. She was afraid of Arabs, and her fears were fuelled by personal memories of pogroms and by the collective Jewish trauma of the Holocaust. Meir saw the world in black-and-white with no intermediate shades of grey. Her position was simple: them or us. She absolutely refused to accept that the Arabs were moved by a sense of injustice, that they felt humiliated, or that they had a different narrative about the conflict in Palestine. Fiercely proud of her people, she never doubted for a moment the justice of the Zionist cause. For her, Arab hostility was not a natural reaction to the loss of Palestine, but simply a manifestation of universal anti-Semitism.

Burkett's biography is readable and fair-minded but rather superficial. It is based largely on secondary sources, newspaper reports and interviews with the subject's family and friends. The book does not break any new ground and, contrary to the extravagant claims of the blurb, it makes hardly any use at all of the official documents released under Israel's liberal 30-year rule. Burkett is better at dissecting the many-sided personality of this unusual leader than at analysing the political context in which she operated. She is at her best when contrasting Mrs Meir's tawdry private life with her sanctimonious public posture. Meir emerges from this account as a terrible mother and a dreadful wife. She spent so little time with her two little children that they were happy when she suffered one of her regular migraine attacks, because it meant she had to stay at home with them. Later on she refused to have contact with one of her own grandchildren, who was born with mild Down syndrome, and insisted that little Meira be sent away to an institution. This sad story is difficult to reconcile with the popular image of the benign Jewish grandmother.

Golda Meir also cheated on her sensitive and long-suffering husband, Morris. Gossip spread that she was 'easy to get'. People sniggered at her nickname – 'the Mattress'. Some suspected that she slept her way up from the lowly position of a cashier in a Histadrut construction company to the top echelon of the Labour Party. Sometimes she had more than one lover on the go. But although she herself was a liberated woman, she never supported feminism as a political cause.

From the beginning Meir belonged to the hawkish wing of the Labour Party. In 1956 David Ben-Gurion chose her to replace the moderate Moshe Sharett as foreign minister in order to clear the decks for the sordid collusion with the colonial powers in the attack on Egypt. Mrs Meir had few qualifications for the job; she was preferred mainly because she accepted Ben-Gurion's conception of the Foreign Ministry as little more than the PR wing of the Ministry of Defence. She was, in fact, the perfect henchwoman for the chief proponent of the policy of clobbering the Arabs hard on the head until they surrendered. Nevertheless, she understandably resented Ben-Gurion's habit of referring to her behind her back as the only man in his Cabinet.

Golda Meir's imperious personality, temper tantrums, uncontrollable urge to didacticism, and disdain for diplomats did little to endear her to her staff at the Foreign Ministry. Nor was she a patch on her predecessor when it came to presenting Israel's case abroad. Abba Eban, who was extraordinarily eloquent in seven languages but had the backbone of a noodle, observed that his boss used only 200 words although her vocabulary extended to 500.

When Prime Minister Levi Eshkol died in February 1969, Golda Meir was 71 years old, retired from politics, in poor health, and undergoing treatment for cancer in Switzerland. The polls showed that only 3 per cent of Israelis favoured her as prime minister. Nevertheless, the Labour Party bosses chose her as a caretaker leader, believing that only she could head off a clash between Moshe Dayan and Yigal Allon. The experience of supreme power, however, acted as a tonic, giving Israel's first female prime minister a new lease of life and sustaining her for five more years at the top. She was an exceptionally strong and decisive leader who tolerated no ambiguity, brooked no opposition, and ruled the country with an iron rod. Like Margaret Thatcher, she was a conviction politician who radiated authority and was nicknamed 'the iron lady'. Also like Thatcher, Meir had a closed and rigid mind. She was intellectually incapable of making the kind of subtle distinctions that are so crucial in the conduct of foreign policy. Her innate personal stubbornness was translated into a national posture in the Middle East conflict, with disastrous consequences for her own people and for the region as a whole. To be fair, Golda Meir did not initiate the building of Jewish settlements in the occupied territories – both a violation of international law and the main obstacle to peace. But she turned the preservation of the post-1967 territorial status quo into a sacred mission which precluded any peaceful settlement of the dispute with the Arabs.

Abba Eban quipped that the Arabs never missed an opportunity to miss an opportunity for peace. The same might be said about Mrs Meir. One does not need a rich vocabulary to say 'no'. She said 'no' to every peace plan during her premiership and she had none of her own to put forward. On 4 February 1971, President Anwar Sadat of Egypt presented a plan for an interim settlement based on a limited Israeli withdrawal into Sinai and the reopening of the Suez Canal to international shipping. Even some of the battle-hardened generals saw merit in this proposal but Meir rejected it at least partly for personal reasons: she did not want to go down in Zionist history as the first leader to retreat from territory. It is probable, to say the least, that progress on Sadat's proposal could have prevented the outbreak of the October War which claimed the lives of 2,656 Israeli soldiers. But Meir was wedded to the policy of attrition, of letting Sadat sweat it out with his range of alternatives constantly shrinking until he accepted her terms for peace. This policy, in fact, had the reverse effect. It left the leaders of Egypt and Syria no option but to resort to military force in order to break the diplomatic deadlock. This is what they did on 6 October 1973, taking the IDF by complete surprise and forcing it on the defensive.

The Yom Kippur War was a famous intelligence failure but at a more fundamental level it was the result of a policy failure, of a monumental strategic blunder. Burkett argues that Meir's iron resolve stood between Israel and surrender after Defence Minister Moshe Dayan lost his nerve in the initial phase of the war. But it was Meir's myopia, arrogance and diplomatic intransigence that were primarily responsible for the outbreak of this war in the first place. A commission of inquiry exonerated the prime minister but the Israeli public took to the streets in protest and her career came crashing down in flames.

Golda Meir combined ignorance and self-righteousness in roughly equal portions. Her most notorious statement, made in 1969, was to deny the existence of a Palestinian people. Professor Yeshayahu Leibovitz retorted that it was not up to that ugly old witch to determine whether there is or there is not a Palestinian people. Another typically asinine statement was that Israel had no responsibility for war 'because all the wars against Israel have nothing to do with her'. Perhaps the worst example of Meir's humbug was her claim that while Israelis might one day forgive the Arabs for killing Israeli boys, they could never forgive them for forcing Israelis to kill Arab boys.

Both as foreign minister and as prime minister Golda Meir never tired of repeating that she was ready to travel to any corner of the earth, at any time of the day or night, to meet any Arab leader who wanted to talk about peace. The reality did not match the rhetoric and most of her officials knew this. Behind her back they used to joke about Golda's launderette which was open 24 hours a day. A fitting epitaph might have been: 'Golda's launderette is closed for the duration!'

# TWELVE

# Arab Nationalism and its Discontents

Fouad Ajami's *The Dream Palace of the Arabs: A Generation's Odyssey* is at once an intellectual tour de force and an intimate and perceptive survey of the Arab literary, cultural and political worlds.* Ajami was born in Southern Lebanon and raised in Beirut, and he has a rare ability to listen to and convey his culture's inner voice. Equally rare is the quality of his English prose. Like Conrad, of whom he is an admirer, Ajami fell under the spell of the English language, and this new book displays his skills as scholar, as stylist and as literary critic.

The title comes from the *Seven Pillars of Wisdom*, the book in which T.E. Lawrence described his campaign in the Arabian desert during the First World War as an attempt to give the Arabs the foundations on which to build 'the dream palace of their national thoughts'. Lawrence, however, dwelt only on the fringe of modern Arab history, and the task that Ajami sets himself is to tell that history from the inside, through the Arabs' own fiction, prose and poetry:

* Fouad Ajami, *The Dream Palace of the Arabs: A Generation's Odyssey* (New York: Pantheon, 1999).

On their own, in the barracks and in the academies . . . Arabs had
built their own dream palace – an intellectual edifice of secular
nationalism and modernity. In these pages I take up what has
become of this edifice in the last quarter-century. The book is
at once a book about public matters – a history of a people, the
debates of its intellectuals, the fate of its dominant ideas – and a
personal inquiry into the kind of world my generation of Arabs,
men and women born in the immediate aftermath of the Second
World War, was bequeathed.

The 'odyssey' of the subtitle is the ideological journey of the
intellectuals and poets who propounded a new vision of Arab
culture, and this vision's gradual disintegration in the second half
of the twentieth century. The battle of ideas is sketched against the
backdrop of Arab politics and enlivened by Ajami's account of his
encounters with some of the protagonists. His central theme is the fit,
or rather the misfit, between ideas and politics in the postwar Arab
world. His method is to use the lives and writings of major literary
figures in order to illuminate the larger themes of Arab history, such
as the revolt against Western dominance, the rise and fall of pan-
Arabism, and the conflict between the liberal tradition and the more
assertive Islamic tendency of recent years. Albert Hourani called his
great work on the history of ideas *Arabic Thought in the Liberal Age,
1798–1939*. Fouad Ajami would deny that there has ever been a
genuinely liberal age in either Arabic thought or in Arab politics.
His view of the Arab condition is comprehensively and irremediably
bleak. His pet hate is Arab nationalism. And he reserves his most
withering critique not for the despots nor the dictators but for the
intellectuals who, in his judgement, have led the Arabs down a blind
alley.

*The Dream Palace of the Arabs* opens dramatically and symbolically
with a nightmarish account of a suicide and of the cultural requiem
that followed it. Khalil Hawi, a gifted Lebanese poet, took his own
life on 6 June 1982, the day on which Israel invaded Lebanon.
'Where are the Arabs?' Hawi had asked his colleagues at the American
University of Beirut before he went home and shot himself. 'Who

shall remove the stain of shame from my forehead?' The eulogists told a simple story, portraying the patriotic poet as the sacrificial lamb for an Arab world that had fragmented. In his death the world of letters saw a judgement on the political condition. 'He was weary of the state of decay,' wrote the Palestinian poet Mahmoud Darwish, 'weary of looking over a bottomless abyss.' But there was more to his death than met the eye, and more to Khalil Hawi than the stereotype this politicisation had turned him into. From Ajami's researches a much more complex and richly textured picture emerges. The poet's life had begun to unravel long before Israel swept into Lebanon, and there had been a suicide attempt a year earlier, when Hawi had taken an overdose of sleeping pills. He had been in the grip of a long, deep depression and never recovered from that earlier suicide attempt.

Khalil Hawi was born in 1919 to a poor Greek Orthodox family from Mount Lebanon. He was forced to leave school at the age of 13 to earn a living as a stonemason. More than a dozen years passed before he would return to school and in 1956 a scholarship took him to Cambridge, England, where he attained a doctorate in literature. Along the road Hawi had fallen for Syrian nationalism, and then pan-Arabism, only to return to a simple love of Lebanon. Literary fame came relatively late in his life. He was much admired as the *batunji* (bricklayer) who became a professor and a poet; but the private pain of the journey had left its mark, merging as it did with a progressively more pessimistic assessment of the prospects for Arab nationalism.

A premonition of disaster ran through his work. By the time the Arab national movement suffered its most spectacular defeat at the hands of Israel in June 1967, Hawi had become a seasoned exponent of the politics of disappointment. But the defeat of the pan-Arabism with which he had become so closely identified was like a descent into a bottomless pit. 'Let me know if Arab unity is achieved; if I am dead, send someone to my graveside to tell me of it when it is realised', Hawi said on one occasion. Death, whether individual or collective, was never far from his thoughts.

Hawi had travelled far only to find great darkness and despair. His poetry reflected the torments and the tribulations of Arab modernity. He had known moments of public exaltation alongside his private pain but a nemesis lay in wait for him. He was an avid reader of foreign books, but all were to no avail. He was a proponent of modernity but his modernity had been a false promise. That dawn ushered in a 'strange morning', wrote Hawi in a volume of verse he published in 1979 under the title *Wounded Thunder*. The sun had reversed its orbit, rising in the West and setting in the East. Hawi wept for himself and for that 'Arab nation' whose rebirth and regeneration he so much wanted to see:

> How heavy is the shame,
> do I bear it alone?
> Am I the only one to cover my face with ashes?
> The funerals that the morning announces
> echo in the funerals at dusk.
> There is nothing over the horizon,
> save for the smoke of black embers.

Earlier writers hailed Khalil Hawi as the voice of a new Arab generation and the expositor of a new kind of reality, but they often missed the underlying gloom and doom. Fouad Ajami shares their admiration for Hawi's poetry but not his politics. Indeed he considers Hawi's life as emblematic both of the rise and of the ebbing of the tide of Arab nationalism. He shows sympathy for Hawi's existential predicament but he also suggests that the ideology of Arab nationalism was doomed to failure from the start, that it was bound to lead into a literary as well as a political cul-de-sac:

The failure of the written word convinced Khalil Hawi that the battle of his generation of Arabs had been lost. The text had sustained the men and women of the Arab nationalist tradition. Sweeping out all that stood in its way, the language of secular nationalism had been heady and sure of itself. It had wished away great timeless truths that were everywhere in Arab life: the truths of the clans and the religious sects; the split between the thin layer of literary and political culture and the popular traditions below that mocked the optimism and bravado of the written word. Hawi was ahead of his time in his despair of writing and the written word. In the years to come, the problems of writing, the difficulty of matching Arab words and Arab things, became a steady lament in the world of letters. Arab men and women of this century escaped into the word, and the word failed them.

Not long after Hawi's death, the romantic poet Nizar Qabbani and the poet and literary critic Adonis offered their own autopsies. For both, the crisis of writing was simply a reflection of the Arab political condition. There was a disturbing discontinuity between the discourse of politics and poetry, and the world Arabs confronted every day. It had become harder to write, both seemed to be saying. Qabbani borrowed the term *jahiliyya*, meaning pre-Islamic ignorance, to describe the reality of the 1980s. In that original time of darkness the poet was his tribe's spokesman, chronicler and scribe. The new *jahiliyya* is darker than the old, however. It has no use for the poet because it wants people to live on their knees. The rulers, 'the sultans of today', want only supporters and sycophants, and this has had the effect of emasculating the language. They fear the word because it is 'intrinsically an instrument of opposition'. The conflict between the word and *al-sulta*, or authority, is inescapable.

Qabbani was born in Syria but made his home in Beirut, the capital of Arab letters and the Arab enlightenment. But having to witness the destruction of the enchanted city of his youth by the civil war prompted him to speak of the death of Arab civilisation. Beirut's wars showed how all the grand ideas resulted in endemic violence and a return to primitive tribalism – his own wife was killed in 1981 in one of the daily episodes of violence. In his grief he wrote 'Balqees', a long lament of heartbreaking intensity:

> Balqees . . . oh princess,
> You burn, caught between tribal wars,
> What will I write about the departure of my queen?
> Indeed, words are my scandal. . .
> Here we look through piles of victims

For a star that fell, for a body strewn like fragments of a mirror.
Here we ask, oh my love:
Was this your grave
Or the grave of Arab nationalism?
I won't read history after today,
My fingers are burned, my clothes bedecked with blood,
Here we are entering the stone age. . .
Each day we regress a thousand years.
What does poetry say in this era, Balqees?
What does poetry say in the cowardly era. . . ?
The Arab world is crushed, repressed, its tongue cut. . .
We are crime personified. . .
Balqees. . .
I beg your forgiveness.
Perhaps your life was the ransom of my own,
Indeed I know well
That the purpose of those who were entangled in murder was
    to kill my words!
Rest in God's care, oh beautiful one,
Poetry, after you, is impossible . . .

Adonis's account of his predicament went beyond Qabbani's grief. It is given in a book of literary criticism, *al-Shi'riyya al-Arabiyya* (*Arabic Poetics*), published in Beirut in 1985. Here Adonis depicts the Arab writer as being under a 'dual siege', caught between Western thought on the one hand and the hold of Islamic tradition on the other. Adonis advances the argument that the marriage between the West, or the kind of modernity that the Arabs imported from the West, and tradition has issued in an arid and artificial world. 'Our contemporary modernity is a mirage', he writes. As long as the Arabs fail to grasp that there is more to the West than they have found in it – its spirit of curiosity, its love of knowledge, its defiance of dogma – the 'Western' modernity of the Arab world is doomed to remain a 'hired' form of modernity. Real modernity can only be attained, says Adonis, when the contrived world of the foreigner and the contrived world of the ancestor are transcended.

Adonis, like Qabbani, endured Beirut's carnage and breakdown, and like him he was driven into exile. Reality had surpassed their worst fears. Is it any wonder that many of those in the Arab world who traffic in words felt that they had so little to say? Moving back and forth in time, Ajami keeps returning to the false premises and the baleful consequences of Arab nationalism. The political crisis of the early 1980s made it difficult for even its most passionate advocates to persist. Arab society, he observes, had run through most of its myths and what now remained in the wake of the proud statements Arabs had made about themselves and their history was a new world of waste, confusion and cruelty. The oil-based economic boom of the 1970s had done nothing to sustain the myth that a collective condition prevailed from one end of the Arab world to another. On the contrary, the windfall created a fault line between those that were able to share in this new wealth, and the 'modernity' that came with it, and the large sectors of the population who were only on the fringe. The petro-era catapulted the Arabs into an unfamiliar world. Ajami himself sees only shadows and no light in the new order:

> Whatever its shortcomings, the old world . . . had been whole: it had its ways and its rhythms. At least people knew who they were and had some solid ground to stand on. The winners may have been a little uppity or cruel, but they could not fly too high. There were things that people were ashamed to do, limits that marked out the moral boundaries of their deeds. The permissible (*halal*) was distinguishable from the impermissible (*haram*). Scoundrels and bullies knew what they could and could not get away with. There was, in sum, a moral order. Then all this was blown away. The continuity of a culture was shattered. All attempts to reconstitute the wholeness, to ignore the great rupture by means of cultural chauvinism or a hyperauthentic traditionalism, brought only greater confusion and breakdown.

Egypt has always held an endless fascination for Ajami because of its subtlety, its resilience, and its civility amid great troubles. His chapter 'In the Land of Egypt' opens with a dramatic, defining episode in modern Egypt's life: the assassination of Anwar al-Sadat on 6 October 1981. For Ajami, the tension in the Egyptian psyche and in the country's history was illuminated by Sadat and the angry young men who struck him down. Years earlier Ajami had been mesmerised by the tale of the assassination and read practically all the court proceedings and police investigations that surrounded it. Something said by the principal assassin, a young lieutenant with strong Islamic convictions, lodged itself in his memory: 'I shot the Pharaoh.'

In *The Dream Palace of the Arabs* Ajami elaborates on the duality of Egypt: the modernity at the core of its national aspirations, and the nemesis that stalks it in the form of theocratic politics. During a recent visit to Egypt Ajami had the good fortune to spend four evenings in the company of the great novelist Naguib Mahfouz. Then in his eighties, Mahfouz was recovering from a knifing by religious fanatics that nearly cost him his life and paralysed his writing hand. To Ajami, Mahfouz epitomises at once the modernity of Egypt and the siege of its men and women of letters. Ajami considers Egypt as too wise, too knowing, too patient and too tolerant to succumb to a reign of theocratic zeal, but he notes with sadness that the theocratic alternative has seeped into the culture of the land. 'The danger here', he writes, 'is not sudden, cataclysmic upheaval but a steady descent into deeper levels of pauperisation, a lapse of the country's best into apathy and despair, Egypt falling yet again through the trap door of its history of disappointment.'

Predictably, Ajami does not think much of the resurgence of Egypt's pan-Arab vocation. The Nasserite revolt against the West, and the series of Arab–Israeli wars, ended in futility and defeat, and then in dependence on America, he argues. He dismisses the calls of intellectuals for Egypt to assume a larger regional role as a mirage and a warmed-over version of the failed pan-Arab creed of the 1960s. Egypt's primacy in Arab politics is a thing of the past; Arab states have gone their separate ways. Egypt was the last of them to proclaim the pan-Arab idea and, under Sadat, the first to desert it. If the country succumbs again to its temptation as a distraction from intractable domestic problems, Ajami warns, pan-Arabism would have afflicted the country twice, the first time as tragedy, the second as farce.

The last part of the book, 'The Orphaned Peace', is devoted to the intellectual encounter with Israel, which for 50 years has both fascinated and repelled its Arab neighbours. Talking about Israel has been an indirect way for Arabs to talk about themselves and to take stock of their own condition. Yet, despite the fascination, the Arabs have remained profoundly ignorant about Israel, its political institutions, its culture and society, its language and literature.

Progress towards a settlement at the diplomatic level has done surprisingly little to break down the psychological barrier that sets the two societies apart or to lift the taboos on direct dealings between them. No sooner was the Oslo Accord signed in September 1993 than a new campaign was launched in the Arab world, fuelled by the fear that Israel's military supremacy would be replaced by Israeli cultural hegemony. The matter of Israel was bound up with Arab modernity. Some Arab intellectuals admitted it was time to cease looking at Israelis as though they were extraterrestrial beings who had descended on the region from an alien world. Adonis was one of their number. But they were a distinct minority.

The Oslo Accord was greeted with dismay in some quarters of the Arab world. It was peace without justice and without honour, charged the critics. But it fell to the Arab world's most popular poet, Nizar Qabbani, to catch the widespread opposition to this particular peace agreement. He did so in a prose poem, 'al-Muharwiluun' (those who rush or scurry), which he wrote from his new home in London and published in the daily *Al-Hayat* in 1995. Qabbani's bitter disappointment with the Oslo Accord, and his anger with the Arab leaders who made it, were given free rein:

> We stood in columns
> like sheep before slaughter
> we ran, breathless
> We scrambled to kiss
> the shoes of the killers. . .

They stole Jesus the son of Mary
while he was an infant still.
They stole from us the memory of the orange trees
and the apricots and the mint
and the candles in the mosques.

In our hands they left
a sardine can called Gaza
and a dry bone called Jericho.
They left us a body with no bones
A hand with no fingers.

After this secret romance in Oslo
we came out barren.
They gave us a homeland
smaller than a single grain of wheat
a homeland to swallow without water
like aspirin pills.

Oh, we dreamed of a green peace
and a white crescent
and a blue sea.
Now we find ourselves
on a dung-heap.

Qabbani's poem reverberated throughout the Arab lands. It also triggered an exchange between the poet and the venerable Naguib Mahfouz. Mahfouz, a supporter of peace since the early 1970s, praised the beauty of the poem while taking issue with its politics. There can be no peace without negotiations, Mahfouz argued, and since the option of war was not available, there was no justification for this attack on the pragmatic Arab negotiators. Qabbani took refuge in poetic licence. 'As a poet I am constitutionally of the party of peace', he wrote in response:

for poetry cannot be written in the shadow of death and desolation. But what we are offered here is not peace but a pacifier made of

rubber with no milk in it, a bottle of wine with no bottom, a love
letter written in invisible ink. What we are offered takes from us
what is above us and what is under our feet, and leaves us on a
mat . . . Nothing remains for us of Palestine in the shadow of this
ruinous peace.

In Egypt, the debate over relations with Israel has been going on
for decades. Sadat's 'pharaoh's peace' was allowed to stand in his
lifetime but his successors have let it wither. A tacit understanding
was reached, however, between Mubarak's regime and the
chattering classes: diplomatic accommodation was to be pursued
but the opposition was allowed to denounce the unloved peace
agreement. Indeed, no one who reads the Egyptian daily *Al-Ahram*
would believe that Israel and Egypt are at peace. Its contributors
wage a steady campaign against normalisation, conjuring up the
spectre of Israel as an enforcer of Pax Americana, and as an enemy
bent on diminishing Egypt's power and influence. On all other
subjects clear limits of the permissible are laid down from above,
but over Israel there is a free-for-all. The intellectual class likes to
resort to wordplay, whereby normalisation, *tatbi*, is equated with
*tatwi* (domestication) and peace, *salam*, dismissed as surrender,
*istislam*.

Muhammad Hasanayn Heikal, a former editor of *Al-Ahram* and a
keeper of the Nasserite flame, argued that just as the 1950s and 1960s
had been an 'Egyptian era' of nationalism and political struggle, the
1970s and 1980s a 'Saudi era' of wealth and petro-dollars, the 1990s
had turned into an 'Israeli era'. The peace that was emerging in the
1990s, Heikal told his readers, was sure to reflect the facts of Israel's
power. It was pointless to blame the Palestinians for their acceptance
of a truncated peace, he said, because they were at the end of their
tether, because the world had wearied of them, and because their
leader was on the ropes. Nevertheless, a new map was being drawn
for the region and this map was a 'birth certificate' for a new order
destined to subjugate the Arab world.

Ajami sees the Mubarak regime's hostility to Israel as a safety valve
for a severely troubled political order, and as an olive branch held out

to its critics in the professional classes and the universities. When he goes back to the pre-Mubarak era, Ajami writes with evident admiration for the intellectuals who sustained Sadat in the 1970s, and the older generation of writers and thinkers who wanted to end the conflict with Israel. Along with Mahfouz, this group included the critic Louis Awad, the playwright Tawfiq al-Hakim, the historian Husayn Fawzi, and the novelist Yusuf Idris. All of them, says Ajami, were individuals with broad horizons and wide-ranging interests. They had seen the pan-Arab vocation of the Nasser era and the wars that followed as an unmitigated disaster for Egypt. They had no love for Israel but they wanted to extricate their country from the conflict and from the authoritarian political culture that it fostered and justified. For them, peace was a precondition of modernity and an open society.

Ajami's own sympathies are clearly on the side of the modernists. Time and again he berates Arab intellectuals for refusing to look reality in the face, for failing to incorporate the logic of power into their programme. For modernity to have a chance, he argues, the Arab political imagination will have to go beyond the old enmity, and start looking more seriously at Israel's place in a region at peace. He concludes with a plea 'for the imagination to steal away from Israel and to look at the Arab reality, to behold its own view of the kind of world the Arabs want for themselves'.

Ajami is no stranger to controversy. With his latest book he is likely to generate at least as much controversy in the Arab world as he did with his first book *The Arab Predicament*. He represents one school of thought, the school that blames the Arab predicament on the Arabs themselves. At the other end of the spectrum there is the much larger school of thought which blames the Arab predicament on the West. In between these polar opposites, there are many intermediate strands of thought on the Arab predicament. Ajami's implicit assumption is that all the failures and frustrations of the Arabs are due to factors that are inherent and innate in Arab society, and this leads him to Cassandra-like conclusions about the prospects for a better future. Another feature of Ajami's analysis is the tendency to exaggerate the role of the intellectuals in shaping Arab politics and the role of poets in shaping, as opposed to reflecting, public opinion in the Arab world. But whatever weaknesses there might be in his analysis, there can be no doubt that this book makes a major contribution to the study of Arab culture and society.

# THIRTEEN

# Israel and the Gulf

T
wo major security challenges confronted the Israeli government headed by Yitzhak Shamir in the second half of 1990: the Palestinian uprising, then in its third year, against Israeli rule in the occupied territories, and the crisis triggered by Iraq's invasion of Kuwait on 2 August. To begin with, the Gulf crisis overshadowed the intifada, but within a short time it also contributed to a serious escalation of the Palestinian–Israeli conflict, pushing it to the brink of an inter-communal war. Increasingly, the solution to the Gulf crisis became linked in the public debate with a solution to the Palestinian problem, giving rise to a new buzz word – linkage.

At the helm in Israel during that turbulent period was the most hawkish right-wing government in the country's 42-year history. Shamir's Cabinet was more purely right-wing in its composition than the Menachem Begin Cabinet of 1977, which achieved the peace treaty with Egypt, or even Begin's second Cabinet, which took the decision to bomb the Iraqi nuclear reactor, formally annexed the Golan Heights, and launched the ill-fated invasion of Lebanon. Between 1984 and 1988, Israel was ruled by a Labour-Likud government, with Shimon Peres and Yitzhak Shamir rotating as prime minister and foreign minister. This curious situation gave each party a power of veto over the more extreme policies of the other. Following the draw between the Likud and the Labour Party in the 1 November 1988 general election, the two parties formed a national coalition government, with Shamir as prime minister; but Labour broke up the coalition in March 1990 because of irreconcilable differences over foreign policy. In June of that year Shamir eventually succeeded in cobbling together a narrow coalition government, with the support of the religious parties and three small secular ultra-nationalist parties.

The key portfolios in the new government went to the members of Shamir's Likud Party. David Levy, a populist of Moroccan origins, became foreign minister. Mr Levy did not speak English. But since little more than a dialogue of the deaf with the United States was likely on the peace process, this was not considered a severe handicap. Moshe Arens, an engineering professor of American origins whose reasonable manner masked unyielding nationalist convictions, moved from the Foreign Ministry to the Ministry of Defence. Ariel Sharon, chief architect of the Israeli invasion of Lebanon, was back at the centre of government as Minister of Housing.

On the fringes of the government, but helping to set the tone, were two renowned hardliners representing tiny but highly vocal Arab-spurning parties with only two or three seats each in the 120-member Knesset. Professor Yuval Ne'eman of the Tehia or Renaissance Party was appointed minister of science, technology and energy, reinforcing his popular image as an Israeli Dr Strangelove. The agriculture portfolio was given to Rafael Eitan, the IDF chief of staff during the Lebanon War who once likened the Palestinians of the West Bank to drugged cockroaches. His party, Tsomet, meant 'crossroads' in Hebrew, though it advocated a straightforward policy of building Greater Israel. The government as a whole was so fiercely nationalistic that Begin's first government seems by comparison a model of tolerance and flexibility.

Mr Shamir himself appeared to want to go down in history, not as the man who extended Begin's peace with Egypt to Israel's other neighbours, but as someone who stood firm and refused to yield any part of the ancestral land, *Eretz Yisrael*. Having abstained in the Knesset vote on the Camp David agreements, he maintained that the conditions that made possible the peace with Egypt did not obtain in relation to the Palestinians ('the Arabs of the Land of Israel', as he preferred to call them) or to any Arab state. He disliked and distrusted the Arabs, and did not believe in the possibility of peaceful coexistence with them, at least not in the foreseeable future. Seeing the Arabs as primitive, volatile and blindly hostile to the State of Israel and its Jewish population, he questioned the power of any diplomatic agreement to bring genuine peace and stability to the region. Personal experience of the Holocaust went a long way to explaining this deeply pessimistic outlook. Although Shamir rarely invoked the Holocaust, he was acutely conscious of his people's vulnerability, and would expect the rest of the world to remain indifferent in the event of a real threat to Israel's existence. For all these reasons, Shamir was an apostle not of peace but of self-reliance, a consolidated Israeli presence on the West Bank, a build-up in Israel's military strength, and steadfastness in relation to international pressures.

The Likud leader and his colleagues did not accept the basic formula of exchanging territory for peace on Israel's eastern front. This formula lies at the heart of UN resolution 242 of November 1967 and subsequent international initiatives to resolve the Arab–Israeli dispute, and is accepted, at least in principle, by the Israeli Labour Party. Historically, the Labour Party has been the proponent of 'the Jordanian option', a settlement with Jordan based on a territorial compromise over the West Bank, so as to deal with the Palestinian problem in a way that involves neither negotiation with the PLO nor the creation of an independent Palestinian state. Labour has also regarded, and continues to regard, the survival of the Hashemite monarchy in Jordan as essential to Israel's security. Likud, by contrast, insisted – and continues to insist – that Judea and Samaria, the official term for the West Bank, are an integral and inalienable part of the Land of Israel, and emphatically rejects any Jordanian claim to sovereignty over this area. Likud's basic thesis is that Jordan is Palestine: that there is already a Palestinian state on the East bank of the Jordan, since the Palestinians there constitute the majority of the population, and that there is therefore no need to create a Palestinian state on the West Bank of the Jordan.

A number of politicians inside the Likud, such as Ariel Sharon, as well as in the parties further to the right, were also known to favour the large-scale expulsion of Palestinians from the West Bank to the East, should a suitable opportunity present itself. This implicit threat of Israeli 'demographic aggression' evokes in Jordan fears that verge on an obsession. It is one of the factors which induced King Hussein to sever legal and administrative links between his kingdom and the West Bank in July 1988. Another significant consequence of this fear was to push Jordan closer to Iraq as the only Arab state capable of providing some sort of deterrent against a possible Israeli move to realise the thesis that Jordan is Palestine.

Another potential partner in the search for a settlement whom the Likud helped to drive into the arms of Saddam Hussein was the PLO. The Likud's rejection of the PLO has always been absolute. In other words, its position is not that negotiations with the PLO would be possible if it met certain conditions, but that the PLO is a terrorist organisation with which Israel should refuse to negotiate under any circumstances. Scarcely less categorical is the Likud's rejection of any Palestinian right to national self-determination in any part of Palestine. Here the difference between Likud and the Labour Party is much less profound than in relation to Jordan. This is why the Palestine National Council's historic resolutions of 15 November 1988, renouncing terror, recognising Israel and offering to partition Palestine between Jews and Arabs, failed to elicit any positive response from the Israeli side.

The PLO's peace offensive, and the dialogue with the US government for which it paved the way, cast Israel more clearly than ever before in the role of the obdurate party, and by harnessing their actions on the ground to the PLO's moderate diplomacy, the local leaders of the intifada further helped to expose the intransigence at the heart of Israel's position. As a result, a reversal of previous roles began to take place. In the aftermath of the June 1967 war it was the Arabs who were widely perceived as the intransigent party and Arab rejectionism was summed up in the three famous no's of the Khartoum summit: no to recognition, no to negotiation, no to peace with Israel. Now Israel was seen as the main obstacle to a settlement, and Israeli rejectionism was summed up by King Hussein as the Likud's four no's: no to the exchange of land for peace, no to negotiations with the PLO, no to an independent Palestinian state, and no to an international conference to deal with the Arab–Israeli problem.

Once the PLO–American dialogue got under way in Tunis, Israel came under growing pressure from the first Bush Administration to show some flexibility in order to reactivate the moribund Middle East peace process. American impatience with Israeli stonewalling was given an uncharacteristically blunt expression in a public statement by Secretary of State James Baker, vouchsafing the telephone number of the White House and telling the Israelis to call when they were serious about peace.

Something resembling a peace initiative was launched by the Israeli government prior to Shamir's visit to Washington in May 1989. The government offered to hold free municipal elections on the West Bank and the Gaza Strip, and to allow the inhabitants a greater measure of autonomy in the running of their daily affairs. The offer was hedged around by restrictions. It did not extend the vote to the Arab inhabitants of Jerusalem. It promised no change in the political status of the territories. It stated that Israel would not conduct negotiations with the PLO, and that it opposed the establishment of 'an additional Palestinian state in the Gaza District and in the area between Israel and Jordan'. Despite these obvious limitations, the Americans welcomed the initiative and wanted to pursue it vigorously. The Palestinians, however, rejected the offer, seeing it as a delaying tactic designed to propitiate American opinion and to take the sting out of the intifada.

There was thus complete deadlock on the Arab–Israeli peace front when Saddam Hussein surprised the world by invading Kuwait.

The Iraqi invasion was greeted by Mr Shamir and his coalition colleagues with an inaudible sigh of relief because it shelved American plans to get Israelis and Palestinians round the negotiating table, and diverted international attention from the intifada. It also seemed to lend credibility to their contention that the principal threat to the stability of the region did not stem from the failure to solve the Palestinian problem, but from the ambition and greed of dictatorial Arab regimes, of which Iraq was only the worst example.

The PLO leadership gave vent to the frustrations that had built up in the Palestinian camp over the previous two years by openly siding with the Iraqi tyrant, instead of standing by the inadmissibility of acquiring territory by force – a principle which would have served its cause better. The Israeli government seized on this, and the anti-Israeli rhetoric which accompanied it, as further vindication of its refusal to have any truck with the PLO. Supporters of a dialogue with them on the Israeli Left no longer had a leg to stand on. Some of them gave public expression to their disillusionment with the Palestinians and closed ranks behind their own government. Yossi Sarid of the Citizens' Rights Movement wrote in the independent daily *Haaretz* that if the Palestinians could support Saddam Hussein, who had executed tens of thousands of his domestic opponents and used poison gas against the Kurds, then perhaps it was not so terrible to support the policy towards the Palestinians of Yitzhak Shamir, Ariel Sharon and Yitzhak Rabin.

When Iraq invaded Kuwait, the Americans advised Israel to keep out of this particular quarrel, while themselves rushing forces to Saudi Arabia and assembling against Saddam Hussein a broad international coalition which included Egypt and Syria. The Americans wanted Israel to keep quiet, to stay in the background and not complicate matters. The Israeli leaders were only too happy to oblige: the last thing they wanted to do was to help Saddam Hussein turn an Arab–Arab conflict into an Arab–Israeli one. So they kept a very low profile during the initial phase of the Gulf crisis. They even took the controversial decision to distribute gas masks to the civilian population in order to underline the defensive nature of their response. It was Saddam Hussein who first made the link between the Gulf crisis and the Arab–Israeli dispute by offering what he called 'new arrangements' between Iraq and Kuwait in return for an Israeli withdrawal from the occupied territories. Both Israel and

America firmly rejected any parallel between the two occupations and any linkage in dealing with them, and world opinion was largely on their side.

The turning point came on 8 October, when the Israeli security forces massively overreacted to a riot in the Old City of Jerusalem and ended up killing 19 Palestinians. Israel was back in the headlines. The massacre on Temple Mount provoked a wave of angry condemnation and redirected international attention to the plight of the Palestinians under Israeli rule. Israeli security forces had thus put an abrupt end to the government's policy of staying in the background. They had also appeared to confirm the link whose existence the government had so strenuously denied, and to underline the urgency of finding a solution to both problems. The massacre strained Israeli–American relations, not least because of the damage it inflicted on US efforts to maintain the coalition against Saddam Hussein. Most Arabs regarded Saddam's occupation of Kuwait as not all that different from Israel's occupation of Arab land, and accused America of double standards in moving so energetically to put an end to the former after doing so little to end the latter. By joining in the universal outcry against Israel, the Bush Administration tried to limit the damage to itself. It even voted in favour of UN Security Council resolution 681 of 21 December 1990, which condemned Israel's treatment of the Palestinians in the occupied territories, and supported a separate appeal for an international conference to settle the Arab–Israeli dispute. The call for a conference was non-binding and did not specify a date, yet it highlighted Israel's growing isolation.

Another victim of the incident in Jerusalem was the policy of restraint in dealing with the intifada which had been inaugurated by Moshe Arens. Whereas his Labour predecessor Yitzhak Rabin had been responsible for the notorious policy of breaking bones, Arens had instructed the security forces to remain as unobtrusive as possible in the occupied territories, to avoid unnecessary provocations and confrontations, and to keep the use of armed force to a minimum. As a result, the death toll was reduced almost to nothing, the intifada appeared to run out of steam and the media began to lose interest.

The indiscriminate shooting of the 19 Palestinians dramatically reversed all these trends, and the intifada was transformed from a mass uprising against Israeli rule in the occupied territories into a low-intensity civil war between Arabs and Jews which no longer stopped at the pre-1967 border, or Green Line, as it is called in Israel. On both sides of the line the extremists started coming to the fore; the upshot was an escalation in the level of violence.

To check the wave of attacks on Israeli civilians and the pervasive insecurity caused by these attacks, the army and police barred Palestinians from coming into Israel. This was officially described as a temporary measure until calm was restored, but it nevertheless carried far-reaching implications. Over 100,000 Palestinians from the West Bank and Gaza used to travel daily to workplaces in Israel. One of the pillars of Israeli rule was the provision of employment to the inhabitants of the occupied territories. What the closure signified was that Arabs and Jews could not coexist peacefully, and that the two had to be separated by confining the Arabs to their areas. Paradoxically, it was a Likud government, ideologically committed to the unity of the land of Israel, which was now forced to revive the Green Line it had done so much to obliterate. The move was widely perceived in Israel as marking the beginning of a new era, and was welcomed as such by both Right and Left, though for rather different reasons. For the hard Right the move was a hopeful prelude to a more drastic policy, which some politicians openly advocate, of expelling the Palestinians from the West Bank and Gaza to clear the area for Jewish settlement. On the Left, the move was taken as the beginning of a separation between Israel and the occupied territories, and as further proof that the Likud's Greater Israel programme is not viable.

The massive influx of Jews from the Soviet Union reinforced the trend towards separation between the Arab and Jewish communities and economies. More than 180,000 Soviet immigrants arrived in Israel in 1990. Between one and two million were expected to arrive by 1995. For the Jewish state, this mass immigration or *aliya* meant fulfilment of the Zionist dream. But it also placed a severe strain on government finances already stretched by the cost of maintaining a military alert in the face of the Gulf crisis. Soviet Jews were taking up some of the jobs Palestinian workers had been forced to relinquish, and this only exacerbated the tension between the two communities. Likewise, Shamir's repeated statements to the effect that large-scale immigration requires a large Israel did nothing to allay Arab fears of Israeli expansionism.

Ever since 2 August 1990 the threat from the east had overshadowed the Israeli government's preoccupation with domestic problems. As the crisis unfolded, differences between Israel and America came to the surface. The new tendency manifest in Washington, of viewing the Gulf in terms of America's own interests and the interests of its Arab allies, fed Israeli anxieties that the influence of these allies over US strategy would grow, and gave rise to complaints that the US was being held captive by the anti-Iraq coalition it had formed.

Israel's commitment to keeping a low profile was based on the expectation that America would act to remove the Iraqi military threat. Any sign that America and its allies might settle for an Iraqi withdrawal from Kuwait and a return to the status quo ante was therefore sure to deepen Israel's concern. Bush's offer to hold talks with Iraq was received in Jerusalem with dismay. David Levy declared that Israel would assume the highest possible profile should its security come under threat. His government informed Washington that it would feel free to deal with the Iraqi military threat if the United States and the international community did not. In the Israeli press this message was read as expressing a new policy in relation to the Gulf crisis. It certainly revealed some tension, not to say mistrust, between Israel and the United States, and it seemed to reserve for Israel the right to take independent action to counter the Iraqi threat.

From Israel's point of view, the best possible scenario for ending the Gulf crisis was an American military strike to destroy Saddam Hussein's regime, his army and his military infrastructure, thereby erasing once and for all the threat from Baghdad, preferably without Israeli involvement. Although the Israeli government was careful to avoid giving the impression that it was egging America on to go to war, its influential friends there, like Henry Kissinger, were publicly advocating this option from the first week of the crisis. A second scenario which might have been just about acceptable to Israel was to maintain the siege of Iraq, and to keep the forces of the US and its allies in the region until someone in Iraq brought down the regime. The worst scenario for Israel was an Iraqi withdrawal from Kuwait which would leave Saddam Hussein with his formidable military machine – army, long-range missiles, chemical and biological weapons and nuclear programme – intact. Such an outcome would permit him to continue to project his military and political power in the region, and it would erode Israel's deterrent capability, which lies at the heart of its security doctrine. The long-term danger would have been greatly magnified if Saddam were to emerge as the victor from the crisis by holding on to parts of Kuwait or by extracting concessions on the Palestinian issue.

But whether the crisis provoked by the Iraqi invasion of Kuwait was to be resolved by war or by containment or by compromise, one thing was certain: in the aftermath of the crisis Israel would come under the most intense international pressure for fresh ideas and for real movement to solve the Palestinian problem. There were signs that even the Bush Administration – while maintaining its refusal to discuss the two problems simultaneously on the grounds that to do so would reward Iraqi aggression – was beginning to bend to pressure to accept linkage between the Gulf crisis and the Israeli–Palestinian conflict.

The Iraqi invasion of Kuwait did not alter the nature of the Palestinian problem in any fundamental way, but it did profoundly alter the international context. By posing the first major challenge to the post-Cold War international order, the Iraqi dictator inadvertently helped to forge a remarkable concert of powers that included the United States, Western Europe, the Soviet Union and some of the most powerful Arab states. All these powers were now committed, in varying degrees, to promoting a negotiated settlement to the Israeli–Palestinian conflict once the immediate challenge from Iraq was dealt with. They were unlikely to tolerate an attempt by Israel to return to the 'do nothing' policies of recent years. A growing number of Israelis also came to recognise that time was not on their side, that there could be no military solution to the intifada, and that bold political initiatives were needed to arrest the slide towards civil war. Yitzhak Shamir, the 75-year-old master of the art of stonewalling, was not of that number.

# FOURTEEN

# Changing Places:
## The Madrid Peace Conference

S ince its origins at the end of the nineteenth century, the
Jewish–Arab battle for the possession of Palestine has been
accompanied by another battle, fought in the international
arena – the battle for hearts and minds. Also since its origins, the
Jewish–Arab conflict has been an existential conflict between two
movements for national liberation, one Jewish and one Palestinian.
It is, in essence, a struggle between two peoples for one land. But
the Zionists who led the Jewish struggle for national liberation
deliberately obscured this essence by portraying Palestine as 'a land
without a people for a people without a land'.

Zionism may have been one of the most successful public relations
exercises of the twentieth century, and Palestinian nationalism one
of the least, but at the Middle East peace conference which convened
in Madrid in late October 1991 the Palestinians, for the first time
ever, began to gain the upper hand in the propaganda battle. It
was a historic reversal which could not fail to affect the course of
the Israeli–Palestinian conflict in the last decade of the twentieth
century and beyond. In this chapter I examine the reasons behind
the apparent shift in the respective fortunes of the protagonists, and

analyse the significance of the Madrid conference for the participants and for the American-led peace process which was set in motion in the aftermath of the 1991 Gulf War.

The early Zionists clearly grasped the power of words in the struggle for independence. Theodor Herzl was not a politician but a failed playwright whose book *The Jewish State*, published in 1896, evoked a powerful response among Jews. On 3 September 1897, Herzl wrote in his diary: 'In Basle I founded the Jewish State.' He was referring to the first Zionist Congress which he had convened in Basle. The 'Basle Programme' stated that 'the aim of Zionism is to create for the Jewish people a home in Palestine secured by public law'. Both the title of Herzl's book and his diary entry suggest that the aim of Zionism, from the start, was an independent Jewish state in Palestine. This long-term aim was deliberately blurred, however, because it would have provoked Arab hostility and been a liability in the struggle to mobilise international support for the establishment of a Jewish national home in Palestine.

Herzl's diary entry highlights a second important aspect of political Zionism, namely, the belief that the commitment to an idea and resolutions passed in international gatherings have a crucial role to play in paving the road to statehood. It was precisely because of the military impotence of their movement that the early Zionists set so much store by winning the propaganda battle and mobilising worldwide the traditional Jewish talents of advocacy and persuasion. They always concentrated their efforts on the leading great power of the day: first, the Ottoman Turks, then the British, and then the Americans. In order to appeal to public opinion as well as the governments of the great powers, the Zionists cultivated an image of reasoned moderation. Their tactics were always flexible even if their long-term aim remained fixed and inflexible. They accepted in principle nearly all the compromise proposals put forward by Britain for settling the Palestine problem, in the process enhancing their reputation for reasonableness. They accepted the judgement of Solomon to divide the disputed land between themselves and the Palestinians. The Zionist leaders, especially David Ben-Gurion, were also adept at presenting the Palestinian position in the conflict as unreasonable. It is not that they were not genuinely interested in a compromise solution. But since the claims of the two sides could not be reconciled, it was preferable that the Palestinians should bear the responsibility for the deadlock.

When the United Nations voted for partition in November 1947, showing that the logic of partition had become inescapable, the Zionists accepted the plan with alacrity, although a Jewish state within the UN borders would have scarcely been viable. Accepting the resolution of the world body put them within the framework of international legality and provided a charter of legitimacy for the Jewish state. They counted on the Grand Mufti to put himself on the wrong side of the international community by rejecting the UN partition plan, and reject it he did. It was this sophisticated Zionist approach to playing the game of nations which helped them to win a state of their own in 1948, just as the diplomatic inflexibility of the Palestinians helped to bring about the greatest disaster in their history.

Israel and the Palestinians did not change places overnight. The reversal of their strategies and tactics was the result of a gradual process which only reached its climax in Madrid. One landmark in this process was the rise to power in 1977 of the Likud Party, which rejected the principle of partition, rejected territorial compromise with Jordan, and staked a claim to the West Bank as an inalienable part of the Land of Israel. Sinai, which was not part of the Biblical homeland, was traded by Menachem Begin for peace with Egypt despite opposition from right-wing colleagues like Yitzhak Shamir, his successor as prime minister.

Another major landmark in this process was the peace offensive launched by the PLO in 1988. In November of that year the Palestinian National Council (PNC) met in Algiers, where it accepted the principle of partition and a two-state solution based on all relevant UN resolutions going back to November 1947. The claim to the whole of Palestine was finally laid to rest and a declaration of independence was issued for a mini-state in the West Bank, East Jerusalem and the Gaza Strip. The passage of these resolutions through the Palestinians' 'parliament' was accompanied by a conscious attempt to project a more moderate image. A special effort was made to gain respectability by dissociating the PLO from international terrorism. PLO chairman Yasser Arafat made a number of statements on the subject, but they failed to satisfy the United States. In the end the US virtually dictated the text of a declaration which Arafat delivered in Geneva. Although it sounded as if Arafat was renouncing tourism, what he actually said was 'we absolutely renounce terrorism'. This statement, coming on top of the PNC resolutions, opened the door to the initiation of the dialogue between the PLO and the US government.

By the time the PLO was prepared to accept partition, Israel had changed its mind. Israel's response to the momentous changes that were taking place within the Palestinian camp was its series of no's: no to withdrawal from the occupied territories, no to an international conference, no to negotiation with the PLO, no to a Palestinian state. The only positive idea to come out of Israel was Yitzhak Shamir's plan of May 1989 for the holding of elections in the West Bank and in the Gaza Strip, leading to limited autonomy. But Shamir only put forward this idea in response to pressure from Washington, and to the latter's intense frustration he retreated from it at the first sign of danger that the Palestinians would accept it.

As mentioned in the previous chapter, the PLO suffered a major setback in its quest for legitimacy during the 1990–91 Gulf crisis. Frustrated by Israel's rejection of all its peace overtures and the suspension of the dialogue with the US, the PLO recklessly bet on Saddam Hussein and lost. While Saddam tried to link Iraqi withdrawal from Kuwait to Israeli withdrawal from the occupied territories, America resisted this linkage on the grounds that the two disputes were unrelated, but it promised to seek a settlement of the Arab–Israeli conflict once the Gulf conflict had been resolved. The convening of the Middle East peace conference in Madrid represented the fulfilment of this promise. The 'mother of all battles' threatened by the Iraqi tyrant in the Gulf was followed by the 'mother of all peace conferences'.

What distinguished Madrid from previous Arab–Israeli conferences was that the Palestinians were represented there for the first time on a footing of equality with Israel. Madrid registered the arrival of the Palestinians, long the missing party, at the Middle East conference table. That in itself was a major gain in international recognition. The Palestinians had to pay a stiff price for their ticket of admission to the conference chamber. Even at the level of symbols, so crucial to a movement for national liberation, no concessions were made to them. No Palestinian flag was displayed and no battle fatigues or *keffiyehs* were worn in Madrid. All the members of the Palestinian delegation wore smart business suits. As far as dress was concerned, they were indistinguishable from the two former Texas oil men who represented the United States at the talks.

The mere presence of official Palestinian representatives in Madrid marked a change, if not a reversal, of Israel's long-standing refusal to consider the Palestinians as a partner to negotiations, as an *interlocuteur valable*. Israel's veto of members of the PLO and residents of East Jerusalem resulted in a Palestinian delegation which was part of a joint Jordanian–Palestinian delegation and an advisory council, with Faisal al-Husseini as coordinator and Dr Hanan Ashrawi as spokeswoman. Ironically, by excluding the PLO, Israel helped the Arabs of the occupied territories to put forward fresh faces. The Palestinian delegation to the conference was the most effective team the Palestinians had ever fielded at an international gathering, and it played the game of nations in Madrid with outstanding skill and flexibility.

The opening speeches by the heads of the Israeli and the Palestinian delegations faithfully reflected the positions of the two sides. Mr Shamir, like the Bourbons of France, seemed to have learnt nothing and to have forgotten nothing. The whole tone of his speech was anachronistic, saturated with the stale rhetoric of the past, and inappropriate for the occasion. He used the platform to deliver the kind of promotional speech for Israel that would normally be heard in an Israel Bonds drive. His version of the Arab–Israeli conflict was singularly narrow and blinkered, portraying Israel simply as the victim of Arab aggression and refusing to acknowledge that any evolution had taken place in the Arab or Palestinian attitude to Israel. All the Arabs, according to Shamir, wanted to see Israel destroyed; the only difference between them was over the way to bring about its destruction. His speech, while long on anti-Arab clichés, was exceedingly short on substance. By insisting that the root cause of the conflict is not territory but the Arab refusal to recognise the legitimacy of the State of Israel, Shamir came dangerously close to rejecting the whole basis of the conference – UN resolutions 242 and 338, and the principle of land for peace.

The contrast between Mr Shamir's speech and the speech of Dr Haidar Abdel-Shafi, the head of the Palestinian delegation, could have hardly been more striking in tone, spirit or substance. This single speech contained more evidence of new thinking than all the other speeches, Arab and Israeli, put together. It was, by any standards, a remarkable speech and its impact was only heightened by the quiet, dignified quality of the delivery. Dr Abdel-Shafi reminded the audience that it was time for the Palestinians to narrate their own story. While touching on the past, his speech was not backward-looking but forward-looking. 'We seek neither an admission of guilt after the fact, nor vengeance for past iniquities,' he explained, 'but rather an act of will that would make a just peace a reality.' In the name of the Palestinian people, Dr Abdel-Shafi went on:

We wish to directly address the Israeli people with whom we have had a prolonged exchange of pain: let us share hope instead. We are willing to live side by side on the land and share the promise of the future. Sharing, however, requires two partners willing to share as equals. Mutuality and reciprocity must replace domination and hostility for there to be genuine reconciliation and coexistence under international legality. Your security and ours are mutually dependent, as intertwined as the fears and nightmares of our children.

Dr Abdel-Shafi accused Israel of brutal oppression in the occupied territories but he sought to portray the Israelis as fellow victims:

> We have seen you anguish over the transformation of your sons and daughters into instruments of blind and violent occupation, and we are sure that at no time did you envisage such a role for the children whom you thought would forge your future. We have seen you look back in deepest sorrow at the tragedy of your past and look on in horror at the disfigurement of the victim turned oppressor. Not for this have you nurtured your hopes, dreams and your offspring.

This stress on the human cost of occupation, and empathy for the other side, was followed by a handsome tribute to those Israelis who had expressed sympathy and solidarity with the Palestinians.

Dr Abdel-Shafi's basic message was that the Israeli occupation had to end, the Palestinians had a right to self-determination, and that they were determined to pursue this right relentlessly until they achieved statehood. The intifada, he suggested, had already begun to embody the Palestinian state and to build its institutions and infrastructure. But while staking a claim to Palestinian statehood, Dr Abdel-Shafi qualified it in two significant ways. First, he accepted the need for a transitional stage, provided interim arrangements were not transformed into permanent status. Second, he envisaged a confederation between an ultimately independent Palestine and Jordan. Dr Abdel-Shafi's speech in Madrid was both the most eloquent and the most moderate presentation of the Palestinian case ever made by an official Palestinian spokesman since the beginning of the conflict at the end of the nineteenth century. The PLO, for all its growing moderation, had never been able to articulate such a clear-cut peace overture to Israel because of its internal divisions and the constraints of inter-Arab politics. No PLO official had ever been able to declare so unambiguously that a Palestinian state would be ready for a confederation with Jordan. The whole tenor of the speech was more conciliatory and constructive than even the most moderate statements of the PLO. In the words of Afif Safieh, a senior PLO official, the speech was 'unreasonably reasonable'.

There was a palpable feeling of history-in-the-making as the soft-spoken doctor from Gaza read his text in the magnificent Hall of Columns in the royal palace in Madrid. Future historians will look back on 31 October 1991 as a landmark in the quest for reconciliation between the national claims of the Palestinians and the Israelis. The origins of the doctor's speech were highly revealing of the strategy adopted by the Palestinian leaders, including the PLO, for the Madrid conference. Suggestions that the speech be read in Arabic were turned down on the grounds that it was not intended for the folks back home but for the world at large. The main aim of the speech was to counter the harmful stereotypes that had become attached to the Palestinians in world opinion, and to humanise the Palestinian cause. The other aim was to convince the Israeli public that the Palestinians are genuinely committed to peaceful coexistence.

Thirteen drafts of the speech were prepared before consensus was reached on the final text. Dr Hanan Ashrawi, Professor of English literature at Birzeit University on the West Bank, was the principal author. She confessed that the speech was written on the assumption that one day it would be taught in primary schools in the state of Palestine. Contributions to the speech were made by fellow Palestinians including Dr Abdel-Shafi, Mamduh Aker, Nabil Sha'ath (an adviser to Yasser Arafat) and the PLO chairman himself. The speech struck just the right note and gave the Palestinians their finest day in Madrid. One Palestinian delegate was even moved to declare, echoing Theodor Herzl nearly a century earlier: 'In Madrid we founded the Palestinian state.' In the international media the speech received every accolade. Even some of the Israeli officials in Madrid professed themselves to be moved by the speech. The calm and reassuring manner of the elderly physician from Gaza only served to underscore the humanity and reasonableness of the message he was bearing.

Abba Eban's old jibe that the Palestinians 'never miss an opportunity to miss an opportunity for peace', was singularly inappropriate on this occasion; if anything, it could be turned against the Israeli side.

Even the composition of the two delegations was indicative of the historic transformation that had taken place on the road to peace. Half the Palestinian delegates to Madrid were doctors and university professors. The Israeli delegation, on the other hand, was led – as the Syrian foreign minister reminded the conference – by a former terrorist who in 1948 was wanted by the British for the assassination of Count Bernadotte, the UN mediator to Palestine. 'This man', he said, brandishing a picture of the 32-year-old Shamir, 'killed peace mediators'.

Shamir's performance in Madrid raised serious questions as to whether he and his generation of Likud Party leaders could ever put the past behind them and work towards a genuine accommodation with the Palestinians. Listening to his speech, one Israeli journalist wondered whether his officials had not, by mistake, taken out of their files one of Golda Meir's speeches from the early 1970s. Shamir's basic thesis was that the Arabs still refused to accept Israel as a permanent entity in the Middle East. But the peace with Egypt and the presence in the conference chamber around him of representatives from all the confrontation states, as well as the authorised representatives of the Palestinians, told a completely different story.

The truth is that the Arabs had recognised Israel when they signed the armistice agreements with it under UN auspices in Rhodes in 1949, and that there had been countless meetings – some secret, some open – between them and Israel ever since. But Israel continued to claim that the Arabs did not recognise it and to insist on direct negotiations. Some people, it would seem, are never satisfied. After the first day of talks, Mr Shamir was asked how it felt to sit down finally face to face with all Israel's Arab adversaries. He answered: 'It was a regular day.' Shamir's presence was as much of a liability to the Israeli public relations effort in Madrid as the absence of the PLO was a boon to the Palestinians. In charge of the Israeli public relations effort was Binyamin Netanyahu, then deputy foreign minister and later leader of the Likud, who had the advantage of speaking in the kind of short sound bites beloved of American television interviewers. Mr Netanyahu maintained the highest Israeli profile in the daily war of the sound bites waged in

Madrid. But he fought a losing battle. As Michael Sheridan wrote in the *Independent* on 2 November 1991:

> The Israelis possessed the best organised, most efficient, least flustered, public relations team at the conference, with Mr Netanyahu, its intellectual bruiser, rushing before the CNN cameras every other minute. But for all its military élan, the Israeli PR machine has without question lost the battle for hearts and minds to the Palestinians this week. Its principal problem was that a million glib sound bites from Mr Netanyahu could not efface the image of Yitzhak Shamir, scowling in repose and truculent in action, a visual epitome of the policy he represents.

Netanyahu was up against Hanan Ashrawi, the spokeswoman of the Palestinian delegation, whose eloquence was matched by patent sincerity and a refreshing habit of answering reporters' questions directly and unambiguously. As spokeswoman, Dr Ashrawi maintained the most visible profile in daily press briefings and numerous interviews to the media. She was clearly the star of the show. Overnight she had become the most prominent woman in the Arab political world. She was every bit as articulate and assertive as the Israelis, and considerably more sophisticated in handling the media. To the American public, in particular, she presented an intelligent and sensitive human face and a powerful Palestinian voice.

The Palestinian spokesmen also cut a much more credible figure than the PLO chairman. The authority of the PLO was never challenged and the delegates from the occupied territories did not set themselves up as an alternative leadership to the PLO. On the contrary, there was very close coordination between the Palestinian delegation and the PLO before, during and after the conference. But in Madrid the Arabs of Palestine showed that they had another group of able and authentic leaders better qualified to present their case before the tribunal of international public opinion than the discredited leadership in Tunis.

If the Palestinians proved to Shamir that he could no longer rely on them to let him off the hook, he had better luck with Farouk al-

Shara, the foreign minister of Syria. Al-Shara played the old record of rejectionism and vituperation. He was without doubt the most militant and radical Arab representative in Madrid, and he was also the most isolated. The conference degenerated into an unseemly slanging match between the Israeli and the Syrian. Shamir denounced Syria as one of the most repressive and tyrannical regimes in the world. Al-Shara replied in kind, denouncing Israel as a terrorist state led by a former terrorist, and later refused to answer questions from Israeli journalists at a press conference. Against the background of this strident display of Syrian rejectionism, the readiness of the Palestinians to engage in constructive dialogue with the Israelis was all the more striking.

After the plenary session was over, stage two of the peace process began in Madrid. It took the form of a series of separate bilateral meetings between Israel and each of the Arab delegations. Here, too, the Syrians were the most rigid and intransigent, while the Palestinians seemed more eager than any of the Arab delegations to forge ahead with the talks in order to bring about a freeze on Jewish settlements in the occupied territories. As a result of these differences, the common Arab front collapsed. Syria held out for a unified Arab position to back its demand for an Israeli commitment to trade the Golan Heights for peace before the bilateral talks began. Among the Palestinian delegates there was considerable irritation with Syria's attempt to set an overall Arab agenda in the talks. They broke ranks with Syria and not only held their meeting with the Israelis but shook hands in front of the cameras. What the Palestinians were saying, in effect, was that Syria had no power of veto over their own moves, and that they would not allow the 'peace process' with Israel to be held hostage to inter-Arab politics.

Another key to Palestinian success in Madrid was the political alliance they formed with the United States, formally one of the co-sponsors but actually the driving force behind the conference. The whole thing was carefully stage-managed by the Americans, with Secretary of State James Baker acting as the chief puppeteer. Despite the unreasonable conditions imposed by Israel, the Palestinians agreed to participate because Baker warned them that this would be their only chance. He also promised them that once the talks were underway, all the pressure would be on Israel to start making concessions. The emergence of an American–Palestinian axis broke the familiar mould of Middle Eastern politics. Of all the delegations to Madrid, the Palestinians were the only ones who agreed to nearly all the American requests on both procedure and substance. It was the US officials who advised the Palestinians to appeal to the American public, and this advice was followed almost to the point of neglecting public opinion in other countries. In what practically amounted to a dress rehearsal, the Americans went over different scenarios with the Palestinians before the conference in order to minimise the risk of an Israeli walkout. The Americans thus had every reason to be pleased with the performance put on by the novices in their début on the international stage.

What mattered much more than the polished performances by the debutants in Madrid was the fact that they were a lot closer than the Israelis to the American position. They explicitly accepted that the negotiations should be based on UN resolutions 242 and 338 and the principle of land for peace, whereas Israel did not. They got on board the bus, which Baker told them would come only once, while Shamir continued to quibble over the fare, the powers of the driver, the rights of other passengers, and the bus's speed, route and final destination.

The reversal of the Palestinian and Israeli positions in relation to US policy in the Middle East carried the most profound historical significance. In the past Israel had been America's principal ally in the region, whereas the Palestinians counted for little in American eyes. 'What about the Palestinians?' John Foster Dulles was asked in 1956. 'Well,' he replied, 'they are unlucky because they fell under the feet of elephants. The old generation will die and the young will forget.' The Palestinians have not forgotten and the then occupant of Dulles's room in the State Department clearly recognised that the Palestinians could no longer be ignored.

A parallel change was also evident in America's attitude to Israel. The collapse of the Soviet Union as a rival superpower and Saddam

Hussein's adventure in Kuwait combined to call into question the special relationship between the United States and Israel. In the past, US aid to Israel, totalling $77 billion, had been justified on the grounds that Israel helped protect American interests in this vital part of the world against the twin threats of communism and pan-Arab nationalism. But the communist threat had vanished and, when the crucial test came in the war with Iraq, America's much-vaunted strategic asset proved to be an embarrassment and a liability.

The official American position towards the Arab–Israeli conflict had remained unchanged since 1967. America supported the exchange of land for peace, refused to acknowledge the Israeli annexation of East Jerusalem and regarded the building of Jewish settlements in the occupied territories as illegal and an obstacle to peace. What changed in the run-up to Madrid was the evident determination of the Bush Administration to do more than repeat these positions like a gramophone record. The moderation shown by the Palestinians in Madrid made it easier for the Bush Administration to tilt further in their direction and away from Israel. At Madrid the Palestinians were on the side of the most powerful man on earth. As America and the Palestinians became closer, Israel and America began rapidly to drift apart. For the leader of a small state so heavily dependent on US support, Shamir behaved in a very odd way. He ignored the golden rule of the leaders of mainstream Zionism: never stage a confrontation with a friendly great power which you cannot hope to win.

Shamir was disturbed by what he described as an increasingly one-sided approach by the United States to the Arab–Israeli conflict. He also felt that he was personally humiliated during his visit to Washington. On 21 November 1991 he came out of a meeting with Baker saying there had been no agreement on the venue and date of the next round of peace talks. He expected to discuss this question at his meeting with President Bush the next day. But before he was able to do so, the Americans formally invited both Israel and the Arabs to Washington to start bilateral talks on 4 December. To make matters worse, the letters of invitation included suggestions on questions of substance designed to narrow the gap between Israel and the Arabs.

The Americans could not afford to lose the momentum of the peace process started in Madrid. They felt they had to keep the pressure on all parties, especially Israel and Syria, to keep moving forward before getting bogged down in the 1992 US presidential election and the Israeli general election. But Shamir and his Cabinet colleagues were outraged by America's failure to consult and by its attempt to force the pace. A meeting in the US capital with all the Arab delegations under the same roof on the same day was not their idea of stage two in the peace process. They responded by asking the US for a delay of five days to allow more time for consultations and clarifications. Some ministers wanted to withdraw from the talks altogether. Yuval Ne'eman, the hardline minister of science, suggested sarcastically that the Cabinet add a chair for the US ambassador to Israel, so he could give the orders directly. Rechavam Ze'evi, a Cabinet minister from the rightist Moledet party, claimed that Washington was treating the Israelis like 'the Cherokee tribe of Indians that was put onto a reservation'. Shamir made a series of contradictory statements but was forced to climb down when the US held firm on the venue and date of the talks.

The Israeli public did not rally behind Prime Minister Shamir during this confrontation with the Bush Administration. Opinion polls revealed that the Israeli public was much more willing to trade land for peace than was its government. Foreign Minister David Levy, within the government the strongest advocate of the talks, said that Israel was acting 'out of anger rather than logic', and 'treating marginal issues as if they were substantive'. Some members of the opposition privately justified the abrasive behaviour of the Bush Administration; without it, they argued, Shamir would pile one delay on top of another. 'On the record? It's horrible what the Americans did', an opposition member of the Knesset said to an American journalist. 'Off the record? I love it. As Woody Allen said, if the end doesn't justify the means, what does?'

The reservations over diplomatic procedure voiced by the Israeli government masked deep-seated unease about the content and direction of the peace process. There was a feeling that the moment of truth was approaching and that Israel would be subjected to mounting pressure to make concessions for peace. Shamir had been suspicious about this process from the start. The last thing he wanted was the kind of brisk and concrete down-to-business approach urged by the Americans. A past master at playing for time, he resorted to all his familiar tricks of obstinacy, obfuscation and procrastination. While calling repeatedly for direct negotiations between Israel and the Arabs, Shamir continued to erect obstacles on the path to such negotiation. The gap between the declaratory level and the operational level of his foreign policy had grown so wide that it was difficult to avoid the conclusion that his real aim was to scuttle the peace talks while ensuring that the Arabs took the blame.

Since 1948, Israel's leaders, of all political complexions, had never ceased to proclaim their readiness to meet the Arabs anywhere, at any time, to discuss peace. When Golda Meir was prime minister, even her officials tired of hearing the refrain endlessly repeated. But at the Madrid conference the moment of truth had arrived. Israel's leaders could no longer hide behind the claim that there was no one to talk to on the other side.

Whatever history's verdict on Shamir's role in the Madrid peace talks, his behaviour amply demonstrated that the rejectionist boot was now firmly on the other foot. The Israeli position as presented by Shamir was not only intransigent but was seen to be intransigent. The Palestinians, on the other hand, appeared to have learnt a great deal from the mistakes of their leaders and from the success of their opponents, and to have distilled new wisdom from past experience. Foremost among the lessons they learnt were the value of good public relations, the importance of not staking out maximalist positions, the advantage of saying 'yes, but' rather than saying 'no', and the virtue of a gradualist approach. Above all, the Palestinians clearly recognised at last the value for a weak national liberation movement of having a powerful sponsor when playing the rough and cruel game of international politics.

Following the historic meeting in Madrid, the peace process encountered severe challenges and met with only limited success. Arab and world reactions to Israel's brutal treatment of Palestinian militants was one complicating factor. The challenge of Hamas to the PLO, and of Jewish settlers in the occupied territories to the Jewish state, further demonstrated the fragility of even the most lauded developments in the search for peace in the Middle East, such as the conclusion of a limited peace agreement between Israel and the PLO in September 1993, and the subsequent achievement of limited Palestinian autonomy in Jericho and the Gaza Strip in May 1994. Such problems threatened the positive outcomes of a peace process, begun at Madrid, which was then widely seen as a watershed in the history of the Israeli–Palestinian conflict. At Madrid and subsequently, the Palestinians not only demonstrated a capacity for moderation, but were seen to be moderate. Perhaps this was the most encouraging outcome of all. If, despite all the difficulties, the Palestinians can still adhere to this quintessentially Zionist strategy, they may well end up with a state of their own – just like the Zionists.

# FIFTEEN

# Prelude to the Oslo Accord:
## Likud, Labour and the Palestinians

The mutual recognition between Israel and the PLO, and the Declaration of Principles on Palestinian self-government in Gaza and Jericho, signed in Washington on 13 September 1993, marked a historic breakthrough in the century-old conflict over Palestine. Here I want to explore the background to this Accord by comparing and contrasting the policies of the Likud bloc and of the Labour Party towards the peace talks that got under way at the October 1991 Madrid conference. Most Arabs believe that there is no significant difference between the two parties. It might be instructive, therefore, to examine the record of the Likud-led and the Labour-led governments in the peace talks with the Palestinians in order to determine whether this is indeed the case.

When the Labour Party emerged as the victor in the Israeli general election in June 1992, a BBC correspondent asked an Arab janitor in Jerusalem for his reaction. 'Do you see my left shoe?' asked the Arab indifferently by way of response. 'That is Yitzhak Rabin. Do you see my right shoe? That is Yitzhak Shamir. Two Yitzhaks, two shoes, so what's the difference?' This feeling that there is not much to choose between the leaders of Israel's two main parties is not confined to

Arabs. When Rabin served as defence minister in the national unity government headed by Shamir from 1986 to 1990, there was a joke in Israel which went as follows: 'What is the difference between a left-wing Likudnik and a right-wing Likudnik? Answer: a left-wing Likudnik is a follower of Yitzhak Shamir, and a right-wing Likudnik is a follower of Yitzhak Rabin.'

The traditional foreign policies of the rival parties led by the two Yitzhaks also display some striking similarities. The critic William Hazlitt compared the Whig and the Tory parties in the early nineteenth century to two rival coach companies that splash mud on one another but go by the same route to the same destination. It is tempting to apply the same analogy to the Labour and Likud parties which have dominated the Israeli political scene since 1948, but to do so would be to take a simplistic view of Israeli politics. No one would deny that Likud and Labour splash mud on one another, and it is true that both parties used to share a blind spot regarding the Palestinians, preferring to treat the Arab–Israeli conflict as an inter-state conflict. It is true that both parties are deeply opposed to Palestinian nationalism and deny that the Palestinians have a right to national self-determination. The notorious statement that there is no such thing as a Palestinian people came not from the Likud but from that old Labour Party battleaxe, Golda Meir. It is also true that, until recently, both parties refused to negotiate with the PLO, and that both remain unconditionally opposed to the establishment of an independent Palestinian state.

Yet the differences between the Likud and Labour are quite significant, both in the realm of ideology and in the realm of practical policy. The final destination of the two parties was different and they sought to get to their respective destinations by different routes. This is why the rise to power of the Likud in 1977, in addition to ending three decades of uninterrupted Labour rule at home, constituted such a sharp break in Israeli foreign policy. And this is why the Labour victory of June 1992, which ended a decade and a half of Likud hegemony, constituted another watershed in Israel's relations with the Palestinians.

As discussed earlier (see Chapter 13), the Labour Party traditionally had a pro-Hashemite orientation. In 1947 its leaders reached an agreement with King Abdullah of Jordan to partition Palestine at the expense of the Palestinians. The Palestinian state envisaged in the UN partition plan of 29 November 1947 never saw the light of day. What was left of Arab Palestine was annexed by Jordan. After 1948, the Labour Party leaders remained actively committed to the survival of the Hashemite monarchy in Amman and to the suppression of Palestinian nationalism. After the war of 1967, the Labour Party adopted the so-called 'Jordanian option'. This posited that there is no room for a Palestinian state west of the Jordan river. The aim of the policy was to reach a settlement with King Hussein based on territorial compromise, on the return of most but not all of the West Bank to Jordanian rule.

The Likud's ideology can also be summed up in two words – Greater Israel. According to this ideology, Judea and Samaria, the biblical terms for the West Bank, are an integral part of *Eretz Yisrael*, the Land of Israel. The Likud categorically denies that Jordan has any claim to sovereignty over this area, or that the Palestinians have any right to self-determination within it. All that the Likud would offer the Palestinians is limited autonomy in running their daily lives. The first Palestinian autonomy plan was put forward by Menachem Begin in December 1977 when negotiating the Camp David Accords with President Anwar Sadat of Egypt. It is essential to understand that, then as now, autonomy as conceived by Likud applies only to the people of the occupied territories and not to the land. Israel retains its claim to sovereignty over the West Bank and Gaza under this plan. Yigal Allon, the late Labour Party leader, remarked of the plan that only in Marc Chagall's paintings do people float in mid-air, free of the force of gravity, and that it is impossible to translate this artistic quirk into any meaningful political reality. It was impossible then, and it remained impossible under Begin's successor, Yitzhak Shamir, who was actually opposed to the Camp David Accords.

One way of summing up the differences between the Likud and Labour is by focusing on their attitude towards the principle of partition. The Likud rejects partition as the basis for a settlement with either the Palestinians or Jordan, laying claim to the whole territory west of the Jordan river. The Labour Party, on the other hand, accepts the principle of partition – the notion of trading land for peace – as a basis for a settlement, but has traditionally preferred Jordan to the Palestinians as a partner. Yitzhak Shamir himself remains something of an enigma despite his prominence in public life during the decade that preceded his crushing electoral defeat. Losing his family in the Nazi Holocaust was a formative experience that could only reinforce his stark, Hobbesian view of the world. Although he rarely mentioned the Holocaust in his public utterances, the experience seared his psyche and continues to colour his attitude to his people's other great adversary – the Arabs. In Shamir's monochromatic picture of the world, 'the Arabs' featured as a monolithic and implacable enemy bent on the destruction of the State of Israel and on throwing the Jews into the sea. Any signs of a change of heart on the Arab side were habitually dismissed by Shamir as the product of purely tactical considerations. 'The Arabs are still the same Arabs,' he was fond of saying, 'and the sea is still the same sea.' A general disbelief in the possibility of peace and a refusal to pay any concrete price for it are part and parcel of this deeply entrenched view of a hostile world, bad Arabs, and permanent danger.

On Shamir's position vis-à-vis the Palestinians, two rather different interpretations were advanced. One interpretation, popular among American Jews, was that Shamir was a tough bargainer, but that if the terms were right he would strike a deal and use his impeccable nationalist credentials to push it through, as Begin had done with Egypt. The other view was that on the Palestinian issue Shamir was a hopeless case, because his ideological commitment to the Land of Israel ruled out any territorial compromise. As Avishai Margalit put it:

Shamir is not a bargainer. Shamir is a two-dimensional man. One dimension is the length of the Land of Israel, the second, its width. Since Shamir's historical vision is measured in inches, he won't give an inch. He will not bargain about the Land of Israel or about any interim agreement that would involve the least risk of losing control over the occupied territories.[1]

While the first Bush Administration worked to convene the Middle East peace conference in Madrid, Shamir continued the policy of building more Jewish settlements on the West Bank. He insisted, as a condition for attending the conference, that the Palestinians could not be represented by Yasser Arafat (or any other PLO leader based in Tunis) or by residents of East Jerusalem, but only by local leaders from the West Bank and Gaza who would form part of a joint Jordanian–Palestinian delegation. It was one of those rare international disputes in which one party chose not only its own team for the match but also that of the other party. Although he succeeded in imposing his own rules for Palestinian representation, Shamir went to Madrid in a defiant and truculent mood. The letters of invitation stated that the negotiations would proceed on the basis of UN Security Council resolution 242 of November 1967, which incorporated the principle of trading land for peace, but Shamir would not explicitly accept either the resolution or the principle as a basis for negotiation.

As noted in the preceding chapter, Shamir used the platform to deliver his speech portraying Israel as the innocent victim of Arab aggression and categorically denying that any change had taken place in the Arab attitude to Israel. The root cause of the conflict, he insisted, was not territory but the Arab refusal to recognise the legitimacy of the State of Israel. Hence he was not prepared to trade territory for peace; all he would offer was peace for peace. Some observers chose to interpret the speech as the opening gambit in a protracted bargaining process. Concessions, they said, would come only once the substantive negotiations got under way. Subsequent events, however, were to prove that Shamir's opening speech in Madrid represented his basic, inflexible, and unchangeable position. For him Palestinian autonomy in what was to be a transitional period of five years was intended to foreclose all other options, not to pave the way to any further Israeli concessions.

Following the Madrid conference, five rounds of bilateral talks under Likud were held in Washington. Throughout these talks, the Shamir government continued to rule out swapping land for peace. A good deal of time was taken up with procedural wrangles and it was not until Israel agreed to negotiate separately with the Palestinian and Jordanian delegations that the substantive issues could be addressed. Even then the negotiations proceeded at a snail's pace and ended in deadlock. The negotiations between Israel and the Palestinians only highlighted the immense gap between them. The Palestinians began with the assumption that they are a people with national rights and that the interim arrangements under discussion were the precursor to independence and should be shaped accordingly. The Israeli government started with the assumption that the Palestinians are the inhabitants of the territories with no national rights of any kind and certainly no right to independence, not even after the end of the transitional period.

During the fourth round of talks towards the end of February 1992, the two sides tabled incompatible plans for the interim period of self-government. The Palestinian blueprint was for a Palestinian Interim Self-Governing Authority, PISGA for short. Israel's counter-proposal was for 'interim self-government' arrangements. Behind the two names lurked irreconcilable positions on the nature, scope, and purpose of 'interim self-government'. Israel's proposal, anchored in the 1978 Camp David Accords, applied only to people, not to territory. In some respects it offered the Palestinians less than Begin's 1977 autonomy plan, which they had rejected scornfully at the time as the power to 'collect garbage and exterminate mosquitoes'. While Shamir's proposal failed to meet the minimal expectations of the Palestinians, it provoked his ultra-nationalist partners in government to quit the coalition. With the departure of Tsomet and Tehiya, the countdown to the next election began. During the subsequent campaign Shamir declared that the settlement drive in Judea and Samaria would continue and that he himself would not be party to any deal that placed this drive at risk. Consequently, the June 1992 election became almost a referendum on the peace issue. Israelis were asked to choose between the territorial expansionism of the Likud and the policy of peace based on territorial compromise offered by Labour.

To this difficult question, the Israeli electorate gave an uncharacteristically clear-cut reply. It returned Labour to power with a clear mandate to put its programme into action and relegated Likud to the opposition. Labour increased its seats in the Knesset from 39 to 44, while Likud seats fell from 40 to 32. One has to go back to the 1977 election for a comparable landslide victory. In defeat Shamir remained as unapologetic about his ideological commitment to the Land of Israel as he had been while in power. Many observers considered this commitment to be incompatible with his other declared aim of attaining peace with the Palestinians, and concluded that the prime minister could not be negotiating in good faith. The US-sponsored peace process, according to this view, served simply as a smokescreen for consolidating Israel's grip on the Golan Heights, the West Bank and the Gaza Strip.

Shamir himself confirmed these suspicions in an interview of blinding candour with the Israeli newspaper *Maariv* only three days after his electoral defeat. It was the true confession of a stonewaller. In it, Shamir noted that the centrepiece of his party's ideology was the Land of Israel, and that on this there could be no compromise. 'Moderation', he explained, 'should relate to the tactics but not to the goal. That is how I acted as prime minister. In my political activity I know how to display the tactics of moderation, but without conceding anything on the goal – the integrity of the Land of Israel.' Shamir disclosed that his secret agenda for the peace talks had been to expand Jewish settlement and to complete the demographic revolution in the Land of Israel, without which there was the danger that autonomy could be turned into a Palestinian state. 'I would have carried on autonomy talks for ten years,' he said, 'and meanwhile we would have reached half a million people in Judea and Samaria.' When reminded that, judging by the results of the recent election, there was no majority for a Greater Land of Israel, Shamir retorted bluntly: 'I didn't believe there was a majority in favour of a Greater Land of Israel. But it can be attained over time. This must be the historic direction. If we drop this basis, there would be nothing to prevent the development of a Palestinian state.'[2]

Shamir's interview was widely reported in the international media and caused outrage among Americans, Arabs, Palestinians and Israelis alike. Some of Shamir's ministerial colleagues felt they had been tainted by his confession. Some of the peace negotiators also felt deceived by him, saying they would not have participated in the talks had they known he was not serious. Under pressure from the Israeli Foreign Ministry, which had been inundated with protests, Shamir's office expressed surprise at the interpretation of his remarks and denied any lack of commitment on his part to the idea of Palestinian autonomy. Shamir's comments, it was claimed, referred only to the negotiations on the final settlement and not to the negotiations on autonomy during the transitional period. But this lame explanation could not erase the impression that Shamir's real aim had been to obstruct the peace process rather than to advance it. Arabs and Palestinians now had it on the highest authority that, from the very start, their partner had secretly hoped to ensure that the peace talks would fail. This was the grim legacy left by Shamir to his Labour successors.

To dissociate himself from this legacy, Yitzhak Rabin emphasised the differences and downplayed the similarities between himself and his predecessor. He presented the election results as marking a break rather than continuity in the country's approach to the peace talks. 'We inherited the framework of the Madrid conference from the previous government', he told the Knesset on 13 July 1992. 'But there is one significant change: the previous government created the tools, but they never intended to use them in order to achieve peace.' The composition of the new government also underscored the sharp break with the legacy of the Likud. Of Labour's 11 ministers, at least six may be counted as doves, Foreign Minister Shimon Peres being the most prominent. Labour's chief coalition partner was Meretz, a left-of-centre party created through a merger of the Citizens' Rights Movement (Ratz), Mapam and Shinui, which won 12 seats in the Knesset. The other coalition partner was Shas, a centrist religious party of mainly Oriental Jews, which increased its representation in the Knesset from five to six seats. Although Rabin's government commanded only a narrow majority of 62 in the 120-member

Knesset, it could also count on support for a moderate foreign policy from the five Arab and Communist MKs. Rabin thus enjoyed considerable latitude in the making of foreign policy.

But Rabin was also the product of the previous half-century of his people's history. He was the first Israeli-born prime minister and, to a far greater extent than any of his predecessors, he was personally involved at the sharp end of the conflict with the Arabs. This direct involvement in the conflict, first as a soldier and then as a diplomat and politician, played a decisive part in shaping Rabin's worldview. Suspicion of the Arabs and a deep sense of personal responsibility for Israel's security were the twin hallmarks of this view. For Rabin, the Arabs represented first and foremost a military threat. Consequently, he tended to view all developments in the region from the narrow perspective of Israel's security needs. A lifetime spent as a soldier inclined him to proceed with caution, on the basis of a 'worst-case analysis', and made him reluctant to assume any political risks. Rabin was not endowed with imagination or vision, and he certainly had no empathy for the other side in the conflict. Like a staff officer, he concentrated on the practical side, examining alternative courses of action, and carefully weighing the costs and benefits of each. This was both his greatest strength and greatest limitation as a statesman.

Within the Labour Party, Rabin always belonged to the hawkish wing, but his pragmatism was such that he was capable of changing his mind even on basic tenets of party dogma. Nothing illustrated this better than his attitude towards the Palestinian issue. To begin with, Rabin was a firm believer in the Jordanian option. He was no less devoted to reaching an agreement with Jordan than Shimon Peres. He was even more outspoken than Peres in his opposition to the idea of an independent Palestinian state. On security issues he was even more hardline than the Likud ministers. When the Palestinian uprising broke out in December 1987, Rabin was defence minister in the national unity government headed by Yitzhak Shamir. Rabin was critical of Shamir for not using sufficient force to crush the intifada, issuing his 'break their bones' order. When this policy failed, the army commanders explained that this was a political problem and that there was no simple military solution to it. It was then that Rabin coined the phrase 'marching with two feet', the military foot and the political foot.[3] This implied stepping up the use of force in order to arrive at the negotiations from a position of strength. But it also implied that Israel would have to negotiate directly with the Palestinians, which amounted to a departure from his party's hitherto exclusive orientation towards Amman. Rabin liked to think of himself as a great strategist like Henry Kissinger, combining the use of force and diplomacy to achieve political ends. Nevertheless, his political thinking was rather crude, his diplomatic style was unsubtle, and his use of force extremely heavy-handed.

Yitzhak Rabin's victory thus inspired both hope and doubts about the prospects of the peace talks. On the one hand, he was ready to move the peace talks forward and to accelerate negotiations on Palestinian autonomy. On the other hand, given his worldview and record, he was likely to act with great caution in order to safeguard what he considered to be Israel's overriding security interests. In a sense, he replaced the ideology of Greater Israel with the secular ideology of national security.

Rabin presented his programme and his government in a major speech before the Knesset on 13 July 1992. He grouped the differences between the outgoing and incoming governments under three headings: national priorities, the peace process, and Israel's place in the world. Whereas the outgoing government had lavished money on the Jewish settlements in the occupied territories, Rabin promised to divert resources to the absorption of immigrants, to social and economic reforms, to the war against unemployment, and to better education. As far as the peace process was concerned, Rabin proposed to move from 'process' to peacemaking and to give priority to the talks on Palestinian autonomy, implying that Syria would have to wait its turn. Peace, however, could not come at the expense of Israel's security. 'When it comes to Israel's security', he said, 'we will concede not a thing. From our standpoint, security takes precedence over peace.'

But the most striking and unexpected part of Rabin's speech concerned Israel's place in the world. Likud leaders had assiduously cultivated the image of a small and vulnerable Jewish state surrounded

by a sea of Arab hostility. Their answer to this sense of permanent
threat was to build up Greater Israel as a citadel for the entire Jewish
people. Rabin not only discarded this policy but directly challenged
the thinking behind it. 'No longer are we necessarily "a people that
dwells alone"', he declared in his historic address to the Knesset,
'and no longer is it true that "the whole world is against us". We
must overcome the sense of isolation that has held us in its thrall for
almost half a century.'[4] These words constituted a sharp departure
from what the American-Jewish historian Salo Baron once called the
lachrymose view of Jewish history.

The effects of the new attitude were felt immediately when the
sixth round of Middle East talks got underway in Washington on
24 August 1992, with all sides reporting a new tone and a more
conciliatory attitude. The Israeli side suggested continuous talks,
and this round lasted a whole month – longer than any of the
five previous rounds – with a ten-day recess in the middle. Before
embarking on the talks, Israel volunteered a number of Confidence
Building Measures (CBMs) such as freeing Palestinian detainees and
rescinding deportation orders. With so much at stake, Rabin took
personal charge of the bilateral talks, leaving his foreign minister
in charge of the less critical multilateral talks. At a fairly early stage
in the bilateral talks, Rabin switched to a 'Syria first' position after
having started the talks from a 'Syria last' position. Having planned
to concentrate on Palestinian autonomy first, he put the autonomy
talks on the back burner.

Rabin's retention of Likud's Eliakim Rubinstein as the head of
the Israeli delegation for the talks with the Palestinians suggested,
intentionally or otherwise, continuity in Israeli policy. Nor were there
any radically different ideas on offer to counter this impression. Real
dialogue replaced sloganeering, but the positions of the two parties
remained wide apart. On the nature of the Palestinian Authority,
the Israeli concept remained essentially unchanged. Israel offered
elections for a 15-member Palestinian administrative council, while
the Palestinians demanded a 120-member parliament with real
legislative authority. Israel kept offering the delegation of tasks to
the administrative council while the Palestinians kept insisting on a

transfer of legislative authority. The Israelis hinted that if agreement could be reached on the concept of the Palestinian Authority, all other issues would become much easier to solve. But they excluded so many key policy areas from the purview of this authority that no agreement could be reached.

Both sides had their own explanation for the lack of progress. The Israelis claimed that the Palestinian delegation was paralysed by personal and factional conflicts, quite apart from the problems of coordination with the PLO leadership in Tunis, and that this rendered them incapable of responding in a reasonable manner to practical proposals. The Palestinians claimed that Israel's policy on the ground, as well as its negotiating position, were intended to perpetuate Israeli control over the West Bank and Gaza. They also suspected that Israel was seeking a separate peace with Syria. But their chief complaint was that the Israeli autonomy proposals applied only to people and not to the land, and that they did not define clearly the geographical boundaries of interim self-government. 'You have to define territoriality', insisted Palestinian spokeswoman Hanan Ashrawi. 'Even if the Israelis want to make us garbage collectors, you have to define the area where you collect your own garbage and where you dispose of your garbage.'

The real problem for the Palestinians was that, while the negotiations with the Arab states were intended to lead to final peace settlements, their talks were designed to produce only an interim solution. To get over this hurdle, they called for a direct link between the interim self-government phase and the final status of the occupied territories. Israel, however, could not or would not clarify which territories were to be under the jurisdiction of the proposed Palestinian council. Shimon Peres explained: 'Instead of attempting to draw up a map of a self-governing territory . . . we have suggested a definitive timetable. While this proposal lacks the clarity of a map, it provides the commitment of a calendar.' For the Palestinian negotiators, this commitment was not enough.

During the seventh round in November 1992, the ambiguity which had obscured the conceptual gap between the Israeli and the Palestinian positions since the beginning of the talks finally disappeared. It was impossible for the two sides to agree on a first step because they were intent on marching in opposite directions. The Palestinians wanted to end the occupation, the Israelis wanted to retain as much control as possible for as long as possible. The Palestinians tried to negotiate the establishment of a pre-state Palestinian state. They wanted the interim agreement to permit and even lay the ground for the development of their sovereign state. Israel was equally determined to prevent the interim agreement from resembling the embryo of a Palestinian state. It insisted on keeping sole control of the Jewish settlements and the roads in the occupied territories during the transition period and to share control only of state land.

Palestinians were outraged by this idea which, they said, would give them control over only about a third of the West Bank, and would legalise the Jewish settlements. Nabil Sha'ath, the coordinator between the negotiating team in Washington and the PLO headquarters in Tunis, protested that the Israeli model offered so little territorial and functional integrity to the Palestinians that it was more like a Swiss cheese – full of holes.[5] The PLO experts regarded the Israeli model not only as unjust but as so complex as to be unworkable. Yasser Arafat dismissed it as a non-starter and blamed Yitzhak Rabin for the deadlock. 'So far', protested the chairman of the PLO, 'Rabin is refusing, like Shamir, to accept that 242 is applicable to Palestinian land. He says we can discuss it later. It seems he doesn't want to accept that these are occupied territories. He's undermining the basis of the peace process.'[6] Al-Quds, a Palestinian paper in East Jerusalem, all but gave up on the peace process and took to calling it the 'Penelope process', after Ulysses's wife who unravelled at night what she wove all day.

When the eighth round opened in Washington on 7 December 1992, in the twilight of the first Bush Administration, the talks between Israel and the Palestinians were virtually at a dead end. Negotiations about interim self-government were resumed but Israel continued to focus solely on the interim arrangements while the Palestinians tried, without success, to shift the focus to self-government. To the American sponsors it seemed that the Israeli concept of interim self-government was fundamentally flawed. But in its dying days the Bush Administration was not well placed to persuade the Israelis that interim self-government means precisely what it says – a stage leading to full self-government.

Lack of concrete results from the peace process added to the frustration of the Palestinians in the occupied territories and boosted popular support for the Islamic resistance movement, Hamas, which is opposed to negotiations with the Jewish state. Round eight in the talks was due to end on 17 December, but it ended abruptly a day early when Rabin announced his government's decision to deport 416 Hamas activists to Lebanon, following the kidnap and murder of an Israeli border policeman. All the Arab delegations angrily suspended their participation in the peace talks and refused to set a date for their resumption. Rabin was widely condemned but unrepentant. Government policy towards the Palestinians, he said, was two-pronged: fighting violent extremists and talking peace to the moderates. But his deportation order was without precedent and in flagrant violation of international law. It outstripped the toughest measures of the Likud and out-Shamired Shamir. None of the alleged Islamic activists had been charged, tried, or allowed to appeal before being driven blindfolded into exile in Lebanon. This act was intended to curb the rising influence of Hamas but it had the opposite effect. It discredited the peace talks, strengthened the extremists, and weakened the moderates. It was worse than a crime – it was a mistake.

The deportation exposed Rabin as an unreconstructed Arab-basher. Having recognised the need to march with both feet, the military and the political, he reverted to his old habit of kicking with the military foot. Far from demonstrating that the only language the Palestinians understand is force, his action revealed that force is the language he himself instinctively resorted to in dealing with the Palestinians. Rabin had plainly stated that for him security took precedence over peace, and in this sense he was true to his word. The problem about his notion of security was that it denied the basic human rights of the Palestinians. This was a major reason for the lack of progress in the peace talks. During the election campaign,

Rabin ran as a candidate who would conclude an agreement on Palestinian autonomy within six to nine months. Yet six months after taking office, he dealt a body blow to the entire peace process by his savage treatment of the Palestinians. The deportations boosted Rabin's domestic popularity but did not stem the tide of violence. In March 1993, 13 Israelis were murdered by knife-wielding fanatics. Rabin's response was to order on 30 March the closure of Israel's pre-1967 border to workers from the occupied territories. Nearly 120,000 families were punished for the deeds of a handful of killers. The closure achieved its immediate aim of reducing the incidence of violence, but it also served Rabin's new aim of bringing about Israel's disengagement from the occupied territories. It recreated the 1967 border and led to the economic and social separation of the Jewish and Palestinian communities. The message was not lost on the Palestinian negotiators. Israeli disengagement could be the prelude to Palestinian autonomy in the occupied territories.

The ninth round of bilateral talks opened in Washington on 27 April, after a hiatus of four and a half months. To get the talks restarted, Israel accepted Faisal Husseini as a negotiator, despite his residence in East Jerusalem, and approved in principle a Palestinian police force in the territories. There was also evidence of greater Israeli flexibility on fundamentals. The Israelis were now willing to admit a link between the interim and the final phase of Palestinian self-government. They indicated that the body elected to govern the Palestinians for the five-year interim period could have some legislative powers. And they affirmed that negotiations on the final status of the occupied territories would be based on UN Security Council resolution 242. Having derided Israel's previous proposals for self-government as Swiss cheese, the Palestinians now had something to chew on. Having previously refused to discuss details before establishing an overall framework for a settlement, they now formed three working groups with the Israelis to discuss self-government, land and water, and human rights.

Despite this auspicious beginning, the document presented by the Palestinian delegation in response to the Israeli proposals revealed persistent divergence on three fundamental issues: the application

of resolution 242; the relationship between the interim phase and
the final phase; and the nature and powers of the interim Palestinian
Authority. First, the Palestinian document treated resolution 242 as
a holy writ, valid at all stages and requiring total Israeli withdrawal
from the territories captured in 1967, including East Jerusalem and
the settlements. Israel, on the other hand, saw 242 as relevant only to
the negotiations on final status and ruled out any withdrawal during
the interim phase. Second, while Israel admitted a link between
the first stage of the agreement and the second stage but insisted
on keeping all the options open, the Palestinians tried to extract
a declaration of intent making it clear that, when the time came,
Israel would withdraw from all the occupied territories. Third, the
two sides could not agree on the powers of the Palestinian Authority
during the interim stage. The Israeli version envisaged an executive
council with limited legislative powers. The Palestinian version
envisaged an elected council which would assume all the powers
exercised by the Israeli Administration.[7]

In an attempt to move the peace talks off dead centre, the
recently elected Clinton Administration stepped up its involvement.
It formulated and presented to the Palestinians a working paper
which proposed new terms of reference for the talks. The Palestinian
delegates, however, detected Israel's thumbprints all over the
American paper. Reversing a 26-year-old American policy, the paper
accepted the Israeli claim that East Jerusalem and the rest of the
West Bank and Gaza are disputed – not occupied – territories. The
Palestinian delegation pointed out that the paper deviated from
the terms of reference under which the talks were initiated and was
therefore unsuitable even as a starting point for talks.

The tenth round, which lasted from 15 June until 1 July, ended in
failure. Little was expected and nothing was achieved. In Israel Rabin
began to attract criticism for his failure to deliver on his promise
of agreement on Palestinian autonomy. One critic accused the
government of missing a rare opportunity for settlement by clinging
to its current five no's: no to a Palestinian state; no to a return to the
1967 borders with only minor modifications; no to discussion of the
permanent settlement; no to withdrawal from the Jordan Valley and

the Etzion bloc; and no to negotiations with the PLO.[8] Government spokesmen tried to evade responsibility for the deadlock by placing all the blame on the Palestinians. At least one thing was clear at the end of the 20 months and ten rounds of Arab–Israeli peace talks: the Madrid formula was not capable of ushering in a new era of peace in the Middle East, and a new formula had to be found.

Although the Madrid formula had involved Israel in indirect negotiations with the PLO, for a whole year Rabin resisted the calls for its formal recognition. He saw Yasser Arafat as the main obstacle to a deal on Palestinian autonomy and did his best to marginalise him, pinning his hopes on the local leaders from the occupied territories whom he considered more moderate and more pragmatic. Experience taught him, however, that the local leaders could not act independently of the PLO chairman in Tunis and that, consequently, if he wanted a deal, he would have to cut it with his arch-enemy. The failure of the official Washington talks on the Palestinian track left Rabin with two alternatives: a deal with President Hafez al-Assad of Syria, which entailed complete withdrawal from and the dismantling of Jewish settlements on the Golan Heights, or a deal with the PLO on interim self-government which did not entail an immediate commitment to withdraw from the West Bank or to dismantle Jewish settlements. He opted for the second alternative.

Rabin knew that back in January Shimon Peres, his foreign minister and erstwhile opponent, had established a secret channel for informal talks with PLO officials in Norway. At first Rabin had showed little interest, but in the course of the summer the talks made considerable progress. It became clear that the PLO was bankrupt, divided and on the verge of collapse, and therefore ready to settle for considerably less than the official negotiators in Washington. Negotiations now began in earnest, with Rabin and Peres directing the secret talks from Jerusalem, and Arafat from Tunis. All together, 15 sessions were held over an eight-month period until an agreement was reached on mutual recognition between Israel and the PLO, and limited Palestinian self-government in Gaza and the West Bank town of Jericho.

This Accord, despite all its limitations, defects and ambiguities, marked a watershed in Israel's relations with the Palestinians. It seemed to signal the beginning of the end of the movement towards Greater Israel. This is why it would have been utterly inconceivable had Yitzhak Shamir remained in power. At the signing ceremony on the South Lawn of the White House, Rabin declared: 'I tell you Palestinians: we are doomed, you and we, to live together on the same plot of land, in the same country.' It is equally inconceivable that Shamir would have uttered these words. True, the two Yitzhaks were both hawks, but there was an important difference: Yitzhak Shamir was an ideological hawk while Yitzhak Rabin was a security hawk. The Israeli–PLO deal compromised the ideology of Greater Israel; it did not compromise Israel's security.

There is historic irony in the fact that it took a leader of Rabin's renowned hawkishness on security to bring the Labour Party back to the path of political moderation. Historically, the Labour Party had been the party of humane and liberal Zionism, of political moderation, of reconciliation and compromise. Under Golda Meir's leadership, however, it veered towards messianic nationalism and territorial maximalism. By reaching an agreement on Palestinian self-government, however limited in scope, Rabin carried his party back to its original acceptance of the principle of partition. By officially recognising the Palestinian people and the PLO as its representative, he took the first step towards correcting the tragic mistake to which his party succumbed in the aftermath of the 1967 victory. By starting the withdrawal from occupied Arab territory, Rabin did not lead Israel to commit suicide, as his critics on the right claimed, but laid the only secure foundation for peaceful coexistence between Israel and the Palestinians.

The very fact that Rabin reached an accord with the PLO demolishes the notion, so prevalent and persistent among Palestinians, that there is no real difference between the Labour Party and the Likud. If the history of the peace talks begun at Madrid can teach us anything, it is that the Labour Party is pragmatic in its approach to the Palestinian question whereas the Likud is not. Indeed, the Israeli–PLO Accord represented the triumph of pragmatism on both sides.

After a hundred years of conflict and bloodshed, the two principal protagonists began to put behind them the ideological dispute as to who is the rightful owner of Palestine, and turned to addressing the practical problem of how to share the small piece of territory on which they are doomed to live together.

# SIXTEEN

# The Rise and Fall of the Oslo Peace Process

The Middle East is the most penetrated sub-system of the international political system. Ever since Napoleon's expeditionary force landed in Egypt in 1798, the region has been an object of rivalry among the great powers. The strategic value of the Middle East was considerable as the gateway between Europe and the Far East. The discovery of oil in the early part of the twentieth century enhanced the region's importance for the global economy. After the Second World War, the Middle East became one of the major theatres of the Cold War. It was constantly caught up in superpower rivalry for political influence, power and prestige. External sources of conflict combined with internal ones to produce frequent crises, violence and wars. One of the most destabilising factors in the affairs of the region is the dispute between Israel and the Arabs, at the core of which lies the problem of Palestine. But the search for a settlement of the Palestinian–Israeli conflict is complicated by inter-Arab relations and by the involvement of outside powers. Here, I will re-examine the peace process that got under way in the aftermath of the 1991 Gulf War and, more specifically, the quest for a settlement between Israel and the Palestinians.

*       *       *

Stalemate in the official talks following the Madrid conference of October 1991 led both Israel and the PLO to seek a back-channel for communicating. The decision to hold direct talks with the PLO was a diplomatic revolution in Israel's foreign policy and paved the way to the Oslo Accord of 13 September 1993. Three men were primarily responsible for this decision: Prime Minister Yitzhak Rabin, Shimon Peres, the foreign minister, and Yossi Beilin, the youthful deputy foreign minister. Rabin held out against direct talks with the PLO for as long as he could. Peres took the view that without the PLO there could be no settlement. He said on one occasion that expecting the PLO to enable the local Palestinian leaders to reach an agreement with Israel was like expecting the turkey to help in preparing the Thanksgiving dinner. As long as PLO chairman Yasser Arafat remained in Tunis, he argued, he represented the 'outsiders', the Palestinian diaspora, and he would do his best to slow down the peace talks.[1]

Yossi Beilin was even more categorical in his view that talking to the PLO was a necessary condition for an agreement with the Palestinians. Beilin had always belonged to the extreme dovish wing of the Labour Party. He was the real architect behind the Israeli recognition of the PLO. Peres backed him all the way and the two of them succeeded in carrying their hesitant and suspicious senior colleague with them. The secret talks in Oslo got under way in late January 1993 with the active encouragement of Beilin, who kept Peres fully informed. Altogether, 14 sessions of talks were held over an eight-month period, all behind a thick veil of secrecy. Norwegian foreign affairs minister Johan Joergen Holst and social scientist Terje Roed-Larsen acted as generous hosts and facilitators. The key players were two Israeli academics, Dr Yair Hirschfeld and Dr Ron Pundik, and PLO treasurer Ahmad Qurei, better known as Abu Ala. Away from the glare of publicity and political pressures, these three men worked imaginatively and indefatigably to establish the conceptual framework of the Israeli–PLO Accord. Their discussions ran parallel to the bilateral talks in Washington, but they proceeded without the knowledge of the official Israeli and Palestinian negotiators.

The unofficial talks dealt initially with economic cooperation but quickly broadened into a dialogue about a joint declaration of principles. That May, Peres took a highly significant decision: he ordered Uri Savir, the director-general of the foreign ministry, and Yoel Singer, a high-flying attorney who had spent 20 years in the IDF legal department, to join Hirschfeld and Pundik on their weekend trips to Oslo. At this point Peres began to report to Rabin regularly on developments in the Norwegian back-channel. At first Rabin showed little interest, but he raised no objection to continuing the explorations either. Gradually, however, he became more involved in the details and assumed an active role in directing the talks alongside Peres. Since Abu Ala reported directly to Arafat, an indirect line of communication had been established between Jerusalem and the PLO headquarters in Tunis.

Another landmark in the progress of the talks was the failure of the tenth round of the official Israeli–Palestinian negotiations in Washington. To tempt the Palestinians to move forward, Peres floated the idea of 'Gaza first'. He believed that Arafat was desperate for a concrete achievement to bolster his sagging political fortunes, and that Gaza would provide him with his first toehold in the occupied territories. Peres also knew that an Israeli withdrawal from Gaza would be greeted with sighs of relief among the great majority of his countrymen. Arafat, however, did not swallow the bait, suspecting an Israeli plan to confine the dream of Palestinian independence to the narrow strip of territory stretching from Gaza City to Rafah. The idea was attractive to some Palestinians, especially the inhabitants of the Gaza Strip, but not to the politicians in Tunis. Rather than reject the Israeli offer out of hand, Arafat came up with a counter-offer of his own: Gaza and Jericho first. His choice of the small and sleepy West Bank town seemed quirky at first sight, but it served as a symbol of his claim to the whole of the West Bank. Rabin did not balk at the counter-offer. All along he had supported handing over Jericho to Jordanian rule while keeping the Jordan Valley in Israeli hands. But he had one condition: the Palestinian foothold on the West Bank would be an island inside Israeli-controlled territory with the Allenby Bridge also remaining in Israeli hands. Jordan, too, preferred Israel to the Palestinians at the other end of the bridge. Arafat therefore had to settle for the Israeli version of the 'Gaza and Jericho first' plan.

Rabin's conversion to the idea of a deal with the PLO was clinched by four evaluations which reached him between the end of May and July. First was the advice of Itamar Rabinovich, the head of the Israeli delegation to the talks with Syria, that a settlement with Syria was attainable but only at the cost of complete Israeli withdrawal from the Golan Heights. Second were the reports from various quarters that the local Palestinian leadership had finally been neutralised. Third was the assessment of the IDF director of military intelligence that Arafat's dire situation, and possibly imminent collapse, made him the most convenient interlocutor for Israel at that particular juncture. Fourth were the reports of the impressive progress achieved through the Oslo channel. Other reports that reached Rabin during this period pointed to an alarming growth in the popular following of Hamas and Islamic Jihad in the occupied territories. Both the army chiefs and the internal security chiefs repeatedly stressed to him the urgency of finding a political solution to the crisis in relations between Israel and the inhabitants of the occupied territories. Rabin therefore gave the green light to the Israeli team and the secret diplomacy in Oslo moved into higher gear.

Rabin and Peres also believed that progress towards a settlement with the Palestinians would lower the price of a settlement with Syria by lessening the latter's bargaining power. Peres reduced the link between the two sets of negotiations to what he called 'the bicycle principle': when one pedal is pressed, the other pedal moves by itself. His formula was not directed at reaching a separate agreement with the Palestinians but at gradual movement towards a settlement with the Palestinians, the Syrians and the Jordanians.

On 23 August, Rabin stated publicly for the first time that 'there would be no escape from recognising the PLO'. In private, he elaborated on the price that Israel could extract in exchange for this recognition. In his estimate, the PLO was 'on the ropes' and it was therefore highly probable that it would drop some of its sacred principles in order to secure Israeli recognition. Accordingly, while endorsing the joint declaration of principles on Palestinian self-government in Gaza and Jericho, and mutual recognition between Israel and the PLO, he insisted on changes to the Palestinian National Charter as part of the package deal.

Peres flew to California to explain the Accord to the US Secretary of State, Warren Christopher. Christopher was surprised by the scope of the Accord and by the unorthodox method by which it had been achieved. He naturally assumed that the US had a monopoly over the peace process. His aides in the State Department had come to be called 'the peace processors'. Now their feathers were ruffled because they had been so thoroughly upstaged by the Norwegians. All the participants in the Oslo back-channel, on the other hand, had the satisfaction of knowing that they had reached the Accord on their own without any help from the State Department. Their success showed that the fate of the peace process lay in the hands of the protagonists rather than in the hands of the intermediaries.

The Declaration of Principles on Interim Self-Government Arrangements was essentially an agenda for negotiations, governed by a tight timetable, rather than a full-blown agreement. The Declaration laid down that within two months of the signing ceremony, agreement on Israel's military withdrawal from Gaza and Jericho should be reached and within four months the withdrawal should be completed. A Palestinian police force, made up mostly of pro-Arafat Palestinian fighters, was to be imported to maintain internal security in Gaza and Jericho, with Israel retaining overall responsibility for external security and foreign affairs. At the same time, elsewhere in the West Bank, Israel undertook to transfer power to 'authorised Palestinians' in five spheres: education, health, social welfare, direct taxation and tourism. Within nine months, the Palestinians in the West Bank and Gaza were to hold elections to a Palestinian Council to take office and assume responsibility for most government functions except defence and foreign affairs. Within two years, Israel and the Palestinians were to commence negotiations on the final status of the territories, and at the end of five years the permanent settlement was to come into force.[2] In short, the

Declaration of Principles promised to set in motion a process that would end Israeli rule over the two million Palestinians living in the West Bank and Gaza.

The shape of the permanent settlement was not specified in the Declaration of Principles but was left to negotiations between the two parties during the second stage. The Declaration was completely silent on vital issues such as the right of return of the 1948 refugees, the borders of the Palestinian entity, the future of the Jewish settlements on the West Bank and Gaza, and the status of Jerusalem. The reason for this silence is not hard to understand: if these issues had been addressed, there would have been no Accord. Both sides took a calculated risk, realising that a great deal would depend on the way the experiment in Palestinian self-government worked out in practice. Rabin was strongly opposed to an independent Palestinian state but he favoured an eventual Jordanian–Palestinian confederation. Arafat was strongly committed to an independent Palestinian state, with East Jerusalem as its capital, but he did not rule out the idea of a confederation with Jordan.

Despite all its limitations and ambiguities, the Declaration of Principles for Palestinian self-government in Gaza and Jericho marked a major breakthrough in the century-old conflict between Arabs and Jews in Palestine. On Monday, 13 September 1993, the Declaration was signed on the South Lawn of the White House and sealed with the historic handshake between Prime Minister Rabin and Chairman Arafat.

The Oslo Accord consisted of two parts, both of which were the product of secret diplomacy in the Norwegian capital. The first part consisted of mutual recognition between Israel and the PLO. It took the form of two letters, on plain paper and without letterheads, signed by Arafat and Rabin respectively on 9 and 10 September. Nearly all the publicity focused on the signing of the Declaration of Principles, but without the mutual recognition there could have been no meaningful agreement on Palestinian self-government. In his letter to Rabin, Arafat observed that the signing of the Declaration of Principles marked a new era in the history of the Middle East. He then confirmed the PLO's commitment to recognise Israel's right to live in peace and security, to accept United Nations Security Council resolutions 242 and 338, to renounce the use of terrorism and other acts of violence, and to change those parts of the Palestinian National Charter which were inconsistent with these commitments. In his terse, one-sentence reply to Arafat, Rabin confirmed that in the light of these commitments, the government of Israel decided to recognise the PLO as the representative of the Palestinian people and to commence negotiations with the PLO within the Middle East peace process.

Taken together, the two parts of the Oslo Accord seemed at the time to merit the overworked epithet 'historic' because they reconciled the two principal parties to the Arab–Israeli conflict. The clash between Jewish and Palestinian nationalism had always been the heart and core of the Arab–Israeli conflict. Both national movements denied the other the right to self-determination in Palestine. Their history was one of mutual denial and mutual rejection. Now mutual denial made way for mutual recognition. Israel not only recognised the Palestinians as a people with political rights but formally recognised the PLO as its representative. The handshake between Rabin and Arafat at the signing ceremony, despite the former's awkward body language, was a powerful symbol of the historic reconciliation between the two nations. This reconciliation was based on a historic compromise: acceptance of the principle of the partition of Palestine. Both sides accepted territorial compromise as the basis for the settlement of their long and bitter conflict. By accepting the principle of partition, they suspended the ideological dispute as to who is the rightful owner of Palestine, and turned to finding a practical solution to the problem of sharing the cramped living space between the Jordan river and the Mediterranean sea. Each side resigned itself to parting with territory that it had previously regarded not only as its patrimony but as a vital part of its national identity. Each was driven to this historic compromise by the recognition that it lacked the power to impose its own vision on the other side. That the idea of partition was finally accepted by both sides seemed to support Abba Eban's observation that men and nations often behave wisely once they have exhausted all the other alternatives.[3]

The breakthrough at Oslo was achieved by separating the interim settlement from the final settlement. In the past the Palestinians had always refused to consider any interim agreement unless the principles of the permanent settlement were agreed in advance. Israel on the other hand, had insisted that a five-year transition period should begin without a prior agreement about the nature of the permanent settlement. At Oslo the PLO accepted the Israeli formula. In contrast to the official Palestinian position in Washington, the PLO agreed to a five-year transition period without clear commitments by Israel as to the nature of the permanent settlement.[4]

The Israeli–PLO Accord had far-reaching implications for the inter-state dimension of the Arab–Israeli conflict. Originally, the Arab states got involved in the Palestine conflict out of a sense of solidarity with the Palestine Arabs against the Zionist intruders. Continuing commitment to the Palestinian cause had precluded the Arab states, with the notable exception of Egypt, from extending recognition to the Jewish state. One of the main functions of the Arab League, established in 1945, was to assist the Palestinians in the struggle for Palestine. After 1948, the League became a forum for coordinating military policy and for waging political, economic and ideological warfare against the Jewish state. In 1974 the Arab League had recognised the PLO as the sole legitimate representative of the Palestinian people. Now that the PLO had formally recognised Israel, there was no longer any compelling reason for the Arab states to continue to reject her.

Clearly, an important taboo had been broken. PLO recognition of Israel was an important landmark along the road to Arab recognition of Israel and the normalising of relations. Egypt, which was first to take the plunge back in the late 1970s, felt vindicated and elated by the breakthrough. When Rabin stopped in Rabat on his way home, after attending the signing ceremony in Washington, he was received like any other visiting head of state by King Hassan II of Morocco. Jordan allowed Israeli television the first ever live report by one of its correspondents from Amman. A number of Arab states, like Tunisia and Saudi Arabia, started thinking seriously about the establishment of diplomatic relations with Israel. And the Arab League began discussions on the lifting of the economic boycott which had been in force since Israel's creation. Nothing was quite the same in the Arab world as a result of the Israeli–PLO Accord. The rules of the game in the entire Middle East had changed radically.

The change was no less marked in Israel's approach to its Arab opponents than in their approach to Israel. Zionist policy, before and after 1948, proceeded on the assumption that agreement on the partition of Palestine would be easier to achieve with the rulers of the neighbouring Arab states than with the Palestine Arabs. Israel's courting of conservative Arab leaders, like King Hussein of Jordan and President Anwar Sadat of Egypt, was an attempt to bypass the local Arabs, and avoid having to address the core issue of the conflict. Recognition by the Arab states, it was hoped, would help to alleviate the conflict without conceding the right of national self-determination to the Palestinians. Now this strategy was reversed. PLO recognition of Israel was expected to pave the way for wider recognition by the Arab states from North Africa to the Persian Gulf. Rabin expressed this hope when signing the letter to Arafat in which Israel recognised the PLO. 'I believe', he said, 'that there is a great opportunity of changing not only the relations between the Palestinians and Israel, but to expand it to the solution of the conflict between Israel and the Arab countries and other Arab peoples.'[5]

On both sides of the Israeli–Palestinian divide, the Rabin–Arafat deal provoked strong and vociferous opposition on the part of the hardliners. Both leaders were accused of a betrayal and a sell-out. Leaders of the Likud, and of the nationalistic parties further to the Right, attacked Rabin for his abrupt departure from the bipartisan policy of refusing to negotiate with the PLO, and charged him with abandoning the 120,000 settlers in the occupied territories to the tender mercies of terrorists. The Gaza-Jericho plan was denounced as a bridgehead to a Palestinian state and the beginning of the end of Greater Israel. A Gallup poll, however, indicated considerable popular support for the prime minister. Of the 1,000 Israelis polled, 65 per cent said they approved of the peace accord, with only 13 per cent describing themselves as 'very much against'.[6]

Within the Palestinian camp the accord also encountered loud but ineffective opposition. The PLO itself was split, with the radical nationalists accusing Arafat of abandoning principles to grab power. They included the Popular Front for the Liberation of Palestine, led by George Habash, and the Damascus-based Democratic Front for the Liberation of Palestine, led by Nayef Hawatmeh. Arafat succeeded in mustering the necessary majority in favour of the deal on the PLO's 18-member Executive Committee, but only after a bruising battle and the resignation of four of his colleagues. Outside the PLO, the deal aroused the implacable wrath of the militant resistance movements, Hamas and Islamic Jihad, who regarded any compromise with the Jewish state as anathema. Opposition to the deal from rejectionist quarters, whether secular or religious, was only to be expected. More disturbing was the opposition of mainstream figures like Farouk Kaddoumi, the PLO 'foreign minister', and prominent intellectuals like Professor Edward Said and the poet Mahmoud Darwish. Some of the criticisms related to Arafat's autocratic, idiosyncratic and secretive style of management. Others related to the substance of the deal. The most fundamental criticism was that the deal negotiated by Arafat did not carry the promise, let alone a guarantee, of an independent Palestinian state.

This criticism took various forms. Farouk Kaddoumi argued that the deal compromised the basic national rights of the Palestinian people as well as the individual rights of the 1948 refugees. Edward Said lambasted Arafat for unilaterally cancelling the intifada, for failing to coordinate his moves with the Arab states, and for introducing appalling disarray within the ranks of the PLO. 'The PLO', wrote Said, 'has transformed itself from a national liberation movement into a kind of small-town government, with the same handful of people still in command.' For the deal itself, Said had nothing but scorn. 'All secret deals between a very strong and a very weak partner necessarily involve concessions hidden in embarrassment by the latter', he wrote. 'The deal before us', he continued, 'smacks of the PLO leadership's exhaustion and isolation, and of Israel's shrewdness.'[7] 'Gaza and Jericho first . . . and last' was Mahmoud Darwish's damning verdict on the deal.

Arab reactions to the Accord were rather mixed. Arafat got a polite but cool reception from the 19 foreign ministers of the Arab League who met in Cairo a week after the signing ceremony in Washington. Some member states of the League, especially Jordan, Syria and Lebanon, were dismayed by the PLO chairman's solo diplomacy, which violated Arab pledges to coordinate their negotiating strategy. Arafat defended his decision to sign the Accord by presenting it as the first step towards a more comprehensive peace in the Middle East. The interim agreement, he said, was only the first step towards a final settlement of the Palestinian problem and of the Arab–Israeli conflict which would involve Israeli withdrawal from all the occupied territories, including 'Holy Jerusalem'. He justified his resort to a secret channel by arguing that the almost two years of public negotiations under US sponsorship had reached a dead end. Some of the Arab foreign ministers agreed with the PLO chairman that the Accord was an important first step, even if they were not all agreed on the next step or the final destination.

Two committees were set up in early October 1993 to negotiate the implementation of the lofty-sounding declaration signed in Washington. The first committee was chaired by Shimon Peres and Mahmoud Abbas, the leader who signed the declaration on behalf of the PLO. This ministerial-level committee was supposed to meet in Cairo every two or three weeks. The other committee, the nuts and bolts committee, consisted of experts who were supposed to meet for two or three days each week in the Egyptian resort of Taba on the Red Sea. The heads of the delegations to these talks were Nabil Sha'ath and Major-General Amnon Lipkin-Shahak, the number-two man in the IDF and head of its military intelligence. The two sides managed to hammer out an agenda and formed two groups of experts, one to deal with military affairs, the other with the transfer of authority.

The IDF officers took a generally tough line in the negotiations. These officers had been excluded from the secret talks in the Norwegian capital, and they felt bitter at not having been consulted about the security implications of the Accord. Chief of staff Ehud

Barak believed that in their haste to secure their place in history, the politicians had conceded too much to the PLO and that when the time came to implement the agreement it would be the responsibility of the army to tackle the security problems.

Underlying the labyrinthine negotiations at Taba, there was a basic conceptual divide. The Israeli representatives wanted a gradual and strictly limited transfer of powers while maintaining overall responsibility for security in the occupied territories in their own hands. They wanted to repackage rather than end Israel's military occupation. The Palestinians wanted an early and extensive transfer of power to enable them to start laying the foundations for an independent state. They were anxious to get rid of the Israeli occupation and they struggled to gain every possible symbol of sovereignty. As a result of this basic conceptual divide the Taba negotiations plunged repeatedly into crisis and took considerably longer to complete than the two months allowed for in the original timetable.

After four months of wrangling, an agreement was reached in the form of two documents, one on general principles, and the other on border crossings. The two documents were initialled by Shimon Peres and Yasser Arafat in Cairo on 9 February 1994. Although the Cairo agreement was tactfully presented as a compromise solution, it was a compromise that tilted very heavily towards the Israeli position. The IDF had managed to impose its own conception of the interim period: specific steps to transfer limited powers to the Palestinians without giving up Israel's overall responsibility for security. The IDF undertook to redeploy rather than withdraw its forces in the Gaza Strip and Jericho. The Cairo agreement gave the IDF full authority over Gaza's three settlement blocs, the four lateral roads joining them to the Green Line and 'the relevant territory overlooking them'. The outstanding feature of the agreement was thus to allow the IDF to maintain a military presence in and around the area earmarked for Palestinian self-government, and to retain full responsibility for external security and control of the land crossings to Egypt and Jordan. Despite these serious limitations, the Cairo agreement formed a first step in regulating the withdrawal of the Israeli Civil Administration and secret services from Gaza and Jericho.

Another round of negotiations resulted in an agreement signed by Yitzhak Rabin and Yasser Arafat in Cairo on 4 May. The Cairo agreement wrapped up the Gaza-Jericho negotiations and set the terms for expanding Palestinian self-government to the rest of the West Bank. Expansion was to take place in three stages. First, responsibility for tourism, education and culture, health, social welfare and direct taxation was to be transferred from Israel's Civil Administration to the Palestinian National Authority. Second, Israel was to redeploy its armed forces away from 'Palestinian population centres'. Third, elections were due to take place throughout the West Bank and the Gaza Strip for a new Authority.

The Cairo document was billed by both sides as an agreement to divorce after 27 years of unhappy coexistence in which the stronger partner forced the weaker to live under its yoke. This was true in the sense that Israel secured a separate legal system and separate water, electricity and roads for the Jewish settlements. It was not true in the sense that the document gave the stronger party firm control over the new relationship. The Cairo document stressed repeatedly the need for cooperation, coordination and harmonisation in the new relationship. A large number of liaison committees, most of which were to have an equal number of representatives from the two sides, gave a superficial appearance of parity. But this parity was undermined in favour of the stronger partner by the fact that Israeli occupation laws and military orders were to remain in force unless amended or abrogated by mutual agreement. What this meant in practice was that any issue that could not be resolved by negotiation would be subject to the provisions of Israeli law rather than those of international law. This was a retreat from the Palestinian demand that international law, particularly the Fourth Geneva Convention, should be the source of legislation and jurisdiction during the transition period.

A week after the Cairo document was signed, a token force of 30 Palestinian policemen entered the Gaza Strip from Egypt to take over control of internal security from the retreating Israelis. This was the first tangible evidence that Israeli occupation was winding down. Until this point all the movement had been unilateral, as the Israeli army redeployed its forces so as to provide continuing protection for the tiny community of Jewish settlers in the strip. Now a new Palestinian police force was to take charge of the nearby Palestinian population centres in accordance with a pre-arranged division of labour. The Israeli withdrawal was greeted with a sigh of relief at home and great joy and jubilation among the Gazans. As the last Israeli soldiers pulled out of their military camps in Rafah and Nusairat to a final barrage of stones, the Israeli flag was replaced by the flag of Palestine. A 27-year-old experiment in imposing Israeli rule over two million recalcitrant Arabs was symbolically and visibly nearing the end of its life.

The Israeli government's policy of controlled withdrawal from Gaza and Jericho enjoyed broad popular support. Hard as they tried, the leaders of the opposition failed to arouse the nation against the government's decisions. As far as the government was concerned, the real paradox was that it needed a strong PLO to implement the Gaza-Jericho settlement, but a strong PLO could only reinforce the determination of the Palestinians to fight for a state of their own. The government maintained its commitment to peace with the Palestinians despite the protests from the Right, and despite the terrorist attacks launched by Hamas and Islamic Jihad with the aim of derailing the peace talks. On 29 August 1994, the Agreement on Preparatory Transfer of Powers and Responsibilities was signed by Israel and the Palestinians. This agreement transferred powers to the Palestinian Authority in five specified spheres: education and culture, health, social welfare, direct taxation and tourism.

Negotiations on the Syrian track proceeded in parallel to those on the Palestinian. Rabin's strategy was to decouple the Syrian from the Palestinian, Jordanian and Lebanese tracks. He controlled the pace of the negotiations with Syria according to what was happening on the other tracks. The Americans offered their good offices in trying to broker a settlement with Syria. For the latter the key issue was full Israeli withdrawal from the Golan Heights, by which it meant a return to the armistice lines of 4 June 1967. The Israelis preferred withdrawal to the 1923 international border, which was more favourable to them. In the second half of 1993 Rabin came close to accepting the Syrian condition if Syria met his demands – the four legs of the table, as he used to call them. Besides withdrawal, the other three legs of the table were normalisation, security arrangements and a timetable for implementation. The Syrian response on these other points did not satisfy Rabin. Consequently, although considerable progress was achieved by the two sides in narrowing down the differences, it was not sufficient to secure a breakthrough on the Syrian track.

Jordan was more directly affected by the Israel–PLO accord than any other Arab country, both because of its close association with the West Bank and because over half of its population is of Palestinian origin. A day after the Accord was presented to the world, in a much more modest ceremony in the State Department, the representatives of Jordan and Israel signed a common agenda for negotiations aimed at a comprehensive peace treaty. Its main components were borders and territorial matters, Jerusalem, water, security and refugees. The document bore the personal stamp of King Hussein, who had been deeply involved in the quest for peace in the Middle East for the preceding quarter-century. A year of intensive negotiations culminated in the signature of a peace treaty in the Arava desert on 26 October 1994. This was the second peace treaty concluded between Israel and an Arab country in 15 years, and the first to be signed in the region. The treaty between Israel and Egypt had been signed in 1979. But whereas Egypt had offered a cold peace, King Hussein offered Israel a warm peace.

On 28 September 1995, the Israeli–Palestinian Interim Agreement on the West Bank and the Gaza Strip was signed in Washington by Yitzhak Rabin and Yasser Arafat in the presence of Bill Clinton, Hosni Mubarak and King Hussein of Jordan. It became popularly known as Oslo II. This agreement, which marked the conclusion of the first stage in the negotiations between Israel and the PLO, incorporated and superseded the Gaza-Jericho and early empowerment agreements. The Interim Agreement was comprehensive in its scope and, with its various annexes, stretched to over 300 pages. From the point of view of changes on the ground, it was highly significant.

It provided for elections to a Palestinian Council, the transfer of legislative authority to this Council, the withdrawal of Israeli forces from the Palestinian centres of population, and the division of territories into three areas – A, B and C. Area A was under exclusive Palestinian control, area C under exclusive Israeli control and in area B the Palestinians exercised civilian authority while Israel continued to be in charge of security. Under the terms of this agreement, Israel yielded to the Palestinians control over nearly a third of the West Bank. Four per cent of the West Bank (including the towns of Jenin, Nablus, Kalkilya, Tulkarem, Ramallah, Bethlehem and Hebron) were turned over to exclusive Palestinian control and another 25 per cent to administrative-civilian control. Oslo II marked the point of no return in the process of ending Israel's coercive control over the Palestinian people.

On 5 October, Yitzhak Rabin gave the Knesset a comprehensive survey of Oslo II and of the thinking behind it. His speech was repeatedly interrupted by catcalls from the benches of the opposition. Two Likud MKs opened black umbrellas, the symbols of Neville Chamberlain's appeasement of Adolf Hitler at Munich. In the course of his speech, Rabin outlined his thinking for the permanent settlement: military presence but no annexation of the Jordan Valley; retention of the large blocks of settlements near the 1967 border; preservation of a united Jerusalem with respect for the rights of the other religions; and a Palestinian entity which would be less than a state and whose territory would be demilitarised. The fact that Rabin sketched out the principles of the permanent settlement in a session devoted to the interim settlement suggested a strong interest in proceeding to the next stage.

The day that the Knesset endorsed Oslo II by a majority of one, thousands of demonstrators gathered in Zion Square in Jerusalem. Binyamin Netanyahu, the leader of the Likud, was on the grandstand, while the demonstrators displayed an effigy of Rabin in SS uniform. Netanyahu set the tone with an inflammatory speech. He called Oslo II a surrender agreement and accused Rabin of 'causing national humiliation by accepting the dictates of the terrorist Arafat'. A month later, on 4 November 1995, Rabin was assassinated by a religious-nationalist Jewish fanatic with the explicit aim of derailing the peace process. Rabin's demise, as his murderer expected, dealt a serious body blow to the entire peace process. Shimon Peres followed Rabin down the potholed road to peace with the Palestinians, but his efforts were cut short by his electoral defeat in May 1996.

The return to power of the Likud under the leadership of Binyamin Netanyahu dealt another body blow to the Oslo peace process. From the very beginning the Likud had been bitterly opposed to the Labour government's land-for-peace deal with the PLO. Netanyahu himself repeatedly denounced the Accord as a violation of the historic right of the Jewish people to the Land of Israel, and as a mortal danger to their security. The foreign policy guidelines of his government expressed firm opposition to a Palestinian state, to the Palestinian right of return and to the dismantling of Jewish settlements. They also asserted Israel's sovereignty over the whole of Jerusalem and ruled out withdrawal from the Golan Heights. In the Arab world this programme was widely seen as a declaration of war on the peace process.

Netanyahu spent his two and a half years in power in a relentless attempt to arrest, freeze and subvert the Oslo Accords. He kept preaching reciprocity while acting unilaterally in demolishing Arab houses, imposing curfews, confiscating Arab land, building new Jewish settlements and opening an archaeological tunnel near the Muslim holy places in the Old City of Jerusalem. Whereas the Oslo Accord left Jerusalem to the final stage of the negotiations, Netanyahu made it the centrepiece of his programme in order to block progress on any other issue. His government waged an economic and political war of attrition against the Palestinians in order to lower their expectations.

Intense American pressure compelled Netanyahu to concede territory to the Palestinian Authority on two occasions. The Hebron Protocol was signed on 15 January 1997, dividing the city into a Palestinian zone and a Jewish zone. This was a milestone in the Middle East peace process, being the first agreement signed by the

Likud government and the Palestinians. The second agreement was
brokered by President Bill Clinton at Wye Plantation in Maryland
on 23 October 1998. By signing the Wye River Memorandum,
Netanyahu undertook to withdraw from a further 13 per cent of the
West Bank in three stages over a period of three months. But a revolt
of his ultra-nationalist and religious partners brought down the
government after only one pullback. The fall of the government was
inevitable because of the basic contradiction between its declared
policy of striving for peace with the Arab world and its ideological
makeup, which militated against trading land for peace.

Under the leadership of Ehud Barak the Labour Party won a
landslide victory in May 1999. Labour's return to power was widely
expected to revive the moribund peace process. During the election
campaign Barak presented himself as Rabin's disciple, as a soldier
who turned from fighting the Arabs to peacemaking. He was given
a clear mandate to resume the quest for peace with all of Israel's
neighbours. Within a short time, however, Barak dashed the hopes
that had been pinned on him. He lacked the vision, the political
courage and the personal qualities that were necessary to follow
through on the peace partnership with the Palestinians. Barak's style
was arrogant and authoritarian, and he approached diplomacy as
the extension of war by other means. The greatest barrier raised by
Barak on the road to peace with the Palestinians was the expansion
of Jewish settlements on the West Bank. Settlement activity is not
contrary to the letter of the Oslo Accord, but it is contrary to its
spirit. True, settlement activity had gone on under all previous prime
ministers, Labour as well as Likud. But under Barak it gathered pace:
more houses were constructed, more Arab land was confiscated, and
more access roads were built to isolated Jewish settlements. For the
Palestinian population these settlements are not just a symbol of
the hated occupation, but a source of daily friction and a constant
reminder of the danger to the territorial contiguity of their future
state.

Another reason for the slowdown on the Palestinian track was
the clear preference articulated by Barak for a deal with Syria first,
on the grounds that Syria was a serious military power whereas the

Palestinians were not. During his first six months in power Barak concentrated almost exclusively on the Syrian track, leaving the Palestinians to twist in the wind. When the then Syrian President, Hafez al-Assad, rejected his final offer, Barak turned, belatedly and reluctantly, to the Palestinian track. His reservations about the Oslo Accord were well known. He argued that the step-by-step approach of trading land for peace does not serve Israel's interests because the Palestinians will always come back for more. This made him wary of further interim agreements and prompted him to insist that the Palestinian Authority commit itself to an absolutely final end to the conflict.

One more interim agreement was necessary, however, before taking the plunge to the final settlement. It took ten months to break the deadlock created by the Likud government's failure to implement the Wye River Memorandum. Once again, Barak proved to be a tough negotiator, applying intense pressure on the Palestinians. His method was described as 'peace by ultimatum'. The accord that he and Yasser Arafat signed at Sharm el-Sheikh, on 4 September 1999, reflected the underlying balance of power between the two parties. It put in place a new timetable for the final status talks, aiming at a 'framework agreement' by February and a fully fledged peace treaty by 13 September 2000.

The February deadline fell by the wayside, fuelling frustration on the Palestinian side and prompting Arafat to threaten to issue a unilateral declaration of independence if no agreement could be reached. To forestall this eventuality, Barak persuaded President Clinton to convene a trilateral summit in the United States. With the announcement of the summit, Barak's chaotic coalition fell apart. Three parties quit the government, robbing him of his parliamentary majority on the eve of his departure for the summit. In a defiant speech, Barak told the Knesset that although he no longer commanded a majority, as the directly elected prime minister he still had a mandate to make peace. But Barak's domestic political weakness inevitably reduced the diplomatic room for manoeuvre that he enjoyed. Once again, as so often in the past, the peace process was held hostage to the vagaries of the Israeli political system.

Negotiations at Camp David started on 11 July 2000 and lasted 14 days. Barak approached the summit meeting in the manner of a soldier rather than a diplomat. He dismissed Arafat's plea for more time to prepare the groundwork, believing that with the help of the American 'peace processors' he would be able to impose on the opponent his terms for the final settlement. In fairness to Barak it must be said that he crossed his own 'red lines' and put on the table a package which addressed all the issues at the heart of the conflict: land, settlements, refugee rights and Jerusalem. Basically, Barak envisaged an independent Palestinian state over the whole of the Gaza Strip and most of the West Bank, but with the large settlement blocs next to the 1967 border being annexed to Israel. The Jordan Valley, long cherished as Israel's security border, would eventually be turned over to exclusive Palestinian sovereignty. Altogether 20.5 per cent of the West Bank was to remain in Israel's hands: 10.5 per cent to be annexed outright and 10 per cent to be under Israeli military occupation for 20 years. Barak agreed to the return of Palestinian refugees, but only in the context of family reunification involving 500 people a year. On Jerusalem he went further than any previous Israeli prime minister, and indeed broke a taboo by agreeing to the partition of the city. But his offer fell well short of the Palestinian demand for exclusive sovereignty over all of the city's Arab suburbs and over Haram al-Sharif/Temple Mount.[8] The problem with this package was that it was presented pretty much on a 'take it or leave it' basis. Moreover, Barak insisted that an agreement would mark the final end of the conflict, with the Palestinians formally renouncing any further claim against the State of Israel.

The Palestinian delegation was divided in its response to the package. Some saw in it a historic opportunity for putting the conflict behind them, others felt that it would compromise their basic national rights, and in particular the right of return of the 1948 refugees. In addition, the Palestinian delegation came under pressure from Egypt and Saudi Arabia not to compromise Muslim rights over the Muslim holy places in the Old City of Jerusalem. At this critical juncture in his people's history, Yasser Arafat displayed neither courage nor statesmanship. His greatest mistake lay in rejecting many of the proposals put to him without putting forward any counter-proposals of his own. Consequently, when the summit ended in failure, Barak and Clinton were able to pin all the blame on Arafat. Arafat returned home to a hero's welcome, but he returned empty-handed.

With the collapse of the Camp David summit, the countdown to the outbreak of the next round of violence began. On the Palestinian side there was mounting frustration and deepening doubt that Israel would ever voluntarily accept a settlement that involved even a modicum of justice. Israel's apparent intransigence fed the belief that it only understands the language of force. On the Israeli side, there was growing disenchantment with the Palestinians and disillusion with the results of the Oslo Accord. Ehud Barak succeeded in persuading virtually all his compatriots that there was no Palestinian peace partner.

It was against this background that Ariel Sharon, the leader of the Likud, chose to stage his much-publicised visit to al-Haram al-Sharif, the Noble Sanctuary which the Jews call Temple Mount. On 28 September 2000, flanked by a thousand security men and in deliberate disregard for the sensitivity of the Muslim worshippers, Sharon walked into the sanctuary. By embarking on this deliberately provocative walkabout, Sharon in effect put a match to the barrel of gunpowder. His visit sparked off riots on the Haram al-Sharif that spread to other Arab areas of East Jerusalem and to other cities. Within a very short time, the riots snowballed into a full-scale uprising – the al-Aqsa intifada.

Although the uprising happened spontaneously, the Palestinian security services became involved and played their part in the escalation of violence. The move from rocks to rifles on the Palestinian side and the resort to rockets, tanks and attack helicopters by the Israelis drove the death toll inexorably upwards. As so often in the past, the sound of gunfire drowned the dialogue of the diplomats. Violence is, of course, no stranger to the region. Even after the signing of the Oslo Accord, diplomacy was sometimes interspersed with bursts of violence. Now fierce fighting was interspersed with small doses of ineffectual diplomacy. Positions hardened on both sides and the tit-for-tat gathered its own momentum. Neither side wanted to be seen as willing to back down. Yasser Arafat saw no contradiction between the intifada and negotiations. On the contrary, he hoped that the intifada would give him more leverage in dealing with the Israelis. Barak insisted that the incitement and the violence had to end before he would return to the negotiating table. His announcement of 'time out' signalled the abandonment of the political track until further notice. In the absence of talks, the security situation steadily deteriorated, clashes became more frequent, and the death toll increased at an alarming rate. Trust between the two sides broke down completely. The Oslo Accords were in tatters.

Why did the Oslo peace process break down? One possible answer is that the Oslo Accord was doomed to failure from the start because of its inherent shortcomings, and in particular because it did not address any of the core issues in the conflict between Israel and the Palestinians. The foregoing account of the rise and fall of the Oslo Accord, however, suggests a different answer. It suggests that the basic reason for the failure of Oslo to resolve the conflict is that Israel, under the leadership of the Likud, reneged on its side of the deal. By resorting to violence, the Palestinians contributed to the breakdown of trust without which no political progress is possible. But the more fundamental cause behind the loss of trust and the loss of momentum was the Israeli policy of expanding settlements on the West Bank, which carried on under Labour as well as Likud. This policy precluded the emergence of a viable Palestinian state without which there can be no end to the conflict.

The breakdown of the Oslo peace process suggests one general conclusion about the international relations of the Middle East, namely, the importance of external intervention for the resolution of regional conflicts. According to a no doubt apocryphal story, Pope John Paul believed in two possible solutions to the Arab–

Israeli conflict, the realistic and the miraculous: the realistic would involve divine intervention; the miraculous a voluntary agreement between the parties. For the reasons explained in this chapter, the PLO and Israel were able to negotiate the Oslo Accord without the help of a third party. But the imbalance in power between them made it exceedingly difficult to carry this agreement to a successful conclusion. America's role as manager of the peace process was therefore essential to the success of the whole enterprise. In the final analysis, only the United States could push Israel into a settlement. And in the event, America's failure to exert sufficient pressure on Israel to withdraw from the occupied territories was one of the factors that contributed to the breakdown of the Oslo peace process.

# SEVENTEEN

# *Woman of the Year*

Of all the presentations of the Palestinian case made by
official spokesmen since the beginning of the Arab–Israeli
conflict, the speech made by Dr Haidar Abdel-Shafi at
the Madrid peace conference in 1991 was undoubtedly the most
eloquent as well as the most conciliatory and the most convincing.
It would have been inconceivable for the PLO, despite its growing
moderation, to make such an unambiguous peace overture to
Israel. The PLO, in any case, had been excluded from the Madrid
conference by the Israeli prime minister, Yitzhak Shamir. Evidently
troubled by the conciliatory tone of Dr Abdel-Shafi's speech, Shamir
passed a note to an aide. An observer speculated that the note could
well have said: 'We made a big mistake. We should have insisted
that the PLO is the sole legitimate representative of the Palestinian
people.'

The principal author of this remarkable speech was Dr Hanan
Ashrawi, the spokesperson for the Palestinian delegation. Hanan was
born in Nablus on 8 October 1946, into a well-to-do middle-class
Christian family. Her father, Daud Mikhail, was a doctor who joined
in the resistance against British control of Palestine. After the loss of
Palestine in 1948, the family lived under Jordanian rule in Ramallah,

in what became known as the West Bank. From the Friends Girls School in Ramallah, Hanan went to study English literature at the American University in Beirut. The Israeli occupation of the West Bank in June 1967 turned her overnight into an exile. It also marked the beginning of her active involvement in the Palestinian revolution. In 1970, barred by the Israeli authorities from returning home, she enrolled as a PhD candidate in medieval English literature at the University of Virginia at Charlottesville. There she combined radical political activism with her academic studies and began to make a place for herself in the US at a time when the word 'Palestinian' was synonymous with 'terrorist'. As the founder and only member of the Charlottesville branch of the Organisation of Arab Students and as head of the American Friends of Free Palestine, she formed coalitions with an anti-Vietnam War group, women's groups, and the Black Students Alliance.

In 1974, a general amnesty for Palestinians enabled Dr Ashrawi to return home to Ramallah and to rejoin her family. She settled into academic life as head of the English Department at Birzeit University. From the outset, she made clear her opposition to the occupation. Following her participation in a few student demonstrations and protest marches, she was arrested and taken before a military judge. 'What are you doing here today?' asked the judge after Hanan chose to take her oath on the New Testament rather than the Koran or the Old Testament. 'That's a good question', she replied calmly. 'A very good question. Maybe you can answer it.' This experience led her to establish the University Legal Aid Committee to provide support for Palestinian students. Outside the university, she and a group of other women started feminist study groups, and held consciousness-raising sessions about the treatment of women in different spheres of Palestinian life.

Hanan's husband, Emile Ashrawi, was not a political activist but a musician, a drummer in a rock band that combined Arabic lyrics with contemporary music. They married in 1975, and had two daughters. With a helpful husband, Hanan was able to continue her many nationalist and feminist activities. Like many of her colleagues at Birzeit University, she had some contact with the leftist political factions of the PLO, but she did not join any one of them. She moved closer to the mainstream Fatah movement while always retaining her political independence.

The intifada of December 1987 drew Ashrawi deeper and deeper into politics. The popular revolt brought together the seemingly irreconcilable elements of Palestinian society in a joint campaign that pitted them against the formidable Israeli military machine. It was a heady experience which, despite all the suffering it entailed, released suppressed energies and gave the participants a sense of power, even of invincibility. Ashrawi was susceptible to the prevailing mood of exhilaration, but she also became more aware of the importance of organisation, discipline, and self-criticism. She took the lead in devising ways to explain the Palestinian case, particularly in the press and on television.

As a matter of policy, Palestinians had refrained from talking to Israelis in a public debate. This was a way of withholding recognition of Israel; but it gave the Israelis exclusive access to the mass media and plenty of opportunities for blaming and misrepresenting the absent Palestinians. An invitation to debate face-to-face with Israelis on Ted Koppel's ABC show *Nightline* in April 1988 gave Ashrawi just the opportunity that she had been looking for to break with the Palestinian tradition of verbal boycott. She seized the opportunity, she writes, to deliver three quite different messages: 'to the world – that we wanted to be heard directly; to the Palestinians – that it was time to take the initiative and speak out; to the Israelis – that we were ready to take them on'. Encouraged by the result of this first public encounter, Ashrawi and a group of other political 'independents' formed the Palestinian Political Committee, which held many of its meetings in her house. The objectives of the committee were to brief journalists and foreign visitors; to provide a pool of accredited speakers who could participate in conferences and seminars throughout the world; to present different options to the unified national leadership of the intifada; and to become a centre for political and diplomatic activity in the occupied territories. Such activity was illegal then, but the danger only encouraged them to persist. Apart from being risky, this activity impinged heavily on

Ashrawi's home life. Zeina, her younger daughter, said: 'I have lent my mother to the peace process.'

The peace process between the Palestinians and Israel, which culminated in the famous handshake between Yasser Arafat and Yitzhak Rabin on 13 September 1993, is the main theme of Ashrawi's revealing and highly readable memoir.* The book, as its title indicates, is not a work of diplomatic history but an inside account by one of the participants. Ashrawi also tells us that she was encouraged to write this account by her friend Edward Said, who often lamented the lack of a Palestinian narrative to reveal their side of the truth.

Hanan Ashrawi is not a politician by choice, politics being her second career. Her literary background, however, inevitably influenced her political style. Her command of English was an obvious asset in putting across the Palestinian case, but precisely because she was not a professional politician, she was able to offer a new perspective on the Palestinian struggle. She raised the level of debate about Palestinian politics by concentrating on issues affecting daily life, by articulating the hopes and fears of ordinary Palestinians, by dwelling on issues of justice and morality – calling attention, for example, to Israel's infringement of academic freedom, its arbitrary deportations and its mistreatment of arrested Palestinians. Being a woman probably made it easier for her to speak about her own feelings and emotions, and the human predicament of people who had been deprived of their land and forced into exile or to live under occupation – and this touched a chord with the Western audiences to whom she addressed herself. Although she presented her case with passion, and although she could be dogmatic, her listeners did not feel threatened or hectored by her. Even under severe pressure, she carried herself with dignity.

As did Edward Said, Hanan Ashrawi understands the importance of Palestinians' telling their own stories; unlike him, she also understands the requirements of pragmatic politics, the necessity of compromise not only with one's enemies but also with one's

* Hanan Ashrawi, *This Side of Peace: A Personal Account* (New York: Simon and Schuster, 1995).

partners. Like Said, Ashrawi is an intellectual with a passionate commitment to the Palestinian cause and considerable expository and oratorical skills. The difference is that Ashrawi can translate ideas into a plan of action. Her approach to politics is informed by practical experience, by a sense of realism, by a capacity to balance conflicting considerations.

It was these political skills and not just her mastery of the English language that commended Ashrawi to Yasser Arafat as an envoy to the US government. Arafat knew that she had no personal ambitions for political power, and that she would not threaten his position as the leader of the Palestinian political movement. Yet their relationship mirrored some of the tensions between the two major components of this movement: those in the occupied territories and those outside, *al-dakhil* and *al-kharij*. Both the Americans and the Israelis wanted the centre of gravity within the Palestinian movement to shift from the leadership in Tunis to the local leadership in the occupied territories, a shift that Arafat was determined to resist. However, in 1989 Arafat himself asked Ashrawi to meet with State Department officials and make a plea for upgrading the status of dialogue between the US and the PLO. That was the beginning of the role she was to play for the next six years, a role which gave her an increasingly visible international presence.

At the State Department, Ashrawi met three of James Baker's aides – Dennis Ross, Dan Kurtzer and Aaron Miller – who were later to be called 'the peace processors'. By her own account, she was not exactly self-effacing:

> Being, and perceiving myself to be, of the people and not official-dom, an envoy though not a diplomat, I exercised my option for directness and honesty. I brought with me an aspect of the innocence of the intifada, its willingness to confront, to take the initiative, to assert itself, and not to succumb to intimidation. But most of all, I brought to that encounter, and subsequently to all others, that one essential *sine qua non* that was to become the most salient quality of Palestinian political discourse: the human dimension.

A year later, Yasser Arafat committed one of the worst blunders of his political career by literally embracing Saddam Hussein, following the Iraqi invasion of Kuwait. That embrace put the PLO once again in the doghouse, and exposed the Palestinians in the occupied territories to physical danger. Publicly, Saddam posed as the champion of the Palestinians; privately, when asked about the safety of the Palestinians should he attack Israel with Scud missiles, he is reported to have replied, 'I am not separating lentils'. The local Palestinian leaders now had to steer a very careful course. For years Ashrawi and her colleagues had been trying to teach the language of peace: 'Like Sisyphus we had laboriously rolled the rock of nonmilitary solutions uphill. Now, it seemed, with the glorification of Mars, the rock was not only about to roll back, but to crush us in the process.'

Following the First Gulf War, Ashrawi and a handful of leaders from the 'inside' – led by Faisal Husseini, a prominent figure in the Fatah mainstream and the PLO in the occupied territories – participated in exploratory talks with Secretary of State Baker. These helped both to launch the Middle East peace process and to ensure that the Palestinians would be part of it. George Bush proudly proclaimed that the Gulf War laid the foundations for a 'new world order'. Baker was charged with convening an international conference to deal with the Arab–Israeli conflict; in this he saw the Palestinians from the occupied territories as a useful ally, but also one that could be disposed of if necessary. As Yitzhak Shamir kept stonewalling, Baker steadily intensified the pressure on the Palestinians, attempting to sell them any proposals that Israel seemed willing to accept, saying that this was the only way of getting Israel into the talks.

Baker and his aides shuffled back and forth between Israel and the Palestinians, carrying, as Ashrawi ruefully observed, a carrot for the Israelis and a stick for the Palestinians. Baker developed a healthy respect for his unconventional interlocutors, as one journalist travelling with him reported to Ashrawi. Rather flippantly she replied: 'After a six-hour meeting with Shamir, he'll find anybody likeable.' In these exploratory meetings, Husseini and Ashrawi resisted every attempt to create an alternative leadership to replace the PLO. Their task, as they saw it, was to represent the PLO not to replace it. While they were forced to yield to most of Shamir's conditions on Palestinian representation at the planned peace conference, particularly the exclusion of Arafat, they maintained their long-term aim to get the PLO recognised as the legitimate voice of the Palestinians, and ultimately to get the PLO leaders to negotiate with Israel directly and officially.

Madrid was by far the most comprehensive of all Middle East peace conferences. It included the United States and the Soviet Union as co-sponsors, United Nations and European Union observers, delegations from Israel and several Arab countries, a joint Jordanian–Palestinian delegation, and some five thousand journalists from throughout the world. As the spokesperson for the Palestinian delegation, Hanan Ashrawi quickly emerged as the star of the show. That the PLO was excluded enabled her to present the Palestinian delegation as one made up mainly of academics and professionals, who had come to Madrid to present the cause of their people. It was Ashrawi who persuaded PLO leaders that the opening address should be delivered in English rather then Arabic, because it was aimed primarily at the American public. In preparing the address, Ashrawi writes, she felt driven by the need to capture in words the essence of the Palestinian experience and to help create an irresistible force for change. So moving was the speech that Dr Abdel-Shafi, a gentleman of the old school, was afraid he would cry when he delivered it. 'Never mind, *ma'lesh*,' said the author, 'go ahead and cry. Heaven knows we have the right to cry; we have enough to cry about.'

In the intervals between plenary sessions Ashrawi was constantly getting attention, giving press briefings and interviews. The Israelis fielded a large professional public relations team, but they clearly lost the game to Ashrawi. One of the Israeli experts described her as terrifyingly articulate, and her handling of the press was nothing short of brilliant. She was not intimidated and she did not suffer from stage fright. She believed that the press was after the truth and that her ally was the verifiable truth about, for example, the ways

Palestinians were deprived of elementary rights. At the final press briefing in Madrid, she ended by saying: 'You have given me and the Palestinian people a fair hearing, and for that I'm deeply grateful.' She received a standing ovation from the reporters.

The second stage in the US-sponsored peace process was the bilateral talks between Israel and the Arab delegations, which got under way in Washington in January 1992. Dr Abdel-Shafi stayed on as the head of the Palestinian delegation, while Dr Ashrawi continued as the spokesperson. One critic called these delegates 'an arbitrary fistful', but the press, on the whole, continued to portray them as intelligent and personally impressive. The PLO leadership in Tunis was still excluded from direct participation in the talks, but was as determined as ever to call the shots. In this complex situation three different Palestinian groups were involved in the peace process: the delegation to Washington that conducted the negotiations; the Leadership Committee, headed by Arafat's adviser, Nabil Sha'ath; and a Strategic Committee consisting of advisers and experts. Thrown together literally overnight, this diverse group of men and women, doctors and academics, functioned as a surprisingly coherent team.

The main constraint that impaired their work was the constant interference from Tunis. Working with the PLO chairman had never been easy because of his autocratic and idiosyncratic style of decision-making, and because he was vain and inept in roughly equal proportions. But Ashrawi makes it plain that he now began to develop an obsession, verging on paranoia, with the threat of an 'alternative leadership'. He feared that any progress made by the 'people's delegation' would undermine the status of the PLO and his own position as the leader of the Palestinian movement. He used the analogy of the drone that serves to fertilise the queen bee and is then left to die; he talked bitterly of the man who is revived in order to make him sign his will and is then left to die or even got rid of. To fend off this imagined threat, Arafat resorted to manipulation, divide-and-rule tactics, and petty intrigues. He was anxious to demonstrate that no progress could be achieved in the talks without his backing. He pulled strings from Tunis, and he went to remarkable lengths to show that only he could make decisions on behalf of the Palestinians.

Hanan Ashrawi had a special position within the Leadership Committee because she was its internationally known spokesperson, and because she had close contacts with American officials. She represented the Palestinian side in many talks, formal and informal, with Baker and his aides in the State Department; consequently she could speak with authority about the American position. But although liaison with the State Department was one of her official duties, it exposed her to the charge of being too close to the Americans. Some members of Arafat's entourage, probably prompted by jealousy, started to question the reliability of her reports on the American position, and they even insinuated that she had sold out. Arafat himself was double-faced. When he saw her in Tunis he would be appreciative and ingratiating, calling her not only 'a dear sister but the crown on our heads, *taj rasna*'. Behind her back, however, he could be every bit as dismissive and malicious as his subordinates.

The attitude of the Israeli negotiators posed quite different problems for Ashrawi. Throughout the first five rounds of the Washington talks, the Palestinians tried to engage the Israelis on substantive issues, such as withdrawal from the West Bank and the future of Jerusalem, but the Israelis remained slippery and evasive. They kept up the semblance of participation without addressing the real issues. That Yitzhak Shamir wanted the talks to go nowhere slowly was soon an open secret. As far as the PLO's backstage involvement in the talks was concerned, Shamir preferred to pretend it did not exist. His intransigence contributed to the defeat of the Likud in the June 1992 elections. Labour's victory gave rise to optimistic forecasts that peace was around the corner. 'The real test is yet to come', Ashrawi cautioned her colleagues: 'whether Rabin the bone-breaker can become Rabin the peace-maker'. To her dismay, even modest expectations of the new Israeli prime minister were quickly shattered when he, too, refused to engage in serious negotiations.

A third source of frustration for the Palestinians was the American reluctance to take a more active part in managing the peace process, except when Israel needed bailing out. The peace process had started with two sponsors at Madrid, but one, the USSR, no longer existed, and the other, the US, became a spectator. With the approach of the 1992 presidential elections, George Bush and James Baker, faced with a strong possibility of defeat, relaxed what control they had over the peace talks and allowed Israel to take advantage of its superior power. Elections aside, moreover, no US Administration was prepared to stand up to Israel, because there was no political advantage to be gained by doing so. The Palestinians, on the other hand, however just their cause might be, were seen as useless in advancing political careers, whether on Capitol Hill or in the White House. Among themselves, Ashrawi writes, the Palestinians joked that Americans only sent them 'nonpapers' because they looked on them as a 'nonpeople', and that the Americans did not respond to most of the Palestinians' memoranda because they regarded them as a 'nondelegation'.

When Bill Clinton succeeded George Bush as president, the pro-Israeli bias in American policy became pronounced. The more even-handed approach of the Bush Administration was replaced by an 'Israel-first' approach reminiscent of the Reagan era. Clinton made it clear that he would not put pressure on Israel and he adopted a 'hands off' attitude to the peace talks. At her first meeting with Secretary of State Warren Christopher, Ashrawi studied closely both what he said and how he said it, and concluded that he had no personal interest in the outcome in the Middle East. The policy of the new Administration, she observed, was characterised by hesitancy and vagueness. On the few occasions when the Clinton Administration presented proposals to break the deadlock, they clearly reflected Israeli views. By the summer of 1993, the Palestinian negotiators gave up hope that the Clinton Administration would have any serious influence on Israel's positions, let alone come up with formulations they considered fair to Palestinians.

Consequently, Hanan Ashrawi became convinced that the basic format of the negotiations had to be changed if serious and discreet talks were to take place between the PLO and the Israeli government. Without her knowing it, America's failure to move the official talks forward in Washington helped to make possible the secret negotiations in Oslo between the PLO and representatives of the Israeli government. The PLO had made numerous attempts to establish a secret means of negotiation with Rabin, but he did not respond. The meetings that Norwegian officials arranged in Oslo provided the first such back-channel that Rabin appeared to take seriously. Arafat, for his part, played a characteristically devious double game. He kept the official Palestinian negotiators in Washington completely in the dark about the secret talks in Oslo. Moreover, when the Oslo talks moved forward, Arafat started issuing hardline instructions to Ashrawi and her colleagues in a deliberate attempt to block the Washington talks.

When Arafat told Husseini and Ashrawi to pass on to Christopher a paper whose terms they considered unacceptable, they obeyed his instructions and then promptly submitted their resignations, which were not accepted. This time Ashrawi made no attempt to conceal her anger. 'We cannot go on', she told Arafat to his face, 'with conflicting instructions, multiple channels, lack of a coherent strategy, inconsistent political decision making, total disregard for our structures, and lack of accountability and openness in our internal work'. Then, at a specially convened meeting, she excoriated the members of the PLO Executive Committee based in Tunis, accusing them of stabbing her and her colleagues in the back.

On her next trip to Tunis, on 26 August 1993, Ashrawi was told about the Declaration of Principles that had been initialled in Oslo. She was not surprised by the existence of a back-channel, only that this particular channel had succeeded. The next morning she and Faisal Husseini went to the office of Mahmoud Abbas, whose *nom de guerre* is Abu Mazen, and studied a copy of the agreement. Her first reaction was one of shock. It was clear to her that the PLO officials who had negotiated this agreement had not lived under occupation. It did not commit Israel to cease all settlement activity, it postponed the question of Jerusalem, and it said nothing about human rights. Like Husseini, she made clear her deep concern about the gaps in the agreement, the ambiguities, the lack of detail, and the absence of any mechanisms for supplementing it. While recognising that the PLO had made some strategic political gains, as Abu Mazen pointed out, she also thought that the agreement had many potentially explosive provisions that could be turned to the disadvantage of the Palestinian side. In any case, it was clear to her when she read the document that one chapter of Palestinian history was drawing to a close and another about to begin, and that she should start preparing to leave.

At the signing ceremony of the Accord between the PLO and Israel on the South Lawn of the White House, Hanan Ashrawi sat in the tenth row. She had offered to write the speech for the former guerrilla chieftain to deliver in his new incarnation as world statesman, and she no doubt had it in her to produce a fitting sequel to the Madrid speech, but her offer was turned down. In the event, Arafat's speech was quite remarkable for its flatness and banality. Yet the choice of this speech, as someone told Ashrawi, was a conscious one. The implicit message was that her kind of language was over. 'The next phase', she was told, 'is not one for poets and intellectuals. It's the era of hard-core politicians, one in which slogans are the weapons of a struggle for power. Self-interest produces clichés, not humanistic visions.'

Arafat offered Ashrawi a number of jobs in his new Administration, which she declined. It was only to be expected that they would break apart. For the self-styled President of Palestine had intended all along to follow the Algerian model, in which the politicians in exile had returned to rule the country after independence, and had excluded from power the local leaders who had fought the French. Ashrawi was wise to preserve her political independence, because Arafat's language, his values, and his vision for the future were quite different from her own. The need for democracy and for protection of human rights are only two of the issues on which they disagreed. She felt, as she writes towards the end of her book, that:

> Our main challenge ahead was an integrated and comprehensive process of nation building and reconstruction, which required more than a police force and a political authority. We had to build the substance of the state, including the institutions of civil society, of participatory democracy and accountability, as well as

the systems and structures that would regulate their work and
bear the weight of statehood. The independence of the judiciary
had to be guaranteed, while free and fair general elections must
be held for a separate legislative council. The mentality, attitudes,
and work procedures of the past were no longer applicable, and
the worst thing our leadership could do would be to superimpose
these on a new reality with a human substance that would reject
them. It was up to us, I was convinced, to ease the transition and
to ensure that the principles we had espoused and defended for
so long would be translated into fact as the operative norms and
systems of our future.

But the reasons she gave Arafat for declining his offer were tactfully
phrased:

We have to turn the page, close one chapter and begin another.
I will not be part of any political structure, nor will I accept any
official post. From now on, I will be pursuing a different vision. I
had entered the public political arena to serve the people and the
cause, and for the last few years I've given it all I had. Now it's
time to move on, for each phase requires its own instruments and
vehicles, its own language and people.

Hanan Ashrawi went on to establish and to head the Palestinian
Independent Commission for Citizens' Rights. She views the work
of the Commission in hearing and investigating complaints of
mistreatment as an important part of the process of institution-
building. On the day Arafat's Palestinian National Authority was
sworn into office in Jericho, her human rights office in Jerusalem
was already receiving 'a flood of cases and complaints'.

In the meantime, the gulf between the expectations that attended
the conclusion of the Oslo Accord and the actual results was
becoming more apparent by the day. Arafat did not renounce his
'revolutionary' mentality in favour of the commitment to 'state-
building' that Ashrawi advocated. His Administration was set up
in an area amounting to about 6.5 per cent of original Palestine.

It was undemocratic and unpopular, and marked by growing repression. Israeli pressure on Arafat to crack down harder on dissidents, especially those from Hamas and Islamic Jihad, led him to create a new state security court. This controversial three-man court threatened the civil rights of the Palestinians and reminded them of Israel's military courts. Critics who used to sneer at Arafat as the Mayor of Gaza took to calling him the Sheriff of the Gaza Strip. As the head of the Palestinian Independent Commission for Citizens' Rights, Ashrawi was bound to take a dim view of this court, which repeatedly flouted the rule of law. When her privately expressed warnings were ignored, she issued a statement at the beginning of May 1994 strongly condemning the court's procedures and practices. She also made it known that she might resign as head of the Commission if nothing was done. Her statement amounted to a direct challenge to Arafat. Her relations with him reached an all-time low.

One puts down Hanan Ashrawi's memoir with admiration for her courage and integrity and astonishment at her achievements. She rose to prominence in the aftermath of the First Gulf War, one of the most difficult phases in Palestinian history since the disaster of 1948. She was an academic without a constituency, party, power base, or organisation; and her support from the leader of her movement was at best erratic. Yet she threw herself into political and diplomatic activity on behalf of her people, and she was spectacularly successful in projecting a new image of Palestinian nationalism as a rational and humane cause. Subjected for years to unrelenting pressures and drawn into a vortex of petty manipulations, she maintained her psychological balance and never lost her political bearings. She was the right person, at the right time, doing the right job, and doing it far better than any of the PLO apparatchiks. Her character and principles contrast sadly with those of Yasser Arafat and some of the men who surrounded him in his seedy little statelet in Gaza. It is tragic that the Palestinians could not have had her as one of their principal leaders at that critical moment in their history.

# EIGHTEEN

# Overtaken by Events

Yitzhak Rabin inflicted more punishment and pain on the Palestinians than any other Israeli leader to date. As chief of staff in 1967, he presided over Israel's spectacular military victory and the capture of the West Bank. For the next 25 years, in various capacities, he tried to hold on to the occupied territories by brute force. Ironically, it was his brutality towards the Palestinians that earned him his reputation inside Israel as a responsible and reliable politician. But the policy of force had been overtaken by events. Consequently, during his second term as prime minister, which began in June 1992, Rabin the predator began to mutate into Rabin the peacemaker.

The policy of force had commanded a very broad national consensus inside Israel; the policy of compromise did not. Rabin's attempt at a limited, gradual and controlled withdrawal from the West Bank was hysterically denounced by the Israeli Right, and especially by the militant settlers, as treason against the Jewish nation, as the beginning of the end of the Land of Israel. When Rabin was assassinated in November 1995, by a right-wing extremist claiming to act in the name of God, the fact that his assassin was an Israeli painfully underscored the deep and persistent divisions among Israelis on relations with their most intimate enemies – the Palestinians.

Meron Benvenisti, the author of *Intimate Enemies: Jews and Arabs in a Shared Land*,* is a member of the Labour Party but also a severe critic of its policy towards the Palestinians. A geographer and historian by training, he is passionately attached to his homeland. He was Deputy Mayor of Jerusalem under Teddy Kollek from 1971 to 1978 and responsible for administering East Jerusalem and the Old City, where the majority of Jerusalem's Palestinian population lives. In 1982 he established the West Bank Database Project and played an influential part in the debate about the occupied territories. Now he is a full-time writer, publishing books in Hebrew and English, including the autobiographical *Conflicts and Contradictions* (1986), and opinion pieces in the independent Israeli daily newspaper *Haaretz*.

In the foreword to this book Thomas Friedman, who won two Pulitzer Prizes for his reporting from the Middle East, describes Benvenisti as 'an oasis of knowledge in the intellectual deserts of the Middle East – deserts where charlatans and ideologues, hucksters and holymen, regularly opine and divine, unencumbered by facts, history or statistics'. Whenever Friedman wanted to find out what was really happening, he would call Benvenisti, 'confident that his take would be original, his data unassailable, and his conclusions delivered without regard to whom they might offend or support'. These qualities have made Benvenisti one of the most quoted and most damned analysts in Israel – a hawk to the doves and a dove to the hawks, 'Jeremiah and Jonah wrapped into one'.

In the late 1980s, after a decade of hectic settlement activity by the Likud, the question of the day was: could Israel still withdraw from the occupied territories or had it reached the point of no return? Benvenisti's conclusion, based on economic, demographic and land-ownership statistics, was that the process of Jewish colonisation in the West Bank and the Gaza Strip had become irreversible. This conclusion both pleased and displeased the various interest groups.

* Meron Benvenisti, *Intimate Enemies: Jews and Arabs in a Shared Land* (Berkeley: University of California Press, 1995).

The settlers were reassured to hear that the roots they had sunk in Judea and Samaria were now so deep that no government would be able to remove them, but resented being told how much they cost the Israeli taxpayer. Labour Party moderates were reassured to hear that the strategically important parts of the West Bank had been secured, but hotly denied the claim that their favoured option – territorial compromise with King Hussein – had been overtaken by events. The Palestinians felt vindicated by Benvenisti's figures on Israeli land expropriation, but didn't want to be told that their own diplomatic intransigence facilitated the task of the expropriators.

Fundamental to Benvenisti's analysis, here and elsewhere, is the distinction between internal, communal conflict and external, inter-state conflict. An inter-state dispute is conducted by the representatives of sovereign states within a defined international framework and in accordance with well-established rules of diplomatic practice. A precondition for negotiations is recognition of the legitimacy and equality of the representatives of the other state. The subject of negotiation is not the status of each side but the ways and means of resolving the conflict of interest between them. An intercommunal conflict, on the other hand, revolves around fundamental issues of identity, competing symbols and absolute justice. It is an existential conflict which is perceived by both sides as a struggle over the supreme value – collective survival – on which there can be no compromise. The Israeli–Palestinian conflict is defined by Benvenisti as intercommunal:

> an ongoing confrontation between two human collectives, struggling for natural and human resources, and competing for exclusive control over symbolic assets, within a territorial unit that both consider their homeland. It is a multifaceted and multilayered conflict. On the one hand, it is a political, national-ethnic struggle for sovereignty. On the other hand, it is typical of divided societies and derives from an unequal division of resources, asymmetrical economic dependency, and a monopoly over state coercive power exercised by one group against the other. Intercommunal conflicts are organic and endemic, a never-ending

twilight war. At best, violence sinks beneath the surface, but the potential for a conflagration is ever present.

Intimate enmity has turned the two communities into mirror images of each other, swaying together in a dance of death. To drive home his point, Benvenisti cites Camus's description of the conflict between the French and the Algerians: 'It is as if two insane people, crazed with wrath, had decided to turn into a fatal embrace, a forced marriage from which they cannot free themselves. Forced to live together and incapable of uniting, they decided at last to die together.'

Given his reading of the Israeli–Palestinian conflict as primordial, irrational, all-embracing and all-consuming, Benvenisti has long been sceptical about the conceptual framework of inter-state relations and pessimistic about the possibility of the conflict's resolution. The Israeli–Palestinian conflict, he argued for two decades before the Oslo Accord, was not susceptible to the ministrations of traditional diplomacy because neither side recognised the legitimacy of the other. Even when the two sides talked in rational, pragmatic language and engaged with each other in a diplomatic context, it was only in order to conceal the hidden agenda of absolute values. Benvenisti's unique perspective is, to use Friedman's terms, that of a tribal realist and a professional pessimist.

In *Intimate Enemies* he examines the implications of two events in the conflict: the massacre of Palestinians by the Israeli police on Temple Mount in October 1990, and the handshake between Rabin and Arafat on the South Lawn of the White House in September 1993. In the process, he also takes up the escalation of the intifada and of intercommunal and internecine violence, the Gulf War, the Madrid peace conference and the Oslo Accord, all of which occurred in the three years separating the massacre and the handshake.

The incident on Temple Mount in which the Israeli police sprayed automatic fire indiscriminately into a crowd, killing 19 Palestinians, exemplifies the tribal and atavistic character of the conflict. In truth, the question of who started it was more controversial than the incident itself, and Benvenisti skilfully conveys the perspectives of the two communities. The Palestinians on the Mount – convinced of a conspiracy on the part of Jewish fanatics to lay the cornerstone of the Third Temple within the al-Aqsa compound and cause damage to the Muslim holy places – were staging a peaceful protest. The Israelis claimed that the protesters attacked peaceful Jewish worshippers by the Wailing Wall. Some Israelis even believed that Saddam Hussein and Yasser Arafat plotted the disturbance in order to mobilise the Muslim world against the United States and its Zionist puppet. 'Context', Benvenisti observes, 'is a matter of ethnic affiliation. The attribution of cause and effect is not a matter of objective-logical derivation but rather of one-sided conceptions. The chain of intercommunal violence is nourished by opposing definitions of the relationship between challenge and response. What one group sees as a challenge looks like a response to another.' Hardly surprising, for were it possible to get the two sides to agree on the order of events, the dispute would evaporate.

In left-wing circles in Israel the massacre on Temple Mount occasioned serious soul-searching. The Left had always externalised the conflict, focusing it on the occupied territories: the problem was Israel's occupation of Arab land and the solution involved ending the occupation and establishing a Palestinian state alongside Israel. Defining the Israeli–Palestinian divide in geopolitical terms allowed the Left to deny the endemic intercommunal nature of the conflict. The Temple Mount incident, in the heart of 'united Jerusalem', could not easily be reconciled with this point of view. While no doubt feeling some genuine sympathy for those on the receiving end of police brutality, left-wing Israelis were primarily concerned with the damage to their own self-image and to Israel's reputation abroad. As such, Benvenisti argues, 'their reaction to the trauma was not a painful confrontation with reality but an almost desperate attempt to reconstruct their web of evasions and excuses and, most of all, to believe in it again'. Nor did the incident have any lasting effect on official Israeli policy towards the Palestinian population. In retrospect, it should be seen not as a watershed in Israeli–Palestinian relations, but as a testimony to the ethnocentrism of the two communities, of both victors and victims.

The Temple Mount incident provides Benvenisti with a magnifying glass under which to examine the tangled question of Israeli–Palestinian relations in Jerusalem, and to expose some of the anomalies and contradictions of the Israeli approach to the city. In the first place, he argues that Jerusalem exemplifies the struggle between two political cultures, between 'the state of Israel – an entity which functions according to liberal Western criteria, and membership in which is determined by citizenship – and the Land of Israel – an entity in which tribal-fundamentalist values rule and membership in which is tested by adherence to Judaism in its religious-traditional and patriotic-nationalist sense'.

Second, in Benvenisti's view there is a contradiction between the Israelis' perception of their rule in the city as just and fair, and the reality, where concern for 'the rule of law' has replaced concern for 'the legitimacy of the law'. The Israeli authorities have, in his opinion, blurred the distinction between 'the rule of law' as a concept embodying universal, liberal and democratic norms of government, and 'rule through law', which is a unilateral and coercive system used by one community to impose its will on another.

Third, there is a stark contrast between the official claim of fair treatment for all Jerusalem's residents, and the discrimination in services, allocation of resources, licensing and environmental development that Arab residents experience. The evidence he musters for this discrimination, both on the part of the regime and at municipal level, is compelling. Of the huge development funds allocated by government ministries in Jerusalem, the Jewish sector gets 95 per cent and the Arab sector only 5 per cent. The united city invested 3 per cent of its development budget in East Jerusalem in 1986 and 2.6 per cent in 1990. In an interview, Teddy Kollek acknowledged the disparity: 'I've done something for Jewish Jerusalem in the past 25 years; for East Jerusalem? Nothing!'

Finally, Benvenisti challenges conventional Israeli wisdom on how the dispute over Jerusalem might be resolved. He notes that since 1917, when the city became a pressing international problem, no fewer than 40 plans have been suggested while the problem has grown steadily more severe. In 1967, when the borders of the city were redrawn, Israel was guided by the wish to include 'a maximum of land with a minimum of Arabs'. Ever since, successive governments have insisted on absolute and indivisible Israeli sovereignty, while offering self-administration of the Jewish, Muslim and Christian holy places and decentralisation of municipal government to allow greater autonomy to the non-Jewish minorities. These offers, however, only address the secondary problems while avoiding the critical question of sovereignty. In the meantime, Israel's policy – for which there is broad national consensus – has been to integrate the hinterland so as to create one continuous Jewish presence in Greater Jerusalem and to cut off the city's Arab residents from the Arabs on the West Bank. This course of action, in Benvenisti's opinion, is a sure recipe for friction and animosity.

But Israel's entire policy of building settlements in the occupied territories was always certain to lead to friction and animosity. Initially confined to the Jordan Valley in accordance with security imperatives and the classic Zionist doctrine of avoiding as far as possible heavily populated Arab areas, Labour's settlement policy soon developed a momentum of its own. It also paved the way for the policy pursued by the Likud and the national religious parties from 1977 onwards, which was to build settlements everywhere in the West Bank, including the heavily populated Arab areas. For them it was out of the question to prohibit Jewish settlements in places of Biblical resonance like Beit El, Shiloh and Hebron. The end result was a settlement map that significantly reduced the scope for carrying out the Labour Party's original plan of territorial compromise.

Benvenisti compares the Israelis' attitude to the territories occupied by their army in 1967 to the idea of the 'frontier' in American history: as a border region beyond the pale of civilisation, inhabited by natives who do not constitute a society with political rights, and who are incapable of spiritual attachment to the land. Ethnic attachment to the 'frontier' region conquered in 1967 was, he claims, instantaneous and endorsed by all elements of the Israeli-Jewish political culture. This is an overstatement. The truth of the matter is that Israeli society was, and remains, deeply divided in its attitude to the 'frontier' region. Some of these divisions come to light in Benvenisti's long chapter on the Palestinian uprising against Israeli rule in the occupied territories. Although the first intifada began in December 1987, nearly three years before the massacre on Temple Mount, Benvenisti retraces his steps to examine its origins, aims and significance. In fact, there is no better illustration of his thesis that the Israeli–Palestinian conflict is an intercommunal one. The intifada broke out spontaneously, without preparation or planning by the Palestinian elite, let alone the PLO, because the Palestinians in the occupied territories felt not only that their human rights were being trampled on but that their very existence as a national community was under threat. It arose out of the conditions of intimate enmity and its aim was to free the territories from Israeli military presence, political control and economic exploitation. The intifada was a general uprising against the Israeli regime.

Was the intifada an anti-colonial national liberation struggle? It certainly had many of the features of such a struggle. It was directed against a country that had occupied a territory which was not its own, colonised it, taken over its natural resources, exploited the cheap labour of the natives, and maintained its rule by an army of occupation. Similarly, Israel's response was hard to distinguish from colonial repression, especially with Defence Minister Rabin's aforementioned order to his soldiers to 'break the bones' of the troublemakers. On closer examination, however, the colonial model appears more problematic. It assumes, for example, that the borders of the hegemonic country are well defined, whereas Israel's post-1967 borders were not. Another significant difference is that the Europeans dismantled their colonial regimes and went home, whereas the Israelis have to negotiate with enemies who share their land.

Pre-intifada Israeli rule was characterised by minimal use of coercion and relative acquiescence on the part of the subject population. Israeli officials considered the situation stable and the outbreak of the intifada took them completely by surprise. Frustrated by their failure to suppress the uprising with force, Israeli officials concluded that they were fighting a new type of war. To Benvenisti, however, a violent confrontation between communities is not a war, and therefore any comparison with Israel's previous wars is invalid. 'In a conventional war', he writes, 'the army defends the country's borders, while in an intercommunal conflict it defends the regime. A conventional war lasts until one side wins, or until both sides tire and everyone goes home. Intercommunal conflicts are chronic, endemic, organic and endless. They just go on and on.' Furthermore, in a civilian uprising there is no frontier, the occupation of territory has no meaning and the distinction between soldier and civilian is blurred.

One tangible result of the intifada was to shift the PLO from confrontation with Israel to negotiation. The PLO leadership in Tunis had nothing to do with the outbreak of the intifada but it was not slow to claim credit or to assume control over its direction. It was the local leaders, however, who pressed Arafat to translate the intifada's achievements into a realistic political programme. They knew the enemy much better than he did and had a much sounder appreciation of the balance of power. Arafat heeded their advice and at the Palestinian National Council meeting in Algiers in November 1988, he won a majority for the recognition of Israel, for a two-state solution and for a Palestinian declaration of independence. The response of the Israeli government was predictably cool. Just as the Palestinians were moving towards territorial compromise, Israel under Yitzhak Shamir's leadership was moving away from it. Intense international pressure induced Shamir to come up, in May 1989, with a Palestinian election plan but it was a plan that he knew would be unacceptable to the Palestinians. His aim in framing it was simply to shift the responsibility for the continuing deadlock onto the Palestinians. In any case, this plan was added to the pile of papers stamped with the initials OBE – overtaken by events.

The Iraqi invasion of Kuwait in August 1990 arrived like a *deus ex machina*. In the Middle East tragedy the god came in the unlikely form of Saddam Hussein posing as the champion of Palestinian independence. Arafat's embrace of the Iraqi dictator was greeted by Israeli officials with relief. Not only did it seem to vindicate their claim that the Palestinian problem was just one component rather than the heart of the Arab–Israeli conflict, they could now also turn their attention from 'the boys with stones' to the external military threat, from the new type of war in their own backyard for which they had no answer to the global crisis unfolding in the Persian Gulf. Prominent members of the peace camp, like Yossi Sarid, revoked their sympathy for the Palestinian cause. 'Saddam Hussein', Benvenisti writes, 'made it possible to revert once again to the sterile vocabulary of inter-state disputes and escape the intercommunal conceptual conundrum.'

The peace process initiated by George H.W. Bush and James Baker in the aftermath of the First Gulf War was different, in Benvenisti's view, from previous US initiatives in that this time it was the Americans who badly needed progress. Shamir, however, failed to discern the fundamental difference between this plan and its predecessors, and this blindness contributed to his defeat in the general election of June 1992. Benvenisti has no difficulty in explaining Rabin's victory. The public, he says, wanted a change of government and voted for Rabin because he represented both extremes – a minister of defence who had employed the iron fist against the Arabs; a statesman who promised peace in six to nine months. Nor is Benvenisti surprised that Rabin, once elected, opted for continuity rather than change and that some of his proposals to the Palestinians in the bilateral talks were the same as those proposed by the Shamir government, warmed up and repackaged. The single event that mystifies Benvenisti is the famous handshake. Disarmingly, he confesses that the event itself and the lead-up to it stunned him: his own romantic perception of the conflict, he now concludes, had given excessive weight to its ideological and emotional elements. Busy fending off attacks from both Right and Left, he failed to realise that the entire ideological debate, including his own contribution to it, had become anachronistic.

A cynic might say that Benvenisti got it all wrong and that his book also should be stamped OBE – overtaken by events. This would be excessive. Benvenisti deserves credit for his serious, sensitive and highly original analysis of the fatal embrace between Israel and the

Palestinians. Although his style is less than elegant, his knowledge of the international and regional context limited, and his account of Palestinian thinking rather sketchy, his discussion of Israeli strategy and tactics is as incisive as it is illuminating. Even on the historic handshake Benvenisti offers an original gloss. It was a 'supremely symbolic act', he writes,

> transforming the Israeli–Palestinian feud from a primordial shepherds' war into a rational, solvable conflict. It has redefined the enmity: Israelis and Palestinians have been transformed from demonic foes into legitimate enemies. Thus a precondition of any negotiations was met: recognition of the legitimacy, autonomy and authority of the representatives of the other collective entity. Nothing has been resolved, but a marketplace had been established, and give-and-take procedures had been defined.

That a professional pessimist could write with such optimism was a good omen. It generated a glimmer of hope that the Israeli–Palestinian feud itself will eventually become just another boring inter-state dispute, conducted by conventional diplomats using the sterile vocabulary of inter-state relations.

# NINETEEN

# The Likud in Power:
# The Historiography of Revisionist Zionism

On 17 May 1977, Menachem Begin and his Likud union of nationalist and liberal parties won their first electoral victory. This election represented a major landmark in Israel's history. It brought to an end three decades of Labour rule and ushered in a new era which was to last 15 years, during which the right-wing Likud dominated Israeli politics. When Likud came to power, the literature on it was very sparse; by the time it fell from power, in June 1992, the literature had expanded considerably. Colin Shindler's book *Israel, Likud and the Zionist Dream* represents a valuable addition to this literature on a number of counts.* First, whereas most of the existing books deal with specific issues such as the peace with Egypt, the Palestinian uprising against Israeli rule, or the war in Lebanon, Shindler tries to explain the Likud phenomenon as a whole. Second, in order to explain what makes the Likud tick, Shindler explores in some depth its historical and ideological background, and particularly the legacy of the founder of the Revisionist Zionist movement, Ze'ev Vladimir Jabotinsky.

---

* Colin Shindler, *Israel, Likud and the Zionist Dream: Power, Politics and Ideology from Begin to Netanyahu* (London: I.B. Tauris, 1995).

Shindler also traces the influence of Pilsudski's Poland, Mussolini's Italy and the Irish struggle against Britain in moulding the outlook of Menachem Begin and his successor, Yitzhak Shamir. Third, while the subject matter of this book lends itself all too easily to partisanship and polemics, Shindler remains remarkably balanced and fair-minded throughout. He picks his way carefully through the tangled history of this fiercely ideological and rumbustious movement, and manages to avoid the twin pitfalls of hagiography and blind hostility.

The 1977 election signified much more than a change of government. It represented the triumph of Revisionist Zionism after half a century of bitter struggle against mainstream Labour Zionism. The two movements were animated by different aims, different values and different symbols. In his acceptance speech in May 1977, Menachem Begin referred to 'the titanic struggle of ideas stretching back to 1931', a reference that must have puzzled most of his listeners. At the 17th Zionist Congress in 1931, Ze'ev Jabotinsky launched a frontal attack on Chaim Weizmann, forcing him to tender his resignation as president of the World Zionist Organisation. Weizmann typified the Zionist establishment's piecemeal approach to acquiring land, building settlements and working in cooperation with the British mandatory authorities towards the final goal of statehood. Jabotinsky's Zionism was primarily a political movement, not an agency for economic development and settlement on the land. He denounced Weizmann's 'Fabian tactics' and insisted on a forthright statement that the aim of the movement was a Jewish state on both sides of the river Jordan. Weizmann was appalled by the utter lack of realism, the romantic melodrama and the myopic militancy of Jabotinsky and his followers. The battle lines were thus firmly drawn between territorial minimalism and territorial maximalism, between practical Zionism and political Zionism, between a gradualist approach to statehood and militant declarations calling for instantaneous solutions. In 1935 the Revisionists seceded from the World Zionist Organisation in protest against its continuing refusal to declare a Jewish state as its immediate aim. They formed their own New Zionist Organisation, which elected Jabotinsky as its president.

Jabotinsky regarded Arab opposition to Zionism as inevitable, and he believed that efforts aimed at reconciliation were doomed to failure from the start. It was utterly impossible, he argued, to obtain the voluntary consent of the Palestine Arabs to the conversion of Palestine from an Arab country into a country with a Jewish majority. Nor would he settle for the partition of Palestine into two states. His version of the Zionist dream demanded a Jewish state over the whole of *Eretz Yisrael*, the Land of Israel. Britain had established the Emirate of Transjordan on the eastern part of the Palestine Mandate in the early 1920s. Jabotinsky bitterly denounced this 'original sin' and remained uncompromisingly opposed to the partition of the Western part of the Land of Israel. Partition, he observed, was unacceptable not only from the point of view of the Revisionist Zionists, but also from that of the Arabs, because both sides claimed the whole country for themselves. Only superior military power, he concluded, could eventually compel the Arabs to accept the reality of a Jewish state. And only an 'iron wall' of Jewish military power could protect the Jewish state against continuing Arab hostility. Disdain for diplomacy and a reliance on military power in dealing with the Palestine Arabs thus characterised Revisionist Zionism from the very beginning.

The Revisionist movement had its own paramilitary force, the National Military Organisation (the Irgun), which was commanded by Jabotinsky until his death in 1940, and by Menachem Begin from 1943 until its dissolution in June 1948. In 1939 the Irgun called off its campaign against the British mandatory authorities for the duration of the Second World War. Some of the more militant members of the Irgun, led by Avraham Stern, broke away to form a small underground movement, 'The Fighters for the Freedom of Israel', better known as the Stern Gang. Stern saw Zionism as a national liberation movement, and advocated an armed struggle as a means of independence. Since he saw the British as foreign conquerors, he was unwilling to wait until the war against Nazi Germany was over before initiating the military revolt against the British occupation of Palestine. On the contrary, he made approaches to Hitler's Germany and Mussolini's Italy in the belief that 'the enemy of our British enemy must be our friend'. Stern's successors, a triumvirate consisting of Israel Eldad, Natan Yellin-Mor and Yitzhak Shamir, continued to resort to terrorist attacks and political assassinations in their campaign to drive the British out of Palestine. After the war they turned to the Soviet Union in the search for allies against Britain.

Immediately following the declaration of independence in May 1948, both of these dissident organisations were dissolved, and many of their members joined the ranks of the new Israel Defence Force. Menachem Begin formed the Herut (Freedom) party, which adopted the Irgun emblem – a hand holding a rifle on the background of a map of Palestine which stretched over both banks of the river Jordan. The veterans of the Irgun continued to call themselves 'the fighting family'. The Stern Gang also turned itself into a political party, 'the Fighters' List', which won one seat in the Knesset in the elections of 1949.

Herut was returned with 14 seats in the first Knesset. The official Revisionist Party was routed, failing to gain even a single seat. A year later, the two parties merged, and Menachem Begin remained the undisputed leader of the augmented Herut party until his sudden withdrawal from political life in 1983, in the aftermath of the ill-fated war in Lebanon. Begin never abandoned the Revisionist dream of a Jewish state over the whole Land of Israel. In this dream, he included the West Bank of the river Jordan, which had been captured by King Abdullah in 1948 and annexed to his kingdom two years later. But, even while preserving his doctrinal purity, Begin proved adept at forming alliances with liberal, nationalist and ultra-nationalist groups, as well as with breakaway groups from the Labour Zionist movement. In this way, Herut later became Gahal in 1965 as a result of a merger with the Liberal Party. Gahal, in turn, became the Likud in 1973 as a result of another merger with three small nationalist splinter groups.

By 1955, Herut had emerged as the second largest party and the principal opposition to the Labour-led government but, until 1967, it remained outside all the coalition governments. The political climate in Israel in the first two decades of independence tended to delegitimise Herut – David Ben-Gurion pursued a deliberate and effective policy of isolating and ostracising the party. His famous principle for forming coalition governments was 'without Herut or Maki' – Maki being the acronym of the Israeli Communist Party. Gahal joined the government for the first time during the crisis of May 1967, and Menachem Begin became minister without portfolio in the government headed by Levi Eshkol. In July 1970, Begin and his colleagues left the national unity government, headed by Golda Meir, in protest against the Rogers Peace Plan, which, they claimed, involved a new partition of the Land of Israel and a betrayal of the historic rights of the Jewish people. Their three years in government, however, had gained them a large measure of political legitimacy and thus helped to prepare the ground for the Likud's rise to power in 1977.

Menachem Begin was 63 when he became prime minister, and he continued to live in the past. No other Israeli prime minister before or since has been so divorced from the political realities of his day. He was an emotional man, who had been deeply traumatised by the Holocaust and was haunted by fears of its recurrence. He understood contemporary events primarily through the filter of his own terrible experiences during the war. Many of his enemies, including Britain, the Arab states and the PLO, featured in his picture of the world as reincarnated Nazis. Haunted by demons from the past, he was unable to make the realistic assessments of the balance of power between Israel and its enemies that were essential to the conduct of a sound foreign policy. The novelist Shulamit Hareven dubbed him 'the High Priest of Fear', because of his psychological compulsion to uncover and play on the innermost anxieties of the population. But it was precisely these anxieties that also made Begin such an ardent believer in Jabotinsky's concept of an 'iron wall' of military power to protect the Jewish people from its many adversaries.

Although his behaviour could be erratic, Begin never wavered in his ideological commitment to the Land of Israel, and he was nothing if not an ideologue. It was an article of faith that stayed with him all his life that the Jewish people had an historic right to the whole of its Biblical homeland. In a speech to the first Knesset he condemned David Ben-Gurion for acquiescing in Jordan's occupation of the West Bank. Restoration of the Jewish state could not begin, he proclaimed, until 'our country is completely cleansed of invading armies. That is the prime task of our foreign policy.' In another speech to the Knesset, on 3 May 1950, Begin referred to the 'vassal-state that exists on our homeland' and, in a Biblical analogy, labelled King Abdullah 'the Amonite slave'.

After Israel's victory in June 1967, Begin became an outspoken opponent of relinquishing the West Bank. He objected to UN resolution 242 because it meant the redivision of the Land of Israel. The Likud's manifesto for the 1977 elections was categorical on this point: 'The right of the Jewish people to the Land of Israel is eternal, and is an integral part of its right to security and peace. Judea and Samaria shall therefore not be relinquished to foreign rule; between the sea and Jordan river there will be Jewish sovereignty alone.' Begin did not recognise the concept of a Palestinian people, because to do so would have implied their right to national sovereignty in the areas where they lived. For him, as for the old guard of Mapai, 'Palestinians' meant Palestinian Jews as understood in the pre-state days. He never spoke of a Palestinian nation. His definition of the Palestinians was quintessentially Jabotinskyian in that it focused on their status as a national minority. They were part of a wider Arab nation that had already realised its right to national self-determination in some 20 countries. Within the Land of Israel they were a minority entitled only to civil and religious rights.

The PLO was perceived by Begin not as a national liberation movement but as a terrorist organisation, pure and simple. He made no distinction between the policies of its different factions, between radicals and moderates. They were all latter-day Nazis, while the PLO's covenant was the equivalent of Adolf Hitler's *Mein Kampf*. This attitude, too, was unambiguously stated in the Likud's 1977 election manifesto: 'The so-called Palestinian Liberation Organisation is not a national liberation movement but a murder organisation which serves as a political tool and military arm of the Arab States and as an instrument of Soviet imperialism. The Likud government will take action to exterminate this organisation.' When

Begin came to power he had the option of giving concrete expression to his lifelong convictions by annexing the West Bank. He did not exercise this option because he also wanted to achieve peace with Egypt. Asked by a reporter whether he intended to annex the West Bank, he replied 'you annex foreign land, not your own country'. Begin was prepared, however reluctantly, to give back the whole of Sinai, and even dismantle Jewish settlements there, in return for peace with Egypt, because Sinai was not part of the Biblical Land of Israel. For Begin, however, the withdrawal from Sinai was not a prelude to or precedent for further withdrawals, but a means of ensuring permanent Israeli control over the West Bank.

Begin passionately believed that the historic right of the Jews to the Land of Israel overrode all other claims. He was unable to distinguish clearly, however, between historic right and a political claim to sovereignty. The Framework for Peace in the Middle East, which he signed at Camp David, used language that was distinctly foreign for the Revisionists and consequently lost him their support. The Framework recognised 'the legitimate rights of the Palestinian people and their just requirements'. Begin, however, insisted that the Hebrew version referred to 'the Arabs of *Eretz Yisrael*' rather than to 'the Palestinians'. Similar sophistry was applied by Begin to the UN resolutions that were said to be the basis of negotiations. UN resolution 242 called on Israel to withdraw from territories 'occupied in the recent conflict' in return for peace. In Begin's view, the June 1967 war had been a defensive war during which the West Bank had been purged of 'foreign aggressors'. Accordingly, while applying to Sinai, resolution 242 did not apply to the West Bank. All that Begin would offer the residents of the West Bank was an autonomy plan, which they rejected out of hand as derisory.

In June 1982, taking advantage of Egypt's disengagement from the conflict, Begin, aided and abetted by Minister of Defence Ariel Sharon, launched Israel on the road to war in Lebanon. In his book Shindler devotes four chapters to the war in Lebanon, brazenly misnamed 'Operation Peace for the Galilee', but the real logic behind this war eluded him. The war was about securing the Land of Israel, and it was directed primarily against the Palestinians, not against Lebanon or Syria. In its 1977 manifesto, the Likud had vowed to 'exterminate' the PLO, and this was the immediate aim behind the invasion of Lebanon. The PLO was both the symbol and the spearhead of Palestinian nationalism, which had been gaining momentum ever since 1967. If the PLO were crushed, Sharon persuaded Begin, the Palestinians on the West Bank would become demoralised, and their will to resist the imposition of Israeli rule would effectively come to an end. The war achieved its immediate aim by destroying the PLO's military infrastructure in southern Lebanon and forcing it to move its headquarters to Tunis, but it failed utterly in its broader aim of defeating Palestinian nationalism.

What Shindler does bring out very vividly is the impact of Begin's Holocaust trauma on his conduct of the war in Lebanon. He gives many examples of Begin's tendency to compare Arabs with Nazis. Following an attack on women and children in Kiryat Shemona by the Popular Front for the Liberation of Palestine, Begin told the Knesset that 'two-legged beasts, Arab Nazis perpetrated this abomination'. But the most bizarre manifestation of Begin's use of analogies from the Nazi period was a telegram he sent to President Ronald Reagan in early August 1982, when the Israeli army was bombarding Beirut:

Now may I tell you, dear Mr President, how I feel these days when I turn to the creator of my soul in deep gratitude. I feel as a Prime Minister empowered to instruct a valiant army facing 'Berlin', where, amongst innocent civilians, Hitler and his henchmen hide in a bunker deep beneath the surface. My generation, dear Ron, swore on the altar of God that whoever proclaims his intent to destroy the Jewish state or the Jewish people, or both, seals his fate, so that what happened from Berlin – with or without inverted commas – will never happen again.

These comments outraged many Israelis. Despite their sensitivity to the Holocaust, they saw that their leader had lost touch with reality and was merely chasing the ghosts of the past. Chaika Grossmann, a Mapam member of the Knesset who had actually fought in the Warsaw Ghetto, made a direct appeal to Begin: 'Return to reality. We are not in the Warsaw Ghetto, we are in the State of Israel.' The writer Amos Oz, who saw the invasion of Lebanon as 'a typical Jabotinskyian fantasy', appealed to Begin to resist the urge to resurrect Hitler from the dead each day so as to kill him once more: 'The urge to revive Hitler, only to kill him again and again is the result of pain that poets can permit themselves to use, but not statesmen . . . even at great emotional cost personally, you must remind yourself and the public that elected you its leader that Hitler is dead and burned to ashes.'

Anchored in delusions and fed by paranoia, Israel's war in Lebanon went from bad to worse. The horrendous massacre in the Palestinian refugee camps of Sabra and Chatila in August 1982, perpetrated by Israel's Christian Lebanese allies, dramatically stepped up both domestic and foreign opposition to the war. Begin's instinctive response was to turn his back on his foreign critics. He appealed to the Cabinet to close ranks in an act of solidarity against a hostile world. 'Goyim are killing goyim', he exclaimed, 'and the whole world is trying to hang Jews for the crime'. But criticism of the war did not die down. Rabbi Arthur Hertzberg, one of the few Jewish-American leaders to openly oppose the war, doubted that Begin could remain in office, since he had squandered Israel's fundamental asset – its respect for itself and the respect of the world. A year later, in September 1983, Begin did resign. 'I cannot go on any longer' was all he could say by way of explanation. It was an odd remark, which said nothing or everything. His Zionist dream shattered, Begin was a broken man and remained a recluse until his dying day. As Shindler observes: 'The emotional and often fanatical dedication which coloured his way of life, with all its deep depressions and high emotions, had finally overcome him.'

Yitzhak Shamir was elected by the Likud to succeed Begin. The contrast of temperament, personality and style could have hardly been greater. One was volatile and mercurial, the other solid and reliable. One was charismatic and domineering, the other dull and dour. One was a spell-binding orator, the other could hardly string two sentences together. Shamir's greyness of character and lack of

charisma may have actually helped him to get elected. Some Likud
members saw him as a sort of Israeli Clement Attlee, a safe pair of
hands and a welcome antidote to the drama and passions of Begin's
Churchillian style of leadership. In terms of outlook and ideology,
however, the difference between Begin and Shamir was not all that
great. Both were disciples of Ze'ev Jabotinsky. Both were dedicated
to the Land of Israel. Both subscribed to the lachrymose version
of Jewish history, seeing it as a long series of trials and tribulations
culminating in the Holocaust. Both were suspicious of outside
powers, sharing the same bunker mentality, and both were strong
advocates of Israeli self-reliance.

In some ways, Shamir was more intransigent than Begin. For
Shamir, there could be no compromise on the borders of the Land
of Israel. He was strongly opposed, for example, to the Camp David
Accords, and he was generally unreceptive to the idea of bargaining
and compromise, his natural instinct being to stand firm in the
face of external pressure. Towards the PLO, Shamir's attitude was
unremittingly hostile. In November 1988, the PLO moderated its
political programme, accepting UN resolution 242 and opting for
a two-state solution. Shamir, however, dismissed any comparison
between Sadat's peace initiative and the PLO's turning over of a new
leaf. He went even further and threatened to imprison Yasser Arafat
if he flew to Israel to talk peace. 'Hitler and Arafat belong to the
same family of demagogues', asserted Shamir, 'enemies of the Jewish
people who think nothing of killing millions in order to achieve
their objective'. Nor did Shamir yield to the pressure for convening
an international conference to deal with the Arab–Israeli dispute. In
his memoirs, Shamir wrote that regardless of all other assessments he
remained as convinced as he had ever been that the only peace the
PLO could offer Israel was the peace of the cemetery.

In Israel's internal history, Shamir was responsible for one
innovation: a rotating prime ministership. The July 1984 elections
resulted in a draw between Likud and Labour. The two parties
consequently joined in a national unity government for a period
of 50 months. During the first 25 months, the Labour Party leader
Shimon Peres served as prime minister and Shamir as foreign

minister; in October 1986, they swapped places. Peres and Shamir were described, unkindly but not inaccurately, as the Odd Couple. Mutual distrust pervaded their relationship from the beginning. But the broad coalition and curious arrangement of rotation was in itself a recipe for political paralysis, for it gave each party a veto power over the policies of its partner. The Labour Party was wedded to the Jordanian option – territorial compromise over the West Bank with King Hussein of Jordan. To overcome the king's reticence to engage in direct negotiations with Israel, Labour agreed to an international conference under the auspices of the five permanent members of the United Nations Security Council. Likud, on the other hand, was totally opposed either to territorial compromise with Jordan or to the convening of an international conference. Shamir believed that an international conference would imperil Israel's very existence.

After Shamir rotated into the top job, he was as indefatigable in scuppering peace initiatives as Peres was in promoting them. Matters came to a head over the London Agreement of April 1987, which was signed at a secret meeting between Shimon Peres and King Hussein at the home of Lord Mishcon in London. The London Agreement envisaged an international conference with a joint Jordanian–Palestinian delegation, and negotiations on the basis of UN resolutions 242 and 338. Peres read the agreement to Shamir but refused to give him a copy, even though by now he was the prime minister. Such was the mistrust between them. Although the London Agreement did not commit Israel to anything of substance in advance, Shamir feared that it might open the door to territorial compromise. He therefore sent a private message to Secretary of State George Shultz in a bid to scupper the agreement.

George H.W. Bush and his Secretary of State James Baker were much less tolerant of Shamir's stonewalling than Reagan and Shultz had been. The eight-year honeymoon in American–Israeli relations was over. Bush and Baker steadily intensified the pressure on the Israeli government to stop building new settlements in the occupied territories and to start negotiating. In May 1989, the impossible happened: Yitzhak Shamir came up with his own peace plan. The plan specified that the peace process would be based on UN resolutions

242 and 338 and on the Camp David Accords (which Shamir had opposed in 1978), and that there would be no participation by the PLO and no Palestinian state. The most important part of the plan was the staging of elections in the occupied territories to select Palestinian representatives for the negotiations with Israel.

Interestingly, the Shamir Peace Plan was not Shamir's idea. It was suggested to him by Moshe Arens, the hardline member of the Likud who became foreign minister following the elections of November 1988, relegating Shimon Peres to the finance ministry in the new national unity government. In his book *Broken Covenant*,* Arens gives a highly revealing account of the rise and fall of the Shamir Peace Plan and of the deepening crisis in US–Israel relations. Arens found Shamir cool and unenthusiastic about the peace process, and wondered how to get this 'reluctant dragon' to lead Israel's peace initiative. Shamir seemed to have difficulty with the idea of Palestinian elections, but his Cabinet endorsed the plan and the Americans welcomed it. The only opposition came from three of Shamir's ministers and party colleagues – Ariel Sharon, David Levy, and Yitzhak Moda'i – who began a rebellion against Shamir, accusing him of leading Israel to destruction. Shamir did not put up a fight for his plan. On the contrary, he allowed this coalition of ambition to constrain him, and he started to back-pedal. This in turn provoked a crisis in the Cabinet, which culminated in the Labour ministers walking out on Shamir in March 1990. Shamir then formed a narrow government, which he led – or rather, failed to lead – until his defeat at the hands of Yitzhak Rabin in the elections of 23 June 1992.

Moshe Arens was probably as close to Shamir as any other Likud leader, but he became increasingly frustrated by Shamir's inability to agree to anything that seemed like a deviation from the party's ideology. Arens himself was less of an ideologue and more of a hardline pragmatist whose central concern was security. He was also a believer in Jabotinsky's iron wall, but he concluded that Israel had reached the point where it could speak to its Palestinian and Arab

* Moshe Arens, *Broken Covenant: American Foreign Policy and the Crisis between the US and Israel* (New York: Simon and Schuster, 1995).

opponents from a position of military strength. Arens sometimes felt that he was talking to a wall. At one point, Shamir spoke of mobilising American Jewry to face 'a threat to Jewish people's very existence. Baker is against us; a new hangman for the Jewish people has arisen.' With the departure of the Labour ministers from his Cabinet, Shamir regained some of his freedom of action – or rather freedom of inaction. In a heart-to-heart talk with Arens, he confessed that he was not even sure that a dialogue with the Palestinians was really necessary. Arens could not understand how his leader envisaged a resolution of the Arab–Israeli conflict without meaningful contact with the Palestinians. Not surprisingly, Arens concluded that Shamir had become a prisoner of his own ideology. One idea that Arens did put to Shamir on a number of occasions was that Israel should abandon the Gaza Strip because it had become a liability, but he was rebuffed by him every time. 'Gaza is part of the Land of Israel', said Shamir.

By his own account, Shamir regarded peace plans as a threat rather than an opportunity.* 'The presenting and rejecting of peace plans', he writes in his autobiography, 'went on throughout the duration of my Prime Ministership; not a year passed without some official proposal being made by the United States or Israel, or even Mubarak, each one bringing in its wake new internal crises, expectations and disappointments – though I had become more or less immune to the latter'. These plans rarely contained new elements, Shamir complains; what they amounted to was 'peace in exchange for territory; recognition in exchange for territory; never "just" peace'. Poor Shamir: not once in his seven years as prime minister was he offered peace on a silver platter; there was always a price to pay.

Evidently, war was much more in tune with Shamir's inner feelings and outlook on the world than peace. Two days before his electoral defeat, he addressed a memorial meeting of the Fighters for the Freedom of Israel at Kiryat Ata. His theme was that nothing had changed since the War of Independence: 'We still need this truth today, the truth of the power of war, or at least we need to

---

* Yitzhak Shamir, *Summing Up: An Autobiography* (London: Weidenfeld and Nicholson, 1994).

accept that war is inescapable, because, without this, the life of the individual has no purpose and the nation has no chance of survival.' The most charitable construction one can put on this statement is that the 77-year-old Revisionist had in mind, not war for its own sake, but war as a means of defending the Land of Israel. The Land of Israel was always at the centre of Shamir's life. His autobiography does not shed much new light on his violent life or sterile political career, but the last sentence is highly revealing. 'If history remembers me at all, in any way,' he writes, 'I hope it will be as a man who loved the Land of Israel and watched over it in any way he could, all his life.'

In the contest to succeed Shamir as party leader, the main contenders were David Levy and two of the Likud 'princes', Binyamin Netanyahu and Benny Begin, the son of Menachem Begin. The other Likud 'princes' were deterred from throwing their hats into the ring by Netanyahu's popularity rating. In the primaries, the serious and dignified Benny Begin called Netanyahu 'a man of tricks and gimmicks', a person who lacked political gravitas. Other members of the Likud also regarded Netanyahu as an intellectual lightweight, as shallow and superficial, as little more than a purveyor of sound bites for American television. Nevertheless, Netanyahu won the contest on the strength of his popular appeal and proven skills at public relations.

A geologist by profession, Benny Begin was elected to the Knesset in 1988 and joined its influential Committee on Foreign Affairs and Defence. *A Zionist Stand* is a collection of his articles and lectures that reflect the mainstream political thought of the Likud Party.* In an article originally published in 1990 under the title 'A Perennial Stream', Begin observes that, 50 years after the death of Ze'ev Jabotinsky, Revisionist Zionism remained a perennial stream, direct and consistent, unlike other Zionist trends, which meander and even retreat as they flow forward. Benny Begin's Zionism rests on two pillars: the right of the Jewish people to *Eretz Yisrael* (the Land of Israel), and the right of the Jewish State to national security.

---

* Ze'ev B. Begin, *A Zionist Stand* (London: Frank Cass, 1993).

In order to realise the latter, Israel must implement the former in all of 'Western *Eretz Yisrael*'. In the introduction to *A Zionist Stand*, he states his political creed even more succinctly: 'This land is ours.' It is an either/or situation, Begin asserts. 'Either Israel controls Samaria, Judea and the Gaza district, or a murderous terrorist state will be set up there, headed by some faction of the PLO or Hamas.'

Using his background in geology, Begin junior describes the Middle East as follows: 'it is a part of the globe in which you will find numerous political volcanoes, randomly distributed in space, which violently erupt, randomly in time'. In his book, a phenomenon that is random both in space and in time should be defined as disorder or chaos. As is usually the case with Likud supporters, Begin's conviction that instability is endemic in the Middle East reinforces an almost instinctive resistance to international peace initiatives. The more they insist, the more we resist, he observes. Like Yitzhak Shamir, he is guided by the conviction that it is better for Israel to be criticised than eulogised. He praises Shamir for cutting 'the solemn diplomatic nonsense' in the aftermath of the First Gulf War, adding that the diplomatic course offered to Israel by the United States was a 'blind alley in a dark neighbourhood, and we considered it both futile and risky'. The demand that Jerusalem should be included on the agenda was anathema to him. 'Jerusalem, D.C. – David's Capital', he asserts, echoing his father, 'shall forever remain undivided under Jewish sovereignty'.

Binyamin Netanyahu also hails from a prominent Revisionist Zionist family. His father, Benzion Netanyahu, is an eminent historian of Spanish Jewry, an ardent nationalist, and long-time supporter of Greater Israel. Netanyahu junior was born in Israel in 1949, received his schooling in Israel and America, and studied business administration at MIT. He served in an IDF elite unit for five years, rising to the rank of captain, so he had some practical experience of fighting Arabs at the sharp end of the conflict. In 1982, he was appointed Israel's deputy ambassador to Washington and later its Permanent Representative to the United Nations, and he was successful at both posts. While serving in the United States, he also gained a reputation for himself as a leading expert on international terrorism, and he became a frequent participant in talk shows dealing with the subject. His family set up the Jonathan Institute, named after his elder brother, 'Yoni', who had served in the same elite IDF unit, and who was killed in the raid to rescue the Israeli hostages in Entebbe in 1976. The main aim of the Institute is to mobilise governments and public opinion in the West for the fight against terrorism. A volume edited by Netanyahu under the auspices of the Jonathan Institute, *Terrorism: How the West Can Win*, greatly impressed President Ronald Reagan and apparently inspired the air strike he ordered against Libya in 1986.

Netanyahu's *Fighting Terrorism* is a little book, forcefully argued and rich in unintended ironies.* Netanyahu defines terrorism as 'the deliberate and systematic assault on civilians to inspire fear for political ends'. Ironically, by this definition both Menachem Begin and Yitzhak Shamir had been leaders of terrorist organisations in the pre-independence period, although Netanyahu is unlikely to have had them in mind when formulating his definition. For him terrorism is not what the weak do to the strong but what dictatorships do to democracies. More precisely, he regards international terrorism as the result of collusion between dictatorial states and an international terrorist network – 'a collusion that has to be fought and can be defeated'. There is, of course, a view which holds that terrorism is the result of social and political oppression, and cannot therefore be eliminated unless the underlying conditions change. Netanyahu mentions this view, only to reject it out of hand. To Netanyahu's way of thinking, the PLO is nothing but a terrorist organisation working in collusion with dictatorial states. Israel's destruction of the PLO base in Lebanon, he claims, deprived the Soviets and the Arab world of their most useful staging ground for mounting terrorist operations against the democracies. Hizbullah (the Party of God), which was born in the aftermath of Israel's invasion of Lebanon and continues to fight Israeli forces and proxies in southern Lebanon, is presented by Netanyahu as a terrorist organisation sponsored by Iran. But although Iran supports Hizbullah, it does not effectively

---

* Benjamin Netanyahu, *Fighting Terrorism: How Democracies Can Defeat Domestic and International Terrorism* (New York: Farrar, Straus and Giroux, 1995).

control it. Moreover, guerrilla warfare would be a better description than terror for Hizbullah's operations, because, for the most part, they take place on Lebanese territory, under battlefield conditions, against Israeli soldiers.

Hamas (the Islamic Resistance Movement), born in Gaza in 1988, fits Netanyahu's definition of a terrorist organisation rather better, because its attacks are mainly directed against Israeli civilians on Israeli territory. On the other hand, Hamas's political links with Iran are much more tenuous than those of Hizbullah, and it receives much less material support from the dictatorships of the region. Far from being part of an international terrorist network, Hamas is essentially an indigenous movement with its own agenda of creating an Islamic state in the whole of Palestine. It is vehemently opposed to the peace process with Israel, and it denounced Yasser Arafat as an Israeli collaborator. Another irony is that, in its early days, Hamas was secretly supported by Israel in what turned out to be a short-sighted policy of 'divide and rule' aimed specifically at weakening Arafat's secular, mainstream Fatah movement.

But the greatest irony of them all is that Binyamin Netanyahu is not just the most outspoken spokesman against Hamas, but was also the principal political beneficiary of its suicide bombings inside Israel. These attacks had the effect of shifting public opinion against the Labour-led government and the peace process and in favour of right-wing politicians like Netanyahu. The assassination of Yitzhak Rabin by a right-wing Jewish extremist dealt a severe political blow to Netanyahu and gave Shimon Peres a substantial lead in the opinion polls. When the elections were called in mid-February 1996, Peres was ahead in the opinion polls by a seemingly unassailable 20 per cent. This advantage was blown to pieces by the Islamic suicide bombings, which killed 63 Israelis and generated an acute sense of insecurity. To put it crudely, Jewish terror, which is not even mentioned in Netanyahu's book, worked against him, while Islamic terror worked strongly to his advantage. It narrowly tipped the balance in his favour in the first direct elections for Israeli prime minister, held on 29 May 1996.

Despite its various permutations since the 1920s, the Likud has always remained an ideological party. The principal difference between Netanyahu and his predecessors is that they were true believers and he is not. They were faithful, not to say fanatical, defenders of the Land of Israel, regardless of the electoral consequences of this stand, whereas he is a pragmatic politician in the American mould who was prepared to dilute his party's ideology for the sake of attaining power. His acceptance of the Oslo Accord appealed to wavering voters, but it plunged the Likud into a deep ideological crisis. In his book, Netanyahu had denounced the Oslo Accord as capitulation by the Labour government to 'the PLO's Phased Plan' of bringing about a gradual Israeli withdrawal to the pre-1967 borders. But he never came up with a coherent alternative to the Plan's limited, gradual and controlled withdrawal from the occupied territories. Since the majority of Israelis continued to support the peace process and the withdrawal from the occupied territories, Netanyahu appeared to be changing his tune in the lead up to the elections. 'The Oslo Accord endangers Israel', he said, 'but one cannot ignore reality'.

It is a reality that may spell the beginning of the end of the Revisionist Zionist dream of Jewish sovereignty over the whole of the Land of Israel. Jabotinsky and Begin turn in their graves.

# TWENTY

# Capital Folly

More than any other capital city, Jerusalem demonstrates the power of symbols in international politics. The conflict between Israel and the Palestinians is one of the most bitter and protracted of modern times, and the Jerusalem question, a compound of religious zealotry and secular jingoism, lies at its heart. The Oslo Accords, which launched the Palestinians on the road to self-government, bypassed the matter of Jerusalem along with the other truly difficult issues in the dispute: the right of return of the 1948 refugees, the future of the Jewish settlements, and the borders of the Palestinian entity. Discussion of these was deferred until negotiations took place on the final status of the territories, due to begin towards the end of a five-year transition period. They were belatedly tabled at the summit convened by Bill Clinton at Camp David in July 2000, but Jerusalem was the issue that ultimately led to the failure of the summit and the breakdown of the Oslo peace process.

Religious rivalries are notoriously difficult to resolve, and Jerusalem's spiritual significance for the three great monotheistic religions has ensured its long and bloody history. And then there is the political prestige that has always gone with possession of the city. Between its foundation and its capture by the Israelis in 1967, it is said to have been taken 37 times, and it has now been on the international diplomatic agenda for a century and a half. When Arthur Koestler visited it during the 1948 war, he was filled with gloom at the 'international quarrelling, haggling and mediation' that he could see looming. 'No other town', he wrote, 'has caused such continuous waves of killing, rape and unholy misery over the centuries as this Holy City.'

Anyone seeking to understand the Jerusalem question in its current form could not do better than read Bernard Wasserstein's thoroughly researched, elegantly written and strikingly fair-minded book, *Divided Jerusalem: The Struggle for the Holy City*.* Its starting point is what psychologists have long been aware of as the 'Jerusalem syndrome' that afflicts some visitors to the city, especially Western Christian tourists, who feel a need to register their presence in the Holy City by assuming the identity of a Biblical character, undergoing mystical experiences or succumbing to the delusion of possessing supernatural powers. Jerusalem, in other words, represents not just a problem but also an emotion: above all, a religious emotion. Veneration for the city among Jews, Christians and Muslims runs deep and it is the duty of the historian, as Wasserstein sees it, to record this fervour without succumbing to it. From here, he goes on to develop his argument that politicians of all three religious affiliations have deliberately inflated the city's religious importance to serve their own political ends.

When the Ottoman Turks captured Jerusalem in 1516 it was a provincial backwater with a population of fewer than 15,000. It didn't acquire any administrative importance over the four centuries of Ottoman rule, but served only as the capital of a district forming part of the province of Damascus. During the reign of Suleiman the Magnificent it acquired the walls enclosing the city that are still almost intact today. But the various religious groups were left to run their own affairs and to administer their own institutions, with little interference from the central government. The Jerusalem question

---

* Bernard Wasserstein, *Divided Jerusalem: The Struggle for the Holy City* (London: Yale University Press, 2001).

in its modern form arose as a byproduct of the slow decline of the Ottoman Empire. The initial struggle was over the Christian holy places. As Ottoman power waned, the other great powers sought to extend their authority and prestige, and in a chapter on 'The Wars of the Consuls' Wasserstein lays bare with a wry humour the methods they employed: religious sentiment was exploited, local protégés were cultivated, dependent institutions such as churches, monasteries, convents, hospitals, orphanages, schools and colleges were founded.

Wasserstein also gives credit where it is due. He notes that in the late Ottoman period, there were no significant instances of mass communal violence in Jerusalem. Relations between Muslims, Christians and Jews, while often fraught and acrimonious, were contained within a framework of law. What the consular wars illustrate rather is the propensity of the Jerusalem question to inflame relations between the powers: 'Seized upon as a sacred cause, Jerusalem proved a handy pretext for warmongers with much larger objectives.' This is not something that has faded with the passage of time.

Britain governed Jerusalem, under the Palestinian Mandate, from 1920 until 1948. Nominally, it was responsible to the Permanent Mandates Commission of the League of Nations but in reality Palestine was governed as if it were a Crown Colony. Although British rule lasted only three decades, it transformed the city and paved the way to its eventual partition. This was Jerusalem's first Christian administration since the Crusades, yet it granted unprecedented privileges to the Supreme Muslim Council and sponsored the establishment of a Jewish national home. Breaking with the Ottoman past, the city became a major administrative centre and the seat of the High Commissioner for Palestine. The result was a profound change in its relationship to Palestine. For the first time in its modern history, Jerusalem was a capital. The status of the local elites, Muslim as much as Jewish, was enhanced by their proximity to the seat of power. The British tried to be even-handed, but reconciling the claims of the two nascent national movements proved beyond them. Both Arabs and Jews became progressively alienated and staged revolts against British rule, the former in the late 1930s, the latter in the late 1940s. By the time the Mandate reached its inglorious end in May 1948, there was precious little goodwill left towards Britain on either side of the divide.

On 29 November 1947, the United Nations passed a resolution for partitioning Palestine into two independent states, one Arab and one Jewish, but with an international regime for Jerusalem, which was to be treated as a *corpus separatum*. Formally the British remained neutral, but in practice they were hostile to the plan for an independent Palestinian state because it was certain to be ruled by the Mufti, who had thrown in his lot with Nazi Germany during the war. Britain's secret objective was partition between the Zionists and King Abdullah of Jordan, their loyal ally – which was the precise outcome of the 1948 war. Towards the end of that war, Jerusalem once again became an issue. Most members of the UN still supported an international regime for the city but the powers on the ground, Jordan and Israel, were united in their wish to partition it between themselves. After the guns fell silent, Jordan continued to rule East Jerusalem and Israel to rule West Jerusalem, until the six days that shook the Middle East in the summer of 1967.

By joining Nasser in the Six-Day War, King Hussein lost the West Bank and East Jerusalem, which his grandfather had incorporated into the Hashemite Kingdom of Jordan by the Act of Union of 1950. Jordan's participation in 1967 was largely symbolic but the price it paid was heavy. On 7 June, Israeli forces captured East Jerusalem as part of their sweep through the West Bank. At noon that day, Moshe Dayan, the defence minister, went to the Western Wall and declared that Jerusalem had been 'liberated': 'We have united Jerusalem, the divided capital of Israel. We have returned to the holiest of our Holy Places, never to part from it again.' Contrary to the view held by most Arabs, Israel had no prior plan for keeping the West Bank or East Jerusalem, but the victory unleashed powerful currents of religious messianism and secular irredentism that no government could have held in check even if it had wanted to. The Zionist movement's moderate position disappeared overnight, and suddenly life in the Jewish state without Zion (one of the Biblical names for Jerusalem) became difficult to imagine. At the end of June, in a remarkable display of unity, the Knesset enacted legislation to extend Israeli jurisdiction and administration to Greater Jerusalem, which included the Old City (the small area inside the walls which is divided into four quarters – Jewish, Christian, Muslim and Armenian). This was annexation in all but name.

Over the next quarter of a century, the central political figure in Israeli Jerusalem was its mayor, Teddy Kollek. A liberal-minded and pragmatic man, he sought practical solutions to the city's many everyday problems and was anxious to achieve harmony among its different groups. But his overriding aim, which he made little effort to conceal, was to secure Israel's permanent hold on Jerusalem as its unified capital. The expropriation of Arab land in East Jerusalem proceeded at a rapid pace and new Jewish neighbourhoods were built in flagrant violation of international law. Driving all this hectic activity was a long-term geopolitical aim: the creation of a ring of Jewish settlements on the northern, north-eastern and southern periphery of the city. As Kollek himself admitted in a newspaper interview in 1968, 'the object is to ensure that all of Jerusalem remains for ever a part of Israel. If this city is to be our capital, then we have to make it an integral part of our country and we need Jewish inhabitants to do that'.

The position of the great powers remained virtually unchanged: they refused to recognise the legality or legitimacy of the Israeli attempt to incorporate East Jerusalem. The United Nations passed a series of resolutions condemning Israeli activities in the Arab quarters. But external pressure failed to dent Israel's confidence in its moral right to impose its rule over a large and recalcitrant Arab population. On the contrary, in nationalist circles at least, it provoked deep resentment and defiance. In July 1980, the Knesset passed the Jerusalem Law, which stated that 'Jerusalem, complete and united, is the capital of Israel.' Its initiator, the ultra-nationalist Geula Cohen, made it clear that her purpose was to foreclose any negotiations over the status of the city. Unlike earlier legislation, the bill was widely criticised within Israel as unnecessary, even harmful. It set Israel on the defensive internationally and drew criticism from all the major powers. On 20 August, the Security Council passed a resolution reprimanding Israel by 14 votes to zero, with the US abstaining. The *New York Times* called the law 'capital folly'.

In the years after this folly was enacted, Israeli leaders of all political shades continued to repeat the mantra that unified Jerusalem is the eternal capital of the State of Israel, and its status non-negotiable. It was to get around this self-imposed constraint that the Israeli participants in the Oslo Accords set the Jerusalem question aside. The Declaration of Principles signed on 13 September 1993 had little to say about it. The Palestinian Interim Self-Government Authority was to have no jurisdiction over Jerusalem, and the status quo was to continue until the 'final status' negotiations. In the meantime, both sides were free to cling to their symbols of sovereignty and their dreams. An optimistic Yasser Arafat said that the agreement was merely the first step towards 'the total withdrawal from our land, our holy sites, and our holy Jerusalem', while an Israeli spokesman insisted: 'Jerusalem is not part of the deal and there has been no weakening on that.'

The framework for a final status agreement was concluded on 31 October 1995 by Yossi Beilin, Israel's deputy foreign minister, and Mahmoud Abbas (also known as Abu Mazen), a close adviser to Arafat. This bold document made a first stab at resolving all the outstanding issues between Israel and the Palestinians. It envisaged an independent but demilitarised Palestinian state, covering Gaza and 94 per cent of the West Bank, with al-Quds (East Jerusalem) as its capital. Four days later, Yitzhak Rabin was assassinated and his successor, Shimon Peres, lacked the courage to adopt the plan, not least because it would have exposed him to the charge of dividing Jerusalem. When Likud leader Binyamin Netanyahu came to power following the elections of May 1996, he abruptly reversed the cautious peace policy of his Labour predecessors, especially with regard to Jerusalem. Oslo was meant to hold Jerusalem back until the end of the process: Netanyahu placed it at the centre of his policy, thereby blocking progress on all the other issues.

The question did not make another significant appearance on the international agenda until the Camp David summit which Clinton convened at the request of Netanyahu's successor, Ehud Barak, in 2000. There, Barak and Arafat negotiated more back to back than face to face. Both had serious internal problems. Barak's coalition was crumbling and he arrived at the conference as the head of a government on the verge of collapse. Arafat was under pressure not to yield on the Palestinian demand for an Israeli withdrawal from the whole of Arab East Jerusalem. The city was the core issue at the summit and the main stumbling block. To break the deadlock, the American mediators put forward 'bridging proposals' broadly based on the Beilin–Abu Mazen plan. But there was no meeting of minds between the two delegations and no real negotiations took place. Arafat stood his ground, failed to put forward any constructive counter-proposals, and refused to give way on Jerusalem and the holy places. Clinton's suggestion that the issue be postponed for later determination was also rejected by Arafat, and a frustrated Clinton likened the whole experience to 'going to the dentist without having your gums deadened'.

With the breakdown of the talks, an inevitable new round of violence began on 28 September 2000 with Ariel Sharon's ostentatious visit to Temple Mount. Claiming he was delivering what he called 'a message of peace', to the other side the message that came across loud and clear was 'Israel rules OK!' The visit sparked off riots which spread from Temple Mount to the Arab quarters of Jerusalem, the West Bank, Gaza, and for the first time, some of the Arab-inhabited regions of Israel. Riots quickly turned into a full-scale uprising. Within ten days, the death toll of what became known as the al-Aqsa intifada was approaching 100. The Oslo Accords were lost to view in the outpourings of collective hatred that accompanied the return to violence.

Against this grim background Clinton made one last attempt, just before the end of his term, to bridge the gap between the sides. At a meeting at the White House with Israeli and Palestinian representatives in late December, he presented his ideas for a final settlement. These 'parameters', as he called them, had moved a long way towards meeting Palestinian aspirations. Israel was to withdraw altogether from Gaza and from 94–96 per cent of the West Bank. There was to be an independent Palestinian state but with limitations on its level of armaments. The guiding principle for solving the refugee problem was that the new state would be 'the focal point for the Palestinians who choose to return to the area'. With regard to Jerusalem, 'the general principle is that Arab areas are Palestinian and Jewish ones are Israeli'.

Negotiations on the basis of the parameters took place at the Egyptian Red Sea resort of Taba in the last week of January 2001. Both sides broadly accepted the proposals but with a long list of reservations. On Jerusalem, Israeli reservations were more substantial than those of the Palestinians. Barak stated publicly that he would not transfer sovereignty over Temple Mount. At this critical juncture, as so often in the past, internal Israeli politics took precedence over everything else. The elections scheduled for 6 February 2001 led Barak to adopt a tough line over the Old City and Temple Mount. Despite these local difficulties, however, the negotiators came closer to a final agreement than they ever had. But then Sharon won the election, and his government immediately declared that the understandings reached at Taba were not binding because they had not been embodied in a signed document. To make things worse, the incoming Bush Administration didn't consider itself bound by the proposals of its predecessor and in any case chose to disengage from the peace process. Most of the achievements of the Taba talks disappeared into the desert sand.

In the preface to this admirable book, Wasserstein observes that the 'eternally unified capital' of the State of Israel is the most deeply divided capital city in the world: 'Its Arab and Jewish residents inhabit different districts, speak different languages, attend different schools, read different newspapers, watch different television programmes, observe different holy days, follow different football teams – live, in almost every significant respect, different lives.' What the book eloquently demonstrates is that the struggle for Jerusalem cannot be resolved without some recognition of the reality and legitimacy of its plural character. It is sad to have to add that such recognition is a more remote prospect today than at any time since the Oslo Accords were signed.

# PART III

*The Breakdown of the Peace Process*

TWENTY-ONE

## *The Lost Steps*

American policy-makers may be divided into two schools of
thought on the Arab–Israeli conflict: the even-handed and
the Israel-first. The even-handed school seeks to play the role
of the honest broker in pushing the two sides towards a settlement
of the dispute between them. It believes that America's most vital
interests lie in the oil-producing Arabian Gulf, and it is reluctant
to jeopardise those interests by being too close to Israel. The Israel-
first school, on the other hand, supports a special relationship with
the Jewish state, hailing it as an island of democracy in a sea of
authoritarianism. Members of this school also seek a settlement of
the dispute between Israel and its neighbours. But their starting
point is that Israel has to assume serious risks on the road to peace
and that America should therefore give it all the support it needs in
order to feel confident enough to assume those risks. George H.W.
Bush was arguably the most even-handed president in American
history. Bill Clinton was by far the most pro-Israel president
until George W. Bush's rise to power. An Israeli newspaper once
described Clinton as the last Zionist. In long historical perspective,
however, George W. Bush may yet emerge with a stronger claim
to this title.

Dennis Ross was the chief Middle East peace negotiator in the Republican Administration of George H.W. Bush and in the two terms of Bill Clinton's presidency. Ross was particularly close to Secretary of State James Baker, so the Democratic victory in the 1992 election was expected to spell the end of his diplomatic career. But Clinton wanted Ross to stay on as head of the American Middle East team under Secretary of State Warren Christopher. Consequently, Ross remained a key player in this political process for the next eight years. He thus has the unique distinction of having served in a prominent capacity both in the most even-handed American Administration since the war and in one of the most ardently pro-Israel ones.

Despite Bush the elder's pedigree, Ross belongs fairly and squarely in the pro-Israel camp. His premises, position on the Middle East and policy preferences are identical to those of the 'Israel-first' school. Indeed, it is difficult to think of an American official who is more quintessentially Israel-first in his outlook than Dennis Ross. In his memoir Ross recounts in minute detail his personal involvement in the Middle East peace process from 1988 to January 2001.* This was an eventful period in the history of the region, which saw the First Gulf War, the Madrid peace conference, bilateral Arab–Israeli negotiations under American auspices in Washington, the Oslo Accord between Israel and the PLO, the conclusion of the Jordanian–Israeli peace treaty, the assassination of Yitzhak Rabin, the rise and fall of Binyamin Netanyahu, the ill-fated Camp David summit and the outbreak of the al-Aqsa intifada. There were also persistent though ultimately unsuccessful efforts to achieve a breakthrough on the Syrian track, the high points being the meetings between Ehud Barak and Foreign Minister Farouk al-Shara in Shepherdstown, West Virginia, and between Bill Clinton and President Hafez al-Assad in Geneva.

During the period covered in this book, there was thus a great deal of peace process and Dennis Ross was the peace processor *par excellence*. Unfortunately, the substantive achievements were not so

* Dennis Ross, *The Missing Peace: The Inside Story of the Fight for Middle East Peace* (New York: Farrar, Straus and Giroux, 2004).

impressive, for there was more process than there was peace. The two major achievements – Oslo and the Israeli–Jordanian peace treaty – were negotiated directly between the parties themselves with virtually no American involvement. Ross indirectly acknowledges the failure to achieve comprehensive peace in the Middle East by calling his book *The Missing Peace*. The main point and the real value of the book are indicated in its subtitle – it is the inside story of the struggle for peace, of the failures as well as the successes, of personalities and policies, of countless crises and confrontations, of backstage manoeuvres and media spin, of betrayals and brinkmanship, of the high points and the low points.

About Ross's dedication and commitment to the cause of peace there can be no doubt, but his influence over the actual course of events is more difficult to measure. Yossi Beilin, the militant Israeli moderate and one of the main architects of the Oslo Accord, published a book around the same time entitled *The Path to Geneva: The Quest for a Permanent Agreement, 1996–2004*.* 'Until Clinton's very last day in office', writes Beilin, 'Ross wanted to believe that it was possible to reach an agreement. The failure of the negotiations with the Syrians and with the Palestinians was the failure of Dennis Ross.' This verdict is surely too harsh. The fact that Ross kept up his frantic efforts to broker an agreement literally until his last day in office does not necessarily saddle him with the responsibility for the failure. More senior players were involved, and it was their choices that determined the final outcome.

Some of the controversy surrounding Ross is related to the fact that he is Jewish. Not so subtle questions were sometimes raised, especially in the Arab world, about his being Jewish and its effect on his fairness as a negotiator. Ross himself tells us that his faith was never an issue with the presidents and secretaries of state with whom he worked most closely. This is obvious: had his faith been a problem, Ross's employers would not have appointed him in the first place or kept him on following the transition from a Republican to a Democratic Administration. On the other hand, Ross tells us,

* Yossi Beilin, *The Path to Geneva: The Quest for a Permanent Agreement, 1996–2004* (New York: Akashic, 2004).

some right-wing American Jews have felt that Israel is in such danger that it should never be subjected to pressure or criticism. When the Bush–Baker team put pressure on the government of Yitzhak Shamir after the Gulf War, Ross received hate mail branding him a self-hating Jew. The gibe could not be further off the mark, for he is in fact a very proud Jew. One can only sympathise with Ross for the crassness of some of his American co-religionists. As Ross himself points out: 'In the Jewish tradition there are few higher callings than to be a seeker of peace – a Rodef Shalom.' Some of Ross's supporters in the Jewish community described him as a Rodef Shalom, and for him there could be no greater accolade.

Arab attitudes to Ross, however, merit a more serious consideration than he allows. His relations with Yasser Arafat were always very strained. Arafat saw Ross as an arrogant man who was too close to the Israelis. In his bad moments Arafat considered Ross to be a real enemy and at one point went as far as to refuse to meet with him. Hafez al-Assad criticised Ross rather more obliquely for not being positive enough in his attitude towards Syria. The Arab media habitually portrays American policy towards the region as biased in favour of Israel, as a result of the influence of the Jewish lobby and Jewish officials, and Ross was held out as a prime example. Other factors, such as the democratic nature of Israel and the lack of democracy in the Arab world, are conveniently forgotten. Nevertheless, Arab leaders' perception of Ross as partial to Israel complicated America's task as the manager of the peace process.

Since Ross was the architect of the first Bush Administration's policy towards the Arab–Israeli conflict and the chief peace negotiator of the Clinton Administration, his assumptions were important. Ross's entire approach to peacemaking is premised on a strong US–Israeli relationship. Given Israel's small size and vulnerability, he argues, it must feel secure if it is to make concessions for peace. Israel would not feel safe enough to give up territory if it doubted the American commitment to its security. Similarly, the Arab world would not accommodate itself to Israel's existence if it had reason to question the staying power of the American commitment to Israel. While peace must ultimately be between the two parties and must therefore be directly negotiated by them, Israel must feel secure if it is to take risks for peace. This, in a nutshell, is Ross's philosophy of peacemaking.

There are three main problems with this approach. In the first place, it puts all the emphasis on Israel's concern for security and overlooks the Arab concern for justice. Given this, it is hardly surprising that the Arabs felt Ross was too sympathetic to Israel's needs and insufficiently attuned to theirs. Second, the Israeli concept of security is so inflated and one-sided that it amounts to a denial of the legitimate security concerns of the other side. Third, the approach advocated by Ross is wide open to abuse by Israel. Israel can absorb any amount of American aid without reciprocating with concessions to the Arabs. In short, Ross's mistake lies in assuming that a confident Israel would embark on the road to peace. History does not support this conclusion.

No one was more confident of Israel's military power than Moshe Dayan, who served as defence minister from 1967 to 1974. Yet he was unwilling to assume risks for the sake of peace. Dayan frankly admitted that he would rather have 'Sharm el-Sheikh without peace than peace without Sharm el-Sheikh' (a strategic point in the Sinai Peninsula, captured from Egypt in the 1967 war and later returned to Egypt under the terms of the 1979 peace treaty). Opportunities for peace during that period were missed not because Israel felt insecure but because America did not lean hard enough on its ally to return the territories it had conquered in 1967.

Before embarking on a detailed narrative of the peace process, Ross outlines the context and the contours of the conflict. This takes the form of a long chapter on 'Why Israelis, Arabs, and Palestinians See the World the Way They Do'. Ross's account of the Israeli narrative is predictably better informed and more sympathetic than his account of the Arab and Palestinian narratives. He repeats, for example, the hoary claim that on the morrow of its spectacular military victory in June 1967, Israel offered to withdraw from the Sinai Peninsula and the Golan Heights in return for peace with Egypt and Syria, only to be confronted with the 'three no's' of the Arab League summit at Khartoum: no recognition, no negotiation and no peace with the State of Israel. In fact, no offer was ever made, and the process of colonisation quickly got under way. Ever since then, Jewish settlements on occupied Arab land have been the main obstacle to peace in the Middle East. The three no's of Khartoum were the excuse for, not the cause of, Israel's relentless intransigence in the post-1967 era.

Ross is however right to stress that the two sides have a fundamentally different approach to peace negotiations. The Israeli mindset focused on practical, highly detailed matters, and on the security dimensions. By contrast, the Arabs and Palestinians were drawn to principles, generalities and broad claims: Return their land, and peace – or at least the absence of war – would result. The onus to start the process was on Israel, not on them, because it was Israel that had occupied their land. From these very different starting points stemmed the two sides' different ideas about peace negotiations, their purpose, and the tactics that should be employed.

Ross's involvement in the story began with the peace conference in Madrid convened by James Baker in the wake of the First Gulf War. The conference itself was in fact more significant at the symbolic than at the practical level. It ended the taboo on direct negotiations between Israel and the Palestinians. But since Yitzhak Shamir had to be dragged to Madrid kicking and screaming, as long as he remained prime minister, the bilateral talks went nowhere slowly.

With the rise to power of Yitzhak Rabin's Labour government in June 1992, the American peace team was back in business. Within a matter of months, Bill Clinton was firmly ensconced in the White House. Both leaders tended to favour a 'Syria-first' strategy, believing that a deal with Syria would change the entire strategic landscape of the region in a way that a deal with the Palestinians could not. Rabin was prepared to contemplate a complete withdrawal from the Golan Heights in return for complete peace and security. This conditional offer became known as 'the pocket', as it was placed in Warren Christopher's pocket. Christopher embarked on a shuttle between Jerusalem and Damascus that brought the two sides to the brink of peace. But the final terms that Assad offered fell short of

Rabin's expectations, leading him to accelerate the secret talks with the PLO that culminated in the Oslo Accord.

The implicit bargain was statehood for security. A historic threshold had been crossed. Having been upstaged by the Norwegians, the American peace processors did not sulk in their tents; they immediately rallied round to promote the PLO–Israel accord, to elevate it, and to generate momentum behind it. Clinton succeeded brilliantly in turning the signing ceremony of the Declaration of Principles into the most spectacular diplomatic event of the 1990s. A year later, Rabin surprised Clinton again by presenting him with a peace agreement with Jordan on a silver platter. But a year after that the assassination of Rabin dealt a body blow to the peace process.

Binyamin Netanyahu's victory over Shimon Peres at the polls in May 1996 was most unwelcome to the Americans. Clinton had told Rabin that if the prime minister ran risks for peace, the United States would act to minimise those risks. Now that Rabin was dead, Clinton felt responsible for preserving his legacy. Netanyahu posed an unmistakable threat to it. As prime minister, Netanyahu was not as bad as people had expected – he was much, much worse. In his first meeting with the president, at which Ross was present, 'Netanyahu was nearly insufferable, lecturing and telling us how to deal with the Arabs. He would respect the Oslo agreement because a democratically elected government in Israel had adopted it, but there would have to be adjustments and new negotiations over parts of it'. After Netanyahu left the room, Clinton observed, 'He thinks he is the superpower and we are here to do whatever he requires.' No one, according to Ross, disagreed with that assessment.

Following Netanyahu's visit, Ross travelled to the region to brief Arab leaders. 'My visits with both Assad and Arafat were successful,' he writes, 'but Netanyahu – believing that his policy of talking tough but not doing anything was working – squandered what I delivered.' Netanyahu also strained relations with Jordan to breaking point for no apparent reason, provoking an uncharacteristically emotional and personal attack from King Hussein. In a meeting at the White House, the King accused Netanyahu of threatening the hopes for peace of Arabs and Israelis alike with his refusal to respect agreements, his immaturity and his poor judgement.

Ehud Barak's 1999 victory over Netanyahu raised expectations sky-high in Israel, both among the Palestinians and within the Clinton Administration. Whereas Netanyahu only scored points, Barak promised to solve problems. Clinton said that he waited for Barak's arrival in Washington like a child waiting for a new toy. The American peace processors were again back in business. Clinton hoped that Barak would fulfil all of Israel's outstanding commitments to further troop withdrawals from the West Bank, and then proceed without delay to negotiations on a permanent status agreement with the Palestinians. But he yielded to Barak's insistence on aiming for a deal with Syria first. Barak and Assad were realists. They knew that what mattered to the Syrians was the land, and that what mattered most to the Israelis was security and water. There was thus a basis for a deal, for 'a peace of the brave', as Assad liked to call it. Barak's initial approach to the Syrians, however, was based on a faulty premise: that he did not have to reaffirm Rabin's conditional commitment to withdraw to the lines of 4 June 1967, which would place Syria on the north-eastern shore of the Sea of Galilee. Barak wanted Israeli sovereignty over the lake and a strip of about 400 yards to the east of it.

When Ross accompanied Madeleine Albright to Damascus in December 1999, it was clear that something had changed. Assad put forward ideas but did not impose any conditions for resuming negotiations with Israel. This paved the way for a meeting between Barak and the Syrian foreign minister, Farouk al-Shara, at Shepherdstown the following month. At Shepherdstown the Syrians were willing to go forward, but Barak held back. Unbeknownst to the Americans, Barak had received the results of a poll that led him to believe that full Israeli withdrawal from the Golan Heights would arouse widespread domestic opposition. He therefore decided to hold fast regardless of the Syrian moves. It was then, Ross later came to believe, that the deal was probably lost – and with it the possibility of an Israeli withdrawal from Lebanon within the framework of an understanding with Syria, rather than under pressure from Hizbullah.

Clinton made one more effort to broker a deal by inviting Assad to a summit meeting in Geneva on 26 March 2000. Prior to the meeting Clinton elicited from Barak his bottom lines. At the meeting, Clinton announced with great drama that Barak, based on 'a commonly agreed border', was prepared to withdraw to the June 4 line as part of a peace agreement. Ross tells us that Assad was simply not interested. But his account of the summit is inaccurate and unreliable. Instead of acting as an honest broker, Ross cooperated with Barak in an attempt to trick Assad. Assad's position was consistent and unswerving: he insisted all along on full withdrawal to the June 4 line in an exchange for full peace, nothing more and nothing less. Barak, on the other hand, played games, using Clinton to intimate to Assad that the Israelis were going to offer this if he came to Geneva. But when everyone assembled at Geneva, the proposal that Barak presented still had Israeli control over the whole of the Sea of Galilee. Barak did not offer to withdraw to the June 4 line. He did offer territory elsewhere in exchange for keeping control of the shoreline, but Assad considered this unacceptable. He claimed that 'the lake has always been our lake; it was never theirs. . . . There were no Jews to the east of the lake.' He could not remain in power for one day, he said, if he were to agree to what Barak was asking.

The meeting in Geneva thus ended abruptly in high-visibility failure. The most charitable explanation of this failure is that a misunderstanding had occurred: Assad expected to have his needs met as he defined them, and he simply shut down when he saw that the US president had not delivered what he expected from Barak. Ross, however, suggests a different explanation. He thinks that Assad, conscious of his failing health, was preoccupied with ensuring a smooth succession for his son Bashar. A deal with Israel was no longer on his agenda. This explanation, however, ignores two facts: Assad had prepared his public at home for an imminent agreement, and he brought a large team of experts to Geneva, including military officials. As they left the conference room, Assad went up to Ross and grasped him by the upper arm. Ross reciprocated this silent gesture of friendship. Though Assad did not seem weak, Ross noticed as he grasped his upper arm that there was next to nothing there – no muscle, no fat, no tissue, just bone. This seemed to confirm the reports about the Syrian dictator's declining health. But whatever the cause of Assad's intransigence, the Syrian track was dead.

Having left the Palestinians to twist in the wind, Barak now had no choice but to resume negotiations with them. Once again he asked for US help, and once again he expected the Americans to do everything his way. As Yossi Beilin testifies, Barak called Clinton often to comment, criticise and complain. Like his predecessor, Barak treated the president of the United States like a clerk, and got impatient when his orders were not carried out immediately. Many of the technical details with which Barak burdened the president could have been safely left to the subministerial level. Barak is a most peculiar individual, combining high intelligence with a complete absence of interpersonal skills. In the army they used to call him 'little Napoleon' both because of the physical resemblance – short and stocky with a pear-shaped head – and the authoritarian personality.

Barak refused to fulfil Netanyahu's commitment to a further troop withdrawal on the West Bank. This undermined Palestinian trust in him. Brushing aside their protests, Barak insisted on a summit meeting between the top leaders to conclude a final status agreement, and Clinton obliged. Arafat felt that a summit was premature and that if it failed, it would make matters worse. He suggested lower-level talks to close the gaps and lay the groundwork for the summit. Clinton persuaded Arafat to attend the summit and promised him that if it failed, no one would be blamed: There would be no finger-pointing. The summit meeting was duly convened at Camp David, the presidential retreat in Maryland, and lasted 14 days, from 11 to 25 July 2000. Ross provides an exceptionally detailed and gripping account of what transpired at the summit, day by day, almost blow by blow. His account demonstrates complete mastery of the issues, considerable psychological insight and a keen sense of drama.

Barak emerges from Ross's account as a man who played his cards very close to his chest, driven by conflicting impulses and utterly exhausting and exasperating to deal with. To be fair to Barak, he did bring to Camp David a set of ideas that touched on all the most sensitive issues at the core of the conflict: Palestinian statehood, borders, Jerusalem and refugees. His great fear was that Arafat would pocket whatever he offered and demand more, forcing Barak to move again beyond his red lines. He could contemplate withdrawal from 90 per cent of the West Bank, but he was worried that the Palestinians would retain the animating grievances of the conflict – Jerusalem and the right of return of the 1948 refugees. In short, Barak was worried that Israel would come under pressure to give up a great deal but get nothing in return. His mood was darkly apocalyptic, seeing everything in life-and-death terms. So stressed was Barak that he choked on a peanut and required the Heimlich manoeuvre to resume breathing. Barak's way of dealing with these anxieties, however, was self-defeating. He would not accept anything that he did not hear directly from Arafat, yet he refused to meet Arafat. In the two weeks at Camp David the two leaders did not have one serious face-to-face discussion. This left Clinton with the unenviable task of serving as a messenger between the two taciturn and surly leaders.

On the seventh day of the summit, Clinton's patience was exhausted and he flipped his lid. Barak gave Clinton a paper that he wanted him to present to the Palestinians as his own. Not only did the paper pose questions as if the Palestinians had a test they must pass, but it drew back from some of the key moves that Shlomo Ben-Ami, Barak's foreign minister, had made earlier. Clinton exploded: 'You want to present these ideas directly to Arafat, to the Palestinians, you go ahead and see if you can sell it. There is no way I can. This is not real. This is not serious. I went to Shepherdstown and was told nothing by you for four days. I went to Geneva and felt like a wooden Indian doing your bidding.' His voice rising and his face red, Clinton shouted, 'I will not let it happen here. I will simply not do it.' This outburst evidently had a sobering effect, for the next day Barak finally presented his bottom lines. Clinton duly conveyed the new ideas to Arafat, underlining their historic significance. Were they a basis for concluding an agreement, yes or no? The answer came back: No. Nor did Arafat make any counter-proposal. This sealed the fate of the summit. Clinton promptly laid all the blame for the failure of the summit at Arafat's door, breaking his promise that there would be no finger-pointing in the event of failure.

With Clinton's support, Barak's version of events rapidly gained ground, particularly in Israel and the United States. According to this version, Israel made the most generous offer imaginable at Camp David, but Arafat flatly rejected it and made a deliberate decision to return to violence. This allegedly demonstrated that there is no Palestinian partner for peace. In *The Missing Peace* Dennis Ross supports this version, sometimes implicitly and sometimes explicitly. During the crisis at Camp David, he muses that Arafat may simply not be up to making a deal: 'He is a revolutionary; he has made being a victim an art form; he can't redefine himself into someone who must end all claims and truly end the conflict.'

The Barak–Ross version of the collapse of the Camp David summit is simplistic, selective and self-serving. It is also contradicted by Ross's own account. If he and Barak didn't think that Arafat was up to doing a deal, why did they convene the summit and pressure Arafat to attend it? Didn't the intimate relationship with the Israelis cast some doubt on America's claim to be acting as an honest broker? Was there no basis for Arafat's suspicion of an Israeli–American conspiracy to corner him at Camp David? Arafat had many faults, but he demonstrated his ability to make historic choices, notably by opting for a two-state solution in 1988 and by signing the Oslo Accord in 1993. By contrast, Barak had been unhappy about the Accord with the PLO; he abstained in the Cabinet vote on the 1995 Oslo II agreement; and he had never been a member of what Yossi Beilin calls 'the peace mafia' in Israel. The most fundamental cause of the failure of the Camp David summit lies not in Arafat's psychological makeup but in Barak's package. On the one hand, he offered only limited concessions on Jerusalem and the refugees; on the other, he insisted on an absolute end to the conflict. He insisted that the Palestinians sign on the dotted line that they had no further claims against the State of Israel. This remorseless insistence on finality was in fact part of the problem, not the solution. Peace by ultimatum did not work.

Barak's package was a reasonable basis for an interim agreement, not for the final end of the conflict, which he wanted so badly. Israelis like to demonise Arafat, but no Palestinian leader, however moderate, could accept the package on offer at Camp David. Arafat, in fact, represented the broadest consensus within the Palestinian community. That was the source of his legitimacy and the secret of his strength. Arafat's real mistake was not to reject the much-vaunted 'generous offer' but to encourage, or at least to tolerate, the resort to violence from his side following the collapse of the Oslo peace process. The Palestinian resort to violence in the al-Aqsa intifada had disastrous consequences. It came close to destroying the peace camp in Israel, convinced the public that there is no partner for peace, and brought to power the most aggressively right-wing government in Israel's history.

*The Missing Peace* is a comprehensive and fascinating memoir about the trials and tribulations of an American peace processor. It covers a period of 13 years on all the tracks, and it ends with some general reflections on the perils and pitfalls of peacemaking. It is easy to pour scorn on a process that absorbed so much time and energy from all the parties involved and yielded such meagre results. But the years since the end of the Clinton presidency have shown all too clearly the cost of not having a peace process. A peace process does not invariably produce a settlement, but it usually keeps the dogs of war at bay. Talking, however protracted and inconclusive, is preferable to fighting and mutual carnage. As Winston Churchill used to say, 'Better to jaw-jaw than to war-war'. Dennis Ross and the other members of his team therefore deserve our gratitude for all their efforts to bring a measure of peace and stability to a region that is notoriously prone to irrational behaviour and violence. And Ross himself deserves special commendation for producing such a revealing record of these efforts.

Yet *The Missing Peace* raises serious questions about the soundness of the Israel-first school of which Ross is a prominent member. The American emphasis on Israel's security at the expense of Palestinian rights was one of the reasons for the failure of the American-sponsored peace process. The asymmetry in power between Israel and the Palestinians is such that a voluntary agreement between the parties is simply unattainable. A third party is needed to push Israel into a settlement, and that third party can only be the United States. What is more, the Americans have the capacity to bring effective pressure to bear on Israel. It simply does not make sense for the US *not* to exert this leverage in the cause of peace. Paradoxically, the most serious charge against the Israel-first school is that it does not serve Israel's true, long-term interests. Israel's real interest, like that of the Palestinians, lies in an end to the occupation and a two-state solution.

# TWENTY-TWO

# George W. Bush and the Israeli–Palestinian Conflict

Major wars have a habit of generating a peace agenda which goes beyond the immediate security objectives of the campaign to outline a vision of a better world, of international order based on universal values such as justice and morality. This is particularly true of wars that are fought not by one country but by a coalition of countries. The broader peace agenda is needed to keep the coalition together and to justify the sacrifices that have to be made in the course of fighting the war against the adversary. Thus, the First World War was the war to end all wars. The Second World War was fought to free the world from the scourge of fascism and to make it safe for democracy. On 16 January 1991, George H.W. Bush stated that military action against Iraq would make possible a 'New World Order, a world where the rule of law, not the law of the jungle, governs the conduct of nations'. Similarly, George W. Bush embarked on the war against al-Qaeda and the Taliban regime in Afghanistan with the broader agenda of freeing the world from the scourge of international terrorism.

There were other striking parallels between the First Gulf War and the war in Afghanistan. In the first place, on the American

side, some of the key positions in 2001 were held by veterans of
the 1991 Gulf War, including Dick Cheney, Paul Wolfowitz and
Colin Powell. Second, in both conflicts the incumbent US president
sought to build a broad international coalition to confront the
aggressor. Third, in both wars Israel was kept at arm's length in order
to preserve the coalition. Fourth, in both cases a link was quickly
established between the conflict at hand and the Palestine problem.

When George W. Bush assumed the US presidency in January
2001, he departed from the approach of his Democratic predecessor
in two respects. First, whereas Bill Clinton was prepared to devote
as much of his presidency as it took to resolve the Israeli–Palestinian
dispute, George W. adopted a 'hands-off' attitude, leaving it to the
two sides to sort out their own differences. Second, whereas Clinton
had a special bond with the leaders of the Labour Party in Israel
as well as with Yasser Arafat, Bush cold-shouldered the Palestinian
leader and established surprisingly warm relations with the right-
wing Israeli leader, Ariel Sharon. After their first meeting at the
White House, Bush commented on Sharon's 'marvellous sense
of history'. More importantly, the Bush Administration seemed
receptive to the Sharon line that Yasser Arafat was a terrorist, that the
Palestinian Authority was a terrorist entity, and that they should be
treated as such. Sharon's refusal to resume the political dialogue with
the Palestinian Authority until there was a complete cessation of
violence struck a sympathetic chord in Washington. Vice-President
Dick Cheney went so far as to justify in public Israel's policy of
assassinating Palestinian activists suspected of orchestrating the
violence.

The terrorist attacks on the World Trade Center and the Pentagon
on 11 September 2001 violently shook the kaleidoscope of world
politics. The attacks had far-reaching consequences for almost all
aspects of US foreign policy, including relations with Israel and the
Palestinians. Many Israelis hoped that the events of September 11
would engender greater sympathy and support in the US for their
own war against Palestinian militants. Ariel Sharon reportedly said
to Colin Powell, 'Everyone has his own bin Laden and Arafat is
ours.' Sharon also hoped to make common cause with the US in

the war against international terrorism. All these hopes, however, were quickly dashed. Colin Powell made it clear that 'Israel will not be part of any anti-terror military action.' The attempt to demonise Yasser Arafat backfired. While Israel was firmly excluded from the emergent anti-terror coalition, some of its enemies, such as Syria and Iran, were being considered for membership. Hizbullah, Hamas and Islamic Jihad were conspicuous in their absence from the list of 27 terrorist organisations that had their assets frozen by Congress. They were treated on this occasion as local movements fighting against occupation, not as global terrorist networks like the one headed by Osama bin Laden. Far from gaining respectability, Israel felt that it was being treated almost as a pariah and as an impediment to the American effort to build an anti-terror coalition.

Worse was to come. Two weeks after the attacks, President Bush issued the strongest statement yet endorsing an independent Palestinian state with East Jerusalem as its capital. The Bush Administration's plan, which was said to have been in preparation prior to September 11, envisaged the handing back of nearly all the West Bank to Palestinian control. Departing from its standard operating procedures, the State Department prepared its own plan rather than forwarding Israeli proposals with minor modifications. The plan itself was anathema to Sharon, who was committed to keeping the whole of Jerusalem under Israeli control. He was reluctant to yield to the Palestinian Authority more than the 42 per cent of the West Bank that it already controlled; and he envisaged a weak Palestinian entity made up of isolated enclaves with no territorial contiguity.

Sharon reacted to the American peace plan with an astonishing outburst of anger which reflected his deep fear that the US might abandon the strategic alliance with Israel in favour of an alliance of convenience with the Arab states and the Palestinians. He warned President Bush not to repeat the mistake of Neville Chamberlain in 1938 of trying to appease Nazi Germany by offering Hitler part of Czechoslovakia. 'Do not try to appease the Arabs at our expense', said Sharon. 'Israel will not be Czechoslovakia. Israel will fight terrorism.' The analogy with Munich was preposterous: Israel is not

Czechoslovakia but an occupying power; the Palestinian Authority is not Nazi Germany; and Yasser Arafat was no Adolf Hitler. After being compared to Neville Chamberlain, of all people, Bush must have regretted his remark about Sharon's marvellous sense of history. In any case, the official American response reflected extreme displeasure. 'The prime minister's comments are unacceptable', said Ari Fleischer, the White House spokesman:

> Israel has no stronger friend and ally in the world than the United States. President Bush has been an especially close friend of Israel. The Unites States has been working for months to press the parties to end the violence and return to political dialogue. The United States will continue to press both Israel and the Palestinians to move forward.

Although Sharon expressed regret for provoking this public row, his allegation of appeasement and of treachery continued to rankle.

Israel's reaction to the assassination in Jerusalem of tourism minister Rehavam Ze'evi – by the Popular Front for the Liberation of Palestine (PFLP) on 17 October 2001 – deepened the crisis in the relations with the US. The radical right-winger and racist former general, who advocated the 'transfer' of Palestinians from Palestine, was a personal friend of Ariel Sharon. The assassination was a straightforward retaliation for Israel's 'targeted killing' of the PFLP leader, Abu Ali Mustapha, in August. Sharon warned Arafat of 'all-out-war' unless he handed over the assassins. Without waiting for a reply, he ordered the Israel Defence Force to reoccupy six cities in Area A on the West Bank in the most drastic assault on Arafat's Authority since limited self-rule had begun seven years previously. The scale and ferocity of the incursion shocked many Israelis, including Shimon Peres, the foreign minister and leading advocate of negotiation as opposed to retaliation. It appeared to serve the not-so-secret agenda of the hardliners in the government and in the army, that of destroying the peace process by banishing Arafat and bringing about the collapse of the Palestinian Authority (PA).

These aggressive moves against the PA placed Israel on a collision course with the US, which denounced the move in uncharacteristically blunt terms and called on Israel to quit the West Bank cities immediately and unconditionally. It also warned Sharon that the war against the Palestinians threatened the fragile coalition against the Taliban regime and Osama bin Laden. Sharon flatly rejected the American demand in a remarkable display of defiance towards an ally that gives his country $3 billion in aid every year. But he was forced to recognise his error in thinking that the terrorist attack on the US provided Israel with an opportunity to redefine the rules of the game in the local conflict with the Palestinians. Having declared that Israel would act unilaterally in defence of its own interests, he was compelled to take American interests into account. A gradual withdrawal from the West Bank cities was set in motion.

The pro-American Arab regimes, led by Egypt, Jordan and Saudi Arabia, viewed the escalation of violence in Palestine with mounting anguish and anxiety. They had been shamed and discredited in the eyes of their own people by their inability to help the Palestinians or to modify the United States' blatant partiality towards Israel. Osama bin Laden was quick to seize on the plight of the Palestinians as an additional stick with which to beat these Arab regimes following the Anglo-American assault on Afghanistan: 'Israeli tanks are wreaking havoc in Palestine – in Jenin, Ramallah, Rafah and Beit Jala and other parts of the land of Islam, but no one raises his voice or bats an eyelid.' Like Saddam Hussein, bin Laden exploited the plight of the Palestinians for his own ends. But his motives did not detract from the centrality of the Palestine question, and his plea struck a sympathetic chord in much of the Arab and Islamic world. By swearing that the US would have no peace until Palestine was free, the besieged bin Laden succeeded in setting the agenda for Arab demands on Palestine.

Yasser Arafat was the first Arab leader to denounce the horrific terrorist attacks of September 11. He had paid a heavy price for his support of Saddam following the invasion of Kuwait, and he was not about to make the same mistake again. Arafat and his colleagues, and all thoughtful Palestinians, sought to distance themselves from bin

Laden, the Lucifer of international terrorism. Bin Laden's war against the West is a religious war, whereas the Palestinians' struggle against Israel is essentially a political and national struggle, although there is an undeniable religious dimension to it. Palestinians also draw a firm distinction between the kind of unbridled terrorism practised by bin Laden and their own resort to violence in self-defence. A further distinction they make concerns Israeli violence, which they regard as illegitimate because its purpose is to perpetuate the occupation of their land and their own resistance to Israeli occupation. The US stands accused of double standards, of subscribing to a definition of terrorism that, until very recently, suited only Israel. Arab and Muslim groups have been pressing for some time for a new definition of terrorism that excludes movements resisting occupation. The lack of one helps to explain their lukewarm response to the American-led coalition against it.

Clearly, a link existed between the war in Afghanistan and the conflict in Palestine. For the majority of Arabs and Muslims, Palestine is a central issue. Their attitude towards the US war in Afghanistan was determined to a large extent by its stand on the Palestine question. And the dominant perception was one of American double standards, of one standard applied to Israel and another to the Palestinians. Consequently, the US did not receive unambiguous Arab support in its war against international terrorism because it did not satisfy the moderate Arab demands on Palestine, meaning the Clinton parameters: a deal that would establish the borders for an independent and sovereign Palestinian state, that would allow for the return of some refugees, and that would divide Jerusalem between Israel and the Palestinians. President Bush took a critical step forward in invoking international justice to justify the war in Afghanistan. To be consistent, he had to uphold the same standard of justice for the Palestinians. Verbal commitments no longer carry much credibility. His father promised justice for the Palestinians after the First Gulf War and failed to deliver. He himself would be judged not by words but by actions.

*        *        *

The experience of the Bush Administration proved once again that a voluntary agreement between the parties is unattainable. The only possible path forward is an externally imposed solution. That sounds rather coercive and brutal towards Israel but it need not be. Indeed, if it is brutal, it will backfire. The key to progress is to bring about a change in Israeli public opinion in favour of ending the occupation and conceding to the Palestinians the right to genuine national self-determination. Improbable as it may look today, such a change is not inconceivable. The Israeli public has never been as resistant to the idea of Palestinian statehood as are the politicians of the Right. At the 2001 elections, Ariel Sharon promised peace with security and decidedly failed to deliver either. He did not have a plan with the remotest chance of being acceptable to the other side, and he knew it. Hence his stubborn opposition to the resumption of the final status negotiations. At the same time, he was subjected to the most intense pressure by his coalition partners, the Left pressing him to quit the West Bank, the Right to reoccupy it. His main aim was survival, which precluded the option of voluntary withdrawal from the West Bank. So once again, as so often in the past, the peace process was held hostage to domestic Israeli politics.

Only the US can break the deadlock in Israeli politics. If it does not, no one else will. The credentials of the US as a friend are impeccable. Since 1967, it has given Israel more than $92 billion in aid; and this aid continues to the tune of $3 billion a year. The US should involve the United Nations, the European Union, Russia and its Arab allies in a concerted effort to generate internal pressure on Israel to move forward on the political front; but its own leadership role is crucial. The key point to drive home in this educational campaign is that the US remains committed to Israel's security and welfare, and that the country's security will be enhanced rather than put at risk by ending the occupation of the West Bank and Gaza. Arguably, the US would have done Sharon a favour by walking him into a peace deal against which, given his ideological provenance, he was bound to protest loudly in public. Moreover, a fair number of sensible, level-headed Israelis would be grateful to the US for liberating them from the colonial venture which has so disastrously distorted the Zionist political project. In the end, it might be a question, as George Ball once put it in an article in *Foreign Affairs*, of how to save Israel against itself.

TWENTY-THREE

# *Ariel Sharon's War Against the Palestinians*

For Ariel Sharon, diplomacy, to invert the famous saying by Karl von Clausewitz, is the extension of war by other means. The Israeli leader had a chequered career as a soldier and a politician but he never thought of himself as a diplomat. The title Sharon chose for his autobiography aptly sums him up in one word – *Warrior*. Bargaining, accommodation and compromise were alien to his whole way of thinking. This makes Sharon unsuited, both by temperament and by conviction, to the task of peacemaking. In a peace process, unlike war, you cannot have a winner and a loser. The resolution of a conflict requires two winners. Sharon, on the other hand, views the relations with the Palestinians as a zero-sum game where a gain by one side is necessarily at the expense of the other. And he was hell-bent on always being the winner. President George W. Bush once described Sharon as 'a man of peace'. But this is about as accurate as describing Sharon as a slim and handsome young man.

A man of war through and through, Sharon perceived the Palestinians not as a partner on the road to peace but as Israel's principal enemy. The roots of Sharon's thinking about the Palestinians go back to Ze'ev Jabotinsky, the spiritual father of the Israeli right. In 1923 Jabotinsky published an article entitled 'On the Iron Wall (We and the Arabs)'. He argued that Arab nationalists were bound to oppose the establishment of a Jewish state in Palestine. Consequently, a voluntary agreement between the two sides was unattainable. The only way to realise the Zionist project was behind an iron wall of Jewish military strength. In other words, the Zionist project could only be implemented unilaterally and by military force.

The crux of Jabotinsky's strategy was to enable the Zionist movement to deal with its local opponents from a position of unassailable strength. The iron wall was not an end in itself but a means to an end. It was intended to compel the Arabs to abandon any hope of destroying the Jewish state. Despair was expected to promote pragmatism on the other side and thus to prepare the ground for the second stage of the strategy: negotiations with the local Arabs about their status and national rights in Palestine. In other words, Jewish military strength was to pave the way to a political settlement with the Palestinian national movement which laid a claim to the whole of Palestine.

The key phrase here is 'iron wall'. It accurately describes the basic Zionist strategy in the conflict with the neighbouring Arab states since Israel was established in 1948. It also provides the title of my book *The Iron Wall: Israel and the Arab World*. There I argue that the history of the State of Israel is a vindication of the strategy of the iron wall. The Arabs – first the Egyptians, then the Palestinians, then the Jordanians – learnt the hard way that Israel could not be defeated on the battlefield and were compelled to negotiate with it from a position of palpable weakness.

The 1993 Oslo Accord marked the transition from the first to the second stage of the iron wall strategy, the transition from deterrence to negotiations and compromise. The Palestinians believed that by signing the Accord and thereby giving up their claim to 78 per cent of pre-1948 Palestine, they would gradually gain an independent state stretching over the Gaza Strip and most of the West Bank with a capital in East Jerusalem. They had moderated their political programme very considerably in the way that Jabotinsky had predicted in his extraordinarily prescient article. But what the Oslo

Accord produced in practice was not the partition of Palestine but a persistent political deadlock. The Palestinians are now bitterly disappointed with the results of the historic compromise they struck on the lawn of the White House with the leaders of the Jewish state. The Oslo peace process broke down in the summer of 2000 and the dream of independence and statehood remained just that – a dream. Having made the peace of the brave, the Palestinians confronted an Israeli prime minister determined to impose on them the peace of the bully.

Ariel Sharon was involved at the sharp end of the confrontation with the Arabs for most of his life. The hallmarks of his career are mendacity, the most savage brutality towards Arab civilians, and a persistent preference for force over diplomacy to solve political problems. After making the transition from the army into politics, Sharon remained the champion of violent solutions. His ideology is the Likud ideology of Greater Israel that claims the whole of the West Bank as an integral part of the Land of Israel. This ideology leaves no room for an independent Palestinian state between the Jordan river and the Mediterranean sea.

In the past, Sharon used to seek a solution to the Palestinian problem at the expense of Jordan, half of whose population is of Palestinian origin. Sharon was in fact one of the most consistent proponents of the Likud policy and the slogan that 'Jordan is Palestine'. This policy denied the need to create a new Palestinian state on the West Bank of the river Jordan, claiming that a Palestinian state in all but name already existed on the East Bank of the river. Consequently, the solution lay in helping the PLO to transform the Hashemite Kingdom of Jordan into the Republic of Palestine. During the crisis in Jordan in September 1970, Sharon was the only member of the IDF General Staff who was opposed to the policy of helping King Hussein beat off the challenge from the PLO. After the signature of the peace treaty between Israel and Jordan in October 1994, the Likud finally abandoned the policy that 'Jordan is Palestine'. Sharon himself may have realised that it was no longer realistic, but his failure to renounce it openly suggests that it may have still been lurking at the back of his mind.

In and out of uniform, Sharon waged a relentless war against the Palestinian people. This is the theme of Baruch Kimmerling's informative and illuminating book *Politicide: Ariel Sharon's War Against the Palestinians*.* Kimmerling defines politicide as 'a process that has, as its ultimate goal, the dissolution of the Palestinians' existence as a legitimate social, political, and economic entity. This process may also but not necessarily entail their partial or complete ethnic cleansing from the territory known as the Land of Israel.' Kimmerling regards Sharon as the most brutal, deceitful and unrestrained of all Israeli generals and politicians, and as one of the most frightening leaders of the new millennium. His book is a devastating indictment of Sharon's attempts to destroy the Palestinian people, including the proposal to forcibly turn Jordan into a Palestinian state, and the infamous invasion of Lebanon in 1982.

As minister of defence in Menachem Begin's government Sharon was the driving force behind the invasion of Lebanon. This was not a defensive war to safeguard Israel's security but an offensive war designed to reshape the geopolitical landscape of the Middle East. The principal objective of Sharon's war was to destroy the PLO as a military and political organisation, to break the backbone of Palestinian nationalism, to spread despair and despondency among the inhabitants of the West Bank, and to pave the way to its absorption into Greater Israel. A second objective was to give Israel's Maronite allies a leg-up to power, and then compel them to sign a peace treaty with Israel. A third objective was to defeat and expel the Syrian army from Lebanon and to make Israel the dominant power in the Levant. Under Sharon's devious direction, an operation that was supposedly undertaken in self-defence developed into a merciless siege of Beirut and culminated in a horrendous massacre in the Palestinian refugee camps of Sabra and Shatila, leading to the removal of Sharon from his post at the ministry of defence.

If brute military force was Sharon's principal instrument in dealing with the Palestinian people, the building of Jewish settlements on

* Baruch Kimmerling, *Politicide: Ariel Sharon's War Against the Palestinians* (London: Verso, 2004).

occupied Palestinian territory was another project that was always close to his heart – or what passed for one. Here he was acting in the best Zionist tradition of 'creating facts on the ground' to pre-empt negotiations. In various capacities – as minister of agriculture, minister without portfolio, minister of industry and trade, minister of housing and construction, minister of national infrastructure, and minister of foreign affairs – Sharon spurned diplomatic compromise and pushed for confiscating more and more Arab land, for building more and more Jewish settlements in the occupied territories, and for the expansion of existing settlements. Not for nothing was he nicknamed 'the bulldozer'. The settlements were a manifestation of Sharon's territorial expansionism, an example of his general preference for unilateral action, and a way of preventing the establishment of an independent Palestinian state. Whereas Labour-led governments tended to construct settlements in areas of strategic importance to Israel, the Likud, and Ariel Sharon in particular, deliberately scattered settlements across the length and breadth of the West Bank in order to render territorial compromise impossible when the Labour Party returned to power.

Sharon's deliberately provocative visit to Haram al-Sharif in the Old City of Jerusalem on 28 September 2000 sparked the Palestinian riots which quickly evolved into the al-Aqsa intifada, paving the way for Sharon's decisive electoral victory against Ehud Barak on 6 February 2001. Israel was now at war and no Israeli leader was more efficient or more ruthless in fighting the Palestinians than this old warhorse. During the election campaign the wily Sharon tried to reinvent himself as a man of peace. He ran on a ticket of 'peace with security'. But it was the same old Sharon. He had not mellowed with age; neither did he appear to have learnt any lessons from his ill-conceived and ill-fated war in Lebanon. Sharon's rise to power thus immediately extinguished any faint light there might have been at the end of the tunnel.

With Sharon ensconced in the prime minister's office, Israel was back to the old strategy of the iron wall in its most aggressive form. Ze'ev Jabotinsky had outlined a sophisticated strategy of change in which Jewish military power was designed to pave the way to negotiations from strength. Like most politicians of the Right, Sharon was dedicated to building up his country's military power but was rather reluctant to engage in peace negotiations with the Palestinians. His strategy was to use Israel's overwhelming military power in order to impose his terms on the opponent. Small wonder that after Likud's victory at the polls in 2001, final status negotiations with the Palestinian Authority were not resumed. The persistence of Palestinian violence against Israeli civilians, especially in the terrifying form of suicide bombings, was Sharon's excuse for refusing to resume political negotiations. The deeper reasons lay in his psychological makeup, his worldview, and the ideology of Greater Israel. One does not negotiate about a nationalist ideology. All -isms eventually lead to war, and right-wing Zionism is no exception.

Ariel Sharon was the unilateralist *par excellence*. This was reflected across the entire spectrum of his government's policies, from the destruction of Palestinian houses to the targeted killing of militant Palestinian leaders, from the expansion of Jewish settlements on the West Bank to the construction of an elaborate network of bypass roads for the exclusive use of the settlers, from habitual violation of UN resolutions to the systematic abuse of international humanitarian law. Arab peace offers were treated with indifference verging on contempt. In late March 2002, for example, all 22 members of the Arab League endorsed a Saudi plan that offered Israel peace and normalisation in return for withdrawal from the territories it occupied in June 1967. Sharon's response amounted to a declaration of war. He launched the fraudulently named 'Operation Defensive Shield' which seriously damaged the PA's capacity to govern and destroyed much of the civilian infrastructure that had been built with foreign aid. On the belligerent prime minister's orders, the IDF marched into the Palestinian part of the West Bank and waged a savage war against its people which included the reoccupation of cities, the bombardment of refugee camps, the demolition of houses, attacks on medical facilities, the rounding up of hundreds of suspects, torture, and summary executions.

One of the most disturbing aspects of the Sharon government's policy was the commencement of the construction of the so-called 'security barrier' or wall on the West Bank. Higher than the Berlin Wall, it winds its way round the main Jewish settlement blocks, and is in flagrant violation of international law. The purpose of the wall is said to be to prevent terrorist attacks on Israel, but the hidden motives behind it have as much to do with land-grabbing as with security. To build the wall Israel expropriated land, demolished houses, separated farmers from their fields and workers from their workplaces, school children from their schools, and entire communities from their sources of water. The wall bites deep into the West Bank with the apparent aim of crowding as many Palestinians as possible into as little territory as possible. Estimates of the area of the West Bank that this wall will gobble up by the time it is completed range from 15 to 25 per cent. What is clear is that the wall is paving the way to the *de facto* annexation of a substantial part of the West Bank to Israel, thereby undermining the possibility of a genuine two-state solution. For Ze'ev Jabotinsky the strategy of the 'iron wall' was a metaphor for dealing with the Arabs from a position of unassailable strength. In the crude hands of Ariel Sharon and his associates, however, this metaphor fast became a hideous and horrendous concrete reality, and an environmental catastrophe.

In an effort to breathe some life into the comatose Israeli–Palestinian peace process, British Prime Minister Tony Blair took the lead in persuading the Quartet (consisting of the US, UN, EU and Russia) to issue the 'road map'. George Bush was not an enthusiast of the road map, and adopted it only under pressure from his allies. The road map was formally launched by the Quartet in June 2003. It envisaged three phases leading to an independent Palestinian state alongside Israel by 2005. The Palestinians embraced the road map with great alacrity, though they found it difficult to come up with a credible security plan due to the death and destruction visited upon them by 'Operation Defensive Shield'. The Israeli position was more ambiguous. Sharon requested and received from President Bush three delays in launching the road map; once it was launched, he submitted 14 amendments that were designed to empty it of any serious political content. The Israeli Cabinet never endorsed the road map as such; it only voted for specific measures that were required of Israel in the first phase. There was also some outright opposition to the road map from ministers who were well to the right of Sharon.

The policies of the Israeli government did not change significantly following this half-hearted adoption of the road map. It continued to order IDF incursions into the Palestinian territories, targeted assassinations of Palestinian militants, demolition of houses, uprooting of trees, curfews, restrictions, and the deliberate inflicting of misery, hunger and hardship to encourage Arab migration from the West Bank. At the same time, settlement activity continued on the West Bank under the guise of 'natural growth' but in blatant violation of the provisions of the road map.

The failure of all official plans to break the deadlock on the Israeli–Palestinian front encouraged private individuals and groups from both sides of the divide to come forward with fresh ideas. Sari Nusseibeh and Ami Ayalon obtained more than 300,000 signatures for their blueprint for the resolution of the conflict. Yasser Abed Rabbo and Yossi Beilin signed a 'peace agreement' between Palestine and Israel in Geneva on 1 December 2003 amid great media and political fanfare. Funded and sponsored by the Swiss government, the Geneva Accord was a 50-page document dealing in detail with all aspects of the dispute. It was enthusiastically received all over the world. Predictably, however, it incurred the wrath of Sharon, who denounced Beilin as a traitor. Ever the soldier, Sharon acted on the precept that the best line of defence is to attack. Sharon's central contention all along was that there is no Palestinian peace partner. The Geneva Accord demonstrated not only that there was a significant body of moderate Palestinians who were prepared to negotiate with Israel for a final settlement to the conflict, but that they had already done most of the groundwork.

At length Sharon reached the conclusion that the occupation in its present form is unsustainable and he began to look for ways of distancing Israel from the main Palestinian population centres while keeping as much of their land as possible. The plan he came up with was not a peace plan but one for a unilateral Israeli disengagement from the Gaza Strip and four isolated settlements on the West Bank. Characteristically, the plan ignored Palestinian rights and interests, and was not even presented to the Palestinian Authority as a basis for negotiations because it would have been rejected out of hand. Sharon presented the plan to the world as a contribution to the road map and to the building of peace based on a two-state solution. But to his right-wing supporters he said: 'My plan is difficult for the Palestinians, a fatal blow. There's no Palestinian state in a unilateral move.' The real purpose behind the plan was to sweep away the remnants of Oslo, to undermine the position of Yasser Arafat and the Palestinian Authority, and to derail the road map. Anchored in a fundamental rejection of the Palestinian national identity, the plan was a pitch for politicide, an attempt to deny the Palestinian people an independent political existence on their land.

Bypassing the Palestinians, the Quartet and the international community, Sharon presented his plan to the only person who counted in his eyes: the president of the United States. As a reward for the offer to pull the 7,500 settlers out of the Gaza Strip, Sharon requested President Bush's support for retaining the six major Jewish settlement blocks, holding 92,000 people, on the West Bank. Indeed, in a remarkable exercise in brinkmanship or blackmail, Sharon threatened not to board the aircraft at Ben-Gurion airport until his demands were satisfied. At their meeting at the White House, on 14 April 2004, George W. Bush granted his guest everything he had asked for and more. Hailing Sharon's plan as a 'a bold and historic initiative' and as a true contribution to building peace in the region, Mr Bush proceeded to give the most right-wing prime minister in Israel's history two specific assurances. First, he promised American support for Israel's retention of choice parts of the West Bank. Second, he rejected the right of return of the 1948 refugees and said that in future they and their families should emigrate to a new Palestinian state. Sharon asked for these assurances in writing and he received them in writing. Taken together, these two assurances amounted to an abrupt reversal of American policy towards the Arab–Israeli conflict, under both Democratic and Republican Administrations, since 1967. They also destroyed irrevocably any residual credibility that the Bush Administration may have had to serve as an honest broker in the resolution of the conflict.

Arab reactions to the Sharon–Bush pact were instantaneous and incandescent with rage. There was a universal feeling that by embracing the Likud's one-sided nationalist agenda, Bush had sounded the death knell of the peace process. Arafat labelled Bush's statements 'a new Balfour Declaration'. King Abdullah II of Jordan cancelled a scheduled meeting with Bush on account of the statements he made during Sharon's visit to Washington. Given Sharon's record as a proponent of the thesis that 'Jordan is Palestine', the king had every reason to dissociate himself from an accord about which he was not consulted, and which could end up destabilising his own kingdom through an influx of Palestinians from the West Bank to the East Bank. President Hosni Mubarak of Egypt said that there was more hatred of Americans in the Arab world now than ever before. The Organisation of Islamic Conferences also condemned Washington for its support of Israel's unilateral initiative. To many Muslims as well as Arabs, the Sharon–Bush collusion was deeply offensive.

Meanwhile, Sharon, the champion of violent solutions, could congratulate himself on a spectacular victory. Virtually single-handed, he had brought about a seismic change in America's position, a change that will redefine the conflict for a generation or more. He persuaded the most powerful man in the world to back his plan to consolidate Israel's grip in the West Bank and to unilaterally draw the borders of an emasculated Palestinian state. Sharon was able to use this backing to overcome opposition to his Gaza disengagement plan from elements in the government and the ruling party, and to hang on to power despite the three separate charges of corruption pending against him and his two sons. As for George W. Bush, his sudden and ill-considered conversion to Sharon's expansionist agenda was largely motivated by political expediency: blind support for Israel went down well in the 2004 US presidential elections not only with Jewish voters but with the much more substantial constituency of Christian fundamentalists. The tragedy is that Bush and Sharon, in trying to protect their domestic power base, only endangered the future of Israel, the Palestinians and the entire Middle East.

TWENTY-FOUR

# *Palestine and Iraq*

P alestine and Iraq are the two most prominent problems
on the rugged political landscape of the Middle East. The
outcome of the conflicts in these two trouble spots will play
a crucial role in shaping the future of the entire region. It is tempting
to look at Palestine and Iraq as two separate and unrelated issues but
to do so would be a grave mistake. Although they are geographically
removed from one another, the two issues are connected in intricate
and important ways. As we have seen, the link between Palestine and
Iraq goes at least as far back as the First Gulf War. In the aftermath
of that war, George Bush senior exerted serious pressure on Israel
to negotiate with the Palestinians and this pressure contributed to
his defeat in the 1992 presidential elections. On his election to the
presidency in 2001, George Bush junior was anxious not to repeat
his father's mistake. From the very beginning, therefore, he adopted
a hands-off approach to the Israeli–Palestinian dispute. The contrast
between the first and the second Bush Administrations could hardly
be more pronounced. When George W. Bush entered the White
House most people expected him to follow in his father's footsteps
with a Bush II Administration. What actually emerged was more
akin to a Reagan III Administration. If Bush senior was the most

even-handed of US presidents, with the possible exception of Jimmy Carter, Bush junior surprisingly turned out to be the most pro-Israeli president in American history. He was more partial to Israel than Harry S. Truman, Lyndon Johnson, Ronald Reagan, and even Bill Clinton, who was once described by an Israeli newspaper as the last Zionist.

The basic premise behind George W. Bush's policy towards the Middle East reflected this strong pro-Israeli bias. The premise was that the key issue in Middle East politics was not Palestine, but Iraq. This was mistaken in at least one respect: for the overwhelming majority of Arabs and Muslims everywhere, Iraq was a non-issue during the build-up to the war. The real issue was Palestine and, more specifically, Israel's oppression of the Palestinians and America's blind support for Israel despite that oppression. In an attempt to win public opinion to their side, American proponents of the war on Iraq promised that action against Iraq would form part of a broader engagement with the problems of the Middle East. The road to Jerusalem, they argued, went through Baghdad. Cutting off Saddam Hussein's support for Palestinian terrorism was, according to them, an essential first step in the quest for a settlement.

Tony Blair went even further when he declared that resolving the Israeli–Palestinian dispute was as important to Middle East peace as removing Saddam Hussein from power. The motion passed by the House of Commons on 18 March 2003 explicitly welcomed 'the imminent publication of the Quartet's road map as a significant step to bringing a just and lasting peace between Israelis and Palestinians and . . . endorses the role of Her Majesty's Government in actively working for peace between Israel and Palestine'. In the year after that motion was passed both the US and UK governments became absorbed in the war in Iraq and its messy aftermath, and the attention they paid to the dispute between Israel and Palestine was intermittent at best. In the absence of sustained engagement, the situation in Palestine went from bad to worse with no end in sight to the vicious cycle of violence and nothing remotely resembling a peace process. Benign neglect is not what was promised, nor is it a viable option on the Israeli–Palestinian front. In this respect nothing has changed since the heady days of regime change in Baghdad.

September 11 changed everything. It set in motion the American war against terror – an open-ended, loosely defined war against an elusive enemy. Ariel Sharon was very quick to jump on the bandwagon of the war against terror. His argument to the Americans was that he was doing in his own little patch what they were doing globally: fighting against terror. The Palestinian Authority was a terrorist organisation, he claimed, and he was going to deal with it as a terrorist organisation. The Bush Administration accepted most of these arguments and abandoned the Palestinians to the tender mercies of General Sharon.

But this close association with the Sharon government was in fact a handicap to Bush in his quest for a global coalition to combat terrorism. As Max Hastings pointed out in the *Guardian* on 11 March 2004: 'More than a few governments are cooperating less than wholeheartedly with America's war on terror because they are unwilling to be associated with what they see as an unholy alliance of the Sharon and Bush governments.' The influence of the Likud and of its friends in Washington could be detected across the entire spectrum of American policy towards the Middle East. Particularly striking was the ideological convergence between some of the leading neoconservatives in the Bush Administration – such as Richard Perle, Paul Wolfowitz and Douglas Feith – and the hardliners in Ariel Sharon's inner circle.

In 1996, a group of six Jewish Americans, led by Richard Perle and Douglas Feith, wrote a paper for incoming Israeli prime minister, Binyamin Netanyahu. Entitled 'A Clean Break', the paper proposed, in essence, an abrupt reversal of the foreign policies of the Clinton Administration towards the Middle East. It argued that pursuing a peace process that embraced the slogan 'New Middle East' undermined Israel's legitimacy and led it into strategic paralysis. Israel was advised to change the nature of its relations with the Palestinians, to ignore the Oslo Accords and to nurture alternatives to Yasser Arafat, presumably collaborators. Israel was

also encouraged to exert military pressure on Syria, especially in
Lebanon, and to reject 'land for peace' on the Golan Heights. But
the authors' most arresting policy recommendation related to Iraq.
'This effort [the shaping of Israel's strategic environment] can focus
on removing Saddam Hussein from power in Iraq – an important
Israeli strategic objective in its own right – as a means of foiling
Syria's regional ambitions.' Thus, five years before the attack on the
twin towers, the idea of regime change in Baghdad was already on
the agenda of some of Israel's most fervent Republican supporters in
Washington.

'A Clean Break' is highly revealing about the mindset of its authors.
It was largely divorced from the regional reality of the time and naive
in its assumption that a clean break could be made without any
regard to what had gone on in the past. It also displayed a curious
inability to view the Middle East through anything but Israeli-made
glasses. While the authors' devotion to Israel's interests was crystal-
clear, their implicit identification of those interests with American
interests was much more open to question. One can debate whether
the occupation of the West Bank and the Gaza Strip serves Israel's
own long-term interests. My own view is that the retention of these
territories after the June 1967 war was a catastrophic mistake that
transformed Zionism from a national liberation movement for
the Jews into a colonial movement that represses and oppresses
the Palestinian people. In my own mind I therefore make a clear
distinction between Israel within the pre-1967 borders and the
Zionist colonial project beyond the Green Line. The former is
legitimate; the latter is not. But whether legitimate or not, what
possible American interest is served by Israel's occupation of these
territories? Israel's friends in America have not yet come up with a
convincing answer to this question.

The Bush Administration's entire policy towards the Middle East
was similarly supportive of Israel's short-term strategic interests.
Bernard Lewis, the 87-year-old Princeton professor, provided the
intellectual underpinning for this policy. Many senior members
of the Administration, notably Vice-President Dick Cheney, were
acolytes of the extraordinarily erudite professor. 'Talking to Mr

Lewis', remarked Richard Perle, is 'like going to Delphi to see the oracle'. The two themes in the history of the Islamic countries most heavily underlined by Lewis are failure to modernise and resentment of the West. Israel and Turkey, two non-Arab countries, are held out as the only successful modern states in the region. Since the Arab countries are incapable of generating reform from within, Lewis recommended an American military invasion to sweep away the existing regimes and spread democracy throughout the region. The conventional wisdom was thus stood on its head: instead of supporting tyrants to promote stability and protect American interests in the oil-rich Arab world, Lewis advocated the seeding of democracy as America's best possible ally in the fight against terrorism. In the aftermath of September 11, he urged a military takeover of Iraq to forestall further and worse terrorist attacks. He wanted to substitute a policy of confrontation for the old and, in his view, ineffectual policy of containment. 'Get tough or get out' was the crux of the Lewis Doctrine.

Paul Wolfowitz, as deputy defence secretary and a leading hawk on Iraq, was one of the most fervent admirers of Bernard Lewis in the inner circle of the Bush Administration. The terrorist attack on September 11 gave Wolfowitz an opportunity to go after Saddam Hussein. Bob Woodward, in his book *Bush at War*, reveals that in the immediate aftermath of the attack, Wolfowitz advocated a war on Iraq as an alternative to the uncertain prospect of a war in Afghanistan. When his view did not prevail, Wolfowitz kept up the pressure for making Iraq the second target in the war on terror.

One of the arguments for regime change in Baghdad was to put an end to Iraqi support for Palestinian militants and for what was seen as Palestinian intransigence in the peace process with Israel. While Iraq was the main target, the neocons also advocated that America exert relentless military pressure on Syria and on Iran. This stood in marked contrast to the EU policy of critical dialogue and critical engagement. Washington's policy of confrontation and regime change was fervently supported in Tel Aviv. Here too the benefit to Israel is much more evident than the benefit to America. And here too, the US agenda towards the region appears to incorporate a right-wing Likud agenda.

Regime change in Iraq was always portrayed by the neocons as a very easy task – as a cakewalk. They predicted that the brittle regime would collapse under the first blow and that the long-oppressed Iraqi people would welcome the coalition forces with open arms as liberators. The proclaimed aim of the invasion of Iraq was to reshape the Middle East in America's image, to turn the Iraqis into a happy nation of Jeffersonian democrats, and to make Iraq a model for the rest of the Arab world. But the expectation that American forces would be welcomed as liberators was at odds with the history of the last 10 or 20 years. Americans may not remember this history, but Arabs certainly do. Iraqis, in particular, remember only too well how the US betrayed them at the end of the First Gulf War in 1991. Bush senior encouraged the Iraqi people to rise up against Saddam Hussein only to abandon them to his tender mercies. With US forces standing idly by, Saddam was able to proceed with his customary brutality to put down the Kurdish uprising in the north and the much more serious Shiite uprising in the south. If ever there was a time for regime change in Baghdad, February 1991 was that time. The abrupt end of the Desert Storm land campaign, however, left Saddam Hussein in power. The Americans had the perfect chance to get rid of Saddam and they blew it, with disastrous consequences all round. We are all still paying the price for this colossal strategic blunder.

The Iraqi and Arab view is essentially the same as the Third World view of the First Gulf War: basically, that America went into Iraq with all sorts of fancy military technology, smashed up the place, left all the problems unresolved, created a whole host of new problems, and then went home to declare victory. The Lewis Doctrine calls for an understanding of the past as the essential basis for building a better future. But failure to view the recent past from the perspective of the Iraqis themselves led the proponents of the 2003 invasion to nurse unrealistic expectations. The war on Iraq could not go according to plan because it was based on a selective and self-serving view of the past.

The Iraq war, for which there was no solid basis in international law, is a good example of the saying in Arabic that something that

starts crooked remains crooked. UN resolution 678 was passed in
1990 for the specific purpose of liberating Kuwait. It could not be
interpreted in good faith as authorising an invasion of Iraq in March
2003. Resolution 1441 of 2002 did not specifically authorise the
use of force by states. It reserved the issue of Iraq for the Security
Council to deal with. A second UN resolution was required to
expressly authorise the use of force by states and this resolution was
never passed. Moreover, a serious international effort was well under
way at the time to disarm Iraq. A team of UN weapons inspectors,
headed by Dr Hans Blix, was carrying out a very thorough, effective
and professional job. They needed another three months to complete
the inspection. They were not given the time. On 17 March 2003,
they were rudely and brusquely elbowed out of the way by the
Anglo-American invaders. Considering the contempt with which
leading members of the Bush Administration treated Dr Blix, he
is remarkably magnanimous towards them in his book *Disarming
Iraq*. He concedes that without the American military build-up, his
inspectors would not have been allowed to return to Iraq or been
given so much freedom. On the other hand, he could not avoid
the suspicion that UNMOVIC's work was intended largely to fill in
time until the military build-up was complete. In one of the many
perversions of logic on the road to war, the unfinished work of the
inspectors was used by the Americans as the pretext for military
action.

Three main reasons were given to justify the war. One was
possession of weapons of mass destruction that allegedly made
Iraq a present and imminent threat to international security. No
WMD were discovered. In this respect the allies went to war on
a false prospectus. David Kay, the head of the Iraq Survey Group,
put it to Congress with blinding candour: 'We were all wrong.' Paul
Wolfowitz admitted in an interview to *Vanity Fair* that the WMDs
were just the most convenient 'bureaucratic' reason for selling the
war to the public.

The second reason was the alleged link between the Ba'th Party
and al-Qaeda. No intelligence was available at the time to confirm
such a link. British intelligence reports made it clear to No. 10

Downing Street that the two were in fact ideological opponents. But, as a result of the invasion of Iraq, a link that did not exist before was created. One did not have to be an expert on international terrorism to predict that this would happen. As Simon Schama had written in the *Guardian*, attacking Iraq was bound to turn the country into a teddy bears' picnic for terrorists.

The third reason occupied the moral high ground: Saddam Hussein was a monster in human form at the head of an evil dictatorship. A humanitarian intervention was therefore called for to rid the Iraqi people of the monster. This description of the man and his regime is indisputable. But Saddam was always a monster, not least in the 1980s, when the West armed and supported him throughout the gruelling eight-year war with Iran that he himself had started. So presenting the invasion of Iraq as an act of humanitarian intervention is disingenuous. There was a strategic decision to invade Iraq and this decision was simply dressed up with moral arguments.

The coalition in this war was very different to the coalition Bush senior assembled in 1990–91. That was a genuine international coalition of 33 nations, including most of the Arab states, led by the US and acting under a clear UN mandate. The 2003 coalition is best described as a cash-register coalition, with American leaders saying to different countries: 'If you support us, we will give you money, and if you don't support us, we will turn against you.' The CIA has been distributing bags of money from Afghanistan to Iraq in pursuit of the war on terror. 'CIA' apparently stands for cash in advance.

Tony Blair's main reason for taking Britain into the war alongside America was the desire to preserve the special relationship and to retain some influence over US actions. Blair realised that, whatever anyone else thought, the US decision had already been made: the Americans were going to 'do' Iraq. The choice for Britain, as he saw it, was to back America in going to war or keep out and risk being sidelined. Blair made the decision to follow America in the face of strong opposition in the Cabinet, the Labour Party and the country. All the information that has come to light since the invasion casts doubt about the wisdom of this decision. Robin Cook, a former British foreign secretary who resigned from the Cabinet in protest against the war, published a book in 2003 with the apt title *Point of Departure*. The book sheds a great deal of light on the many contradictions in Blair's thinking and actions in the lead up to the war. The greatest contradiction is that Blair always presented Britain as a bridge between the two sides of the Atlantic yet, by siding with America over Iraq, he helped to create one of the deepest rifts in the history of transatlantic relations.

Removing Saddam Hussein from power also failed to generate the promised momentum for political reform in the Arab world. Calls for reform from within the region have become more urgent in recent years. A major landmark was the publication in the summer of 2002 of the UN-backed Arab Human Development Report in which 30 intellectuals from the region exposed the dismal failures of the Arab world. The report identified three cardinal obstacles to human development: the widening deficit in freedom, women's rights and knowledge. Prepared by Arabs for Arabs, the report fuelled a much-needed debate in the Arab world. But it also proved useful for US policy-makers whose foreign policy agenda included the transformation of the Middle East. President Bush cited it in a major speech in November 2003, setting out his plans to promote democracy in the region. 'In the words of a report by Arab scholars,' Bush said, 'the global wave of democracy has – and I quote – "barely reached the Arab states".' A draft of the Greater Middle East Initiative, a series of measures unveiled by the US at the G8 summit of rich countries in the summer of 2004, drew heavily on the report and tried to address the three deficits identified by its authors. The American paper, published in full in the London-based *Al-Hayat* newspaper, called for sweeping economic, political, cultural and educational reforms in the Arab world.

Arab intellectuals reacted negatively to Washington's attempt to commandeer their self-critical report. They liked the message but they totally mistrusted the messenger. They claimed that Washington had been selective with the report, ignoring criticism of its own policies before September 11 of supporting authoritarian regimes that helped to breed the religious extremism that now threatened its security. Washington's new ideas were seen as the product of the 'new colonialism' designed to change the values of Arab and Islamic society and to impose reform from above. They have no legitimacy in Arab eyes because they come from a power that has invaded two Muslim countries, Afghanistan and Iraq – a power that has done nothing to promote the interests of the Arab people. Arab intellectuals recognised the urgency of reform but demanded ownership of the process, rejecting America's one-size-fits-all blueprint. In short, they saw the US reform agenda as driven by American priorities and American interests.

Arab rulers were also suspicious that the Bush Administration planned to push ahead with changes in the region before resolving the Arab–Israeli conflict. President Hosni Mubarak of Egypt rebuffed the US proposals for the region at a meeting with Tony Blair at Chequers on 9 March 2004. Mubarak insisted that any modernisation has to stem from the traditions and culture of the region. He also stressed that the Israeli–Palestinian conflict was at the heart of the region's problems. Making reforms while ignoring the Palestinian issue, he warned, will not produce the desired stability. Bush Administration officials, for their part, were critical of Arab governments for using the Arab–Israeli conflict as an excuse for denying democracy, freedom of expression and other rights to their people. They had a point. Arab leaders, on the other hand, believe that Israel's friends in Washington seek to create a string of client-states in the region who would allow Israel to retain the occupied territories. They too have a point. There is only one way to dispel this suspicion, namely by re-engaging in the Middle East peace process and by exerting real pressure on Israel to withdraw from the occupied territories.

This brings us back to the link between Iraq and Palestine. The war on Iraq has not gone according to plan. Wars rarely do. When leaders take their countries to war, they know how the war will start but they can never know how the war will end. Saddam Hussein and his henchmen have been removed from power but the goals of democracy, security and stability have proved persistently elusive. Today the shadow of civil war hangs over Iraq. It has been converted from a country that had no links with international terrorists into a magnet for terrorists from all over the Muslim world. Regime change in Baghdad has thus been a hindrance rather than a help in the struggle against international terrorism. In particular, it heightened the threat from al-Qaeda, as most intelligence services predicted it would.

Nor did the Anglo-American invasion of Iraq help to resolve the Palestinian problem or to promote democracy in the rest of the Arab world. To promote world peace the US and Britain would have done better to try to put an end to the Israeli occupation of Arab lands than to start a new occupation of their own. They destroyed the Ba'th regime in Baghdad in three weeks, but they could not persuade the Likud government to give up one settlement in three years. However flimsy the legal justification, by resorting to military force to topple the Ba'th regime America and Britain raised great expectations. They cannot stop now. Precisely because they invested so much in Iraq, they have a moral as well as a political duty to deliver justice to the long-suffering Palestinians. Their credibility is on the line.

# TWENTY-FIVE

# *Israel's War Against Hamas: Rhetoric and Reality*

I srael's war on Gaza, begun at the end of 2008, lasted 22 days and claimed the lives of over 1,300 Palestinians and 13 Israelis. The only way to make sense of this senseless war is through understanding the historical context. When the State of Israel was established in May 1948, on the basis of a UN resolution, it involved a monumental injustice to the Palestinians. British officials bitterly resented American partisanship on behalf of the infant state. On 2 June 1948, Sir John Troutbeck wrote to the Foreign Secretary Ernest Bevin that the Americans were responsible for the creation of a gangster state headed by 'an utterly unscrupulous set of leaders'. I used to think that this judgement was too harsh, but Israel's vicious assault on the people of Gaza, and the Bush Administration's complicity in this assault, have reopened the question.

I write as someone who served loyally in the Israeli army in the mid-1960s and who has never questioned the legitimacy of the State of Israel within its pre-1967 borders. What I utterly reject is the Zionist colonial project beyond the Green Line. The Israeli occupation of the West Bank and the Gaza Strip in the aftermath of the June 1967 war had very little to do with security and everything to do with territorial expansionism. The aim was to establish Greater Israel through permanent political, economic and military control over the Palestinian territories. And the result has been one of the most prolonged and brutal military occupations of modern times.

Four decades of Israeli control did incalculable damage to the economy of the Gaza Strip. With a large population of 1948 refugees crammed into a tiny strip of land, with no infrastructure or natural resources, Gaza's prospects were never bright. Gaza, however, is not simply a case of economic under-development but a uniquely cruel case of what Sara Roy termed deliberate de-development. To use the Biblical phrase, Israel turned the people of Gaza into the hewers of wood and the drawers of water, into a source of cheap labour and a captive market for Israeli goods. The development of local industry was actively impeded so as to make it impossible for the Palestinians to end their subordination to Israel and to establish the economic underpinnings essential for real political independence.

Gaza is a classic case of colonial exploitation in the post-colonial era. The building of civilian Jewish settlements on occupied Arab territories began in the immediate aftermath of the Six-Day War. These settlements are both illegal and an insurmountable obstacle to peace. They are at once the instrument of exploitation and the symbol of the hated occupation. In Gaza, the Jewish settlers numbered only 8,000 in 2005 compared with 1.4 million local residents. Yet the settlers controlled 25 per cent of the territory, 40 per cent of the arable land and a disproportionate share of the desperately scarce water resources. Cheek by jowl with these foreign intruders, the majority of the local population lived in abject poverty and unimaginable misery. Eighty per cent of them still subsist on less than $2 a day and rely for food rations on UNRWA, the United Nations Relief and Works Agency. The living conditions in the strip remain an affront to civilised values, a powerful precipitant to resistance, and a fertile breeding ground for political extremism.

In August 2005 the Likud government headed by Ariel Sharon staged a unilateral pullout from the Gaza Strip, removing all the 8,000 Israeli settlers and destroying their houses. Hamas, the Islamic resistance movement, conducted an effective campaign to drive the

Israelis out of Gaza. The withdrawal was a victory for Hamas and a humiliation for the Israel Defence Force. To the world, Sharon presented the move as a contribution to peace based on a two-state solution. But in the year after the withdrawal, another 12,000 Israelis settled on the West Bank, further reducing the scope for an independent and territorially contiguous Palestinian state. Land-grabbing and peacemaking are simply incompatible. Israel had a choice and it chose land over peace.

The real purpose behind the move was to redraw unilaterally the borders of Greater Israel by incorporating the main settlement blocs on the West Bank into the Sate of Israel. Withdrawal from Gaza was thus a prelude not to a peace deal with the Palestinian Authority but a prelude to further Zionist expansion on the West Bank. It was a unilateral Israeli move undertaken in what was seen, mistakenly in my view, as an Israeli national interest. Anchored in deep-rooted hostility to Palestinian national aspirations, the withdrawal from Gaza was part of a long-term effort to prevent any progress towards an independent Palestinian state.

Israel's settlers were withdrawn but Israeli soldiers continued to control all access to the Gaza Strip by land, sea and air. Gaza was converted overnight into an open-air prison. From this point on, the Israeli air force enjoyed unrestricted freedom to drop bombs, to make sonic booms by flying low and breaking the sound barrier, and to terrorise the inhabitants of this prison. Israel likes to portray itself as an island of democracy in a sea of authoritarianism. Yet it has never in its entire history done anything to promote democracy on the Arab side and has done a great deal to undermine it. Israel has a long history of secret collaboration with reactionary Arab regimes to suppress Palestinian nationalism. Despite all the handicaps, the Palestinian people succeeded in building the only genuine democracy in the Arab world with the possible exception of Lebanon and Morocco. In January 2006, free and fair elections to the Palestinian Legislative Council brought to power a Hamas-led government. Israel, however, refused to recognise the democratically elected government, claiming that Hamas is purely and simply a terrorist organisation.

The United States and the European Union shamelessly joined Israel in ostracising and demonising the Hamas government and in trying to bring it down by withholding tax revenues and foreign aid. A surreal situation thus developed, with a significant part of the international community imposing economic sanctions not against the occupier but against the occupied, not against the oppressor but against the oppressed. As so often in the tragic history of Palestine, the victims were blamed for their own misfortunes. Israel's propaganda machine persistently purveyed the notion that the Palestinians are terrorists, that they reject coexistence with the Jewish state, that their nationalism is little more than anti-Semitism, that Hamas is just a bunch of religious fanatics, and that Islam is incompatible with democracy. But the simple truth is that the Palestinian people are a normal people with normal aspirations. They are no better but they are no worse than any other national group. What they aspire to, above all, is a piece of land to call their own on which to live in freedom and dignity.

Like other radical movements, Hamas began to moderate its political programme following its rise to power. It persisted in its refusal to recognise the Jewish state. But from the ideological rejectionism of its charter and its call for an Islamic state over the whole of mandatory Palestine, it began to move towards pragmatic accommodation of a two-state solution. Its spokesmen said many times that they would accept a Palestinian state within the 1967 borders and offered a long-term truce on that basis. In March 2007, Hamas and Fatah formed a national unity government that was ready to negotiate a long-term truce with Israel. Israel, however, refused to deal with a government that included Hamas. It rejected all negotiations with the political leadership of Hamas and preferred to try to smash its military wing instead.

At the same time Israel continued to play the old game of divide and rule between rival Palestinian factions. In the late 1980s, it had supported the nascent Hamas in order to weaken Fatah, the secular nationalist movement led by Yasser Arafat. Now it began to encourage the corrupt and pliant Fatah leaders to overthrow their religious political rivals and recapture power. Aggressive US neoconservatives participated in the sinister plot to instigate a Palestinian civil war. Their meddling was a major factor in the collapse of the national unity government and in driving Hamas to seize power in Gaza in June 2007 to pre-empt a Fatah coup.

The war unleashed by Israel on Gaza on 27 December 2008 was the culmination of a series of clashes and confrontations with the Hamas government. In a broader sense, however, it was a war between Israel and the Palestinian people, because the people had elected the party to power. The declared aim of the war was to weaken Hamas and to intensify the pressure on it until its leaders agreed to a new ceasefire on Israel's terms. The undeclared aims were to drive Hamas out of power, and to ensure that the Palestinians in Gaza are seen by the world simply as a humanitarian problem, thus derailing their struggle for independence and statehood.

The timing of the war was determined by political expediency. A general election was scheduled for 10 February 2009 and, in the lead-up to the election, all the main contenders were looking for an opportunity to prove their toughness. The army top brass had been champing at the bit to deliver a crushing blow to Hamas in order to remove the stain left on their reputation by the failure of the war against Hizbullah in Lebanon in July 2006. Israel's cynical leaders could also count on apathy and impotence of the pro-Western Arab regimes and on blind support from President Bush in the twilight of his term in the White House. Bush readily obliged by putting all the blame for the crisis on Hamas, vetoing proposals at the UN Security Council for an immediate ceasefire and issuing Israel with a free pass to mount a ground invasion of Gaza.

As always, mighty Israel claimed to be the victim of Palestinian aggression, but the sheer asymmetry of power between the two sides leaves little room for doubt as to who is the real victim. This is indeed a conflict between David and Goliath but the Biblical image has been inverted – a small and defenceless Palestinian David faces a heavily armed, merciless and overbearing Israeli Goliath. The resort to brute military force is accompanied, as always, by the shrill rhetoric of victimhood and a farrago of self-pity overlaid with self-righteousness. In Hebrew this is known as the syndrome of *yorim ve-bokhim*, 'shooting and crying'.

To be sure, Hamas is not an entirely innocent party in this conflict. Denied the fruit of its electoral victory and confronted with an unscrupulous adversary, it resorted to the weapon of the weak – terror. Militants from Hamas and Islamic Jihad sporadically launched Qassam rocket attacks on Israeli settlements near the border with Gaza until Egypt brokered a six-month ceasefire in June 2008. The damage caused by these primitive rockets is minimal but the psychological impact is immense, prompting the public to demand protection from its government. Under the circumstances, Israel had the right to act in self-defence, but its response to the pinpricks of primitive rocket attacks was totally disproportionate. The figures speak for themselves. In the three years after the withdrawal from Gaza, 11 Israelis were killed by rocket fire. On the other hand, in 2005–7 alone, the IDF killed 1,290 Palestinians in Gaza, including 222 children. The IDF developed a culture of impunity, which extended to the shooting of international volunteers like Rachel Corrie and Tom Hurndall.

Killing civilians is a gross violation of international humanitarian law. This law applies to Israel as much as it does to Hamas, but Israel's entire record is one of unbridled and unremitting brutality towards the inhabitants of Gaza. Following the Hamas seizure of power, Israel clamped Gaza in an economic blockade, closing all the border crossings and allowing no movement between Gaza and the West Bank. Even after Egypt brokered the ceasefire in June 2008, Israel refused to lift the blockade. It prevented any exports from leaving the strip in clear violation of a 2005 accord, leading to a sharp drop in employment opportunities. Officially, 49.1 per cent of the population is unemployed. At the same time, Israel restricted drastically the number of trucks carrying food, fuel, cooking-gas canisters, spare parts for water and sanitation plants, and medical supplies into Gaza. It is difficult to see how starving and freezing the civilians of Gaza could protect the people on the Israeli side of the border. Even if it did, it would still be immoral, a form of collective punishment that is strictly forbidden by international humanitarian law. The hidden purpose of the blockade was to undermine Hamas and to strengthen the position of the discredited Fatah leaders on the West Bank.

The brutality of Israel's soldiers and the inhumanity of its leaders were fully matched by the mendacity of its spokesmen. Eight months before launching the so-called 'Operation Cast Lead', the Israeli government established a National Information Directorate. The core messages of this directorate to the media were that Hamas broke the ceasefire agreements; that Israel's objective was the defence of its population; and that its forces were instructed to take the utmost care not to hurt innocent civilians. Israel's spin doctors were remarkably successful in getting this message across. But, in essence, their propaganda was a pack of lies. A wide gap separated the reality of Israel's actions from the rhetoric of its spokesmen.

In the first place, it was not Hamas but the IDF that broke the ceasefire. It did so on 4 November 2008 by launching a raid into Gaza that killed six Hamas fighters on the flimsy excuse that they were digging a tunnel. It is a little known but crucial fact that Hamas enforced the ceasefire very effectively on its side until Israel sabotaged it. The first four months of the ceasefire were in fact a stunning success. A graph on the website of the Israeli Ministry of Foreign Affairs proved this beyond the shadow of any doubt. The graph showed that the average monthly number of rockets in the preceding period of 2008 was 179 and that this number dropped dramatically to an average of three per month from July to October. Once the offensive got under way, the graph was removed from the website to erase the memory of the ceasefire that had so effectively curtailed the rocket attacks on Israeli civilians. The lesson that these official figures teach us is a simple one: If Israel wants calm on its southern border, the way to get it is through indirect talks with the political leaders of Hamas rather than through military confrontation. They also show that the Hamas leaders have a solid reputation for observing agreements, whereas Israel's leaders do not.

Second, Israel's objective was not just the protection of its population from Qassam rocket attacks but the eventual overthrow of the Hamas government in Gaza, by turning the people against their rulers. Third, far from taking care to spare civilians, Israel was guilty of indiscriminate aerial bombardment and of an 18-month-old blockade that brought the inhabitants of Gaza, now 1.5 million, to the brink of a humanitarian catastrophe.

The Biblical injunction of an eye for an eye is savage enough. But Israel's insane offensive against Gaza seemed to follow the logic of an eye for an eyelash. After eight days of bombing, with a death toll of more than 400 Palestinians and four Israelis, the gung-ho Cabinet ordered a land invasion of Gaza. This was phase II of 'Operation Cast Lead'. Columns of Israeli tanks and ground forces crossed the border into northern Gaza. Their mission was to destroy the rocket launch facilities, to hit Hamas offices and command and control centres, and to kill leading figures in both the political and military wings of the movement. The aim was to 'behead' the organisation without getting entangled in a prolonged occupation. Israeli officials were reluctant to admit that the attack was intended to force Hamas from power, out of concern that doing so would undermine the international support they had won by portraying the assault as a purely defensive measure to stop the Hamas rockets. But there was growing confidence in the upper echelons of the defence establishment that the assault would cripple Hamas and eventually drive it out of power.

Intelligence chiefs told the Cabinet that Hamas was fatally weakened by the destruction of a large part of the physical infrastructure of its Administration, including the parliament building and many government offices. The Cabinet instructions to the IDF, however, stopped short of calling specifically for the overthrow of the Hamas Administration. 'We are not in the regime change business', remarked one official. The intelligence services also told the Cabinet that the Israeli bombardment was turning popular opinion against Hamas. But this assessment was probably coloured by a large dose of wishful thinking. In the short term, at any rate, the trapped, terrified and terrorised people rallied behind their embattled government. Those at the receiving end were shocked by the scale, the ferocity and the indiscriminate nature of the Israeli attack. Israeli spokesmen repeatedly proclaimed their concern to spare innocent civilians. Prime Minister Ehud Olmert stated at the outset that Israel would use the iron fist with Hamas but treat the civilian population with velvet gloves. But in view of the death and destruction that the IDF rained down on Gaza, his words rang rather hollow. Throughout the war, the number of civilian casualties kept escalating. This was no accident. It was the direct result of applying a new IDF doctrine which sought to avoid losses among its soldiers by the ruthless destruction of everything in their path.

The Palestinian Bureau of Statistics estimated after the first two weeks of fighting that of Gaza's 143,437 buildings, 4,000 were totally destroyed and 16,000 were partially destroyed, including 13 mosques, 18 schools and universities, and 30 security buildings. John Ging, the head of the UN relief agency in Gaza, accused Israel of destroying public buildings vital to the administration and governance of Gaza. 'The whole infrastructure of the future state of Palestine is being destroyed', he said. 'Blowing up the parliament building. That's the parliament of Palestine. That's not a Hamas building.'

War crimes were another deplorable feature of this deplorable war. Those who sent soldiers to conduct intensive warfare in the most densely populated area on earth must have known that the result would be a bloodbath, the killing and maiming of innocent civilians caught in the crossfire. In waging this savage war, the Israeli soldiers committed not one or two but a large number of war crimes. The list includes the bombing of the UN school in the Jabaliya refugee camp and the massacre of 44 people who sheltered there; herding a hundred civilians into a house in the village of Zeitoun southeast of Gaza City and then bombing and killing a third of them; the dropping of white phosphorus bombs; the use of civilians as human shields; and firing on hospitals, mobile clinics, ambulances and medical personnel. Navi Pillay, the UN high commissioner for human rights, told the BBC that the incident in Zeitoun 'appeared to have all the elements of a war crime' and called for an independent and transparent investigation. These war crimes alone sweep away any moral or legal justification for the war.

In this war Israel had violent tactics but no coherent strategy. Its strategy was both indecent and self-defeating. The strategy of seeking military solutions to what are essentially political problems had been tried and failed in Lebanon, and it was doomed to fail again in Gaza too. No amount of military escalation could break the spirit of Hamas or its hold on power. Despite all the death and destruction that Israel has inflicted on them, the Hamas fighters kept up their resistance and they kept firing their rockets. This is a movement that glorifies victimhood and martyrdom. In dealing with such a movement, military force has its limits. Israel invariably justifies its resort to force by invoking its right to security. The problem with the Israeli concept of security is that it denies even the most elementary security to the people of Gaza. The only way for Israel to achieve security on its southern border is not through bombing and burning but through talks with Hamas, which has repeatedly declared its readiness to negotiate a long-term ceasefire with the Jewish state within its pre-1967 borders for 20, 30, or even 50 years. Israel has rejected this offer for the same reason it spurned the Arab League peace plan of 2002: it involves concessions and compromises.

Israel's war in Gaza ended with a unilateral ceasefire and a declaration of victory. But the war constituted a massive moral defeat for Israel and its army. Hamas ended the war bruised and battered but still in power, still defiant, and holding the moral high ground. The war inadvertently weakened Fatah and boosted the credentials of Hamas as the only leader of Palestinian resistance to Israeli aggression. Israel damaged not only its own interests through the unrestrained use of force but those of the West as well. Engendering such high levels of anger throughout the Arab and Muslim worlds was neither in its interest nor in that of its allies.

As Fawaz Gerges pointed out in his article 'Hamas Rising' in the *Nation* on 17 January 2009, the assault on Gaza had the immediate effect of radicalising mainstream Muslim opinion. The images shown by Arab and Muslim television stations of dead children and distraught parents kept fuelling rage against Israel and its superpower patron. Israel's inhumanity effectively silenced critics of Hamas and legitimised the radical resistance movement in the eyes of many previously sceptical Palestinians and Muslims. Moreover, more than any previous Arab–Israeli war, this one undermined the legitimacy of pro-Western Arab regimes like Egypt, Jordan and Saudi Arabia in the eyes of many of their citizens. The main beneficiaries of the war were Iran, Syria and the advocates of global jihad against the Jewish state like al-Qaeda leader Osama bin Laden.

This brief review of Israel's record as an occupying power over the past four decades, and especially of its conduct during the 22-day assault on Gaza, makes it difficult to resist the conclusion that it has become a rogue state with 'an utterly unscrupulous set of leaders'. A rogue state habitually violates international law, possesses weapons of mass destruction and practices terrorism – the use of violence against civilians for political purposes. Israel fulfils all of these three criteria; the cap fits and it must wear it. Israel's real aim is not peaceful coexistence with its Palestinian neighbours but military domination. It keeps compounding the mistakes of the past with new and more disastrous ones. In Gaza it went too far: it sowed the wind and it will surely reap the whirlwind.

# PART IV

*Perspectives*

# TWENTY-SIX

# His Royal Shyness: King Hussein and Israel

In the autumn of 1996 I wrote to King Hussein and asked to talk to him about his meetings with Israeli leaders. I explained that I was writing a book on the Arab–Israeli conflict since 1948. The reply came from Brigadier Ali Shukri, the director of the king's private office: 'His Majesty has agreed to grant you an audience.' On 2 December, I had a phone call from Elizabeth Corke, the king's secretary in Britain, asking if I could meet His Majesty in his house, Buckhurst Park, in Surrey the following morning, 3 December. I accepted the invitation with alacrity, although it gave me little time to prepare for an interview spanning four decades of tangled and tortuous Middle East history. I asked Ms Corke how long the audience would last, and she replied with a question: 'How long do you hope for?' 'Two hours', I said, but she thought that this might be too long.

A chauffeur in a silver Mercedes came to collect me in the morning from my house in Oxford. Passing through two security gates, we arrived at an attractive country estate, surrounded by lawns and flower beds. The butler opened the door and led me to a large room with a huge fireplace and three sofas around a square coffee table in the middle of the room. I was offered something to drink, and was

then joined by Brigadier Shukri. Shukri emphasised at the outset
that this was indeed the first time that King Hussein had agreed to
talk about his meetings with Israeli officials in the era preceding the
1994 peace treaty. I asked whether I could record the interview, and
after a few seconds of hesitation, Shukri agreed and helped me to set
up the recorder.

Brigadier Shukri looked to be in his mid-forties, and he spoke
perfect English. He said that King Hussein had excellent relations
with Yitzhak Rabin because Rabin was a military man, and as such
he was a great believer in directness. People knew where they stood
when they spoke with Rabin, Shukri emphasised. Shimon Peres, on
the other hand, is a politician, and one never knew where one stood
with him. Many subjects that were discussed with Peres remained
unclear and subject to different interpretations. His Majesty did not
like that.

After a short while King Hussein came into the room and shook my
hand warmly. He treated the meeting between us not as a favour to
me, but as an exchange of views between equals. He was particularly
keen to talk about the June 1967 war, and to explain that he actually
had no choice but to throw in his lot with the other Arabs. A different
decision would have provoked a civil war in Jordan.

During the interview the one question that seemed to make King
Hussein uncomfortable concerned the warning that he is alleged to
have given Golda Meir towards the end of September 1973 about
the planned Arab attack on Israel. The King denied this, maintaining
that he was surprised by the outbreak of war, and that there was
never any question of Jordan joining the other Arab states in 1973.
On other matters – for example, his meeting with Yitzhak Shamir
on the eve of the First Gulf War and his relations with Yitzhak Rabin
– King Hussein provided historically important information that
had previously been unknown.

The interview lasted two hours and the transcript runs to 36 pages.
The interview explains a good deal of the king's thinking about Israel
and individual Israeli leaders, about his troubled relations with the
PLO and with various Arab rulers, about regional and international
politics, and about the major stages in his struggle for peace.

When the interview was over, the king invited me to contact him at any time and added with a smile: 'I think we covered quite a lot of ground.' Brigadier Shukri said: 'You will probably need two or three more sessions with His Majesty to cover the ground.' This was very reassuring because I had a long-term plan to write a book on King Hussein and the quest for peace in the Middle East. Earlier I had indicated to King Hussein that after finishing the book I was writing on Israel's foreign policy, I planned to write a book about him, and he gave me every encouragement. He invited me to visit him in Amman and volunteered to share with me his notes on the secret meetings that I found so fascinating. But I was too slow: he fell ill; he died of cancer on 7 February 1999 when he was 63 years old; and I lost my chance for further privileged access to Hussein and his papers. After his death I decided to expand the scope of my project into a full-scale biography. The result was *Lion of Jordan: King Hussein's Life in War and Peace* published in 2007. The transcript that follows was a major source for this biography.

Avi Shlaim: Let me start with a general question. When you ascended the throne in 1953 what were your initial impressions and thoughts about Israel?

King Hussein: My initial thoughts and impressions were ones of not knowing very much of what actually the Israelis and their leadership thought or had in mind regarding the future of our region. At the same time it was a period of violence. There had apparently been from time to time some incursions [by Arabs] over the long ceasefire line. We had the longest line, longer than all the Arab ceasefire lines with Israel put together. And Israel's responses were extremely severe, extremely devastating, with attacks on villages, on police posts and civilians along the long ceasefire line. Obviously, I was not very happy with that and it caused us a great deal of difficulty in terms of the internal scene in Jordan.

Egypt's attitude towards us was another problem, especially given the rise of Gamal Abdel Nasser as the leader of the Arab world. Jordan was placed in the position of the conspirator or the betrayer and this was the perpetual thrust of the Egyptian propaganda machine. So that undermined even further the situation within Jordan itself. The Palestinians looked towards Egypt as the major power in the area and treated whatever was said there as the gospel truth. The Israeli raids worsened the situation in Jordan. They showed us as being incompetent and unable to defend our territory. And the Israeli attacks continued although we had done everything that we could to prevent infiltration and to prevent access to Israel.

So this was the atmosphere in which I lived my first years – plus the loss of my grandfather, which was another factor. I knew that he [King Abdullah] had tried his best for peace and that he had not achieved it. But I did not have any details. When I assumed responsibility, I looked for papers to do with my grandfather's reign, but unfortunately no documents were found. So I didn't have any idea as to what exactly had happened.[1] But gradually there was more and more of a feeling that, for whatever reason, we had a neighbour, a people who were close to us historically, whom circumstances in the world had forced into our region. The dilemma was how to avoid mutual destruction and how to find a way of living together once again and not to continue to pay the high price which was not fair on either side. That was in fact what went on in my mind at that time, apart from the thoughts on how to strengthen my country.

In 1967 I had the impression that various events happened without one having anything to do with them and that this was going to be a problem. We came under pressure to hand over the control of our army and our destiny to a unified Arab command as part of the Arab League. And when Nasser moved his forces across the Suez Canal into Sinai, I knew that war was inevitable. I knew that we were going to lose. I knew that we in Jordan were threatened, threatened by two things: we either followed the course we did; or alternately the country would tear itself apart if we stayed out, and Israel would march into the West Bank and maybe even beyond. So these were the choices before us. It wasn't a question of our thinking there was any chance of winning. We knew where we were. We knew what the results would be. But it was the only way and we did our best and the results were the disaster we have lived with ever since.

A.S.: I believe that your first meeting with an Israeli official was with Yaakov Herzog – then the Cabinet Secretary in the Levi Eshkol government – in September 1963. What was the background to this meeting and what was the purpose?

K.H.: My purpose throughout and since the 1960s was to try to see if there is any way to resolve the problem. I felt that, as a person in a position of responsibility, next door to Israel, there was no way that I could live with myself just sitting idly by and not knowing what I am dealing with. I had to explore, I had to find out what is the thinking in Palestine. There is no future in war, there is no future in further suffering for people, either them or us. So one had to know. One had to break that barrier and begin a dialogue whether it led anywhere immediately or not. But it was important to have it direct and first-hand and not to let other players manipulate us. By chance I had a very, very good friend who looked after my health here [in England], Dr Emmanuel Herbert.[2] He was a man who really believed in peace in our region and wished to see it happen. So I think he offered the possibility of some contact and I said 'fine'. That is how it started. Trying to explore, trying to find out what the other side of this issue was like. What was the face of it?

A.S.: The second meeting was apparently with Foreign Minister Golda Meir in Paris in autumn 1965.

K.H.: Yes, I recall that meeting. It was following our decision, on the Arab side, at least, to divert the waters of the Jordan river and I tried to explain that we were acting to preserve what rights we had and that I hoped that eventually these contacts would enable us to figure a way out of the entire dilemma. And we were not talking about a country hundreds of miles away. We were talking about two peoples who were destined to live together in a very small region and who had to figure out how to resolve our common problems. If we looked at water, it was a problem that both of us suffered from. If we looked at even a flu epidemic, it affected both of us. Every aspect of our lives was interrelated and interlinked in some way or another. And to simply ignore that was something I could not understand. One had to do something, one had to explore what was possible.

A.S.: What was your impression of Golda Meir? Was it a beneficial meeting?

K.H.: It was a good meeting. It was really just a meeting to break the ice, to get to know one another. And we talked about our dreams for our children and grandchildren, to live in an era of peace in the region. And I think she suggested that maybe a day would come when we could put aside all the armaments and create a monument in Jerusalem which would signify peace between us and where our young people could see what a futile struggle it had been and what a heavy burden it had been on both sides. Essentially it didn't go beyond that. There wasn't very much indeed that happened, just an agreement to keep in touch whenever possible.

A.S.: In November 1966 Israel carried out the raid against the West Bank village of Samu. Did you feel betrayed by Israel?

K.H.: Yes, I did. In fact that happened on my birthday. One of my very close friends, an air force pilot, was shot down on his way out of that engagement. It really created a devastating effect in Jordan itself. The action that led to the Israeli attack was not something that Jordan condoned or sponsored or supported in any form or way. I couldn't figure out if a small irrigation ditch or pipe in Israel was blown up – assuming it was, which I didn't necessarily know for sure – why the reaction in this way? Was there any balance between the two? I felt we needed to figure out a way of dealing with the threats in a different way, in a joint way. So the Israeli attack was a shock and it was not a very pleasant birthday present.

A.S.: You have already talked about your predicament during the crisis of May/June 1967. The Israelis always stress that they sent you a message to keep out and then you would not be harmed. Presumably you received this message but you chose to ignore it.

K.H.: I did receive the message but it was too late in any event. I had already handed over the command of the army to the unified Arab command. There was a unified Arab command with an Egyptian general in army headquarters in charge of the Jordanian armed forces as a part of the defence effort. The Syrians were not ready, the Iraqis were far away; eventually they moved, even before the Syrians, and already the first wave had gone in from Jordan into Israel when the UN general called to say that there is a message to keep out of it. I said: 'Tell him it's too late.' I don't know that the message made any difference because at that time I had these options: either join the Arabs, or Jordan would have torn itself apart. A clash between Palestinians and Jordanians might have led to Jordan's destruction and left the very clear possibility of an Israeli takeover of at least the West Bank and Jerusalem. We did the best we could in the hope that somebody would stop this madness before it developed any further and help us out.

A.S.: What did you do to recover the West Bank?

K.H.: I met with Nasser immediately after the war and we met at the Arab League summit at Khartoum later. And at Khartoum I fought very much against the famous three no's [no recognition, no negotiation, no peace with Israel]. But the atmosphere there developed into one where all the people who used to support Nasser, who never criticised him on anything, now [following the Arab defeat] turned on him and turned on him in such a vicious way that I found myself morally unable to continue to take any stand but to come closer to him and defend him, and accuse them of responsibility for some of the things that happened. That was the first collision I had with many of my friends in the Arab world. But then we talked about the need for a resolution and the need for a peaceful solution to the problem. And Nasser's approach was: 'I feel responsible. We lost the West Bank and Gaza, and that comes first. I am not going to ask for any withdrawal from

the Suez Canal. It can stay closed until such time as the issue
of the West Bank and of Gaza is resolved. So go and speak of
that and seek a comprehensive solution to the problem and a
comprehensive peace and go and do anything you can short
of signing a separate peace.' And I said that in any event I was
not considering signing a separate peace because we wanted to
resolve this problem in a comprehensive fashion. So we went to
America and our negotiations with the Americans started and
with all the members of the Security Council.

A.S.: You had a meeting in May 1968 in London with Foreign
Minister Abba Eban and Yaakov Herzog. What was said?

K.H.: I think there was one immediately after the adoption of
UN resolution 242 in November 1967, on my way back from
New York – I have to go back to my notes and really find
out the dates.³ What was said then didn't give me very much
encouragement because the Israeli attitude was different from
what we had expected. We were told by the Americans that
we will have to accept 242 as is because the Israelis accepted
it. It is a question of negotiating the implementation of 242.
But unfortunately the Israelis withdrew from that position of
negotiating withdrawal on all fronts.

A.S.: In September 1968 you had a meeting with Abba Eban,
Yigal Allon and Yaakov Herzog. Was this your first meeting
with Allon? Was this the first time he presented to you the
Allon plan, and what was the reaction?

K.H.: I don't think it was on the first meeting that he presented
his plan. But again, we were trying to figure how to get out of
that situation [Israel's occupation of the West Bank after the
1967 war], particularly as there was a lot of violence. We were
constantly under attack. The *fedayeen* movement of Palestinian
guerrillas started, and people were disenchanted with the regular
armies in the region as a whole and turned to that approach.
I tried my best to control this movement. On the one hand, I
believed that people have a right to resist occupation. But on
the other hand, we had a very turbulent internal situation, we
had continuous reprisals and firefights on the long front from

the Dead Sea to the northernmost part. And we were hit by both sides.

A.S.: The number of Israeli participants seemed to increase with every meeting because there was another meeting, in March 1970, attended by Eban, Herzog, Moshe Dayan and the Israeli chief of staff Chaim Bar-Lev. This meeting was in Aqaba. Do you remember that meeting and what was on the agenda?

K.H.: I have all the details back at home and I will be more than happy to check them. The main point was that the Israelis considered that they had to retaliate against all actions from Jordan. I kept saying that these actions were by people resisting occupation and that it didn't necessarily mean that Jordan was fighting. Jordan was deployed on the longest border and its army was trying its best to see what could be done. We were having our own problems but that was our responsibility. I was very worried about the increase of what was almost perpetual fighting until the Egyptians started the so-called War of Attrition and that eased the pressure on Jordan a little bit.

A.S.: The next landmark is Black September in 1970 when the PLO challenged your regime. How significant was Israel's help during that crisis?

K.H.: The main help lay in the fact that Israel did not take advantage of the moment. We were in the fight which I believe was a turning point in the life of Jordan. We didn't want it. We tried our very best to avert the deterioration [of the situation]. But the Palestinian resistance gained strength. They had moved from the Jordan Valley into the towns. What provoked the Israelis were [Palestinian] rockets that were run to a timer from behind our forces that would go off and our forces would be hit [in retaliation by the Israelis]. We had thousands of incidents of Palestinians breaking the law, of attacking people. It was a very unruly state of affairs in the country and I continued to try to restore order. I went to Egypt. I called on the Arabs to help in any way they could, particularly as some of them were sponsoring some of these movements in some form or another, but without much success. And towards the end I felt I was losing control. The army began to rebel. I had to spend most of my time running from one unit to another. I think that the gamble was probably that the army would fracture along Palestinian–Jordanian lines. That never happened, thank God.

A.S.: You met with Golda Meir after the events of Black September. Was this the first meeting in Tel Aviv and can you tell me anything about it?

K.H.: A cordial meeting, the first time since a long time had passed. I don't think the meeting was held in Tel Aviv. It might have been in the south, but later on I did go to Tel Aviv.

A.S.: What was the purpose of this meeting?

K.H.: In 1970 we came up in Jordan with three possible solutions to the Palestinian problem: [a return to the pre-1967] status quo, or there could be a federation called the United Arab Kingdom, or an independent Palestinian state. So it was in this context that we had that meeting but she was totally opposed to these ideas at that time.

A.S.: Yigal Allon suggested a territorial compromise, dividing the West Bank between Israel and Jordan. What was your reaction?

K.H.: This was totally rejected. And in point of fact, in the subsequent period of negotiations, I was offered the return of something like 90-plus per cent of the territory, 98 per cent even, excluding Jerusalem, but I couldn't accept. As far as I was concerned, it had to be every single inch that I was responsible for. This was against the background of what happened in 1948 when the whole West Bank was saved by Jordan, including the old city of Jerusalem but with the loss of Lydda and Ramleh. Yet my grandfather eventually paid with his life for his attempts for peace. If it were to be my responsibility, I had to return everything, not personally to me, but to be placed under international auspices for the people to determine what their future ought to be. We were perfectly happy with that. But I could not compromise. And so this deadlock repeated itself time and time and time again throughout the many years until 1990.

A.S.: The Israelis kept talking about the Jordanian option between 1967 and 1973. From your perspective, was there ever a Jordanian option?

K.H.: I never thought that there was a Jordanian option. The Palestinians can settle in Jordan. They could, as far as I am concerned, be citizens of Jordan, and I believe that this is our greatest contribution towards a peaceful solution because physically it can't be any other way, but psychologically there was always a choice. The Palestinians had a choice: those who wanted to could stay in Jordan and begin their lives again. But there are also many Jordanians who are worse off than the Palestinians in terms of the standard of living, in terms of their needs, and their ability to survive. So Jordan was not a vacant lot.

Jordan had done more than many others by taking these people, treating them as Jordanians, giving them chances and opportunities they never had anywhere else, not keeping them in camps. And that was one of the worst images I ever had of the whole Arab approach, practically keeping them in camps surrounded by barbed wire, unable to work, unable to partake, unable to have a nationality, unable to do anything. But that didn't mean Jordan has to cease to exist as a result of doing that in any form or way. And any solution would have to have Palestinian rights on Palestinian soil. Eventually the Palestinians decided they wanted to move on their own. This absolved us of any further responsibility other than looking after our own damaged population with regard to Israel and peace. But at the same time we continued to work for a comprehensive peace in the area as best we could, starting with the Madrid conference in 1991.

A.S.: Just before the outbreak of the October War you had a meeting with Golda Meir and it was reported in Israel that you warned her in general terms about an Arab attack. Can you throw any light on that warning?

K.H.: I can only say that, as far as I was concerned, I was caught completely off guard [by the October War]. I was riding a motorbike with my late wife behind me in the suburbs of Amman when a security car behind started flashing us to stop, and then I was told that a war had started. I had no idea that anything of that nature would happen and certainly not at that time. I had met with Anwar Sadat and Hafez al-Assad in Cairo shortly before the outbreak of war. We didn't have relations with either of them at the time. Egypt restored relations [with us] and Assad didn't until the day before the war, if I am not mistaken. He wanted the *fedayeen* to be permitted back into Jordan and I refused that. At the same time we were told that [the Syrians] were afraid of an Israeli attack through Jordan and I said that if that ever happened, we will fight it. We are not going to leave our territory open for anyone. So they seemed satisfied with that and I returned to Jordan and a few days later we had the October War. We were totally excluded from any knowledge of what the plan was.

A.S.: Ezer Weizman said you made two mistakes: one was in joining the other Arabs in the war against Israel June 1967 and the other in not joining them in the October 1973 War.

K.H.: I never had the chance to speak to him about that. He is a very, very dear friend and I have said several times I have a great deal of respect for him. We have so many common interests, have always had in our lives.

Maybe people will view 1967 as a mistake but again the Israeli impression was that we did it because we were going to throw them into the sea. That is totally untrue. We went to war hoping that it would not happen until the last possible moment, and that if it did start, it would soon be stopped. But we knew full well what the consequences were. The West Bank was going to be lost one way or the other. We either stuck to our word and our commitment to help others, or we would have had an internal upheaval that would have torn the country apart. That was the choice, and we made our choice not under any illusion that the results would be different.

In 1973 I wasn't a part of it and, in any event, I had embarked on a course of trying to achieve peace and I could not be double-faced about it even if they had told me about the plan to go to war. Thank God I wasn't told anyway.

A.S.: In the period from 1974 until 1976 you had about six meetings with Israeli leaders. Can you cast your mind back to that period and throw some light on these meetings?

K.H.: Yitzhak Rabin [who had succeeded Golda Meir as prime minister after the October War] was very rigid – very polite, very cordial, but very rigid, and impossible to alter. But let me come back to the very recent past when we first met in Aqaba with Rabin, [after] having started the peace process. He said, 'You were very stubborn', and I said, 'Yes I was because I could not give an inch of Palestinian territory or an iota of Palestinian rights. But now that the Palestinians have been able to speak for themselves and they have assumed their responsibilities, we can do business.' This really sums up the whole dilemma. I remember in my last meeting with Rabin, in his first government, he said, 'Well, there is nothing that can be done, wait for ten years, maybe things will change on the ground.' I said, 'Well, too bad.' We agreed to do what we could to help the Palestinians on the humanitarian level, but I refused to go back on 242. He said in that case just leave it and we left it at that. So we could not get anywhere.

A.S.: After the Likud came to power in May 1977, did you sense an abrupt reversal of Israel's attitude towards Jordan?

K.H.: I saw my friend Moshe Dayan, who had become the foreign minister of the Likud, here in London. His attitude was even harder than it had been earlier and that was the end of that. We never had any contacts for a long period.

A.S.: Did Anwar Sadat consult you before his trip to Jerusalem in 1977?

K.H.: Not at all. Or about his contacts or about anything. I did tell him when I saw him that I had been in touch with our neighbours. I wondered whether he was going to ask me about these contacts. But he said that he wanted to assume responsibility only for his own relations with Israel.

A.S.: And when Sadat eventually concluded the Camp David Accords with Israel in 1978, what was your reaction?

K.H.: I was very angry. I really was utterly upset about it. I will tell you why. Before he went on this venture, we had been working with President Carter on the idea of a summit meeting in Geneva with all the countries concerned, together with the Americans and Soviets. I had gone to Egypt and from there Sadat asked me to go to Damascus and see whether I could persuade Assad to join. Assad was his usual self. He was a little bit difficult and hardly responded. I had a feeling that Assad might have driven Sadat to move [on his own] the way he did. Sadat's move shocked me, especially against a background of Nasser saying that he won't move on his own with Israel until he could make up for the damage he caused Jordan in that unrealistic and terrible war. So Sadat was the exact opposite, but there we are.

Yet I went and saw him. I said fine. And he went to Washington and I called him there. By that time I had heard that things were not going all that well and I said, 'Good luck and keep a tough position, if you can.' And then I was on my way back and as we passed through Spain, the Camp David Accords were signed. So we were never a part of it in Jordan, and the Camp David Accords imposed on us in Jordan a role that we had not been consulted about, of essentially providing security in the West Bank, with joint patrols and this and that and the other, but without even having a say in it. And that is where we couldn't take it.

A.S.: What went wrong after you and Shimon Peres reached the so-called London Agreement in April 1987?

K.H.: Shimon Peres and I met here in London and we tried to involve the Palestinians in the search for a settlement with us. We reached an agreement on an international conference and we initialled it. Peres came as foreign minister in a national unity government headed by Yitzhak Shamir. The London Agreement floundered on two levels, the American and the Israeli. Peres told me that he would go back home with the agreement we worked out and he would send it immediately to [US Secretary of State] George Shultz, and within 48 hours it would come back as an American plan. Peres also said that 'the American plan' would be accepted by Israel, and I promised it would be accepted by Jordan. So he left.

Two weeks later nothing had happened. And then a letter was sent by Shultz to Yitzhak Shamir, the Israeli prime minister at the time, telling him that this is the agreement reached between Peres and me, and asking Shamir for his views. And of course Shamir took a negative stand against the London Agreement and the whole thing fell apart. But as far as I was concerned, Peres was the Israeli interlocutor. I talked with him. I agreed with him on something and he couldn't deliver.

A.S.: Let us move on to the Gulf crisis of 1990 when Iraq invaded Kuwait. Did you have any contact with Prime Minister Shamir during the crisis, before the war?

K.H.: Just before the war. We had at that time given up. We were utterly frustrated, utterly angry. It happened during my watch. I was heading the Ittihad al-Arabi, the Arab Union, at the time. And then suddenly out of the blue came this Iraqi attack on Kuwait. I felt that it was my duty to do whatever I could to see if we could resolve this problem within the Arab context. I wanted to get a definite Iraqi commitment of withdrawal from Kuwait. But I was not given a chance to mediate. The Arab League took a hard line. And then there was Iraq's attitude. You couldn't budge them right until my last meeting with Saddam Hussein. Yasser Arafat was there and the president of South Yemen, and we argued and argued. No way. Eventually we managed to get the so-called guests [the Western hostages] out of Iraq. That is the only positive thing that came out of the meeting.

At the airport, as I was leaving, Saddam Hussein said to me: 'Look, Abu Abdullah, don't worry. The whole world is against us but God is with us, and we are going to win.' I said, 'This is beyond my ability to comprehend or to deal with. I leave very saddened and very distressed and I know that the results as they appear to me are going to be disastrous everywhere. I will go back home. But if there is anything further I can do, then you know how to get in touch with me.' He never did and the war broke out.

When I got back we mobilised and the Americans had taken the attitude that you are either with us or against us, and there was no other way. Somehow it turned out that our position had been undermined in the Arab world. In the preceding year and a half, there were rumours of Jordan conspiring with Iraq. Totally unfounded. We had never done so and if we had, we would have done something much better than that. That wouldn't have been the case. It is against our nature. All we were trying to do is to avert the human disaster, the economic disaster, the breaking of bones that until now we [still] can't get repaired in the region. It will take a long time to ever get [what was damaged] back in shape. And all we wanted was a chance to work out an Arab solution to the crisis. If we had been given that chance and Iraq had proved that we couldn't succeed, we probably would have been among the first troops to enter Iraq because it was made very, very clear at all summits that if any Arab country used military force against another, it would need to be faced by all of us. It was in direct contradiction to that that they acted. But we weren't given the chance.

However, the pressure built up on us in such a way that we were totally isolated, but we mobilised, and that was another one of the best moments I have ever seen in Jordan. Our people came together and we of course received 400,000 refugees, the *bidduns* who had no rights, from Kuwait, and from the Gulf, on top of all the other problems we had to cope with. We were encircled, we mobilised almost a quarter of a million Jordanians and through that we controlled the situation, in a way; and we made it very clear to the Iraqis, we spoke to the Israelis, we spoke to everybody else: we may be small, but anybody who attacks us will suffer a lot of damage. We are not saying we are invincible, we are not. But neither can our land or our air be used by [either of] them. We had our forces deployed facing Iraq and facing Israel and facing north and south.

At that time, just before the [Gulf] war there was a suggestion of a meeting with the prime minister, Yitzhak Shamir, and we met here in London. Shamir brought with him Ehud Barak, the [deputy] IDF chief of staff. Shamir said to me, 'Look, I have a dilemma. In 1973 our people were not vigilant enough and the Arab attack came in and a lot of damage occurred. Now we see that you have your troops mobilised and my generals are calling for me to do the same and to have our troops facing yours. There isn't much distance in the Jordan Valley and it would be totally irresponsible, they say, if I did not take the same measures.'

So I said, 'Prime Minister, you are perfectly within your rights to take the same measures if you feel like it, but let me suggest that if that happens then the possibility of an accidental war developing between us is very real.' He said, 'Well, what is your position?' I said, 'My position is purely defensive.' I made it very clear that we will try to stop anyone who transgresses against Jordan from any direction. He said, 'Do I have your word?' I said, 'Yes, you have my word.' He said, 'That is good enough for me and I will prevent our people from moving anywhere.' And he did. And that was one of the events I will always remember. That he recognised that my word was good enough and this is the way people [ought to] deal with each other.

A.S.: In June 1992 the Labour Party won the election and Yitzhak Rabin became prime minister a second time. When were your contacts renewed with him and through what channel?

K.H.: Through direct means, through the help of some friends. We established a way of being able to communicate directly. In fact we had a Jordanian–Israeli agenda worked out but we held back until the Palestinians moved. The Oslo Agreement came out of the blue. Yasser Arafat had told me that he had been in touch with Shimon Peres but suddenly it came out. At one point I was rather upset again. Why not coordinate? How can you work that way? But then I decided, that's what the Palestinians wanted always and the only thing I could do was to support them.

And that freed us so we immediately began our talks. We had a meeting here in London and I asked Rabin if he was ready to move, and he said he was, so we said fine, and we began a process of working on what turned out to be the Washington Declaration [which ended the state of war between Israel and Jordan]. In the meantime, Peres came to Amman and went back, and despite our prior commitment on both sides to keep it quiet until it was appropriate to announce it, it was leaked. So I continued with Rabin.

A.S.: Why did you insist on secrecy?

K.H.: We did not announce peace contacts publicly all through the past because of a mutual agreement. At first we were so far apart, there was no benefit from announcing these meetings. They enabled us to get to know each other. They enabled us to examine the possibilities of positions every now and then to see if there is any chance for progress. They certainly changed the atmosphere, but it was a mutual agreement from the word go that we keep them quiet until we had something of substance.

A.S.: What was the background to the Washington Declaration of July 1994?

K.H.: I was not against a public meeting with Rabin; that's the way people do business, no other way. And we prepared the document, formally ending the state of war between Israel and Jordan. I wanted the first meeting to be held in Wadi Araba so that Rabin would get esteem. I planned to invite him to come and sign what turned out to be the Washington Declaration. At that point President Clinton invited us to the White House. Both Rabin and I felt the Americans had been our partners in trying to get somewhere for so long that we could not turn down their invitation. So we accepted. And we went with the paper already agreed to its last detail and we did not show it to anyone and we gave it to the president's office after the last newspaper came out.

A.S.: Shimon Peres has claimed the credit for the breakthrough with Jordan which produced the Washington Declaration.

K.H.: He had nothing to do with it. He had no knowledge of it. And he was very upset about that unfortunately. And he took it in the wrong way.

A.S.: And next was the actual peace treaty between Israel and Jordan. Who negotiated the peace treaty?

K.H.: Essentially Rabin and us.

A.S.: And did you feel you got a fair deal?

K.H.: I felt we did, yes. I think so, we had a unique relationship. I felt he placed himself in my position many times. I placed myself in his position. We did not try to score points off each other. We tried to work something that is workable, that is acceptable to both our people, something that was balanced, something that was reasonable. And that's the approach we had and we managed to get that.

A.S.: How do you evaluate the progress of the peace process between Israel and Jordan in the year between the signature of the treaty and the assassination of Rabin in November 1995?

K.H.: I think it was rapid, promising and very satisfying, at that period of time. It was preparing the ground for a lot that would happen later. But certainly the last time I met Rabin was at the economic summit in Amman. It was a landmark event: we tried to present to the world the two countries in a state of peace, and hopefully as taking a step towards comprehensive peace in the area. To tell the world: 'Come and be our partners and benefit with us in the dividends of peace.' A few days later we lost it.

A.S.: Was it your intention that the peace between Jordan and Israel would be a warm peace, unlike the cold peace between Israel and Egypt?

K.H.: I can't understand the term cold peace. I don't understand what it means. You either have a war or you have a state of no war, and no peace or you have peace. Peace is by its very nature a resolution of all the problems. It is the tearing down of barriers between people. It is people coming together, coming to know each other. There were so many instances, like the children of martyrs on both sides embracing in Wadi Araba. We saw soldiers who fought each other coming together and exchanging reminiscences about the impossible conditions they had before in a totally different atmosphere. People began to know each other, to have a feeling that their worries were the same. People started meeting and doing business together, and that is peace. What other peace has a meaning? It is not between governments, it is between people. Suddenly they realised they have the same worries, they have the same concerns, they have suffered the same way, there is something that they can both put into creating a relationship that would be of benefit for everybody.

A.S.: After Rabin's assassination what kind of relationship did you have with Shimon Peres and what is your evaluation of Peres as prime minister?

K.H.: The fact that he did not like the peace treaty, I suppose, alienated him to a degree.[4] I don't think he was very happy with that and I am sorry about it because I know he has served his country. Peres has always been a believer in peace, and he has so many thoughts and ideas for progress in every field and area and he would never cease to present them. But the relationship was different and it cooled down constantly.

A.S.: When Binyamin Netanyahu was elected prime minister in 1996, did you think that heralded the end of the peace process in the Middle East?

K.H.: I did not necessarily think that. I thought that the peace process was irreversible and I still hope it is. I remember talking with Rabin once about the approaching elections and he said, 'When the peace treaty with Jordan passed through the Knesset, it was approved by an overwhelming majority. We have never had such a sweeping majority on any other issue. And so it wasn't a peace between Jordan and Labour; it was a peace between Jordan and the whole people of Israel.' I respected that, and that is why I did not interfere in the Israeli elections in any form or way. And I believe that the national consensus in support of peace will continue. But until now obviously we have been moving very slowly, and we are facing a different atmosphere from the one that existed before.

A.S.: At the Washington Summit in late September 1996 you were reported to have spoken very sternly to Netanyahu. What did you say to him?

K.H.: It was probably leaked, not by me, but the leak was essentially correct. I spoke of the arrogance of power, I spoke of the need to treat people equally, I spoke of the need to make progress. I spoke about my concerns and my worries and they were accurately reported.

A.S.: And what was Netanyahu's response?

K.H.: He didn't say anything, but towards the end, as we were leaving, he said, 'I am determined to surprise you.'

A.S.: Finally, you have been dealing with Israel for over 40 years. Do you have a concluding comment on Israel as a neighbour?

K.H.: I believe that there is so much potential for benefits that would result from our coming together. The descendants of the children of Abraham in that region had such an impact on the world and on mankind. There is so much that we achieved together in the past in terms of history, in Spain and elsewhere, and within the region itself. And I think there is so much that could be achieved and could be done. The talents and abilities of peoples coming together should be channelled to do something worthwhile and worthy of them. Now against that, we have the few, but unfortunately effective, people who are against this vision and against this dream on either side of the Arab–Israeli divide. I felt that the divide had changed. It wasn't Israel and Jordan. It was those who believed in peace, and believed in the future, and those who are opposed to it. So we have opponents here and there.

But now, I feel I am in a dilemma. I really feel as responsible to Israelis as I feel to Jordanians. I have had many contacts with Israelis, I have felt the warmth of people, I have felt they are yearning for the same things that our people are yearning for. And I don't know, we are still waiting for positive developments. They haven't happened. How far can I keep quiet? When do I have to speak out to Israelis and Jordanians, to everyone and to share with them my fears and anxieties regarding our mutual future? I don't think one can remain the way we are indefinitely; but I hope somehow that there will be a breakthrough before long and we can start again. That is where we are at the moment.

# TWENTY-SEVEN

# Edward Said and the Palestine Question

E dward Said was an extraordinarily versatile and prolific scholar whose work ranged over a number of academic disciplines. While his principal field was comparative literature, he was also a student of culture and society. His 1978 book *Orientalism* exposed the ideological biases behind Western perceptions of 'the Orient' and helped create a distinctive sub-field of what came to be called post-colonial studies. In addition to these literary pursuits, Said was a pianist of concert-playing standard and a leading music critic. Last but not least, he was a politically engaged intellectual and the most eloquent spokesman on behalf of the dispossessed Palestinian people.

Edward Said's attachment to the Palestinian cause had deep emotional roots. He was born in Jerusalem in late 1935 to a wealthy Christian Palestinian family and spent his childhood in what is today one of the more opulent Jewish districts of the city. In December 1947, after the United Nations voted for the partition of Palestine, the family moved to Cairo where his father already had a branch of his business. The immediate family was thus spared the worst ravages of the catastrophe which turned more than 700,000 Palestinians into refugees. But the cataclysmic quality of this collective experience, of the catastrophe or al-Nakba, seared itself in the boy's mind.

Although Said was only 12 years old at the time, with no more than a semi-conscious awareness of what was happening, he recalled some memories with special lucidity. One was that many of the members of his extended family on both sides 'were suddenly made homeless, some penniless, disoriented, and scarred forever'. He saw some of them again after the fall of Palestine, 'but all were greatly reduced in circumstances, their faces stark with worry, ill-health, despair'. Yet they bore their suffering as not so much a political as a natural tragedy. This etched itself in Said's memory with lasting results, mostly because the faces he had once remembered as content and at ease were now worn with the cares of exile and homelessness. 'Many families and individuals had their lives broken, their spirits drained, their composure destroyed forever in the context of seemingly unending, serial dislocation.'[1] All this remained for Said of the greatest poignancy.

The second thing that Said recalled was the one person in his family who somehow managed to pull herself together in the aftermath of the Nakba. She was his paternal aunt Nabiha, who devoted her life to working with Palestinian refugees in Cairo. In the memoir of his childhood *Out of Place*, Said gives a vivid account of this formidable relative who never discussed the political aspects of the dispute in his presence. A middle-aged widow with some financial means, Nabiha saw it as her lifelong task to help the refugees – battling with the indifferent Egyptian bureaucracy, getting their children into schools, cajoling doctors into giving them treatment, finding jobs for the men, providing constant sympathy and support for the women. For Nabiha, being Palestinian imposed a duty to assist the unfortunate refugees, many of whom ended up penniless, jobless, destitute and disoriented in the neighbouring Arab countries. From her Said learnt that whereas everyone was willing to pay lip service to the cause, only very few people were prepared to do something practical about it. She remained an exemplary figure, a person against whom his own efforts were measured and always found wanting.[2]

Although he was born in Palestine, Edward Said spent most of his life in the United States, progressing steadily through Princeton and Harvard to a chair of English and Comparative Literature at Columbia. Until his early thirties, he was too focused on his academic career and on his passion for music to take much interest in the politics of his homeland. It was the trauma of the Arab defeat in June 1967 that, by his own account, shook him out of his earlier complacency and reconnected him to his people. Despite the shattering consequences of the defeat, which set in motion a new wave of refugees, Said felt invigorated by the Palestinian national movement whose influence began to spread throughout the Arab world in the aftermath of the war: 'We were the first Arabs who at the grass-root level – and not because a colonel or a king commanded us – started a movement to repossess a land and a history that had been wrested from us.'[3]

Said's direct involvement in the tangled history of the Palestinian national movement is not easy to summarise. He first met Yasser Arafat when the chairman of the PLO came to the United Nations in 1974. He translated Arafat's speech from Arabic into English, and he became acquainted with the various officials of the PLO at the time, notably Shafiq al-Hout and the famous poet Mahmoud Darwish. During the 1980s, Said became publicly identified with Arafat, especially in Europe and the United States where he began to be called upon regularly by the mainstream media. The choice Said faced was a difficult one. He could defend the PLO and Arafat as the main instrument of the Palestinian struggle against the overwhelmingly hostile media that denied that the struggle was anything more than terrorism and anti-Semitism. Or he could join in the general racist chorus in the US of attacks on the Palestinians, Islam, the Arabs and Arab nationalism in general. Said chose the former and, as a result, he was fiercely attacked by right-wing American Jews, one of whom gave him the soubriquet 'the Professor of Terror'.[4]

Gradually, Said started to play a more active role as a spokesman for the Palestinians. In 1974 he became a member of the Palestinian National Council (PNC), the nearest thing to a representative assembly of the Palestinians in exile. Elected as an independent intellectual, he steered clear of the endemic factional struggles and used his authority to try to influence the overall direction of the

movement. He rejected the policy of the armed struggle and argued
for recognition of the State of Israel.[5] In 1979, Said expounded his
moderate philosophy in print in *The Question of Palestine*. The main
purpose of the book was to counter the massive accumulation of
lies, distortions and wilful ignorance that surrounded the Palestinian
struggle at the time. Yet Said was savagely attacked by both the
mainstream Fatah and the more radical Popular Front for the
Liberation of Palestine for urging the recognition of Israel.[6]

Edward Said was well ahead of his colleagues in conceding that
the Jews had some historic claim to Palestine. This claim was not
an exclusive one and it most certainly did not entail the right to
dispossess the Palestinians. Nevertheless there was a significant
difference between Said's position and that of the hardliners who
insisted on an exclusive Palestinian right to the whole of historic
Palestine. Said's anti-colonial critique of Israel took into account
the persecution of the Jews in Europe and the strong impact of
the Zionist idea on the European conscience. He understood that
the Holocaust meant that Israel could not be judged by exactly
the same standards as other nations. But he could not see why the
Palestinians should be deprived of their natural rights for crimes
against the Jews that they had not perpetrated.[7] Compassion for
Jewish suffering was thus accompanied by the demand that Israel
recognise its own culpability for the plight of the Palestinians. In a
public debate with Salman Rushdie in the late 1980s, in a phrase
that was to become famous, Said described the Palestinians as 'the
victims of victims'.[8]

In *The Question of Palestine* Said returned to this fundamental
injustice. The Palestinians, he noted, had been associated with
opposition to Zionism, with being the 'heart' of the Middle East
problem, with being terrorists, with being intransigent. But it was
extraordinary bad luck to have a good case in resisting colonial
invasion of their homeland combined with 'the most morally
complex of all opponents, Jews, with a long history of victimisation
and terror behind them'. The absolute wrong of settler colonialism,
he pointed out, was greatly diluted by using it to straighten out the
destiny of the Jews at the expense of the Palestinians.[9] Yet, despite

its trenchant critique of Israeli nationalism, *The Question of Palestine* should be read as an essay in reconciliation.

Although Said's calls for accommodation and peaceful coexistence earned him the displeasure of Arab radicals and few adherents on the Israeli side, he never abandoned the struggle. On the contrary, he continued to articulate his inclusive vision at every conceivable opportunity. In 1983 he was unable to attend the PNC meeting in Algiers but he sent a long memorandum to the group, arguing that they should accept the reality of Israel in order to be able to resist and put limits to its dominance over them and, secondly, in order to be able to put forward a clear goal of their own.[10] The world must see, he wrote, that 'the Palestinian idea is an idea of living together, of respect for others, of mutual recognition between Palestinian and Israeli'. This one sentence encapsulates the essence of Edward Said's thinking. It is the most consistent theme in his voluminous writing on the subject, from *The Question of Palestine* to the last article.

One of the most unfortunate aspects of the dispute, in Said's view, was that even the word 'peace' acquired a sinister meaning for the Arabs. According to the standard Zionist narrative, Israel fervently desired peace, while the Arabs – ferocious, vengeful and gratuitously bent on violence – did not. The reality was rather more complicated and therefore more difficult to convey to the uninformed public: 'In fact, what was at issue between Israelis and Palestinians was never peace but the possibility for Palestinians of restitution of property, nationhood, identity – all of them blotted out by the new Jewish state.'[11] Moreover, for the Palestinians, peace on Israel's terms meant accepting as definitive the military verdict of 1948, the loss of their society and homeland.

Preserving the Palestinian national identity was all-important. Said described his 'most specific task' as simply that of making the case for a Palestinian presence in a world that tended to deny it. The task was to insist, again and again, 'that there was a Palestinian people, and that, like all others, it had a history, a society, and, most important, a right of self-determination'.[12] Like his friend Mahmoud Darwish, Said repeatedly reasserted the distinct identity and the presence of his people. The constant refrain in one of Darwish's

best-known poems is *Sajjil Ana 'Arabi* – 'Take note, I am Arab.'
Said's writings convey the same insistent message on behalf of the
Palestinian people not as individuals but as a collective entity.

If asserting the Palestinian presence was one primary task,
mapping out a path to reconciliation between the Palestinians and
their opponents was another. Said's ideas about paths to peace,
however, were neither fixed nor always consistent. His thinking
about a settlement evolved constantly and took into account the
changing reality on the ground. Four main phases may be discerned
in Said's thinking and writing on the subject. Initially, he favoured
a one-state solution, a bi-national state for both Jews and Arabs
over the whole of historic Palestine. Then, at the PNC meeting in
1988, he advocated a two-state solution, based on the partition of
Palestine. In 1993, at the time the Oslo Accord was signed, he came
out decisively against the two-state solution that was implicit in
it. Finally, towards the end of his life, he reverted to the one-state
solution. His thinking had come round full circle.

In *The Question of Palestine* Said expounded the rationale for a
one-state solution with great clarity and conviction. The 1967 war,
he observed, placed the whole question of Palestine in a direct
adversarial position vis-à-vis Israeli Zionism. The moderate forces
in the Palestinian resistance movement formulated an idea and a
vision that broke away sharply with all past ideas in their camp. This
was the idea of a single secular democratic state over the whole of
Palestine for both Arabs and Jews. Although this idea was derided
in some quarters as a mere propaganda ploy, Said considered it of
tremendous importance for the following reason:

> It accepted what generations of Arabs and Palestinians had never
> been able to accept – the presence of a community of Jews in
> Palestine who had gained their state by conquest – but it went
> further than mere acceptance of Jews. The Palestinian idea posited
> what is still, to my mind, the only possible and acceptable destiny
> for the multicommunal Middle East, the notion of a state based
> on secular human rights, not on religious minority exclusivity
> nor . . . on an idealised geopolitical unity . . . The ghetto state,

the national security state, the minority government, were to be transcended by a secular democratic polity, in which communities would be accommodated to one another for the greater good of the whole.[13]

Two major events in the 1980s led Said to re-examine his position and to move from a one-state to a two-state solution. First, following the Israeli invasion of Lebanon in 1982, the PLO was forced to move its headquarters from Beirut to Tunis. Its stature was so diminished and the organisation became so enfeebled and reclusive that it was hardly capable of providing effective political leadership. Then, in December 1987, the first intifada erupted in Gaza and rapidly spread to the West Bank. It was a spontaneous, full-scale civilian uprising against Israeli rule that took the PLO leaders in Tunis by complete surprise. The intifada refocused world opinion on the plight of the Palestinians. It gave them the status of a people dispossessed and under brutal military occupation. A group of Palestinian moderates began to argue for a bold initiative to translate the success of the intifada into a more lasting political achievement. Edward Said was one of them.

In the months leading up to the crucial PNC meeting in Algiers in November 1988, Said discussed with his colleagues the wisdom of abandoning the rhetoric of the liberation of Palestine by means of the armed struggle and offering a historic compromise based on the partition of the country. Even after its expulsion from Lebanon and the loss of its last front against Israel, the PLO continued to pretend that the goal was the liberation of Palestine. To the majority of Jews and Americans the liberation of Palestine was synonymous with the extermination of the State of Israel. Said saw no point in maintaining a formula that was neither possible nor really their goal. He felt that this was the most significant moment in Palestinian life since 1948 and that the issue had to be faced head-on.[14]

A Palestinian declaration of independence was drafted. Yasser Arafat asked Edward Said to translate it from Arabic into English.[15] On 15 November 1988, a majority vote on the PNC carried the motion: divide historic Palestine into two states, one Israeli and one

Palestinian. The PNC formally recognised Israel's right to exist; it accepted all relevant UN resolutions going back to November 1947; and it opted unambiguously for a two-state solution to the dispute between the two nations. The vote amounted to a transformation of the Palestinian national movement from a liberation movement to an independence movement. It is an exaggeration to claim, as Christopher Hitchens has done, that Edward Said was the intellectual and moral architect of this mutual recognition policy.[16] But Said certainly contributed to this revolution in Palestinian political thinking. He was bitterly disappointed, however, that this move to moderation elicited no response from Israel and only a short-lived dialogue between the PLO and the United States.

In June 1992 Edward Said visited Israel and Palestine. It was his first visit to the country since 1947 and it turned out to be an eye-opener. For the first time Said was exposed directly to the grim reality of life under Israeli occupation. He was forcibly struck by the scope and solidity of the Jewish settlements on the West Bank and by the pervasive presence of Israeli soldiers. What he witnessed at first-hand planted doubts in his mind about the viability of an independent Palestinian state alongside Israel. The Israeli presence looked too deeply entrenched to be rolled back. Israeli settlements across the Green Line gave every appearance of being there to stay and the two communities seemed too closely intertwined to be separated. As a result of the visit, Said was no longer confident that the two-state solution represented a realistic option.[17]

Just as Edward Said was moving away from the two-state solution, the Tunis-based PLO leadership made the decision to embrace it. Secret negotiations in the Norwegian capital culminated, on 13 September 1993, in the Oslo Accord. In an article in the *London Review of Books*, Said launched a frontal assault on the Accord. Some of his criticisms related to Arafat's autocratic, idiosyncratic and secretive style of management. Others related to the substance of the deal. The most basic criticism was that the deal negotiated by Yasser Arafat did not carry the promise, let alone a guarantee, of an independent Palestinian state. 'Let us call the agreement by its real name', thundered Said, 'an instrument of Palestinian surrender, a

Palestinian Versailles'. His description of the signing ceremony mixed contempt and anger in roughly equal measures: 'The fashion-show vulgarities of the White House ceremony, the degrading spectacle of Yasser Arafat thanking everyone for the suspension of most of his people's rights, and the fatuous solemnity of Bill Clinton's performance, like a 20th-century Roman emperor shepherding two vassal kings through rituals of reconciliation and obeisance: all these only temporarily obscure the truly astonishing proportions of the Palestinian capitulation.'[18]

In a series of newspaper articles Said argued that the Oslo Accord compromised the basic national rights of the Palestinian people as well as the individual rights of the 1948 refugees. He lambasted Arafat for unilaterally cancelling the intifada, for failing to coordinate his moves with the Arab states, and for introducing appalling disarray within the ranks of the PLO. 'The PLO', wrote Said, 'has transformed itself from a national liberation movement into a kind of small-town government, with the same handful of people still in command.' The clear implication was that Arafat and his corrupt cronies had sacrificed principle to grab power. Furthermore, this was not a deal between two equal parties: on the one hand there was Israel, a modern state and a military superpower, on the other hand there was the PLO, a leadership in exile with no maps, no technical expertise, no territorial base, and no friends. 'All secret deals between a very strong and a very weak partner', wrote Said, 'necessarily involve concessions hidden in embarrassment by the latter. . . . The deal before us smacks of the PLO leadership's exhaustion and isolation, and of Israel's shrewdness.'[19]

Said's critique of the Oslo Accord may have looked unduly harsh and pessimistic at the time, but it was fully borne out by subsequent events. Indeed, the critique was almost prophetic. The accuracy of Said's predictions is surprising: he even surprised himself. One explanation for his prescience is that he read the text of the Declaration of Principles very carefully – and he was a past master in analysing texts. Reading the text made it patently clear that this Accord was not the product of negotiations between equals: Israel imposed its will on the PLO. There was no mention of Palestinian self-determination or sovereignty or an end to the expansion of Jewish settlements.[20] Not only were Said's judgements vindicated but, to his chagrin, his worst fears came to pass. The Oslo Accord had inspired high hopes of an independent Palestinian state living in peace and security alongside Israel. Seven years later, however, the Accord was in tatters and the hope had all but evaporated amidst the violence and the bloodshed of the second intifada.

In the years after the conclusion of the ill-fated Oslo Accord, Said gradually reverted to his initial position, namely, that the only fair and viable solution to the dispute between Arabs and Jews is a secular bi-national state over the whole of Palestine from the Jordan river to the Mediterranean sea. A single state would address the root problems of the conflict, the problems created by the 1948 war, especially the right of return of the Palestinian refugees, whereas the Oslo Accord of 1993 and Oslo II of 1995 only offered partial solutions to the problems created by the 1967 war. Said recognised that emotions on both sides were strongly against a single state, but he considered a bi-national democratic state to be the only real alternative to the bloody impasse of the al-Aqsa intifada.

The outbreak of the intifada in September 2000 signified the final failure of the Oslo Accords to bring about a genuine reconciliation between the two communities. The main flaw in these Accords, according to Said, was their total obliviousness to the interests of the Palestinian people, as well as their enhancement of Israel's position by propaganda and relentless political pressure. Said called the Oslo peace process a phoney peace because it perpetuated the inequality between the Palestinians and the Israelis. The Israelis were allowed sovereignty, territorial integrity and self-determination while the Palestinians were not.

In a long series of articles in the Western and Arabic press, subsequently gathered in a book entitled *The End of the Peace Process*, Said returned again and again to two main themes. One theme was to elaborate on the consequences of the Oslo Accords. Here he painted a discouraging picture of the deteriorating situation in the aftermath of Oslo: the increase in Palestinian poverty and unemployment; the restrictions on freedom and the abuses of human rights; and the continuation of the worst aspects of the Israeli occupation, including land appropriation and settlement expansion. A second and related theme was disenchantment with Yasser Arafat and the Palestinian Authority. Said could be blunt in his comments on Israel and the United States but he reserved his most scathing criticisms for Arafat and his tight band of loyalists, excoriating them for their subservience to Israel, venality, corruption, lack of accountability and fatal yet characteristic mix of incompetence and authoritarianism. 'Yasir Arafat', in Said's bitter conclusion, 'neither has the vision nor courage to lead anyone anywhere except into more poverty and despondency.'[21]

Disappointment with Oslo and with the Palestinian leadership that was associated with it led naturally and logically to the fourth and final stage in the evolution of Edward Said's thinking on solutions to the Palestinian–Israeli dispute – advocacy of a bi-national state. He spent the last few years of his life trying to develop an entirely new strategy of peace, a new approach based on equality, reconciliation and justice. 'I . . . see no other way than to begin now to speak about sharing the land that has thrust us together, and sharing it in a truly democratic way, with equal rights for each citizen', Said wrote in a 1999 essay in the *New York Times*. 'There can be no reconciliation unless both peoples, two communities of suffering, resolve that their existence is a secular fact, and that it has to be dealt with as such.' This did not mean the diminishing of Jewish life or the surrendering of Palestinian aspirations and political existence. On the contrary, it meant self-determination for both peoples.[22]

The question for Said was not how to devise means for persisting in trying to separate the two peoples but to see whether it was possible for them to live together peacefully. Azmi Bishara, the Israeli Arab and former member of the Knesset, talked about enlarging the concept of *citizenship* as a way of getting beyond ethnic and religious criteria that in effect make Israel an undemocratic state for 20 per cent of its population. Said built on this idea to develop a vision of a secular, democratic, non-exclusive bi-national state. The intellectual roots of this idea went back to the inter-war period when Jewish intellectuals like Judah Magnes and Martin Buber argued and agitated for a bi-national state. The logic of Zionism defeated their efforts but the bi-national vision had not lost its appeal, at least not for Edward Said. 'The essence of that vision', he wrote, 'is coexistence and sharing in ways that require an innovative, daring, and theoretical willingness to get beyond the arid stalemate of assertion, exclusivism and rejection. Once the initial acknowledgement of the Other is made, I believe the way forward becomes not only possible but attractive.'[23]

Thus, after three decades of reflecting, debating, writing and meandering around the Palestine question, Edward Said had come full circle. He had began by favouring a one-state solution; in the late 1980s, for pragmatic reasons, he made an abrupt transition to a two-state solution; the experience of Oslo convinced him of the unworkability of this, so, finally, he reverted to his initial position by embracing the one-state solution. Indeed, he emerged as the most passionate and eloquent proponent of that solution on either side of the Palestinian–Israeli divide. In a series of searing essays that refracted the reality of those terrible years, Said elaborated on this theme with extraordinary insight and compassion.[24]

In his final years, as illness ravaged his health and the violence in Israel–Palestine kept escalating, Edward Said made a conscious decision to channel his energies into music. In 1999 he and Daniel Barenboim, the Israeli pianist and conductor, established the West-Eastern Divan Orchestra. The two friends were united in their belief that art and music transcend political ideology. They also shared a cosmopolitan outlook and a commitment to musical education.[25] Their orchestra is made up of young Israeli and Arab musicians who meet every summer in Seville for intensive rehearsals and a concert tour. Raised in enmity, these talented young men and women set an example by their devotion to their common craft. Together they play with wonderful energy and unanimity in an orchestra that is larger than life. When looking at the orchestra, it is utterly impossible to tell the Israelis from the Arabs or Palestinians. The workshop is a brilliantly successful experiment in breaking down national stereotypes and in artistic collaboration across the battle lines. It was a beacon of hope amidst all the doom and gloom that surrounded the Arab–Israeli conflict in the era of Yasser Arafat and Ariel Sharon.

The thinking that led to the orchestra was eloquently exposed by Said in a lecture he gave in London at the School of Oriental and African Studies in 2003 to inaugurate the Sir Joseph Hotung Project on Law, Human Rights and Peace Building in the Middle East:

> In our work and planning and discussions our main principle is that separation between peoples is not a solution for any of the problems that divide peoples. And certainly ignorance of the other provides no help whatever. Cooperation and coexistence of the kind that music lived as we have lived, performed, shared and loved it together, might be. I for one am full of optimism despite the darkening sky and the seemingly hopeless situation for the time being that encloses us all.

The orchestra was Edward Said's proudest achievement. It stood in marked contrast to the countless conferences he had attended with Israeli moderates, conferences that produced no tangible results and sometimes ended in mutual recrimination. Music, on the other hand, was an exercise in harmony. It brought welcome relief from the frustrations of a debate and a dialogue that went over and over the same ground and seemed to lead nowhere. The orchestra corresponded to Said's conviction that we know best what we make and to his inclusive vision of society. It gave concrete expression to his belief that playing music together can change attitudes and shift the boundaries of the mind. But his passionate devotion to the orchestra also stemmed from the lesson he had learnt from his aunt Nabiha in his childhood: that being a Palestinian means, above all, not pontificating but doing something useful, not engaging in futile argument but rendering practical service to the community. The orchestra was the noblest service that Said could render to his beloved Palestine. It was also one of his most striking successes in engaging meaningfully with the Other.

Edward Said described the orchestra as 'one of the most important things I have done in my life'. He believed that the orchestra, even more than the two dozen books he had written, would be his most significant legacy.[26] It is therefore a fitting epitaph for an intellectual who spent a lifetime grappling with the complexities and contradictions of the Arab–Israeli conflict yet never gave up hope on coexistence and peace. For Said – the private person, as opposed to the public intellectual – helping young men and women from societies at war with one another to rise above the political divide in order to meet and make music together was a deeply rewarding experience. It went beyond politics, beyond polemics, beyond argument, beyond words.

# TWENTY-EIGHT

# Four Days in Seville

Of the countless symposia on the Israeli–Palestinian conflict that I have attended in the last 33 years, the one convened by Daniel Barenboim in Seville in 2004 was by far the most stimulating, constructive and encouraging. The symposium proceeded alongside the rehearsals of the West-Eastern Divan Orchestra that Barenboim created in 1999 with his friend Edward Said, who died in September 2003. The orchestra was Said's proudest achievement. It is made up of young Israeli and Arab musicians who meet every summer for intensive rehearsals and a concert tour. The reunion a year later was tinged with sadness as it was for an Edward Said memorial concert.

Participants in the symposium included some militantly moderate Israelis and Palestinians, Felipe Gonzalez, the former socialist prime minister of Spain, and members of Edward Said's family. Mariam explained that her late husband devoted to this project a large part of his life both because of his commitment to the Palestinian cause and because of his belief in the power of music to break down national barriers. Wadie added that his father got involved in this workshop because of the unique talent of Daniel Barenboim and because it offered an opportunity to do something concrete and constructive involving the two sides. Najla recalled that her father always used to tell her that he and his generation are too deeply enmeshed in the history of this tragic conflict and that the only hope of change lay with the young people of her generation.

Culture is a huge resource for power, and Barenboim and Said used this resource towards a positive end: peaceful coexistence between Jews and Arabs in Palestine. Said described the Palestinians in a memorable phrase as the victims of victims. The Palestinians, he emphasised, have to understand the impact of the Holocaust on the Jewish psyche, and especially the obsession with security, if they are to make sense of Israel's attitude towards them. The Israelis, on the other hand, have to acknowledge that the establishment of their state in 1948 involved a monumental injustice to the Palestinians. What Said wanted was not to draw a line over the past but to gain a broader understanding of the roots of this conflict, to adopt a contrapuntal approach to their parallel histories, as he liked to put it. This was a consistent thread in Said's writing from *The Question of Palestine* to his last article. Said himself combined great humanity with a strong sense of dignity. Cooperation between the two warring tribes in Palestine was his ultimate goal but not at the expense of the dignity of his own people. This stress on the need for mutual respect was an important part of his legacy.

The discussions that preceded the drafting of a declaration in Seville ranged far and wide, but there was complete consensus on one point: the interdependence between the two parties to the conflict. Like it or not, Israelis and Palestinians are simply fated to live together cheek by jowl on the same small piece of land. It follows that what is good for one side is good for the other. All previous efforts to solve this conflict failed because they treated it as a zero-sum game whereby a gain by one side is necessarily at the expense of the other side. Our aim was to move from a zero-sum game to a positive-sum game in which both sides simultaneously reduce their costs and enhance their benefits. The ideas we put forward were not directed against anyone; they were designed to help the parties break out of the cycle of violence, bloodshed and mutual destruction. We are in the construction business, not in the destruction business.

Our purpose was not to propose new solutions but to offer a new definition of the old problem. Together we worked to create a new narrative of one of the most bitter and protracted conflicts of modern times.

It was noted at the outset that while the destinies of the two parties are inextricably linked, the imbalance in their power could hardly be more pronounced. Israel is a sovereign state and a military superpower, whereas the Palestinians are a weak and vulnerable community still at the stage of struggling for statehood. This enormous imbalance of power is ultimately injurious to both peoples. It permitted the crushing of Palestinian institutions, the abuse of human rights, and a relentless assault on their collective identity. On the Israeli side, the occupation brings no security, undermines its democratic foundations, and tarnishes the country's image abroad. As Karl Marx observed, a people that oppresses another cannot itself remain free. Real peace between Israel and the Palestinians can only be based on freedom and democracy on both sides, and on a relationship between equals.

It was against this background that all the participants in the symposium, led by Barenboim and Gonzalez, joined in a passionate plea for a more active European role in settling the dispute between Israel and the Palestinians. Europe has the moral duty, the direct interest and the material capability to contribute to the resolution of this conflict. The part that the European powers played in bringing about the conflict between Jews and Arabs in Palestine imposes on them the moral duty to do everything in their power to bring about a just and equitable solution. But this is not simply a question of morality. Europe is home to a significant number of Jews and a more substantial number of Muslims. The festering conflict in the Middle East is feeding hatred, intolerance and anti-Semitism in Europe. If Europe does not go to the Middle East to tackle the problem at its roots, the repercussions of the conflict will be felt ever more strongly in Europe. Finally, the European Union is the principal provider of foreign aid to the Palestinian Authority and Israel's largest trading partner. It is thus well placed to bring its influence to bear on the diplomatic front.

The sound of classical European music provided the most exhilarating backdrop to the discussions of the symposium. Raised in enmity, the exceptionally talented young men and women set an example by their devotion to the demands of their common craft. Neither the Arab nor the Israeli members of the orchestra need the other to put on an impressive performance. But the collaborative and cosmopolitan character of the project enhances the quality of their music. The West-Eastern Divan Orchestra is thus a beacon of hope on the dismal political landscape of the Middle East. The challenge lies in translating this imaginative artistic concept into the realm of politics. No one under-estimated the magnitude of the challenge, and yet there was a palpable sense of optimism in Seville. By the personal example he set, both in the workshop and in the symposium, Daniel Barenboim infected many of us with his confidence that the impossible is easier to achieve than the difficult.

# TWENTY-NINE

# Benny Morris and the Betrayal of History

'A nation', wrote the French philosopher Ernest Renan, 'is a group of people united by a mistaken view about the past and a hatred of their neighbours.' By this definition, Benny Morris may now be counted as a true member of the Israeli nation. In his account of his 'conversion' in the 22 February 2002 issue of the *Guardian*, Benny explains that, although he had not undergone a brain transplant as far as he can remember, his thinking about the current Middle East crisis and its protagonists had radically changed during the past two years.

Willingness to re-examine one's thinking is always a commendable trait in a historian. Unfortunately, in Benny's case the re-examination is confined to only one protagonist in the Middle East conflict: the Palestinians. As a consequence, his new version of the recent history of the conflict has more in common with propaganda than with genuine history. Like most nationalist versions of history, it is simplistic, selective and self-serving.

By his own account, Benny's conversion was a pretty dramatic affair. He imagines that he feels a bit like those Western fellow-travellers rudely awakened by the trundle of Russian tanks crashing into Budapest in 1956. But there is surely some mistake in this analogy.

Benny could not possibly have heard the trundle of Palestinian tanks crashing into any Israeli city because there are no Palestinian tanks. What he might have heard is the sound of Merkava tanks invading Palestinian cities on the West Bank and refugee camps in Gaza, in the most flagrant violation of a long series of agreements that placed these areas under the control of the Palestinian Authority. Another minor flaw in Benny's analogy is that the Palestinians, by any reckoning, can only be seen as the victims, while Israel is the aggressive and overbearing military superpower. If we are going to look for historical antecedents for this grossly unequal contest, it would make more sense to update the biblical image of David and Goliath: a Palestinian David facing an Israeli Goliath.

There is a historical irony in Benny's conversion to the orthodox Zionist rendition of the past, for he was one of the trailblazers of the 'new history' which placed Israel's political and military conduct under an uncompromising lens. Indeed, it was he who coined the term 'the new historiography' in order to distinguish it from the traditional pro-Zionist literature about the birth of Israel and the first Arab–Israeli war of which he was so savagely critical. His 1988 book, *The Birth of the Palestinian Refugee Problem, 1947–1949*, drove a coach and horses through the claim that the Palestinians left Palestine of their own accord or on orders from their leaders. With a great wealth of recently declassified material, he analysed the role that Israel played in precipitating the Palestinian exodus. Three or four subsequent books consolidated Benny's reputation as the standard-bearer of the new historiography. The hallmark of his approach was to stick as closely as possible to the documentary evidence, to record rather than to evaluate. While his findings were original and arresting, he upheld the highest standards of historical scholarship, and he wrote with almost clinical detachment.

Sadly, the article in the *Guardian* does not display any of Benny's former scholarly objectivity or rigorous use of evidence. Instead of evidence we are treated to a rambling and self-pitying monologue, seething with contempt and hatred for the Arabs in general and Palestinians in particular. The message, pithily summed up in a long interview that Benny gave to *Yediot Aharonot* about his highly publicised conversion, is that 'the Arabs are responsible'. Where no evidence is available to sustain the argument of Arab intransigence, Benny makes it up by drawing on his fertile imagination. According to him, what stayed the hand of Hafez al-Assad of Syria, and that of his son and successor Bashar, from signing a peace treaty was not quibbles over a few hundred yards but a basic refusal to make peace with the Jewish state. The evidence? Benny can see the father, on his deathbed, telling his son: 'Whatever you do, don't make peace with the Jews; like the Crusaders, they too will vanish.' It would appear that Benny can no longer tell the difference between genuine history, and fiction or fabrication along the lines of *The Protocols of the Elders of Zion*. At this rate Benny is in danger of becoming what Isaiah Berlin once described as 'a very rare thing – a genuine charlatan'.

Most of Benny's venom and vitriol are, however, reserved for the Palestinians in what amounts to a remarkable attempt to blame the victims for their own misfortunes. He trots out again Abba Eban's tired old quip that the Palestinians have never missed an opportunity to miss an opportunity, blithely disregarding all the opportunities for peace that Israel has missed since 1967. But the main figure, we are told, around which Benny's pessimism gathered and crystallised was that of Yasser Arafat, leader of the Palestinian movement since the late 1960s. Arafat-bashing was by now something of a national sport in Israel, and Benny has a field day, calling him, among other things, an 'implacable nationalist and inveterate liar'. To be sure, Arafat was no paragon of virtue, but it is far too easy and too simplistic to place the entire blame for the failure of the Oslo peace process on the shoulders of one individual.

Like Benny, I was cautiously optimistic after Israel and the PLO signed the Oslo Accord in September 1993, but our interpretation of the subsequent history is very different. For Benny the principal reason for the collapse of this historic compromise is Palestinian mendacity; for me it is Israeli expansionism. Israel's protests of peaceful intentions were vitiated by its policy of expropriating more and more Palestinian land and building more Jewish settlements on this land. By continuing to build settlements, Israel basically went back on its side of the deal that had been concluded at Oslo.

The main landmarks in the breakdown of the Oslo peace process are the Camp David summit of July 2000 and the outbreak of the intifada towards the end of September of that year. Israel's official history is full of myths, as Benny knows so well from the earlier stage in his career when he was in the business of exploding national myths and slaughtering sacred cows. The latest national myth is that of the generous offer that Ehud Barak is said to have made to Arafat at Camp David, only to be confronted with a flat rejection and a return to violence. There is a broad national consensus behind this myth, including the left and the peace camp, but popular support is not the same as evidence.

The role of the historian is to subject the claims of the protagonists to critical scrutiny in the light of all the available evidence. In this instance, however, Benny seems to have swallowed the official Israeli line on Camp David hook, line and sinker. Benny's account of the next phase in the 'final status' negotiations is hopelessly inaccurate. On 23 December 2000, President Bill Clinton presented his 'parameters' for a final settlement of the conflict. These parameters reflected the long distance he had travelled from the American bridging proposals tabled at Camp David towards meeting Palestinian aspirations. The new plan provided for an independent Palestinian state over the whole of Gaza and 94–96 per cent of the West Bank (with some territorial compensation from Israel proper); Palestinian sovereignty over the Arab parts of Jerusalem, Israeli sovereignty over the Jewish parts; and a solution to the Palestinian refugee problem in which the new state would be the focal point for the refugees who choose to return to the area.

According to Benny, the Palestinian leadership rejected 'the Barak–Clinton peace proposals of July–December 2000'. In fact, they rejected Barak's proposals of July and accepted in principle Clinton's proposals of December, as did the Israeli leadership. Both sides had their reservations. On Jerusalem, the Israeli reservations were more substantial than the Palestinian ones. Benny not only conflates two entirely separate sets of proposals; he makes no mention at all of the negotiations at Taba in the last week of January 2001.

At Taba the two teams made considerable progress on the basis of the Clinton parameters and came closer to an overall agreement than at any other time in the history of this conflict. But by this time Clinton and Barak were on their way out and Sharon was on his way in. During the run-up to the elections, Barak hardened his line on Jerusalem. At this critical juncture, as so often in the past, the peace process was held hostage to internal Israeli politics. With Sharon's election, all the progress made at Taba towards a 'final status' agreement was rendered null and void. A new and grisly chapter in the history of the conflict was about to begin.

Benny's conclusion follows naturally from his deficient and defective account of the history of the last decade, and especially of the last two years. His conclusion is that the root problem today is the Palestinian leadership's denial of the legitimacy of the Jewish state. The conclusion that I draw from my version of history is that the root problem today is the Jewish state's continuing occupation of most of the Palestinian territories that it captured in June 1967.

All the neighbouring Arab states, as well as the Palestinians, recognise Israel's right to exist within its pre-1967 borders. None of them recognises the legitimacy of the Jewish colonial project beyond the Green Line. Nor do I. This is where Benny Morris and I part company. His post-conversion interpretation of history is old history with a vengeance. It is indistinguishable from the propaganda of the victors. He used to have the courage of his convictions. He now has the courage of his prejudices.

# THIRTY

# Free Speech? Not for Critics of Israel

As a member of the British academic community, I find it distressing that some of the more dismal aspects of the American academic environment seem to be coming our way. Nowhere is this more pronounced than on the question of Israel. That country is no stranger to controversy, but the attack on the rights of academics to criticise Israel is a relatively recent phenomenon. Another feature of the American academic scene which is rearing its ugly head on our shores is a tendency towards character assassination of opponents instead of engagement with their arguments.

Israel is often portrayed by its supporters as an island of democracy in a sea of authoritarianism. But these very same supporters, in their excessive zeal for their cause, sometimes end up violating one of the most fundamental democratic principles – the right to free speech. While accepting free speech as a universal value, all too often they try to restrict it when it comes to Israel and its treatment of the Palestinians. The result is to stifle debate.

Defenders of Israel often accuse those critical of the Jewish state of a lack of balance. But the insistence on balance in relation to an unbalanced international actor like Israel raises more questions than it answers. Israel's policies towards the Arabs can hardly be described as balanced. The central theme of my book *The Iron Wall* is that Israel has throughout its history too readily resorted to military force, and has been unwilling to engage in meaningful diplomacy. Cruelty towards civilians is another unjustified feature of Israeli policy.

Israel's recent siege of Gaza is a case in point. It involved severe restrictions on food, fuel and medical supplies to its 1.5 million inhabitants. The aim was to starve the people of Gaza into submission. This was presented to the world as an act of self-defence against the Qassam rocket attacks from Gaza on the residents of Sderot. But rocket attacks on innocent Israeli civilians, utterly deplorable as they are, do not justify the official targeting of civilians. Israel's measures were a form of collective punishment, which is unlawful under the Fourth Geneva Convention; they have caused a humanitarian catastrophe, and are completely counter-productive. If Israel wants a permanent ceasefire in Gaza, the only way to get it is through negotiations with Hamas – the democratically elected representative of the Palestinian people.

The majority of British Jews share the British tradition of civilised debate on all subjects, including that of Israel. There are differences of opinion among them, but the debate is mostly conducted responsibly. Moreover, it is widely accepted that criticism of Israel does not necessarily involve disloyalty to Jews in general or to the values of Judaism. Independent Jewish Voices and Jews for Justice for Palestinians, for example, succeed in combining a critical position on Israel with a strong Jewish identity. Chief Rabbi Jonathan Sacks is another notable example of this fair-minded, liberal and pluralistic tradition. He knows better than most that among the most fundamental values of Judaism are truth and justice, and that Israel's record in this respect leaves something to be desired. Sir Jonathan is also a great believer in inter-faith dialogue. One of the 16 books he has authored is called *The Dignity of Difference: How to Avoid the Clash of Civilisations*.

But on the other side of the Atlantic, public debate about Israel is much more fierce and partisan, leaving relatively little space for the dignity of difference. The passion with which many prominent

American Jews defend Israel betrays an atavistic attitude that is often blind to other points of view. One example is Alan Dershowitz, Harvard law professor and crusader on behalf of Israel. One of his books is called *The Case for Israel* (2003). This is not an objective, academic treatise but a lawyer's brief for his client. This particular lawyer is no friend of free speech when it comes to criticism of Israel, however well-substantiated.

Recent events in Oxford suggest that those of us who thought that attempts to stifle free debate about Israel are confined to American campuses need to think again. The Oxford Union prides itself of being a bastion of free speech. In the Autumn of 2007, however, the Union failed to live up to its lofty ideals. A debate was scheduled for 23 October on the motion 'This house believes that one-state is the only solution to the Israel–Palestine conflict'. Professor Ilan Pappé, Dr Ghada Karmi and I agreed to speak for the motion. I have always been a supporter of the two-state solution, but I planned to argue that since Israel is systematically destroying the basis for a genuine two-state solution by its expansion of Jewish settlements, the one-state is fast becoming a reality. I wanted to expose the contradiction between Israel's acceptance of a two-state solution at the rhetorical level and its ongoing territorial expansionism. These nuances were lost in the media reports that surrounded the collapse of the debate.

Norman Finkelstein, an American-Jewish academic; Lord Trimble, a Northern Irish politician; and Peter Tatchell, a gay-rights activist, were to speak against the motion. In the end, the debate took place without any of the scheduled speakers after an acrimonious American-style row over the panel's makeup. Various friends of Israel had complained to Luke Tryl, president of the Oxford Union, that the debate was 'unbalanced' because it included Professor Finkelstein, a well-known critic of Israel, on the 'pro-Israel' side. What they failed to grasp, or chose to ignore, was that the motion was not for or against Israel but about alternative solutions to the Israeli–Palestinian conflict. Alan Dershowitz was the most aggressive of the protesters. He had been invited to speak, but said he would participate only if he could dictate the motion and approve the other speakers – conditions which were rejected. Nevertheless,

Dershowitz wrote to Tryl complaining that it was outrageous for the Union to give Finkelstein a platform, and later called Finkelstein 'an antisemitic bigot'.

Four days before the debate, Tryl abruptly revoked the invitation to Finkelstein. My colleagues and I then withdrew in protest against the shabby treatment of an academic colleague and the violation of the principle of free speech.

Finkelstein's career illustrates the venom with which the debate about Israel is conducted in America. Finkelstein is one of the most hard-hitting critics of the official Zionist version of the Arab–Israeli conflict. But while he uncompromisingly rejects the Zionist colonial project beyond the Green Line, he fully accepts Israel's legitimacy within its pre-1967 borders. His position is coherent and consistent. Finkelstein specialises in exposing spurious American-Jewish scholarship on the Arab–Israeli conflict. He established his credentials when he was still a doctoral student at Princeton with a savage review article of Joan Peters's *From Time Immemorial* (1984). Her influential book set out to prove the Zionist claim that Palestine was 'a land without a people for a people without a land'. Finkelstein demonstrated conclusively that the book was preposterous and worthless.

In 2005, Finkelstein published a book entitled *Beyond Chutzpah: On the Misuse of Anti-Semitism and the Abuse of History*. This is a frontal attack on more recent works by American Jews about Israel that are written in the vein of 'my country right or wrong', except that they rarely admit any wrong. Finkelstein highlights the biases, distortions, misquotations, selective use of evidence and, in some cases, downright dishonesty of the authors. As the subtitle indicates, he places particular emphasis on the use of the Holocaust and of anti-Semitism to confer upon Israel moral immunity against criticism.

Above all, the book is a devastating indictment of Alan Dershowitz. The most serious charge, denied by Dershowitz, is that Dershowitz plagiarised from Joan Peters, of all people. Finkelstein included an appendix which claims that 22 out of the 52 quotations and endnotes in Chapters 1 and 2 of *The Case for Israel* match almost exactly those in *From Time Immemorial*. Dershowitz's false claims in the rest of the book are nailed down systematically. The main bone of contention is Israel's record in relation to Palestinian human rights. In assembling the case against Dershowitz, Finkelstein perused thousands of pages of human rights reports on Israel over a two-decade period and juxtaposes them with Dershowitz's claims. By the time Finkelstein had finished, very little is left of the case Dershowitz had constructed. *Beyond Chutzpah* is not about the Arab–Israeli conflict per se; it is part of the debate in the American-Jewish community about Israel. It is a brave and highly disturbing study of the lengths to which some American Jews would go to justify Israel's human rights abuses. Readers of the *Jewish Chronicle* may find Norman Finkelstein's style provocative and his views unpalatable, but the basic issue here is one of academic freedom and of academic standards.

I was one of several readers who recommended *Beyond Chutzpah* for publication to the University of California Press. The Press consulted an unusually large number of independent experts on the merits of this manuscript because it was bombarded by threats of lawsuits for libel from Professor Dershowitz and his lawyers. When the Press stood firm, Dershowitz appealed to Arnold Schwarzenegger, the governor of California, to intervene. On 22 December 2004, the professor wrote to the governor:

> I know that you will be interested in trying to prevent an impending scandal involving the decision by the University of California Press to publish a viciously antisemitic book by an author whose main audience consists of neo-Nazis in Germany and Austria. The book to which this is a sequel was characterised by two imminent [sic] historians as a modern-day version of the notorious czarist forgery *The Protocols of the Elders of Zion* . . . If you can do anything to help prevent this impending tragedy, I know that many of your constituents would be very pleased.

Governor Schwarznegger declined to intervene on the grounds that this case involved an issue of academic freedom. The governor apparently understood something that the learned professor did not.

The campaign against Finkelstein reached a crescendo when he was under consideration for tenure at DePaul University in Chicago in 2007. Assistant Professor Finkelstein had an excellent record as a publishing scholar, as a lecturer and as a teacher, as well as the support of the Political Science department. But illegitimate outside pressure evidently contributed to the decision to deny tenure. Alan Dershowitz personally intervened in this process, compiling a 60-page dossier against the candidate, which he sent to every faculty member at the university.

The sorry saga of the Oxford Union debate and the Finkelstein affair are symptomatic of another phenomenon: the propagandistic ploy of equating anti-Zionism with anti-Semitism. Here America is in a league of its own, with institutions such as Campus Watch, which 'monitors' Middle East studies on campus. As its mission suggests, this organisation is incompatible with the core values of higher education such as tolerance, free speech, and the dignity of difference. Mercifully, there is not yet anything remotely resembling Campus Watch in the UK.

There is, however, an ongoing campaign for an academic boycott of Israel. Considerable confusion surrounds the boycott proposal, which is not directed against individual academics; neither does it call for scrutiny of their political views. What it calls for is the withdrawal of institutional collaboration with Israeli universities. This implies refusal to participate in conferences and research projects organised by Israeli universities and opposition to research grants by the EU to Israeli institutions. The strongest argument in favour of the boycott is that the Israeli authorities interfere with the academic freedom of Palestinian universities. For example, a resident of Gaza who studies or teaches on the West Bank is prevented by the Israeli siege from getting to his or her university.

Fortunately, only a tiny fraction of British academics support the call for an academic boycott. One does not have to be an academic to understand that two wrongs do not make a right. My own view is that an academic boycott is an oxymoron: you do not have a boycott on dialogue, debate, or the free circulation of ideas. In fact, I am strongly opposed to a selective boycott precisely because it would violate the freedom of Israeli academics. Freedom of speech is indivisible and inviolable. It is a great gift which we still enjoy on this island and we should all take great care to ensure that no political cause, however dearly cherished, is allowed to override it.

# Notes

## 1 The Balfour Declaration and its Consequences

1 Quoted in Daphna Baram, *Disenchantment: The Guardian and Israel* (London: Guardian Books, 2004), p. 43.

2 Elizabeth Monroe, *Britain's Moment in the Middle East, 1914–71* (London: Chatto and Windus, 1981), p. 43.

3 Elie Kedourie, *In the Anglo-Arab Labyrinth: The McMahon–Husayn Correspondence and its Interpretations, 1914–1939* (Cambridge: Cambridge University Press, 1976).

4 Isaiah Friedman, *Palestine: A Twice-Promised Land? The British, the Arabs, and Zionism, 1915–1920* (New Brunswick, NJ: Transaction, 2000), vol. 1.

5 Ibid., p. xlvii; George Antonius, *The Arab Awakening: The Story of the Arab National Movement* (London: Khayat's College Book Cooperative, 1938), p. 269.

6 Timothy J. Paris, *Britain, the Hashemites, and Arab Rule, 1920–1925: The Sherifian Solution* (London: Frank Cass, 2003), p. 44.

7 Antonius, *The Arab Awakening*, pp. 267–9 and 331–2.

8 Auni Abd al-Hadi, *Mudhakkirat Auni Abd al-Hadi* (The Memoirs of Auni Abd al-Hadi), Introduction and research by Khairieh Kasmieh (Beirut, 2002), pp. 56–7 and 292.

9 Ibid., p. 57.

10 Ibid., pp. 141 and 164.

11 Ibid., p. 139.

12 Ibid., p. 161.

13 Leonard Stein, *The Balfour Declaration* (London: Vallentine, Mitchell, 1961).

14 Mayir Vereté, 'The Balfour Declaration and its Makers', *Middle Eastern Studies*, 6 (1) (January 1970).

15  Jon Kimche, *The Unromantics: The Great Powers and the Balfour Declaration* (London: Weidenfeld and Nicholson, 1968), p. 69.
16  Ibid.
17  Tom Segev, *One Palestine, Complete: Jews and Arabs under the British Mandate* (London: Little, Brown, 2000).
18  Ibid., p. 33.
19  Ibid., p. 43.
20  Ibid., p. 45.
21  Quoted in Margaret MacMillan, *Peacemakers: The Paris Conference of 1919 and Its Attempt to End War* (London: John Murray, 2001), p. 427.
22  Segev, *One Palestine, Complete*, p. 47.
23  Quoted in David Gilmour, 'The Unregarded Prophet: Lord Curzon and the Palestine Question,' *Journal of Palestine Studies*, 25 (3) (Spring 1996), p. 64.
24  Ibid.
25  Segev, *One Palestine, Complete*, pp. 116 and 142.
26  Ibid., p. 141.
27  Bernard Wasserstein, *The British in Palestine: The Mandatory Government and the Arab–Jewish Conflict, 1917–1929* (Oxford: Basil Blackwell, 1991, 2nd edn), p. 71.
28  Gilmour, 'Unregarded Prophet'.
29  A.J. Sherman, *Mandate Days: British Lives in Palestine, 1918–1948* (London: Thames and Hudson, 1997); and Naomi Shepherd, *Ploughing Sand: British Rule in Palestine* (London: John Murray, 1999).
30  Wasserstein, *The British in Palestine*, p. 16.
31  Bernard Wasserstein, *Herbert Samuel: A Political Life* (Oxford: Clarendon Press, 1992), p. 204.
32  Segev, *One Palestine, Complete*, p. 155.
33  Sahar Huneidi, *A Broken Trust: Herbert Samuel, Zionism and the Palestinians, 1920–1925* (London: I.B. Tauris, 2001).
34  Wasserstein, *The British in Palestine*, pp. 16–17.
35  Ibid., p. 17.
36  Quoted in Avi Shlaim, *The Politics of Partition: King Abdullah, the Zionists, and Palestine, 1921–1951* (Oxford: Oxford University Press, 1990), p. 54.
37  Segev, *One Palestine, Complete*, pp. 334–5.
38  Sir John R. Chancellor to Lord Stamfordham, 27 May 1930, Middle East Centre Archive, St Antony's College, Oxford.
39  Ibid.
40  Ibid.
41  Segev, *One Palestine, Complete*, pp. 335–8.
42  Palestine Royal Commission, *Report*, Cmd. 5479, p. 370.
43  Segev, *One Palestine, Complete*, p. 147.
44  Ibid., p. 495.
45  Edward W. Said, *The Question of Palestine* (New York: Vintage Books, 1979), pp. 15–16.
46  Peter Gubser, *Politics and Change in Al-Karak, Jordan: A Study of a Small Arab Town in its District* (Oxford: Oxford University Press, 1973), p. 22.
47  Richard Crossman, *A Nation Reborn: The Israel of Weizmann, Bevin and Ben-Gurion* (London: Hamish Hamilton, 1960), pp. 31–2.

48 Wm. Roger Louis, *The British Empire in the Middle East: Arab Nationalism, The United States, and Postwar Imperialism, 1945–1951* (Oxford: Clarendon Press, 1984), p. 39.
49 Arnold Toynbee, 'Arnold Toynbee on the Arab–Israeli Conflict', *Journal of Palestine Studies*, 2 (3), (Spring 1973).

# 3 The Rise and Fall
# of the All-Palestine Government in Gaza

1 For a revisionist biography of the Mufti that stresses his essential moderation in the period up to 1937, see Philip Mattar, *The Mufti of Jerusalem: Al-Hajj Amin al-Husayni and the Palestinian National Movement* (New York: Columbia University Press, 1988).
2 For two recent studies see Mary C. Wilson, *King Abdullah, Britain and the Making of Jordan* (Cambridge: Cambridge University Press, 1987); and Avi Shlaim, *Collusion Across the Jordan: King Abdullah, the Zionist Movement, and the Partition of Palestine* (New York: Columbia University Press, 1988).
3 Muhammad Amin al-Husayni, *Facts About the Palestine Question* [in Arabic] (Cairo: Dar al-Kitab al-Arabi, 1956), pp. 22–3. For a comprehensive and well-documented survey of the deliberations of the Arab League on the Palestinian question, see Walid Khalidi, 'The Arab Perspective', in Wm. Roger Louis and Robert W. Stookey, eds, *The End of the Palestine Mandate* (London: I.B. Tauris, 1986), pp. 104–36.
4 Khalidi, 'The Arab Perspective', p. 126; Pamela Ann Smith, *Palestine and the Palestinians, 1876–1983* (London: Croom Helm, 1984), pp. 84–6; Barry Rubin, *The Arab States and the Palestine Conflict* (New York: Syracuse University Press, 1981), Chapter 11; Naji Allush, *Arab Resistance in Palestine, 1917–1948* [in Arabic] (Beirut, 1970), pp. 157–62; and Izzat Tannous, *The Palestinians: A Detailed Documented Eyewitness History of Palestine under British Mandate* (New York: IGT Company, 1988), pp. 507 and 609.
5 Muhammad Khalil, *The Arab States and the Arab League* (Beirut: Khayats, 1962), vol. II, pp. 566–68; and Samikh Shabib, 'Introduction to the Official Palestinian Sources, 1948–1950', *Shu'un Filastiniyah*, no. 129–131 (August–September 1982).
6 'The All-Palestine Government', in *Al-Mawsuah al-Filastiniyah* (Encyclopaedia Palaestina), (Damascus, 1984), vol. III, pp. 342–44; 'How the All-Palestine Government Was Established in Gaza in 1948', *Filastin*, no. 30 (August 1963), pp. 6–11; and interview with Akram Zuaitar, *Al-Quds*, 10 November 1988.
7 Evans (Beirut) to FO, 21 September 1948, FO 371/68376, Public Record Office (PRO).
8 Minute by B.A.B. Burrows, 17 August 1948, FO 371/68822, PRO.
9 Ilan Pappé, *Britain and the Arab–Israeli Conflict, 1948–51* (London: Macmillan, 1988), p. 83.
10 Muhammad Nimer al-Hawari, *The Secret of the Catastrophe* [in Arabic] (Nazareth, 1955), p. 271.
11 *Al-Ahram*, 26 September 1948.

12 Muhammad Izzat Darwaza, *The Palestinian Problem* [in Arabic] (Sidon: al-Maktaba al-Assriya, n.d.), vol. II, pp. 211–12.

13 *Filastin*, no. 30 (August 1963).

14 Aref el-Aref, *The Catastrophe* [in Arabic] (Sidon: al-Maktaba al-Assriya, 1956), vol. III, pp. 703–4; Hawari, *The Secret*, pp. 275–83; Darwaza, *The Palestinian Problem*, pp. 211–14; Khalil, *The Arab States*, vol. II, p. 579; 'The Gaza Congress', *Al-Mawsuah al-Filastiniyah*, pp. 398–9; and *Al-Ahram*, 3 October 1948.

15 Tannous, *The Palestinians*, p. 658.

16 Joseph Nevo, *Abdullah and the Arabs of Palestine* [in Hebrew] (Tel Aviv: Shiloah Institute, 1975), p. 100.

17 Shabib, 'Introduction', pp. 77–79; and *Al-Ahram*, 3 October 1948.

18 Nevo, *Abdullah and the Arabs*, pp. 108–10.

19 Ibid., pp. 271–2; and *New York Times*, 25 September 1948.

20 Beirut to FO, 9 October 1948, FO 371/68862; Beirut to FO, 10 October 1948, FO 371/68862, PRO.

21 *Foreign Relations of the United States*, 1948, vol. V (Washington DC: US Government Printing House, 1976), p. 1447; Kirkbride to FO, 25 September 1948, FO 371/68641, PRO; and King Abdullah, *My Memoirs Completed: 'Al Takmilah'* (London: Longman, 1978), pp. 11–12.

22 Sir H. Mack (Baghdad) to FO, 30 September 1948, FO 371/68642, PRO.

23 Kirkbride to FO, 2 October 1948, FO 371/68642, PRO.

24 Chapman Andrews (Cairo) to FO, 2 October 1948, FO 371/68642, PRO.

25 Kirkbride to FO, 12 October 1948, FO 371/68642, PRO.

26 FO to Baghdad, 28 September 1948, FO 371/68641, PRO.

27 Minute by K.C. Buss, 11 October 1948, FO 371/68642, PRO.

28 Zvi Elpeleg, *Grand Mufti* [in Hebrew] (Tel Aviv: Ministry of Defence, 1989), p. 107. Chapter 3 of this biography, 'The Struggle for an Independent Palestine', ends with a highly informative section on the All-Palestine Government that draws extensively on Arabic sources. See also the same author's 'Why Was "Independent Palestine" Never Created in 1948?', *Jerusalem Quarterly*, no. 50 (Spring 1989), pp. 3–22.

29 John Bagot Glubb, *A Soldier with the Arabs* (London: Hodder and Stoughton, 1957).

30 Abdullah al-Tall, *The Palestine Tragedy* [in Arabic] (Cairo: Dar al-Qalam, 1959), Chapter 11; Kamil Ismail al-Sharif, *The Muslim Brotherhood in the Palestine War* [in Arabic] (Cairo: Dar al Kitab al-Arabi, 1951); and Issam Sakhnini, 'The Annexation of Central Palestine to East Jordan, 1948–1950', *Shu'un Filastiniyah*, no. 42–3 (February 1975).

31 Al-Tall, *The Palestine Tragedy*, Chapter 11.

32 Glubb, *A Soldier with the Arabs*, p. 192; and Sir Alec Kirkbride, *From the Wings: Amman Memoirs, 1947–1951* (London: Frank Cass, 1976), Chapter 5: 'The Government of All-Palestine', p. 59.

33 Glubb to Colonel Desmond Goldie, 16 October 1948. I am grateful to Colonel Goldie for giving me access to this letter; Glubb, *A Soldier with the Arabs*, p. 192; and Sir Alec Kirkbride, *From the Wings: Amman Memoirs, 1947–1951* (London: Frank Cass, 1976), Chapter 5: 'The Government of All-Palestine', p. 59.

34 Chapman Andrews (Cairo) to FO, 6 and 8 October 1948, FO 371/68642, PRO. See also Pappé, *Britain and the Arab–Israeli Conflict*, pp. 86–9.

35 Al-Husayni, *Facts About the Palestine Question*, pp. 83–7.

36 Interview with Anwar Nusseibeh, East Jerusalem, 18 June 1982.

37 *Filastin*, no. 30 (August 1963); and *Al-Quds*, 10 November 1988.

38 Beaumont (Jerusalem) to FO, 29 October 1948, FO 371/68643, PRO.

39 Elpeleg, *Grand Mufti*, p. 109.

40 Khairiya Qasmiya, ed., *Awni Abdel Hadi: Private Papers* [in Arabic] (Beirut: PLO Research Centre, 1974), pp. 148–9.

41 Avi Plascov, *The Palestinian Refugees in Jordan, 1948–1957* (London: Frank Cass, 1981), pp. 8–9; Abu Iyad with Eric Rouleau, *My Home, My Land: A Narrative of the Palestinian Struggle* (New York: Times Books, 1981), pp. 137–8; Smith, *Palestine and the Palestinians*, pp. 90–1; and A.H.H. Abidi, *Jordan: A Political Study, 1948–1957* (London: Asia Publishing House, 1965), p. 52.

42 Smith, *Palestine and the Palestinians*, p. 87.

43 El-Aref, *The Catastrophe*, vol. IV, p. 877; Nevo, *Abdullah and the Arabs*, pp. 111–12; and Issa Shuaybi, *The Palestinian Entity* [in Arabic] (Beirut: PLO Research Centre, 1979), p. 22.

# 5   Husni Zaim and the Plan
## to Resettle Palestinian Refugees in Syria

1 Patrick Seale, *The Struggle for Syria* (London: Oxford University Press, 1965), Chapter 5.

2 Eliezer Beeri, *Army Officers in Arab Politics and Society* (New York: Praeger, 1970), p. 59; and Tabitha Petran, *Syria: A Modern History* (London: Ernest Benn, 1972), p. 97.

3 *Al-Ahram*, 25 August 1949.

4 Wm. Roger Louis, *The British Empire in the Middle East, 1945–1951* (London: Oxford University Press, 1984), pp. 621–5.

5 *The Near East, South Asia and Africa*, vol. 6 of *Foreign Relations of the United States*, 1949 (Washington DC: US Government Printing Office, 1977), p. 906 (henceforth this volume will be cited as *FRUS*).

6 Khalid al-'Azm, *The Memoirs of Khalid al-'Azm* [in Arabic], vol. 2 (Beirut, 1973), p. 183.

7 Miles Copeland, *The Game of Nations* (London: Weidenfeld and Nicolson, 1969), p. 42.

8 George McGhee, *Envoy to the Middle East: Adventures in Diplomacy* (New York: Harper and Row, 1983), pp. 35–6.

9 Interview with Moshe Sasson, Jerusalem, 29 March 1983; interview with Gershon Avner, Jerusalem, 6 September 1983; interview with Ezra Danin, Hadera, 15 August 1982; and interview with Yehoshua Palmon, Jerusalem, 26 September 1983.

10 Interview with Yehoshua Palmon, Jerusalem, 14 June 1982.

11 Record of Consultation held on 19 April 1949, Record Group 130.02, Box 2441, File 7, Israel State Archives, Jerusalem (henceforth cited as ISA).

12 David Ben-Gurion, *Ben-Gurion's Diary*, 16 April 1949, Ben-Gurion Archives, Sede Boker.

13 Ben-Gurion, *Ben-Gurion's Diary*, 30 April 1949.

14 *FRUS*, vol. 6 (1949): 965–66.

15  Ben-Gurion, *Ben-Gurion's Diary*, 8 May 1949.
16  *FRUS*, vol. 6, p. 990.
17  Armistice Negotiations with the Arab States, December 1948–July 1949, vol. 3 of *Documents on the Foreign Policy of Israel* (Jerusalem: Israel State Archives, 1983), pp. 581–3 (henceforth cited as DFPI); and Ben-Gurion, *Ben-Gurion's Diary*, 18 May 1949.
18  *DFPI*, p. 584.
19  *FRUS*, vol. 6, pp. 1031–2.
20  *DFPI*, p. 589.
21  Foreign Minister's Talk to Heads of Departments, 25 May 1949, Record Group 130.02, Box 2447, File 3, ISA.
22  *DFPI*, p. 592.
23  *DFPI*, p. 597.
24  *Al-Ahram*, 25 August 1949.
25  Elias Sasson to Ziama Divon, 16 June 1949, Record Group 130.02, Box 2447, File 2, ISA.
26  Ben-Gurion, *Ben-Gurion's Diary*, 9 July 1949.
27  Ben-Gurion, *Ben-Gurion's Diary*, 14 July 1949.
28  Ben-Gurion, *Ben-Gurion's Diary*, 18 July 1949.
29  *FRUS*, vol. 6, pp. 1226–8.
30  Benny Morris, 'The Crystallization of Israeli Policy Against a Return of the Arab Refugees: April–December, 1948', *Studies in Zionism* 6, no. 1 (1985).
31  Interview with Yehoshua Palmon, 18 August 1982.
32  Interview with Ezra Danin, 15 August 1982.
33  Interview with Ezra Danin, 15 August 1982; and extract from memoirs dictated by Ezra Danin before his death and published in *Davar Hashavua*, 22 June 1984.
34  Ben-Gurion, *Ben-Gurion's Diary*, 14 August 1949.
35  Interview with Gideon Rafael, Jerusalem, 17 May 1982.
36  Yaacov Shimoni, 'Syria Between Revolutions', *Hamizrah Hehadash* 1 (October 1949) [in Hebrew].

# 15   Prelude to the Oslo Accord:
## Likud, Labour and the Palestinians

1  Avishai Margalit, 'The Violent Life of Yitzhak Shamir', *The New York Review of Books*, 14 May 1992.
2  Yitzhak Shamir, interview with Joseph Harif in *Maariv*, 26 June 1992.
3  Avishai Margalit, 'The General's Main Chance', *The New York Review of Books*, 11 June 1992.
4  *Divrei Haknesset* (Proceedings of the Knesset), 13 July 1992.
5  Yezid Sayigh, 'Israel and the Palestinians: Reinstating Occupation, Legalizing Annexation', *Middle East International*, no. 440, 8 December 1992.
6  Interview with Ian Black, *Guardian*, 7 December 1992.
7  Dani Rubinstein, 'Significant Gap Regarding the Nature of the Settlement', *Haaretz*, 13 June 1993.
8  Shmuel Toledano, 'The Illusion Celebrates', *Haaretz*, 9 July 1993.

## 16 The Rise and Fall of the Oslo Peace Process

1  Shimon Peres, *Battling for Peace: Memoirs* (London: Weidenfeld and Nicolson, 1995), pp. 323–4.
2  'Declaration of Principles on Interim Self-Government, Washington, 13 September 1993', in Meron Medzini, ed., *Israel's Foreign Relations: Selected Documents, 1992–1994*, vol. 13 (Jerusalem: Ministry of Foreign Affairs, 1995), pp. 319–28.
3  Abba Eban, 'Building Bridges, Not Walls', *Guardian*, 10 September 1993.
4  Yossi Beilin, *Touching Peace* [in Hebrew] (Tel Aviv: Yediot Aharonot, 1997), p. 152.
5  Israeli Prime Minister's Statement, *International Herald Tribune*, 11–12 September 1993.
6  *Guardian*, 16 September 1993.
7  Edward W. Said, *Peace and Its Discontents: Gaza-Jericho, 1993–1995* (London: Vintage, 1995), p. 2.
8  Charles Enderlin, *Shattered Dreams: The Failure of the Peace Process in the Middle East*, 1995–2002 (New York: Other Press, 2003), pp. 213, 270, and 324.

## 26 His Royal Shyness: King Hussein and Israel

1  See Avi Shlaim, *The Politics of Partition: King Abdullah, the Zionists, and Palestine, 1921–1951* (Oxford: Oxford University Press, 1990; reissued with a new preface, 1998).
2  Dr Herbert was Jewish. The first, and some of the subsequent, meetings between King Hussein and the Israeli officials took place at his home in London. It is interesting to note that the initiative for these face-to-face meetings came from the Jordanian rather than the Israeli side.
3  Resolution 242 was passed by the UN Security Council on 22 November 1967, and called in part for 'withdrawal of Israeli armed forces from territories occupied in the recent conflict' and 'respect for and acknowledgment of the sovereignty, territorial integrity and political independence of every State in the area'.
4  It is unlikely that King Hussein intended to imply that Shimon Peres did not like the peace treaty between Israel and Jordan. What the king probably meant to suggest was that Rabin's exclusion of Peres from the negotiations that led to the treaty had alienated Peres.

## 27 Edward Said and the Palestine Question

1  Edward W. Said, 'Afterword: The Consequences of 1948', in Eugene L. Rogan and Avi Shlaim, eds, *The War for Palestine: Rewriting the History of 1948* (Cambridge: Cambridge University Press, 2001), p. 206.
2  Ibid., p. 207, and Edward W. Said, *Out of Place* (London: Granta Books, 1999), pp. 118–21.

3 Edward W. Said, *The Politics of Dispossession: The Struggle for Palestinian Self-Determination, 1969–1994* (London: Chatto and Windus, 1994), p. xv.
4 Obituary for Edward Said, *Daily Telegraph*, 26 September 2003.
5 Said, *The Politics of Dispossession*, pp. xxiv–xxv.
6 Ibid., p. xxv.
7 Malise Ruthven, Obituary for Edward Said, *Guardian*, 26 September 2003.
8 Christopher Hitchens, 'My Friend Edward', *Observer*, 28 September 2003.
9 Edward W. Said, *The Question of Palestine* (New York: Vintage Books, 1979), p. 119.
10 Said, *The Politics of Dispossession*, p. xxv.
11 Said, 'Afterword: The Consequences of 1948', p. 212.
12 John Higgins, 'He Spoke the Truth to Power', *Times Higher Education Supplement*, 10 October 2003.
13 Said, *The Question of Palestine*, p. 220.
14 Said, *The Politics of Dispossession*, p. xxv.
15 Ibid., pp. xx and 145–51.
16 Hitchens, 'My Friend Edward'.
17 Said, *The Politics of Dispossession*, pp. 175–99; and conversation with Mariam Said, Seville, Spain, 27 July 2004.
18 Edward Said, 'The Morning After', *London Review of Books*, 21 October 1993.
19 Edward W. Said, *Peace and its Discontents: Gaza-Jericho, 1993–1995* (London: Vintage, 1995), p. 2.
20 Conversation with Mariam Said, Seville, Spain, 27 July 2004.
21 Edward W. Said, *The End of the Peace Process: Oslo and After* (London: Granta Books, 2000), p. 181.
22 Ibid., p. 318.
23 Ibid., p. 319.
24 Edward W. Said, *From Oslo to Iraq and the Road map* (London: Bloomsbury, 2004).
25 Daniel Barenboim and Edward W. Said, *Parallels and Paradoxes: Explorations in Music and Society* (London: Bloomsbury, 2002).
26 Jacqueline Rose, 'Simply the Most Wondrous, Loyal, Warm-hearted Friend', *Observer*, 5 October 2003.

# *Acknowledgements*

In my work on the Israeli–Palestinian conflict I have received much support over the years from institutions as well as individuals. It is my pleasure to acknowledge it here. My greatest debt is to the British Academy for awarding me a research readership in 1995–97 and a research professorship in 2003–6 which freed me from my teaching and administrative duties at the University of Oxford and enabled me to write two books and a fair number of the articles that are reprinted in this volume.

During the last twenty-one years the Middle East Centre at St Antony's College, Oxford, has been my very happy academic home. I would like to thank all my colleagues and students at the centre and especially the director, Eugene Rogan, the administrator, Julia Cook, the librarian, Mastan Ebtehaj, and the archivist, Debbie Usher. My wonderful research assistant and friend, Noa Schonmann, rendered invaluable help in collecting, organising, editing, and proofreading the pieces that make up this volume.

The editors of numerous books and journals gave me the benefit of their experience and advice. I am grateful to all of them. The majority of the articles, however, first appeared in the *London Review of Books* and in the *Journal of Palestine Studies*. I would therefore like to record my special thanks to Mary-Kay Wilmers of the former and to Linda Butler of the latter.

Next, I would like to express my warm thanks to the staff at Verso: to Tom Penn for his wise editorial direction; to Tim Clark for copyediting the book with such meticulous attention to detail; to Mark Martin for managing so efficiently the entire production process; and to Andrew Lopez for compiling the index.

My heartfelt gratitude goes to my wife, Gwyn Daniel, who has accompanied me on my scholarly meanderings round the Palestine question for over a third of a century. I thank her for her interest in my work, incisive criticism, perceptive comments, and encouragement throughout many seasons. Last but not least, I wish to thank my daughter, Tamar, a keen student of Middle East politics, for many stimulating conversations and for being so helpful in so many different ways. It is to her that this book is lovingly dedicated.

All the above institutions and individuals deserve a share of the credit for this book, if any credit is due. For the shortcomings that remain, I alone am responsible.

*Avi Shlaim*
*July 2009*
*Oxford*

# Index